FREIGHTING BY WAGON SOUTHEAST OF BEND, OREGON, 1913

(Photograph from Judge R. J. Williams of Burns, Oregon, through V. M. Tanner, Yellowstone Cut-Off Association.)

AMERICAN GEOGRAPHICAL SOCIETY

SPECIAL PUBLICATION NO. 13

Edited by G. M. WRIGLEY

THE PIONEER FRINGE

BY

ISAIAH BOWMAN

33486

AMERICAN GEOGRAPHICAL SOCIETY

BROADWAY AT 156TH STREET

NEW YORK, N.Y.

1931

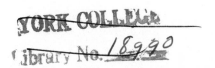

THE COMMONWEALTH PRESS, WORCESTER, MASS.

TO THE MEMORY OF
MY FATHER AND MOTHER

PREFACE

Pioneering today does not conform to the American frontier traditions of the nineteenth century. Most of the land of the United States was occupied before modern machine agriculture was developed. There has been but one big thrust of machine-equipped farmer-settlers in the country since 1900—the determined advance in the dry-farming region of the present wheat growers of western Texas and Oklahoma, western Kansas and Nebraska, and central and eastern Montana. The tools of conquest no less than new fields of conquest are now in the mind of the enterprising settler. Mere land is no longer a boon. No one is looking for rough fare and homespun. Nowadays even the pioneer wants to have. To produce and to sell are the forerunning conditions of having. And "everybody wants everything because there is so much to want."

The pioneer belts of the world are regions of experiment— "experimental zones" we might call them. Settlement habitually advances and retreats on the outer fringe of land occupation. One kind of crop and then another may be grown to see which will best withstand the hazards of uncertain climate: a short growing season that in any year may prove to be too short or a limited rainfall that may prove to be too small. Range land is broken into farm land and then reverts to range again. Whether to raise livestock or grow crops, or how to combine them, are questions that are never settled in the mind of the pioneer because the climate is never settled and the relative market prices of what he has to produce are never settled.

"Marginal" is a term frequently applied to the man who is on or beyond the fringe of normal settlement. Frontier or pioneer living is more than that: it may become economically marginal at last, but it is characteristically a search for the combination of untried or little-known land and climate and crops that will provide a fresh chance to gain an acceptable standard of living. It is also luck-hunting, the habit of "always moving along," the willingness to believe that fortune will be kinder in the wilderness, the desire to give children a better chance. The whole of a country and all of agriculture are experimental in a broad sense; but on the frontier the chances of success or failure in land use are greatest.

The pioneer lands of the world are of great extent. They are to be found in every continent. They include some of the best soil and some of the most promising young communities. One must also admit that some pioneer regions have become "slums of settlement." It is the purpose of this book to sketch the outlines of a "science of settlement" to set forth the ideas that have moved men to take such diverse paths, and to provide a description of the different environments in which so many men elect to meet destiny.

The national policies of a dozen countries involve questions of immigration and land use and the thrust of settlement into pioneer areas. No country desires to add idle men to its city populations. Yet if newcomers turn to the land will they not increase the volume of production that has now flooded the world? The drop in commodity prices and the idle acres of appalling extent in settled communities may lead us to take the narrow view. Not alone high prices for farm products incite men to occupy new land. When the prices of farm products are lowest men are also induced to look for new and more promising sites that mean less capital required to buy, less labor with which to produce, less taxes to pay. A severe drop in crop prices is as likely to lead to new land occupation by settlers from the older communities as a severe drought is likely to drive them back or end their prosperity in the semiarid fringe.

A science of settlement is not desirable merely to provide means by which to attract men to new land. The ultimate withdrawal of the borders of settlement in the least favorable situations is also one of its objects. It is unintelligent to grow everything that can be grown in a given place. Pioneering is an acute question of national magnitude not only because men have gone to the frontier but also because they are now going in large numbers. Science no less than government seeks to follow them in their advance and in their community building. In addition to the science of the pioneering process there are the phenomena themselves—a stream of mankind on some of the newer roads to fortune, having experiences on the way, seeing in new communities the realization of dreams, and willing to pay the price of realization.

ISAIAH BOWMAN

THE PLAN

Six years ago, encouraged by David White, at that time the Home Secretary of the National Academy of Sciences and an officer of the National Research Council, I presented a plan of research in pioneer settlement to the latter organization. After two years' consideration by a special committee, and by the Division of Geology and Geography, the National Research Council approved the plan and recommended it to the Social Science Research Council. The latter organization, after similar consideration for two years, gave its approval and provided generously for the support of the first project. This made it possible for the members of the Advisory Committee of the American Geographical Society to prepare a detailed plan of research in the Canadian field, a plan that has since been vigorously prosecuted by Canadian scholars through the Canadian Pioneer Problems Committee, with results that will be published in the near future.

At the same time the Council of the American Geographical Society generously set up a separate fund for the support of related work on a more limited scale in several other regions.

The Social Science Research Council and the American Geographical Society have also contributed to a joint fund for the publication of a series of papers entitled "Pioneer Settlement" by thirty authors who are specialists in the field and familiar with the regions with which they deal. "The Pioneer Fringe" is intended as an introduction to this companion volume and to the various publications that the plan will call into being and deals with the ideas that moved the three supporting organizations to give their approval.

I cannot express thanks in terms that adequately convey my sense of gratitude to the Social Science Research Council, the National Research Council, and the Officers and Councilors of the American Geographical Society for their endorsement and financial support of the undertaking. In equal measure thanks are due the Advisory Committee of the Society, a group of specialists in geography, history, economics, and sociology, who helped prepare the detailed plans and launch the enterprise.

CONTENTS

PAGE

PART ONE: THE GENERALITIES

Chapter One
THE ROAD TO THE BORDER I

Chapter Two
PIONEERING: MODERN STYLE II

Chapter Three
DOES IT PAY? 21

Chapter Four
THE INVITATION OF THE LAND 34

Chapter Five
METES AND BOUNDS 48

Chapter Six
RAILWAYS AS PIONEERS 64

Chapter Seven
SCIENCE PLAYS A PART 76

PART TWO: REGIONAL EXAMPLES

Chapter Eight
WESTERN ZONES OF EXPERIMENT IN THE UNITED STATES 93

Chapter Nine
THE CANADIAN FRINGE OF SETTLEMENT 143

Chapter Ten
THE PROSPECT IN AUSTRALIA 169

Chapter Eleven
THE WHITE MAN'S LANDS OF SOUTHERN AFRICA . . 200

Chapter Twelve
IMPRISONED SIBERIA 241

Chapter Thirteen
A MODERN INVASION: MONGOLIA AND MANCHURIA . . 267

Chapter Fourteen
SOUTH AMERICAN HINTERLANDS 296

PART ONE

THE GENERALITIES

CHAPTER ONE

THE ROAD TO THE BORDER

And luck—is it yonder?
—CARL SANDBURG, *Abraham Lincoln,*
the Prairie Years

PIONEERS are all sorts of people, a cross section of society
at an advancing border; but they are principally young folks
with children. Those that succeed are strong and hopeful and
confident, willing to buy their dreams with hard labor. In this
sense, pioneers are settlers upon the land whether for agriculture
or grazing, not hunters or mineral prospectors or traders or missionaries, though all these may be the bold forerunners of land-
hungry pioneers. The land-tilling pioneer is at once a home
maker and a breaker of the mold of the society that he leaves behind.
Timothy Dwight thought the frontier type crude beyond the
endurance of a gentleman; while John White's "Planters Plea"
(1630) held to the compensations: ". . . the spirits and hearts of
men are kept in better temper by spreading wide, and by pouring,
as it were, from vessell to vessell." Always in the foreground of
pioneer ambition is a better future for the family: ". . . they
were intent that their children should have a chance."

The whole of America is a land of pioneering tradition; the
western communities are sprinkled with the family names that
make up the honor rolls of the local historical societies. Almost
every other man of us treasures the story of his pioneering forbears:
endless miles over rough roads, mud and snow and storm, the log
hut or the sod "house" at the end of the journey, wild land to
tame, long years of struggle, the flame of hope unextinguished at
the end of the days of strength. "They let life go, [threw] it away
for the benefit of the generation to come after . . ." (Bushnell).

Multiply this story by a million and you have the tale of America
in the pioneering epoch. Elsewhere the tale is not yet ended. The
attack upon the conquerable lands continues on a wide front. Tens
of thousands of men of varied breeds still seek the frontier zone of
every continent. The land of their dreams includes, besides babies
and the end of the rainbow, approximately three million square
miles of productive soil. Its extent and variety would make it a

I

rival of the United States if all of it were gathered together. Millions now live in the pioneer lands, and millions more can be accommodated there. The question of their destiny is a most engaging one to the farmer near the border who has heard of opportunities over the next ridge; to geographers and economists and

FIG. 1—Two-horse team and covered wagon on a mountain road in the colonization country between São Bento and the Hansa Colony (west of Joinville), Santa Catharina, Brazil. (Photograph by Fritz Hofmann.)

colonial administrators; to biologists and eugenists intent on improving the breed and aware of the higher birth rate among pioneers; to politicians who, like nature, abhor empty space; and to a certain type of city dweller, that modern thrall, who would exchange a desk for a bark canoe and whose bright vision of a home in the wilderness rarely outlasts the first rainy night.

The pioneers of today include millions of Chinese, hundreds of thousands a year, on the move, half of them—men, women, and children—walking 400 miles after a journey at sea to reach the edge of settlement in Manchuria; remote Scotch, Welsh, and English sheep herders, and equally isolated farmers, living in the belt of grassland along the eastern foot of the Patagonian Andes; tens of thousands of settlers of many sects and nationalities in the Canadian Northwest, among others, Icelanders, Scandinavians, and Ukrainians; Dukhobors, Hutterians, and Mennonites; Australians (and others of English speech) on the endless grasslands of their sun-baked continent; Boers and Englishmen and Portuguese in southern Africa, on the dry veld and the cooler tropical highlands as well as in the rich hot valleys that border them, where there is a reservoir of cheap black labor; Russian cart trains trailing into

FIG. 2—Russian land settlers emigrating to Siberia. (Photograph copyright by Underwood & Underwood.)

the plains of western Siberia and the Steppe Region and shoving the untamed Kirghiz nomads before them or persuading them to accept the servitude of the plow as they turn virgin grasslands into grainfields.

The remaining pioneer lands are not merely crumbs for the poor man. To be sure, some of them are not the most desirable places in which to meet destiny. All of them mean *border living* for the home seeker, at least for a time. There are chances to take: with rain in Australia and western Siberia; with frost in the Peace River Valley and Northern Manchuria; with the rise of a black proletariat in southern Africa where the planter finds the native useful because he can better endure the hot sun in the fields and his cheapness lowers the cost of production; and with drought and sun and wind and frost at intervals in the long pioneer hinterland of South America that extends from the Brazilian border of the hot Amazon forest to tidewater glaciers in southern Patagonia.

If there are chances to take there are also great ends to gain by those who expect to get independence by toiling for it. Pioneering means hard labor. For the pioneer, life has validity because there is a living to be earned.

John Ball, in the fourteenth century, wrote of the painful contrast between rich and poor in the cities. But he was carried away in the rush of his argument, and, not foreseeing the outward thrust of English-speaking pioneers in the colonial era and its vast economic effects, including, ultimately, a higher standard of living, he really maligned country life when he said: "We have pain and labour, the rain and the wind in the fields." "Rain and wind" came naturally to him as an island and city dweller in the midst of that "stormy Northern sea" of *Ave Imperatrix* and all the geographies. The pioneers of Australia would have less pain if they had more rain; those of windy Patagonia and Manchuria escape the worst effects of disagreeable weather by adapting their culture to the soil and the rainfall habit; and those of southern Africa have less labor because the blacks do most of it. For those that have either black or peon labor, life is made tolerable if not sweet on the principle so long applied to land cultivation by Spaniard and Portuguese: "God bless those who labor and us who guide them!"

Pioneers are explorers of more than material realms. Someone in each community of them is a leader capable of magnificent moments of decision. Someone in distant pioneer groups is forever illustrating the Emersonian principle: "Let one man in a company be wise and all are wise, so great is the contagion." Sometimes it is the pastor of a church community who sees the pillar of cloud. Sometimes it is a merchant who, seeing a better future in "plantations," organizes a company and stakes everything he owns on its success. Here a philosopher seeks Utopia on the border. Rarely does a band of men and women have the courage to go without its strong man who is able to impart the mystic quality inseparable from all great decisions. The Portuguese navigator Quiros, in the service of Spain, immortalized the mood when he sailed his fleet westward out of Callao to be the first to explore the South Pacific, unknown leagues of water ahead of him, no man among his crew knowing the way: "Let her roll; God will take us somewhere."

Writing of Alaska, Davis sounds the immemorial note: "The *Mayflower* sails today for many a northward-facing port." The kind of men aboard her: "If your racial memory includes fiord, moor, fen, proud highland or gravid valley, endless spruce forest, roaring canyon, or nameless rivers, then you will be at home here." The epigram that sets off the pioneer on the ground: "An Alaskan is not a piece of something manufactured."

Some leave the best behind them, for conscience' sake and other and worldly reasons, when they go pioneering, and not a few leave the worst. "Ireland is me country—an' by the help of God, may I niver see it agin!" Some sentimentalize the thing they leave, and their opposites store up sentiment for the land of the future. Memory of the thing behind sometimes plays tricks on hope for the thing ahead. The oversea migrant nowadays may go to his new home in a luxurious steamship; and this last bit of his past, dear in retrospect, may persuade him back to the old accustomed place whose drabness was temporarily forgotten. When so many kinds of men respond so differently to so many kinds of land it must be more than the land that calls.

On the border, men see a chance to live life over again or to begin it without the handicaps of other men's devising. For them the solution of life becomes nascent once more. Opportunity defies its own law and knocks twice. If the border appeals to a man it is because there is a border in his own mind. I speak not of the whole but of the leaders, not of blind mass movements but of purposeful settlement by men who have their eyes on the economic and social order that they hope to create or improve, as in Canada, Australia, and South Africa.

There is no handy rule to pioneering. No one has found a master key. The reasons that impel men to seek the border are as varied as humanity itself. There, as everywhere today, a man must accept his "dissimilars." A colony of Dukhobors finds isolation and independence in the Canadian pioneer zone only to learn that a group of Icelanders or Swedes is moving into the next township. The Mennonites of the Gran Chaco of eastern Bolivia migrated from Canada, fleeing "the world"; but the wilderness isolation they sought is an affair of hours almost, because the settlement of the boundary dispute between Bolivia and Paraguay will surely bring worldly development to their front door and deflect the spirit of their young men.

Economic gain is the most general motive of the pioneer—cheap land with high native fertility, low taxes, and an environment that makes the best economic use of the family unit. On the land, boys and girls are useful at eight and ten years and at sixteen can take the place of men and women. Hunger forces the pioneering

FIG. 3—Telephone line on temporary tripods and new track in undeveloped country, Hudson Bay Railway. (Canadian National Railways.)

Chinese out of crowded Shantung—and the graves of his ancestors may call him back if he prospers by the way. But it is not hunger that drives a man that has five or ten thousand dollars to leave civilization behind and search for the good life on the far margins of settlement. If capital goes, as well as the strong hands of hopeful youth, it is because there is business inducement. There is at least a sprinkling of all kinds of men on the border who are there for all kinds of reasons.

For a long time the pioneer beat science at its own game. He did not wait for the government surveyor or the verdict of the agricultural specialist as to the best lands available for settlement. A large part of the advantage of pioneering lies in getting there first, because the essence of the thing is to get good land cheap. If the settler waited till a printed report became available, he could be quite sure that others would be ahead of him. It is not enough to be on the heels of the surveyor; let him be on your heels. Pioneers speak of a certain man as having "a good eye for land," and picked committees or individuals— naturally endowed Joshuas and Calebs—have often gone ahead of a group that has decided to migrate, in order to choose the best land. Of course the method was not scientific. Often it consisted merely in finding soils and slopes that resembled those back home that were known to be good.

When the land looked right it was taken. The historian E. G. Bourne tells of an early member of his family who settled in eastern

Tennessee because the camp site near by "looked like the country back home in Pennsylvania." The geographer H. H. Barrows notes the tendency of the early settlers of Illinois to avoid the prairies, thought to be poor because they were timberless, and to stick to the timbered river bottoms where there was wood and spring water. They had come from timbered country where the presence of hardwoods was regarded as an index of soil fertility. Gradually the prairies between the rivers became settled as valley-bottom land became scarce. Then it was discovered that it was easier to haul logs and lumber for house building to a prairie site ready for the plow than to clear valley-bottom land of heavy timber. Thus the pioneer makes his case by the method of

FIG. 4—Road near Clairmont, Alberta. (Canadian National Railways.)

trial and error. The scientist has often come along afterward.

To most men, opportunity is not a thing one philosophizes about or seeks beyond some far horizon. Most of the pioneer land of today represents a growth at the *fringe* of settlement. A farmer who made a wrong start by paying too much for his land or who chose a bad site, with poor soil or difficult drainage, casts about for a better place. He hears of former neighbors who have succeeded in a new "country" not far away, and he sets out to better himself. New land just opening up has for the farmer a lure akin to the attraction of a new gold field for the adventurer. I remember with what interest young Gonzales inquired about the *playa* lands (flood-plain strips with deep soils) after my return to his hacienda from a journey down the Urubamba Valley in eastern

Peru. He wanted to know in minute detail just where each *playa* was located, how large it was, what kind of wood or brush grew on it, how many Indians were there on whom one could draw for labor. His father's hacienda at Sahuayaco, on the floor of the Urubamba Valley, was a princely estate, ten miles by forty, and had been bought for only twelve thousand dollars. In a few years the best of it had been cleared, houses and furniture built, and crops of coca, cacao, coffee, rice, pepper, and cotton raised for the Cuzco market accessible at that time by pack train only. Instead of keeping a large family in the city he had become, in a few years, a wealthy landowner. Yet even in these fortunate surroundings his son was absorbed with the possibilities of new land miles away. A pioneer at the fringe, he wanted to get still farther into the undeveloped country.

Modern science has outdistanced the pioneer only in the past few decades and in a limited sense, for it affects chiefly what we may call the second wave of pioneering. When the first wave subsides the scientist can tell *why* certain sections have succeeded and others have failed. From the experimental results of the first pioneers he can derive a basis for soil mapping and land utilization, for example. Or he can help in finding local sources of road-making materials or recommend the best types of livestock for a given combination of climate and grass. The scientist can improve the seed, recommend improvements in the educational and social life, and perhaps reorganize the agricultural practices of a community. It is very like the evolution of an oil field. Before there can be a field someone must strike oil. That someone is the "wildcatter," a close relative of the "squatter," the man who is out ahead of the rest and risking everything, even the title to his farm, on his own guess or judgment.

But "the science of settlement" now enters on a new phase, and that is why it is so tremendously important for government today. This new phase is dependent on a new condition in pioneering—that the best land has been taken in all but a few regions and the rest of it has to be occupied by departures from the commonly accepted standards of agricultural practice. Perhaps dry farming in the United States is the best example, outside of the discovery or development of frost-and-drought-resisting strains of wheat, of the service of science to the fringe of settlement. But science can go very much farther than that today because we now have for the first time data from all the pioneer lands to assess and compare.

Many kinds of experiments have been made in the past: group settlement in Australia, seed improvement in the United States, soil studies in Russia, immigrant colonization in Argentina, soldier settlement in Canada, and the use of native labor in Rhodesia. It is true that in each of these cases the conditions are special and that a uniform type of agricultural or pastoral practice cannot be evolved. It is also true that modern pioneers differ from country to country

FIG. 5—Immigrants traveling on foot to their future homes in Manchuria. (*Canadian Geogr. Journ.*, July, 1931, and the South Manchuria Railway Co.)

and that each type has its own standards of comfort and success. But it is equally true that there are many things in common, provided we take the pioneering lands of the temperate and near-temperate zones and leave out those in the tropics. It is this common body of experience that science is trying to discover. When all the pioneering experiences of the world are pooled, some very useful generalizations and even "principles" can be reached. At any rate we shall know of many things it will *not* pay to try.

Scattered along the edge of settlement through thousands of miles of the world's pioneer communities, experimentation is being carried forward at different rates and has had different degrees of success. We ought to capture each experiment, each technique of living, in process of development—to see how forest land is occupied here, grazing land there, and the relation of short-lived mining towns to the settlement of border communities whose occupation would otherwise be indefinitely delayed. Here too one can find those two most interesting facts of pioneer life, the "social density" and the "economic density" required by the modern pioneer. More than ever, the pioneer dislikes to be out of touch with neighbors. People must see their own kind. What is the present limit of tolerance in this respect? What are the critical densities from the social standpoint?

By "economic density" we mean a distribution not widely scattered but, on the contrary, economically assembled. There are efficient and inefficient densities of population. How far can land be settled from a railway line? In Western Australia ten miles seems to be the economic limit; in Rhodesia it is twenty-five miles; in Argentina, fifteen miles. The individual can accept as low a standard of living as is tolerable to him, but the labor he employs may not go so far. Wheat farming of the extensive type requires the employment of seasonal labor. Here questions of social and economic density overlap. Some races are tolerable to social isolation; others are not. Hints and suggestions about this element of the life of the pioneer are to be had; but laboratory cases remain to be studied. We need both diagnosis and cure.

From the political standpoint the question of subsidy to the pioneer settler is now gravely troubling the makers of government policies. When the state steps in to help settlement how far should it go? What is the measure of state aid? At what point does it become a mere tax upon the people of better-favored lands to the advantage of the people in ill-favored lands? Those in charge of government policies are working haphazardly if they work on the basis of theory alone; they work in a narrow way if they work on a basis of purely local studies; they work in a political not a scientific way if they seek large appropriations merely to throw them into new, untried, and uncritical projects on the theory that any development is better than none.

The economics of marketing and of labor-saving machinery, how far it pays to breed the best strains of livestock under the rough conditions of a new land, what is the geographical extent of repellent or succulent grasses, what is the extent of soils found by local experiment to be good for specified crops—these are among the problems that can be worked out in a new "science of settlement." They are problems that not only can but must be worked out if the marginal lands that are left to our generation are to be permanently occupied, because otherwise the waste of capital and the hardships of settlement would be too great and government would be called upon to provide relief. The better way is clearly to survey the country, analyze conditions, and guide settlement in order that stable communities may develop from the start.

CHAPTER TWO

PIONEERING, MODERN STYLE

I drove my wife to wander with the wind.
—S. V. BENÉT, *John Brown's Body*

WHEN he had told the man's side of the pioneering story of the Middle West, Hamlin Garland turned to the epic of the pioneering woman in "A Daughter of the Middle Border." What pioneering does to family life and education is largely written in terms of what it does to women. Probably the change that has come over the humans who seek life at the frontier, especially in their attitude toward help from the government for roads and schools, is largely due to the unwillingness of the women to stand the hardships and primitive life of the untamed land beyond the settled communities.

We borrow the lines of Stephen Vincent Benét to describe the earlier land-seeker and chronic wanderer in relation to his mate:

I took my wife out of a pretty house,
I took my wife out of a pleasant place,
I stripped my wife of comfortable things,
I drove my wife to wander with the wind.

If "everybody she'd ever known was moving along," it was "because the land was always better elsewhere." The social result was obvious. You can't make a home in a dusty wagon. Murchie warns of the handicap of few educational facilities in the poorer regions of Manitoba which may lead to "a marginal people on the marginal land." The English in Rhodesia make school facilities one of their first concerns, and the women deserve the credit for it. Nowadays, and to an increasing extent, women are responsible for the flow of culture into the pioneering lands of the world; that is the case at least with white women and lands held by English-speaking sovereignties.

At the unveiling of the statue of The Pioneer Woman at Ponca City, Oklahoma, on April 22, 1930, President Hoover and Secretary Hurley made radio addresses in which there is reflected an appreciation of the woman's part in pioneering.

There are few men of the West of my generation who did not know the pioneer woman in his own mother. . . .

FIG. 6

FIG. 7

FIG. 8

FIG. 6—Greek Orthodox Church and bell tower, Ukrainian settlement north of Winnipeg.
FIG. 7—Well-built rural school in the Ukrainian settlement north of Winnipeg.
FIG. 8—Nursing home at Cranberry Portage, Hudson Bay Railway. (Photographs from the Canadian National Railways.)

It was those women who carried the refinement, the moral character and spiritual force into the West. Not only they bore great burdens of daily toil and the rearing of families, but they were intent that their children should have a chance, that the doors of opportunity should be open to them. It was their insistence which made the schools and the churches.[1]

The woman has held the objectives gained by the man. She has been the bulwark ever standing between civilization and barbarism. The pioneer woman has played her part in the conquest of nature through all the ages.

We cannot evaluate her character without any appreciation of her intelligence. Here was an intelligence that quickly and clearly recognized that the three great pillars of democratic government are religion, education, and the home.[2]

The first question the modern pioneer asks of a land where he is to dwell and create a home is, "What is the *quality* of the life I shall have to live there?" Such a question rarely inter-

[1] Herbert Hoover, in a radio address on the occasion of the unveiling of a statue of The Pioneer Woman at Ponca City, Oklahoma, April 22, 1930.
[2] P. J. Hurley, on the same occasion.

ested the pioneer of an earlier day because he left comparatively little behind him. The settlers that followed Boone over the Wilderness Road, the men of Tennessee who freighted their families into Texas when it was still Spanish territory, and the first settlers of the Old Northwest left very little behind them in the way of society. In their home communities early families had only a low level of medical skill, and there were no telephones, no bathtubs, no movies, and no many-other-kinds-of-things for them to relinquish in order to become pioneers. If they subjected their families to the dangers of the wilderness they also offered them such advantages as there may be in an outdoor life. Today it requires courage to leave the telephone behind, for at the other end of it is a skilled specialist, not merely an herb doctor, who may save the life of a member of the family in a crisis. To leave a modern physician behind is to incur

FIG. 9

FIG. 10

FIG. 11

FIG. 9—School and children at a group settlement, Western Australia. (Agent General for Western Australia, London.)

FIG. 10—New log schoolhouse on Missouri River terrace near mouth of Gilbert Creek, Montana.

FIG. 11—Sod house in dry-farming and range country of western Kansas between Leoti and McAllister.

risks as great as those of an early settler in Indian country. Social pleasures and social communication have increased enormously in recent years, and these the pioneer can enjoy only in greatly attenuated forms.

The man in between, who might be persuaded to move either way—to the wilderness or to the city—decides for the city, where these safeguards, comforts, and pleasures are known to be. The means of communication have multiplied to such an extent that he knows they exist, he hears about them constantly, he desires them, his family urge them upon him. He regards his own comforts of living also. To become a pioneer he has to turn his back on many more things than his forefathers did. "People didn't want so much then—there wasn't so much to want," said a mother recently who contrasted her own first simple household with that of her very modern daughter.

Indeed, life for all of us is almost wholly different from what it was for even the generation just before us. It is now so complex that we move along the diagonal of contending forces rather than in answer to a single stimulus such as "religious freedom," or "cheap land," or "democratic institutions in the New World."

We once thought of our world as a three-dimensional thing; but today almost every fact of life shows that we live in a world of at least five dimensions. To the three classical dimensions of space we now add a "fourth dimension" of *time* and a "fifth dimension" of *quality*. From the earliest days of civilization to the present, quality has been the counsel of perfection. Only the occasional philosopher promulgated the truth that it is better not to know how to do a thing than to know how to do it badly. With the growth of democracies in the modern era we have had for the first time whole communities of men raised to a level of education and control over material power that enabled them to believe themselves to be at least moderately critical of the *quality* of their cultural world. Not only have whole masses of men here and there been raised above the level of mere literacy, they have acquired *high speed* and *organized knowledge*. The effect has been felt upon the edge of settlement everywhere, upon all the "frontiers" of the world. In some it has pushed the pioneer forward into new lands; in others it has drawn millions off the land and gathered them into the cities. Excessive city growth is a world-wide phenomenon. The statesmen of every country deplore it and still it continues, irresistible as an elemental force of nature.

FIG. 12

FIG. 13

FIG. 12—Church festival in one of the settlements of the Hansa Colony, Brazil.

FIG. 13—A German colonist farm in mixed woodland and pasture country, Hansa Colony, Brazil. (Photographs by Fritz Hofmann.)

The modern pioneer takes account of time and quality in the same way if not to the same degree as the city dweller. It's no use trying to grow wheat that must be cut by a sickle when your neighbor employs a self-binder or a harvester-thresher combine. A one-horse sled for winter use will do to haul wheat to the railroad station in Siberia, but you have to live like the rest of the peasants

FIG. 14—The old and the new means of conveyance in western Canada. (Canadian National Railways.)

if you haul wheat that way. To compare an ox team of the earlier pioneer with a motor car of the modern farmer is like comparing a rowboat with a liner. The living to be obtained from the one represents a world totally unlike that of the other. When the earlier pioneer set out for the wilderness he left an animal-transport community; he now leaves a motor-car community. To ask him to pioneer without motor or rail transport is to ask him to go back to the living not of the year 1900 but of 1700 relatively. Pioneering is now a somewhat definite business as it certainly is a political and social question of real importance to the governments that have to deal with it—Canada, Australia, South America, South Africa and adjacent territories, and Russia.

Many of our first pioneers went into the Middle West because they didn't fit into the accepted scheme of things back home. Others didn't ask and didn't care how they fitted into any scheme—social, political, or economic. Some didn't even know that there was a scheme. A few saw how the old scheme worked and wanted to create a new one that would work differently, for it is the way of people suited to a new environment to have flexible habits of thought. They are in a creative mood most of the time, since what they have is of their own making. At least this is the classical mood of pioneering. There are many exceptions, and they are rapidly increasing nowadays.

FIG. 15—Fairbanks, Alaska, 1929; looking over circular field built to receive the Graf Zeppelin on its projected polar flight. (Marier Bros., Fairbanks.)

Adventure likewise makes its gravitative pull felt upon the minds of youth; and pioneers are in the main young people who are willing to take risks. "The cowards never started, and the weak ones died by the way" (Sandburg). A sense of crowding is quickly created in the minds of people in a new country, and the pioneering fringe is rapidly extended toward the wilderness. To a man owning an ox team a horse seems fast. Hall thought the people of Brazil back in 1824 showed "that premature 'wear and tear' so strongly and painfully characteristic of a high civilization." Cotton Mather spoke of the crowding in the Massachusetts Bay settlements when the density of population was hardly enough to take up even the best land. To him the colony already seemed like a hive of bees, and the settlers "swarmed" westward through the upland wilderness into the Connecticut Valley. Reading the inscriptions on the stone tablets of Old Deerfield one wonders why such cruel risks were borne when land and opportunity could not have been wanting nearer the established settlements of New

England. The explanation is a matter for scientific analysis and the setting forth of "factors" one by one in orderly array, but it is also a matter for the poet to deal with because each pioneering generation has ingredients of blood and spirit that drive youth to realize fresh visions and to live life more abundantly.

A marginal people in a marginal land is a thing to beware of not merely because the standards of the settled communities are desirable things to maintain but also and chiefly because the pioneering stock generally has some markedly sturdy qualities and a notably higher birth rate. It takes courage to run risks, it takes character to endure hardship, and if only we provide educational facilities for young and selected pioneering stock there is no reason why the second and third generation should not constitute a much stronger people. Whether the stock improves or retrogrades is largely a matter of education, perhaps a much more important thing than economic condition. The pioneers of the Middle West were devoted to the idea of schooling—not the first wave of pioneers but the second that provided a continuous chain of communities along the old historic roads, trails, and watercourses and sowed denominational colleges all the way from the Hudson River and Massachusetts Bay to the edge of the Kansas dry belt. Theodore Roosevelt may have exaggerated when he said that "no American settlement has ever succeeded without a church," but he was shooting close to the mark. That is why the conclusions of the Reverend Horace Bushnell (1846) seem out of perspective: "Whatever man of family moves to any other country . . . makes a larger move also toward barbarism. He has gone beyond the pale of society." That depends upon how much of society he takes with him: the church was, on the whole, a great cementer of social forces.

The leading names in the humanities in the universities of the country, Eastern as well as Western, would have surprised the writer in *Blackwood's* who in 1819 predicted barbarism for pioneer children and grandchildren.[3]

It is true that ne'er-do-wells are also on the frontier. Even early New England had its share of carousing dissenters, "perticulers" and "stuborne fellows." Timothy Dwight[4] has supplied the classical description of

. . . the enterprising, the ambitious, and the covetous. Many of the first, and some of all these classes, are found in every new American

[3] F. J. Turner: The Children of the Pioneers, *Yale Review*, July, 1926.
[4] Timothy Dwight: Travels in New-England and New-York (4 vols., London, 1823), Vol. 2, pp. 439–440.

country, within ten years after its settlement has commenced. From this period, kindred, friendship, and former neighbourhood, prompt others to follow them. Others, still, are allured by the prospect of gain, presented in every new country to the sagacious, from the purchase and sale of lands; while not a small number are influenced by the brilliant stories, which everywhere are told concerning most tracts during the early progress of their settlement. A considerable part of all those, who *begin* the cultivation of the wilderness, may be denominated foresters, or pioneers. The business of these persons is no other than to cut down trees, build log-houses, lay open forested grounds to cultivation, and prepare the way for those who come after them. These men cannot live in regular society. They are too idle, too talkative, too passionate, too prodigal, and too shiftless, to acquire either property or character. They are impatient of the restraints of law, religion, and morality; grumble about the taxes, by which rulers, ministers, and school-masters, are supported; and complain incessantly, as well as bitterly, of the extortions of mechanics, farmers, merchants, and physicians, to whom they are always indebted. At the same time they are usually possessed, in their own view, of uncommon wisdom; understand medical science, politics, and religion, better than those, who have studied them through life; and, although they manage their own concerns worse than any other men, feel perfectly satisfied, that they could manage those of the nation far better than the agents, to whom they are committed by the public. After displaying their own talents and worth; after censuring the weakness and wickedness of their superiors; after exposing the injustice of the community in neglecting to invest persons of such merit with public offices; in many an eloquent harangue, uttered by many a kitchen fire, in every blacksmith's shop, and in every corner of the streets; and finding all their efforts vain, they become at length discouraged; and under the pressure of poverty, the fear of a gaol, and the consciousness of public contempt, leave their native places, and betake themselves to the wilderness."

The Dutch who went to South Africa have developed into one of the finest stocks in the world, but the offshoots on the pioneer fringe have in some cases sunk to incredibly low levels of ignorance and superstition, largely as a result of lack of educational opportunities coupled with extreme isolation and indulgence in the habit of wandering, "trekking," after a few crops have been grown at a temporary halting place. With what force it comes to a man, after he has pitched his tent in far corners of the world, that civilization needs *continuity of effort in place*. This means that we must take even crowding as a fact and not run away from it. Walden Pond is a romantic spot, but it takes more than a Thoreau to make a civilization. Growing density of population means a growing necessity for coöperative effort in which men learn how best to get on with one another.

It is one of the qualities of the new pioneering stock that it so often prefers to take its risks and work out its economic and social problems in groups. Group settlement is an outstanding feature of modern pioneering. For one thing, women have the society of other women and find life more tolerable. The community or village form of settlement is also much more favorable for the education of children. These are not advantages just recently discovered. Compact settlement was typical in the New England environment, and the villager was alive to the social advantages of the village. Group settlement was a feature of colonization in new lands probably before the Greeks went out to people the Mediterranean border. Religious sects furnish many examples of group settlement in the past and today. Racial groups such as Italians, Poles, Scandinavians, and Russians are scattered through the Canadian Northwest. The society of one's kind is particularly desirable in a new environment. In addition, there are land laws to be understood, business arrangements to be made, roads to be built, and much lending of costly machinery and other items of scanty equipment from neighbor to neighbor.

The group idea has been fostered by government, at least so far as contracts with new settlers go, because that makes an easier administrative problem out of it. Implements, stock, temporary food supplies, seed, and land surveys, all can be distributed much more easily to a group with its own domestic organization. Moreover, one successful group attracts another to settle near by. Churches and schools are more easily organized when the whole community desires only one kind of church service or school system in contrast to multiple churches, especially in a mixed and poor population having a variety of religious practices. The diffusion of the group is a later process. The "young folks" are quick enough to find the city and its lighter employments, its varied social life, its amusements and luxuries. Eventually the group breaks away from its old needs and standards and generally becomes part of a larger grouping in a mixed and stable if not permanent form of society.

CHAPTER THREE

DOES IT PAY?

I tell you that we are going to make land.
—Louis Hemon, *Maria Chapdelaine*

THE economics of pioneering used to be very simple. It was embodied in the phrase "cheap land." Capital costs were low because the land at first was free or at least cheap. If the buyer knows how to make a living on the land, a few dollars an acre is a tempting price, and most pioneers buy too much of it. The overhead of local government is low, or absent altogether if one keeps a jump or two ahead of it as a squatter. One accepts, as a matter of course, a lower standard of living for one's self and of schooling for one's children. The margin on a marketable product, between production cost and market price, is wide, but the trick is to get the product to market. For a road means coöperation, and coöperation spells government, and government is unthinkable without taxes.

A third of the sale price of the wheat from La Esperanza, the first Argentine colony of pioneer farmers, was absorbed in the cost of the haul—three days to reach the Paraná, twenty-four miles away over bad roads. The trails of colonial times from Bahia and Pernambuco on the coast of Brazil led two thousand miles westward to the Bolivian frontier on the farther borders of Matto Grosso. Sixty years ago they were still well traveled; many of them are much used today. A hundred years ago cotton was carried from the Brazilian interior by a muleback trip of three or four months to Rio de Janeiro. Nash writes that eighty years ago "the merchants of Arryas, in Goyaz, imported their goods from Rio only once in two or three years, the journey occupying from six to nine months."[1] But, when good roads are built in a pioneer region, and transport becomes easier and cheaper, the price of land goes up; and, if one has enough of it, one can sell a part to improve the rest. Or one can sell out at a profit and take one's place at the front of the wave of advancing pioneers, a sort of capitalist among them, with all that is implied of added comforts and brighter prospects.

The process of advancing into the pioneer fringe is now so

[1] Roy Nash, The Conquest of Brazil, New York, 1926, p. 218.

21

different that wholly new terms are required to describe it. In Rhodesia a prospective settler is advised to bring not less than *seventy-five hundred dollars* with him, and he is much better off with *twelve thousand dollars*. In the Canadian Northwest twenty to forty or sixty dollars an acre is the price of new land. The Canadian Pacific Railway offers special inducements and assistance to a man with a family who has had some farming experience

and possesses a minimum capital of twenty-five hundred dollars. That amount of capital will buy productive but now unused land in parts of the Middle West and New England where first-class crops can be grown and where school and church are accessible. Why should a man take his family to the ends of the earth under such conditions? First let us look at the tax question.

FIG. 16—The inducement of low taxes is advertised by the leading settlers' organization of South Africa.

In many long-settled districts in the Middle West half the rental value of land is absorbed by taxes, and in many more districts the taxes amount to a third of the rental value. To be sure, there are community schools, good motor roads, rural free delivery, and a settled and comfortable way of life if only there could be found an income large enough to enjoy it. High local taxes for good roads are often the source of the trouble. A road may be too good for the purpose it serves. The district engineers of the Panama Canal could not employ the men who insisted on making good roadbeds for the temporary railways needed in canal construction. The principle involved was not to do the thing "as well as it could be done" but rather "as well as it need be done for the purpose." Arkansas has discovered that a state may have too many miles of first-class road. A race horse is unsuited for plowing, and a Rolls-Royce is not required for the marketing of vegetables.

No one has yet worked out fully the economics of road building, chiefly because it is a hard subject and involves the economics of the whole region. We take the easier course and advance our complex civilization by a series of guesses. Santayana once said "I suspect all high guesses"; but this is a philosopher's notion, not the world's practice. Most great discoveries have been the result of high guesses mixed with some scientific knowledge and a great deal of common sense. We try one thing after another to see how it will work; and if all seems well the politician is quick to attribute a general good result to specific new measures and in the mass we are as quick to believe him. The Liberal party in England promised the electorate in the campaign of 1929 to reduce unemployment by engaging in a great system of public improvements, largely roads, with no look forward to see how the charges on the capital costs of such roads were to be met and without knowledge as to what relation the improvements would bear to future economic needs or resources. If temporary relief were provided for several years and new additions to population were made, the end of relief measures would see a worse condition, not a better, except for such limited classes as made specially heavy use of the roads—motor-truck companies, tourists, and the like.

FIG. 17—A chance for children is the most nearly universal of settlement appeals. An advertisement designed for parents.

With high taxes farm rents must be high, and savings are accumulated by the renter with painful slowness. If he has a family that includes several children he knows that his expenses will increase. And he has at heart the future of his children. He wishes to give them a fair start in life. He knows that his strength is now at its greatest as a young man and that he must seize quickly whatever opportunity there may be for the realization of a brighter future, including comforts for his whole family and especially for his wife. That was the logic that impelled the home-making pioneers, as distinct from the adventurers, land speculators, and timber robbers, to occupy the Middle West.

The terms "high taxes" and "high rents" are employed in a relative sense. If all of the new population of an early settlement continued to live in a close-packed community, a pure capitalist state would evolve and every laborer would be a peasant or serf. In an old country "The amount of capital locked up in the results of the past prevents the free adoption of the advances of the present."[2] Capital grows with incredible slowness in a civilization

[2] H. R. Mill: New Lands: Their Resources and Prospective Advantages, London, 1900, p. 16.

FIG. 18

FIG. 19

FIG. 20

FIG. 18—Royal Bank building at Fort Churchill, Hudson Bay Railway. (Canadian National Railways.)

FIG. 19—Bacon's Two Bit Flop ("hotel"), Hudson Bay Railway. (Canadian National Railways.)

FIG. 20—Cranberry Portage, 51 miles from The Pas, a railway junction for the Flin Flon and Sherritt-Gordon mines. (Harold A. Innis, *Geogr. Rev.*, Vol. 20, 1930.)

dependent on land. Those that have a margin quickly become a caste. If labor has no alternative but to work in the fields, the wage will only be sufficient for a bare livelihood. The scarcity of labor in pioneer settlements is a constant source of complaint—the annals of pioneering are filled with the story. From the old hive swarmed new stock that by leaving kept the balance with capital. There was left to the labor that remained a better chance to requite its toil, that is, a lower rental value of land owned by another or a higher wage for a farm laborer or an artisan. Not at once actually higher, of course, but relatively higher than it would have been had there been no overflow of population.

When such a migrant took his small store of savings and implements, his livestock, and his household furniture to the new El Dorado, he had heavier work to do but could stand it for some years at least. He had poorer schools and roads, less social life, a cheaper house, indeed oftener not a house at all but a hut. But he had land that was his own, and he had enough of it for a living. The comforts could wait, and he could be cheerful because he knew that he could secure them in time. A well-defined cycle of benefits, in the period between 1840 and 1890 in the Middle West country, was widely expected. Land was bound to increase in value. In time the railroad would come nearer with its grain elevator and higher prices for livestock. When, for example, a new state road was built farm produce could be more cheaply, that is more profitably, marketed; and in the meantime the lumber companies paid good wages for winter labor in the camps. More neighbors meant increasing social exchanges that satisfied "the women folks."

Hard work, plain living, poorer schools, and a meager social life for his wife were the price the pioneer paid for a new chance on the frontier. All expected to pay the price for a few years only, because the air was full of stories of wealth quickly acquired by those fortunates who sold out in other communities. Some succeeded, some failed, others—and they were most numerous—had their dreams realized only at the end of life when the capacity for enjoyment was over and the habit of hard work had become so ingrained they could not be happy without it. Character was forged by the struggle even if good fortune proved elusive.

The economics of the case has changed entirely. The modern pioneer talks in terms of markets, capital values, and social life and asks "What is government going to do for me?" The older pioneer thought in terms of labor rather than of government. The percentage of failures is higher today (perhaps not higher than in the early pioneering period), but the failures are now more obvious because those who fail run away—to the sheltering cities and the old steady job and a regular wage. They abandon their venture in freedom. To be sure city work is lighter, even if inexorable, social pleasures and institutional privileges are relatively abundant. The serfdom of the cities is based largely upon the fact that so many men and women prefer the company and the shelter of the cities. A longish log-hut "Who's Who" of city-dwelling sons of pioneers can still be compiled: but the list is not composed of those who ran back to the city for shelter but of those to whom the city itself is a "pioneer" zone.

In the older pioneering days the ne'er-do-well was left on the

land to lead whatever sort of life he could. Every neighborhood
had its quota of the shiftless. In the isolation of the Kentucky
and Tennessee Mountains the whole stock stood still. In those
regions Shaler found squirrel-hunting with the crossbow not more
than seventy years ago, and a speech flavored with Elizabethan

FIG. 21—Peace River, Alberta. (Canadian National Railways.)

terms. Backwater settlements are known in every region. For
fifty years at least the Ossipee mountaineers were written up for
the Boston newspapers about as regularly as the Shinnecock
Indians or the Long Island whalers for the New York press when
news was at summer ebb.

   Mark Jefferson, describing the San Carlos settlement founded
in Argentina in 1859, has put the case clearly: "It is to be expected
that there will be vicious people, lazy people, average people,
industrious people, and exceptional people in any colony. When
prosperity comes it comes mainly to the 'fortunate' colonists of
the last three classes. Industry, thrift, and persistence count
much more than intellectual quickness or education. A number
of modern Italian visitors have commented on the fact that a
good many of the immigrants who have attained real wealth have
been ignorant and far from quick-witted but always endowed with
those three qualities. . . . The first step toward wealth has
invariably been the painful saving of a small capital under conditions of real hardship and privation."[3]

   The brightest page in pioneering records the spirit of unquench-

   [3] Mark Jefferson: Peopling the Argentine Pampa, *Amer. Geogr. Soc. Research Ser. No. 16*, New
York, 1926, pp. 81–82.

able hope. No matter in what land we follow the trail of the pioneer, it is always the same story—incredible hardships overcome, discomforts endured, cases of failure and retreat to the cities or the established communities, but in the face of them no relinquishment of set purpose to work out destiny in a new land. Hopefulness

FIG. 22—Wheatfield, Peace River country, Alberta. (Canadian National Railways.)

is epidemic among those who stick. There is a contagion of hope as well as a contagion of failure. Next year will be better than this. When the railroad comes and a town begins to grow, the boosting spirit has its birth. On all sides men see the things they have created with their own hands. They know with what toil they have tamed the land, built the roads, and brought community life into being through church and school. The sense of proprietorship and accomplishment is theirs. And naturally there is also the sense of independence and a flexibility in habits of thought and speech.

It is characteristic of the creative spirit that it dwells on the edge of expectancy. Hope is one of the great driving powers of mankind. There stands the cloud-wrapped, if distant, city of imagination. The pioneer, driven to create, took few elements from his past— it was not rich enough for that. These few served him as germinal forces around which to build the dream of the future, to give shape to it in the midst of the hard realities of the present. The occasional pioneer may be a pessimist, but he is never a decadent. If all of the present is bad to a man, it is because he is tired of the hard work of creation and seeks refuge in a more reassuringly idealized form of a past that is acceptable to him because it is no longer experimental but fixed and known and probably touched by romance.

FIG. 23

FIG. 24

FIG. 23—Typical setting of dry-land farm in Kahlotus-Connell region, southern Washington. Originally this was sagebrush country.
FIG. 24—Fort Rock Valley, Oregon, looking east to Fremont, now deserted. The Fremont School is shown at the extreme right. See page 105.

The challenge has gone out of such an age. It is as comfortable as an accustomed chair, and it has as little to do with creation and the living edge of experience. It lacks the essential "talent for work."

A pioneering folk unwilling to experiment and to turn readily from one thing to another could not succeed. In a large sense pioneers reflect the whole history of the race. Man could not have possessed this earth of his if he had not been willing to experiment region by region endlessly. Here a grass was found that could be turned into grain, there an animal that could be domesticated, and again a new plant was tried for its medicinal qualities. Folk history is full of experiment with the forces of nature and of exchange from tribe to tribe of ideas and materials, so that culture has always traveled farther than the people who gave birth to its elements.

The contrast in the spirit of older and newer communities now reveals the part that spirit plays in the affairs of men as opposed to the so-called "environmental influences." In the belt of sandy country north of a line drawn between Saginaw and Big Rapids, Michigan, the stripping of the timber was accompanied by a wave of settlement that began to recede almost as soon as the timber cutting was over and a supplementary source of livelihood was withdrawn. Whole counties began to go backward, and as soon as a start was made the movement became a landslide. When one's neighbor leaves, one is also inclined to go. It is a self-stimulating process. A change takes place in the spirit of the whole community. The effect has been practically to depopulate whole townships to the point where local government fails entirely. There are literally not enough people remaining to manage roads, schools, and tax lists. Men could still live on the land, but that would mean closing their eyes and ears to the advantages of other places and particularly the towns. Rather than pay the taxes the owners abandon their land to the state. Because there is no one to buy the state cannot sell: everyone wants to move out. Thus the state finds itself with growing acreages of abandoned land to deal with and in consequence is compelled to frame a new afforestation policy to redeem the land from the blight of the timber barons and subsequent effects.

The same result may be seen in some of the New England communities. I have in mind one that came to grief through the medium of a cheap motor car. The roads had been improved, and a stream of summer tourists set an example of hitherto undreamed-of luxury and fun. Cars were bought on the instalment plan, and scores of farmers found that they could pay the instalments only by getting city work. A season in the city and they were lost to the land. Hours were shorter in the city, work was lighter, there was money available week by week. They left their farms to the automobile dealer who has been unable to find tenants. There is something shocking in a process of this sort as it plows its way through an entire community or group of communities. In the case I have in mind, the hardware store was closed first, then a physician moved away, finally the drug store was closed. Daily the community gathered up the children in buses and transported them to a distant school and paid tuition for them rather than try to operate a school of its own. "Recoil from standards once reached is the gesture of a community touched by decay" (Beveridge).

The process of decay has not been measured statistically except in a very few cases. Perhaps the most interesting one is the town of Lyme in New Hampshire, as recently described by Goldthwait.[4] By comparing the house sites of old dated maps and those of today, and correlating the results with the abandoned roads, he obtained a graphic picture of the rate and extent of the downhill process. Schools and churches have gone the way of the farmer. Settlement has run downhill like the drainage. The main valley floors have the best farms today, the best roads, the schools and churches. The hilltop farm and the hillside meadow are in brush, and the old stone-fence boundaries of valuable farms are now almost unrecognizable trails of stone running through deep thickets or dense forest.

In a declining community the tax rate keeps mounting. To the servitudes already laid upon it is added that of maintaining the machinery of the town and the county. Declining productivity has been found to be the cause for such a change in spirit in certain parts of Manitoba. Below a certain critical level of productivity, schools, churches, and hospitals close, and there is a rapidly mounting rate of increase in the number of mortgage foreclosures and bank failures. The pioneer, on the other hand, has virgin soils and, apart from misfortunes due chiefly to the weather, as we shall narrate more fully hereafter, has better crop yields, a smaller capital outlay for his land, and a lower tax rate because he still has a low social and governmental overhead. His taxes represent a much smaller part of the salable product of his farm. If he rents

[4] J. W. Goldthwait: A Town That Has Gone Downhill, *Geogr. Rev.*, 1927, pp. 527–552.

FIG. 25

FIG. 26

FIG. 27

FIG. 25—Deserted schoolhouse of the Acorn Hill district, Lyme township, New Hampshire. (J. W. Goldthwait, *Geogr. Rev.*, Vol. 17, 1927.)

FIG. 26—Unoccupied farm, Reading, Vermont. (H F. Wilson, *Geogr. Rev.*, Vol. 21, 1931.)

FIG. 27—An "agricultural frontier of today in course of reclamation from land abandoned by the lumbermen." Silver Cliff to Blue Mountain, northern Wisconsin. There is one farm in the center foreground and not another in sight. (Guy-Harold Smith, *Geogr. Rev.*, Vol. 18, 1928.)

his land to a newcomer who serves an apprenticeship of a year or
two before advancing in his own name to the border, the taxes are
a much smaller percentage of the rental income than they are in
areas of close settlement. As more people come into a pioneer
region there is a wider and wider spread of the tax burden, so that
government is really cheap. People take care of their own sick,
neighbor helps neighbor in a way that excels mere philanthropy,
the community is fresh and young, and there is no excessive burden
of cost for jails, insane asylums, and the like.

An index of agricultural welfare might well be found in the tax
rate. A map showing the relation of taxes to the overhead of
civilization would disclose some striking things in favor of pioneer
lands. It would reveal one of the economic elements that incites
the pioneering spirit today when there are astounding acreages
of unused land in all of the older communities: north, south, east,
and west you can find them. O. E. Baker argues that we do not
need more land and supports his argument with a wealth of reliable
statistics. Yet, despite the known facts, men keep moving towards
the frontier! New countries do not follow the principle of securing
the greatest possible return per unit of land but rather the greatest
possible return per unit of capital and labor.

It is hard to think of a feature of modern life more extraordinary
than the rival ideas now working in men's minds, the one leading a
man to undertake settlement in the undeveloped or poorly developed pioneer belts of the world, the other drawing him toward
his own kind in cities and thus creating a host of social problems
that challenge the invention and statesmanship of public leaders.
At the moment when there has been a complete abandonment of
the old colonial idea that landed wealth implies stability of capital
value, at the moment when the unused land of every region is
creating emergencies for local government, there is the keenest
interest in the pioneering lands where virgin soil must be cleared or
broken. An equally keen interest is felt in *land as a social and
political problem*. This generation has seen the first acute appearance of the question in the western world—already responsible for
the revolution in Mexico.

When we look into pioneering in South America in a later chapter
we shall see that the land question is a troublesome one throughout
Hispanic America. It has undergone a profound change in Europe.
We think at once of Russia and nationalization of the land, but the
"green revolution" is of far wider scope than that. Men have

denied the right of the individual to own land unless it is put to
social use. Land is conceived of as a thing of public concern,
and the right of the individual to own and manage it is restricted
in the public interest. It cannot be reserved for play when it is
needed for food. In Czechoslovakia a private estate is not permitted to exceed 475 hectares; in Rumania, 550 hectares; while
in Austria and Yugoslavia there has been a similar breaking up of
the old landed estates—one of the little-heralded but fundamental
results of the World War, more revolutionary in its effects than
changes in governments, tariffs, and boundaries, for it affects the
foundation principles of organized social living.

This is land hunger, if you please, but something of vastly more
importance. It is a change in social philosophy, as is clearly revealed
in Chancellor Snowden's budget speech of April, 1931. It implies
that the masses have not yet done with the question but will pursue
it through further experimentation until the use of the land and the
products of the land are as strictly controlled in the general welfare
as they are in Denmark today. It is there regarded as socially
undesirable and a crime against the whole social body that a member
of it should market abroad an inferior product. It will be a nice
question for the future as to whether such control can be carried
out in an industrial country like England in contrast to an agricultural community like Denmark. How will the balance of interests
deflect the course of social events? No such questions yet trouble
the pioneer, because governments with cheap or vacant land *entice*
him to occupy it and leave social problems of the larger sort to be
settled as they arise.

A country with vacant land limits individual holdings only in
the large and generous sense of the term and in the interest of the
individual in order that the speculator may not have too abundant
a harvest. In respect of social control the pioneer is still the pam-
pered child of fortune. Not merely the chance to create a large
estate is his but also direct assistance from the government in
return for the *chances* that he is willing to take. Men hunger for
land only when they can get it under favorable conditions. They
ask much more of government today than the mere opportunity
to own land. As Ely has put it: "The principle of inducement
operates in agriculture as in industry."

CHAPTER FOUR

THE INVITATION OF THE LAND

I am glad that the earth is not all Iowa
or Belgium or the Channel Islands.
—L. H. BAILEY, *The Holy Earth*

IT is often forgotten that Columbus and da Gama dealt in ideas, not merely in maps and ships. They demonstrated dramatically what has always been true, that the world is as new as its newest idea. I commend these reflections to the man who is chained to a desk; and to the ten millions of young men who long for freedom in the wilderness. If you want a new experience it is unnecessary to go to Patagonia for it unless you happen to want precisely the kind of experience that Patagonia affords. Adventure is bound to attend the man who deals with ideas because of the ring of resistance that grows up around them. It will be found that most of the "authorities" are against a really new idea. The Duke of Wellington (and who could dispute him after Waterloo?) "proved" by a speech in the House of Lords that a locomotive could not pull more than its weight unless provided with cog wheels. An experienced Arctic explorer described Fridtjof Nansen's proposed plan of drifting across the Arctic Basin—later so brilliantly executed—as an "illogical scheme of self-destruction" and declared that the ship could not be built that could withstand the pressure of the ice. When steamships were first invented as much was said against them as against dirigibles today. The submarine had as hard a time of it; and even the airplane and the horseless carriage were at first put in a class with perpetual motion and squaring the circle. As a biological group we hate to be fooled by someone's mousetrap, and we are afraid. On the whole, man has given himself a very hard time through his fears. The commonest of expressions, "I am afraid that I can't do it," reflects a deep residual trait.

That is why there is always a fighting border to human experience. To do anything one must overcome. There is the overcoming of ignorance; and there is the overcoming of the shock of the new idea to one's rather fixed notions of things—the experience of the individual tends to be circumscribed by the traditions of the community or the age-old experience of the race. Sir William Beach Thomas, troubled by the state of the English countryside, said recently, "Nothing interferes with progress like not wanting to make it." In most of life's affairs it's what one thinks a thing is that makes it so. Perhaps no area of human experience shows this more clearly than pioneering: not because of the pioneers but because of those who stay at home and argue the failure of each succeeding venture in pioneering. In the last few centuries the white man has rushed headlong into a wilderness of territory and of experiment and of economic theory and made a new world for himself every decade or two with an incalculable amount of mental as well as material adaptation.

The greatest single fact about humanity—despite all its fears and hesitations—is its willingness to advance across the border of experience. However long the catalogue of failures and fears, there have been pioneers in every generation to question and to venture. To the fears of others they reply "Let's see!". They rub out the dictum "Seek peace and ensue it," and write "Seek life and pursue it." The world is on a hinge, and they want to swing it.

Bacon is said to have unrolled "a programme of aggressive search for the hitherto unknown," and the remark has raised the question whether land pioneering may not date from the Age of Discovery. But I think the thing was more widespread than that. It reminds us rather of those great "revolutions" of earth history when a whole species suddenly bolted the familiar or was upset by a cataclysm of nature and had to adapt itself to a new state of things or perish. The world was ready for the idea of pioneering and colonization, and the Atlantic fringe of Europe teemed men of many nationalities. No local cause moved types as distinct as Englishmen and Spaniards to explore and to settle.

With a complacency and an ignorance that matches anything in the history of thought which we now condemn, the end of pioneering is announced. "No more of it left to do anywhere in the world," said the head of a United States government bureau only two or three years ago. A historian takes a bookful of words to prove the same thing with equal conclusiveness. An economist tells us that we *need* no more land: witness the millions of arable acres now left untilled in regions of close settlement in the United States.

The answer to this statistical conclusiveness is made not by a few wandering bands of chronic pioneers but by a host that numbers

millions. The Chinese stream of migration—now the greatest in
the world—that pours out of crowded Shantung into thinly peopled
Manchuria, the thousands of new farmers on the pioneer fringe of
the Canadian Northwest, the wide-ranging settlers of Rhodesia
and Australia—all are living in a stage of pioneering like that of

Fig. 28—A truck farm in a Ukrainian settlement north of Winnipeg. (Canadian National
Railways.)

Kansas fifty years ago. Their world is still one of experimental
development of new land. Following them for a long time will
be streams of folk who accept the life of the frontier in fulfillment
of the age-old dreams of cheap land and homes for children. To
them the unplowed border is a good place even if it is empty. They
have no use for other men's "facts": they make their own.

Wise is the man who has learned not to put his faith in statistics
alone. Not all of the achievements of civilization can be "expressed
in tonnages." We need not despise the frontier because the
population is scattered. Its influence is greater than its crops and
its acreages: it is as great as its men. First they are young men,
and next they are courageous men—those that stay. In his
inspiring and devotional book, "Holy Earth," Bailey has given us
the scientific as well as the poetic view of the fringe of settlement
as a border of experience and hope as well as a place of livelihood,
with so many bushels of something per acre. "We are likely to
think that all these outlying and thinly peopled places are wastes.
I suspect that they contribute more to the race than we think.

I am glad that there are still some places of mystery, some reaches of hope, some things far beyond us, some spaces to conjure up dreams. I am glad that the earth is not all Iowa or Belgium or the Channel Islands."[1]

For another reason land settlement cannot be understood

FIG. 29—The country along the Hudson Bay Railway at mile 42. (Royal Canadian Air Force.)

in terms of economics alone. If land use is the thing you know best, your faith in it is undimmed by what the professionals say when you plan for your future and that of your children. All kinds of better opportunities may exist somewhere in the settled places, but they are distant and vague and uncertain. They involve a knowledge or a technique you do not possess. But the technique of farming, if well known to you, is the one you can put into practice without misgiving. Your estimate is not based upon all the values but upon a few which involve your time and strength and the best way to make a living. The horizon is limited. You measure opportunity in terms of the near and familiar.

Advancing the frontier results in raising the standard of living in the immediate hinterland. This is a process in large part indifferent to world-transport conditions or the tillage system employed or production or overproduction elsewhere. Each type of agriculture and each group, in a neighborhood sense, has a certain *range*. This is determined by what people know of their surroundings (their

[1] L. H. Bailey: The Holy Earth, New York, 1923, p. 152.

habitat) and by their cultural qualities. A Chinese community may be told of a large acreage of land in the next province that would grow a useful crop with machine tillage. But the group refuses to move. To ask the Chinese to machine their land is like asking American farmers to discard the disk harrow for the hoe.

The first occupation of new land goes on to a large degree at the fringe of the tilled land. Just beyond, at a distance not too great, there beckons an opportunity that is understood, that can be realized through a familiar technique. The chances of failure seem limited there. This is what we might call the "invitation of the land." It is an invitation to those who understand the ways of the land, and *it is accepted because it is familiar and not because it is the best thing to do from every standpoint.* The "invitation of the land" is made up of elements that are in part elusive. It cannot possibly be true that the settler sees the *ultimate* possibilities of the land. He has faith in certain things he has heard. His imagination plays with both fact and rumor. What he thinks the land may be, that it is to him in large degree. With electric effect, information about new territory passes almost instantly through a whole chain of communities and starts in many cases a movement of settlers that continues until the new land is filled up or the tide is turned by years of drought and hardship.

The love of the soil that one may see in China or France, the desire to honor it, to keep it in possession no matter how small the plot may be, is a thing born of familiarity and tradition, what we might call a part of the folk spirit in a long-settled agricultural community. It is quite different from the restless response to the "invitation of the land" in a pioneer region.

At all times government has concerned itself with the process of settlement so as to strengthen the appeal of the land; that is, government makes ready the way by protecting the frontier, ascertaining the basis of land titles, surveying the likeliest territory, administering sales, laying out the boundaries of local governments and assisting in local organization, building roads, and actively interesting itself in transportation conditions. It is only after these things are done that the land can be occupied in a permanent sense and settlements established. Then, with the growth of population, institutions play their part. Social life comes into being that was impossible when settlements were in a state of extreme isolation. Community reacts to community. A state of constant change is observable as the social and economic densities increase.

Life on such a border is a process of infinite variety, not merely a walking in the ways of the fathers.

The pioneer settler is presented with a choice of alternatives— the land is new, shall the road or the railway run this way or that; is the soil suitable for the familiar crops of the colonist, or are there native crops better adapted by centuries of trial to the special conditions of the region. The penny must do acrobatic feats and not merely lie in the bank at four per cent. Appreciate the spirit of freedom and enterprise which the pioneer brings to his problem, and one is in the way of seeing how vastly important are the marginal belts of desert, grassland, tundra, and forest where man ventures greatly under new and hard conditions to make a home in what the city dweller would call a wilderness.

At all times pioneering has been closely associated with a change in the point of view of society. Promoters pick up the catchwords of the day, and the settlers themselves are impregnated with the ideas that move the social and economic systems of which they are a part. Hall, who wrote in 1825 on Colombia as a land that offered "inducements to emigration," dedicated his book to Jeremy Bentham in these terms: "I am convinced there is no one more aware of the evils of a crowded population and defective social institutions."[2] Such invitations to settlers were frequent and indicated a state of mind about homes for poor people that represented the land hunt in full swing. More than a hundred years ago Humboldt saw the need of the growing populations of the world for new sources of food supply, and he regarded the boundless energy of plant life in the tropics as of great potential usefulness to the white race. It was thought that the Malthusian doctrine would soon engage the immediate interest of statesmen and that the opportunities for pioneering made it possible for a man now to make the "great choice" between the crowded city and the open field. ". . . Europe must for centuries be the workshop of the New World, as long at least as the latter has lands, the cultivation of which will be a more grateful as well as more profitable occupation, than the unwholesome toils of the manufacturer, 'in close pent-up cities.'"[3]

What has changed the world, that city populations have grown in such disproportion? First of all, the "pent-up" cities have been studied from the social standpoint and have been improved. The

[2] Francis Hall: Colombia: Its Present State, . . . and Inducements to Emigration . . . , Philadelphia, 1825.
[3] *Ibid.*, p. 43.

FIG. 30

FIG. 31

FIG. 32

FIG. 30—German immigrants in a forest clearing, Hansa Colony, Brazil.

FIG. 31—Public square of Humboldt, Hansa Colony, 10 years after the founding of the town.

FIG. 32—The same square 25 years after founding. (Photographs by Fritz Hofmann.)

enjoyments of cities have increased until they outweigh in the minds of the masses any that may be ascribed to the open fields. The stranger in the city is a less important phenomenon than the loneliness of life on isolated farms. The "unwholesome toils" of an eighthour city worker's day in a five-day week would amuse a farmer accustomed to work in summer from 6 a. m. to 9 p. m. The cities have drawn men also because the growing needs of a country building up its plant have been met by a coal-iron-limestone combination that has fed the workshops of America until they have grown out of all proportion to any past expectation, to the point where their products reach into every corner of the world.

But perhaps the most fundamental change of all has resulted from a full cycle of change in our social point of view. Even the humblest and the poorest have a degree of luxury and comfort that was

unthinkable a genera-
tion ago. Not the long
look ahead that marked
earlier pioneer days, but
living in the present is
now the impelling
thought. When the
poor man in the city
had only the far distant
prospect as a source
of hope he could think
of pioneering as a way
out. Today the prefer-
ence for city living is
inspired by much more
than an antipathy for
toil upon the land; in-
deed the comparison of
city and country living
helps but little toward
an understanding of the
greater pull of the cities.
A city is a readier means
of access to civilization
than the country affords,
and universal education
makes possible the diffu-
sion at high speed of
a knowledge of its every
conceivable comfort or
allurement.

The boundless pos-
sibilities of a new land
in the heroic age of
pioneering in America
made an appeal to the
imagination that drew
forth confident proph-
ecy. The plains of
Venezuela were de-
scribed as "this grassy

FIG. 33

FIG. 34

FIG. 35

FIG. 33—Temporary houses and general view of a group
settlement, Western Australia. (Agent General for Western Australia, London.)

FIG. 34—Typical home on Brooklands Estate between
Balingup and Nannup, Western Australia. (Agent General
for Western Australia, London.)

FIG. 35—State Farm, Denmark, near Albany, Western
Australia. (Commissioner for Australia in U. S. A.)

ocean," and it was said of them that "could 20,000,000 of inhabitants be transferred from Europe they could find land to cultivate
and abundance to recompense their labors." Only a modest
warning was set up: "In no corner of the world, whatever may be
its natural advantages, 'is a table spread in the wilderness.'"[4]
Colombia (which then included Venezuela) was said to have land
equal in quantity to that of the United States, and decidedly
superior in quality owing to the high value of tropical products.
This was a common fallacy. It matched the error in judgment
that at one time made Jamaica seem more valuable than all of
Canada. The sugar beet was then an unknown thing, and imagination has always had to play its tricks upon the prophet.

Even the great natural advantages of the New World could not
conceal the cultural deficiencies. Hall made a list of the things that
"stifle and fetter commerce" in the Colombia of his day: want of
population, want of industry, want of capital, want of knowledge,
want of internal communications. The critic might have replied
that he would get all of these things in abundance in the home
country and in the cities whose life he deplored. Hall was moved by
hope rather than by realities and recognized, as all writers about
pioneering lands have done, that in a new country social luxury and
social life, what little exists, are confined to a very few places—seaport towns or the border of denser settlement, that capital is hard
to accumulate by savings. He saw the pulling-down process, how
life goes to seed if man lives apart from his kind. "Throughout the
whole of the interior, the comforts and even the decencies of life
are unvalued because unknown. The man who can eat beef and
plantains, and smoke segars as he swings in his hammock, is possessed of almost everything his habits qualify him to enjoy, or to
which his ambition prompts him to attain—the poor have little
less, the rich scarcely covet more."[5]

This is the outer fringe of pioneer experience. It is no more
diagnostic of the best pioneer lands than the decline of civilization
here and there is a test of the capacity of the earth to feed people.
It may be shown that there has never been a civilization that
declined because it exhausted the possibilities of the land. No
nation has ever fully developed its "frontier." The earth has
never gone back on man, but man has found himself entangled in
the unpredictable effects of his own system.

[4] Hall, *op. cit.*, p. 53.
[5] *Ibid.*, pp. 36–37.

What really happens is that knowledge at the moment of strain is not great enough to control the forces of nature and of systems of government combined. Take the case of Egypt. There is a land whose every square mile of arable soil seems to be known. The latest official statistics assure us that if the productivity of a given unit of land is increased, through additional water, by the amount of ten dollars, one more person is added to the population.[6] So closely as that can the additional water be correlated with the population increase in Egypt. The population, during the period of British occupation, has bred up to every new and higher soil productivity attained by British irrigation engineers. The net effect is merely a change in the numbers of the population without a corresponding change in their welfare. There is the same mud hut, coarse cotton tunic, meager fare. There are no fewer toilsome days.

But the possibilities of Egyptian agriculture are by no means ended now. Modern engineering in Egypt is an affair of a few decades: see its astounding effects as contrasted with the natural limitations accepted by the Egyptians for whole millenniums! In the headwater region of the Nile there are water supplies many times as great as those already impounded by artificial works. The possibilities of the land do not lie in the fertility of the soil alone, and they never did; in Egypt they lie in the available water supply. It can no more be said that Egypt is fully populated or overpopulated than it can be said that England is overpopulated merely because she has to import most of her food supply. Egypt may be overpopulated in an immediate sense, but it is not because her own soil is incapable of growing an adequate food supply for the present population. Egypt has to import water from the southern highlands and has always done so. The only serious question is, How much can she import? When she depended upon the natural flow and flood of the Nile she experienced recurrent famine, and that is a thing of the past because there are now water-storage works which regulate the delivery of water to a certain degree. Larger works have enabled her to put more and more land under cultivation or, what amounts to the same thing, increase the number or size of the crops grown in a single year. We do not yet know the full extent of the development that may take place, and we shall not know until the headwater streams are measured in greater detail and the rainfall gauges tell us more about the *reliability* of the rainfall from decade to decade.

[6] Atlas of Egypt, Giza, 1928, descriptive text accompanying the "Economic Maps."

In the meantime another power must be considered. What England does to the water supply of the Nile through increasing cotton culture in the Sudan will affect Egypt profoundly. Moreover, Egypt alone, if she were wholly free to use the Nile waters unrestrainedly, has at present neither the technical skill nor the

FIG. 36—Farms reclaimed from the forest along the Rio Maullín, near Puerto Varas, Province of Chiloé, Chile. (G. M. McBride, *Geogr. Rev.*, Vol. 20, 1930.)

degree of power in maintaining domestic peace that will guarantee the fullest use of the water. The human system and the political conditions in which Egypt is now enmeshed have far more to do with the control of her destiny than has the fertility of the land.

The case of China is still clearer. The prevailing type of hoe culture makes it impossible for her people to occupy semiarid regions that are suited to extensive machine cultivation, like the western fringe of settlement in the United States. It has been estimated that if China were to employ such lands they would add more than five hundred million acres to the present total. Such a use of pastoral and cereal lands would increase the population very greatly or, better still, supply an outlet to the crowded millions in the densely populated sections. But the required change in type of farm practice would be as revolutionary to the Chinese as migration to a new land. Moreover, it would demand a beginning with capital for machine equipment, and this cannot be got from either private sources or government at this time. So the population stays bound to the crop and land cultivation system created through

the ages—in its present intense form a product of the last century
or two.

We set up the proposition that man has occupied the earth
only in a limited sense. He takes the best of it and lets the rest go.
In Argentina during the earlier pastoral days an animal was

Fig. 37—Crop of Dutch clover at a group settlement, Western Australia. (Agent General for
Western Australia.)

slaughtered for its hide alone. Or the tongue might be cut out
and the bones eventually gathered together to be shipped abroad
to fertilizer plants. The meat was the least valuable part of the
carcass. The same thing was reported from the plains of the Orinoco
a century ago. The system and the need had not been created
that makes the meat valuable as it is today. The land use that
worked in that earlier time demanded ranches as wide as a kingdom.
A certain scale of operations was then required if there were to
be profits that the owner could translate into a standard of living
acceptable to him. In time new systems became available whereby
he could maintain that standard without operating on so vast
a scale and using the land in so superficial a way.

A similar change has taken place in our own West in the scale of
both ranching and farming; just as it has operated in timber cutting
in New England and through the Great Lakes region. Beside the
standard-of-living element we have the desire for great wealth.
Men's minds outrun their need in the face of opportunity. The
timber barons who stripped the land of pine in central-northern

Michigan, and left it a place of desolation, had no need to do it for a living. They saw in the lumbering system, plus a virgin forest that could be bought for a song, a chance to make fortunes. This particular breed of man is a developer only in the sense that his operations may bring in people that exploit the permanent resources of the region. He is no benefactor. Bailey would call him a "skinner of the earth." A true builder strives for balanced development of the sort that James J. Hill had in mind for the Northwest. Cecil Rhodes had a like vision of the future of South Africa.

Kipling's farmer was intent upon his own system because it was "for the honor of the land." The earth has endured all manner of dishonor from soil-wasting and timber-cutting men. Despite all this we cannot say that the earth has ever failed man by circumscribing his empires or leading him to stagnate and decay. She has continued to be his bountiful mother. She has always offered him a frontier. His limitations have been set by his wasteful ways, his dark systems, his mutual enmities, and, above all, by his ignorance of the earth and what she sometimes vainly tries to reveal to him. To the pioneer belongs high praise because he has sought new ways in the face of hardship and has experimented with the earth and with himself. His eye has been on the future, on "the seasons whose feet are in the furrows." The soil under his feet is a primal source of welfare. He has experimented with one crop after another, with a new method of tillage after the earth had scantily rewarded him for his efforts with another. He has been an explorer of homesteads and regions, a discoverer of the earth's bounty and of the places where she withholds it.

Despite all the pioneering of the ages and that phenomenal burst of speed which took place during the eighteenth and nineteenth centuries, there are still, today, incredible acreages of good land awaiting the settler. It is man's privilege to occupy the best of them under conditions of which the earlier pioneer could not have dreamed. This does not mean merely the application of engineering technology; it means also the setting up of social systems from the start that turn the edge of the isolation that so often meant defeat in the past. Pioneering today is not a mere farming venture but a field of social and engineering and agricultural experimentation. It is not a mere extension of farm population but a thrust of an entire civilization with all its qualities—a new form of nation building. As such it affects all and interests all who care about life, the living things at the edge of experience.

These *thrusts of culture* into the pioneer lands are also of wide political significance, as we shall see more clearly when we learn their relation to immigration policy in Canada and to empire building in South Africa. As the pioneer lands come into full production they will also have their effect upon the markets of the world; they will materially increase the potentialities of city growth. The full occupation of the unused lands of the earth will not greatly change the present balance of peoples, at least the shifts of power will not be revolutionary because the pioneer lands are mainly fringes at the border of better-endowed tracts already well-populated.

The field of prophecy is rather wide, and we should do well to be conservative in estimating what people will do on this old earth. The trend of land occupation may be inferred from what we now know of present instruments of power. Given new instruments (and invention and discovery cannot have come to an end in this generation!) new sources of power will be disclosed. We cannot suppose that of all the generations we are without inhibitions and ignorances. Every new idea recreates the earth. A new thought is as new as newly discovered territory. On one college faculty there is said to be a man who invariably begins the discussion of a new idea with the dictum "I am unalterably opposed" . . . That is a more general quality than we like to think. It expresses an instinctive aversion to a new thing. To the best of the pioneer lands are drawn young, eager, courageous stocks. These are in search of the new, not averse to it. They form a better foundation of citizenship than a crowded peasantry. From this standpoint a pioneer fringe is an asset of exceptional value to the country possessing it.

CHAPTER FIVE

METES AND BOUNDS

Mr. Adams talked about latitudes and longitudes.
—Daniel Webster

THE pioneer is not, as we might suppose, a romantic creature that has run off into the wilderness to lead a simple life. He has gone there to better himself materially, but in going he has reduced the number of instruments of power at his command and his degree of control over them. He hopes to enjoy them more fully later on and in the meantime reap other advantages: a homestead, an independent life, and a future for his children that he could not expect to gain if he remained back home in a severely competitive community. Under what conditions of living may one call oneself a pioneer? Where does close settlement end and the open type of occupation begin? How does one recognize a pioneer area? To answer these questions we need to set up a definition: *Pioneer living means a low degree of control by the land settler over instruments of power.* The full enjoyment of such instruments means modern power civilization.

If we trace across the map the whole extent of pioneer lands from shore to shore of each continent we shall realize what enormous distances and acreages are involved in them. Not less than twenty-five thousand miles of "border" come into play—an extent that would girdle the earth if all the parts were placed end to end. The most striking fact about the boundaries of the pioneer lands is the variety of conditions that determine them. Almost every physical fact has a part to play in determining the boundary at some point or other. Imagination plays a vital rôle. Prejudice and inertia may also hold men in restraint. In not a few pioneer regions man has stopped far short of the possible limits of occupation. In others he has exceeded profitable limits and is holding out precariously and uneconomically in the face of drought or excessive rainfall or frost or too great a distance from market.

In every age it has been a question how far men would go beyond the frontier to reap advantages, what risks they would take, what instruments of power and what amenities and securities of life they would forego. One sort of pioneer has no telegraph line or he has merely a telegraph line and no railroad. He has no made roads or he has only poor roads, not motor roads. City mail travels with high velocity, and the velocity is increasing yearly. When the airplane has reached its limit an underground mail chute between New York and Chicago will be projected. These are the needs of dense agglomerations of folk. The mail of the pioneer may take a week to reach the railroad. In the city a telephone call is made, and forthwith an expressman is at the door. If the pioneer wishes to use modern facilities of transport it costs him more to reach those facilities than to make use of them. We enjoy civilization in full panoply, drawing power out of a gasoline tank and a base plug for an endless variety of operations on the farm and in many a farm home as well as in the city. We turn a switch or press a button, but the pioneer has to ride a mule or drive a horse or at best a motor car over new-made roads to accomplish an object of equal worth to him. The pioneer must be above all things industrious, yet his life is slower in accomplishment and enjoyment *in the present*. He is like a man who saves that he may spend later, accepting a sort of pain now for the pleasure to follow.

If we were fully equipped for a statistical comparison, we should find an astonishingly wide gap between an area of close settlement and a pioneer area in their use of the instruments of power.

In tracing a pioneer area we must also take account of climatic possibilities and the limitations set by the vegetation, the nature of the soil, the presence or absence of woodland and natural sources of power. Not all of the remaining pioneer lands are the best in the world. For one reason or another they have been passed by or *they have not yet been reached*. This does not mean, therefore, that they always and everywhere represent extreme conditions. It is true that some of them are the least desirable lands capable of settlement, but it is also true that other tracts are in the nature of pockets, isolated or distant regions, as good as the best when once they have been reached.

The rich farming and ranching country about Lake Nahuel Huapi in northern Patagonia (Fig. 338) is such an isolated region now in process of successful development. It lies so far to one side of the Argentine pampa that none of the apparatus of civilization was accessible when the first colonists settled there. There was no railway, no telegraph line, no motor roads, no machinery of markets and credits and the like. But the soil is excellent, and there are wide pastures for the herds of cattle and sheep on which the colonists

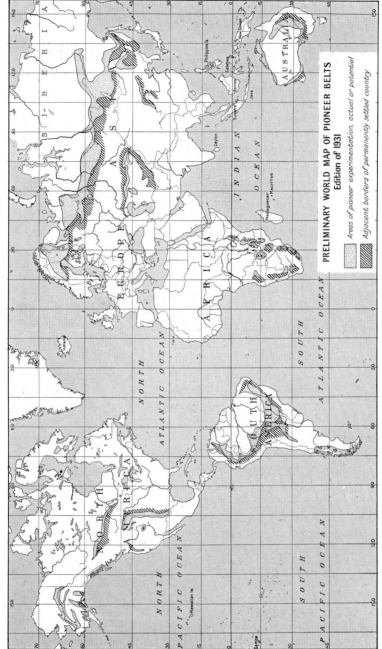

FIG. 38—World map of pioneer belts. The outlines of the different areas are shown diagrammatically and are based upon criteria that vary in combination from region to region. Detailed maps and explanations will be found in the seven regional chapters that form Part Two of this book. The North African and Sudanese belts have been omitted and many smaller areas also. The stippled areas in Alaska and northern Siberia are much exaggerated in size on this projection in comparison with other areas in lower latitudes.

mainly subsisted. Civilization would come in time. The land was so cheap that it cost less to get it than to stock it, to say nothing of fencing it. The rainfall (40 inches or more) is sufficient, the latitude that of New York. The first settlers had everything in their favor but accessibility to market and a proper share of the instruments of power. The region had not been left to one side as poor land: it had been simply unknown. The Peace River Valley in northwestern Canada long illustrated the same condition; and Rhodesia likewise. Yet by far the greater part of the pioneer lands are not of this class.

It is precisely because the remaining pioneer lands are of the less desirable sort that they make their challenge to science and government. When there is the best to choose from in the way of location and soils a government need not concern itself with settlement so much as with law and order. But when conditions of settlement become difficult the safe extension of the well-settled communities demands government aid. That is why we have a direct official interest today in the process of pioneering on the part of governments and scientists alike. Australia has appointed a Commonwealth commission to study the resources of the whole Australian realm, but of course with special attention to the land still capable of settlement by farmers and pastoralists. Heretofore government in most countries having frontier lands has been content with special measures for emergencies as they arise: a railway line here, a telegraph line there, assistance in case of drought in a given district.

Without wading too deeply into the sea of technology we may define the remaining pioneer areas of the world as regions of potential settlement in which man may have a reasonably safe and prosperous life; but regions in most of which he is required to make certain special adaptations. What these adaptations are the settler may discover by painful experiment, as in the past, or by less painful experience if government and science step in to help him. The rainfall of the undeveloped pioneer lands is on the whole not so favorable as in most of the settled areas of the earth, but it is sufficient if the settler uses it rightly. The temperature may be too hot or too cold to suit him, but it is tolerable.

If we look at the southern half of South America, Figure 39, we shall see how the boundaries of pioneer areas are drawn in a specific case. The heavy black line running across Brazil shows the northern limit of tolerable temperatures, that is, it shows the limits within which it is hot in summer and neither hot nor cold but warm in winter. The settler has one season of relaxation of high temperatures in which to recuperate. Along the base of the Andes the same heavy continuous line runs down into Patagonia, including most of that territory in the belt of tolerable country to the east, because though the winters are severe the summers are

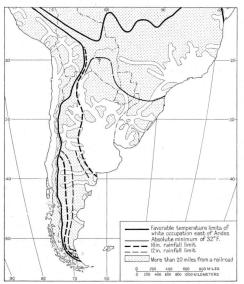

neither hot nor cold but cool and thus provide a season of relaxation of severe conditions. It will be seen from the map that the close net-work of rails and the densest population of Argentina and Brazil are found in the territories farthest removed from the extremes of climate indicated by the heavy continuous line. It would look at first sight as if this meant quite extreme heat and cold at the line itself.

FIG. 39—Some factors that influence habitability in a part of South America. Rainfall and temperature extremes set up outer limiting conditions.

As a matter of fact both the Brazilian High-lands and the northern part of Patagonia offer better temperature conditions than either the pampas of Argentina or the coastal lowlands of Brazil. Why were they not overflowed by the first wave of pioneers? Settlement and the machinery of civilization have a certain inertia. When they once get established they tend to persist in the same place. A shift of the center of gravity takes place as a rule only gradually. Landholding and cultivation began at Buenos Aires and at Rio de Janeiro largely for reasons of accessibility. The natural environment—fertile and flat plains or pampas in Argentina combined with a favorable (though not exceptionally favorable) climate, and a passable harbor—promoted the spread of population from the seaport. The Brazilian settlements were at first almost purely coastal. Sugar and woods provided the economic stimulus. The real foundations of the country were laid when the population of one of the southern captaincies saw the value of the uplands of the São Paulo region and established there a center of economic power that has had a dominating growth down to our time.

Only when its system of living—social and economic—has worked through a natural cycle and come out to the limits of recognized possibilities is a people ready for experimentation with a new system or with serious modifications of the old one. Coffee culture in Brazil, for example, has reached the economic limit set by world demand and capacity to buy. When production exceeded demand, a valorization scheme was put into force at the same time that limits were set by government upon production. Only at this stage was there a real interest in more balanced production, in industrial development and the resources to support it, and in the pioneer lands of the interior.

The cattle-raising and grain-growing types of farming in Argentina have used up the best of the arable land, though by no means all of it; and today one of the greatest social and political concerns of Argentine leaders is with a modified land use that will give the small farmer a chance and avoid the violence of the change in land tenure that took place in Mexico. One way of doing it is to send the excess immigration, or the men who desire small farms, to the outposts, the fringe of settlement, or to help them experiment with a wholly new country like the Nahuel Huapi region already described.

Probably both Brazil and Argentina have paid more attention to the fringe of settlement in the past twenty years than in all the rest of their history put together. The droughts of the Ceará country have impelled the government at Rio to import and to develop the best technical irrigation skill. A telegraph system now reaches into the grassy uplands of the interior and puts the most distant haciendas in touch with the capital. Awakened at last to the needs of its frontier communities, the government of Argentina made a three-year study of its water resources. Borings for water are carried out widely by the hydrological section of the ministry of agriculture. The meteorological service of that country gained an international reputation, in part because its studies have been directed toward long-range weather forecasting. This was inspired by the needs of the grain growers, but the basic studies benefit the frontier also.

In pushing out to the limits of occupation it is not temperature alone that limits settlement. Rainfall or water for irrigation, the kind of grass that stock may depend on, and even the insect life

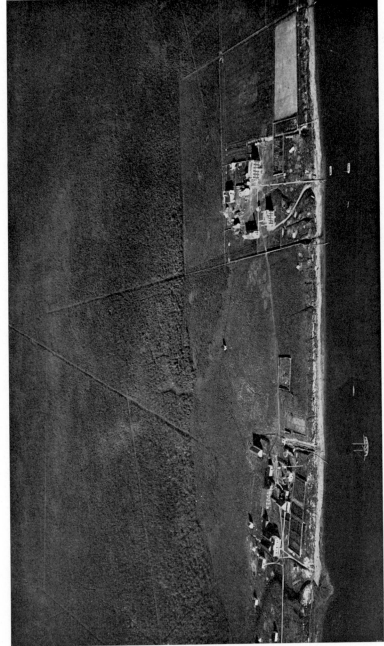

FIG. 40—Fort Albany, James Bay, and heavily forested island back of it. The straight lines are surveyors' lines cut through the forest. Example of settlement on the pioneer fringe. (Photograph by Fairchild Aerial Surveys Co. E. M. Kindle, *Geogr. Rev.*, Vol. 15, 1925.)

FIG. 41—Isolated settlement on the west bank of the Yenisei, opposite Upper Imbatsk. (Luftschiffbau Zeppelin.)

play their part. Portions of the Gran Chaco are so infested with insects that cattle do not thrive. The same must be said of the swampy grasslands of the upper Paraguay River as well as the lowland strips that border the Matto Grosso. In consequence, the fringe of settlement is broken or feebly occupied, for a pastoral life is the only one suited to a country so distant from the railways. Ordinary farming is here impossible because of the extreme droughts of the dry season, and the irrigation of a hacienda requires capital in substantial amounts from the start.

Within the area of tolerable temperatures there are further limitations. Parts of the Matto Grosso of Brazil have a porous soil that absorbs the rainfall so quickly that it is markedly sterile or semiarid, supporting only drought-resisting vegetation. In another part of the country saw grass grows in substantial amounts. It lacerates the mouths of grazing animals, and this tends to restrict the grazing industry and still further limit the area of possible development. In Patagonia patches and strips of agricultural land are found along the base of the mountains and on the transverse valley floors that extend eastward from the base of the Andes. An investigation of each pioneer belt would show the limits of those rigorous conditions of too porous soil, of repellent vegetation, of distant and inaccessible tracts regarding which expert knowledge is demanded if intelligent communities of people are expected to settle there.

Outside of the temperature limits shown in Figure 39 (i.e. equatorward of the one and poleward of the other), man is by no means excluded, but his handicaps are much greater and his activities much more specialized and restricted. His form of living is so highly adapted that he does not possess the soil in the thoroughgoing way of full agricultural development. It is true that the rain-forest belts of the tropics, and the drier subtropical lands about their borders, have large areas of land capable of high development. But to the white man a tropical settlement is still like the medieval walled town: the wild beasts of legend are the microbes, and the wall is medical science. It still costs too much to keep the wall in repair, and commercial development is aimed primarily at money making, not the conquest of tropical diseases.

The discussion that has raged over Queensland and Northern Territory (Australia), as well as their present condition, show that tropical settlement by the white man is still in the laboratory stage. The magic productivity of the tropics is a myth if the

FIG. 42

FIG. 43

FIG. 44

FIG. 42—Harvesting wheat in the valley of Esquel in the colony of 16 de Octubre, Patagonia. (Bailey Willis, Northern Patagonia. Photo supplied by Ministerio de Obras Públicas, Buenos Aires.)
FIG. 43—German model farm at Rio Negro, Paraná.
FIG. 44—A new settlement on the Tokachi Plain, Hokkaido. (R. B. Hall, *Geogr. Rev.*, Vol. 21, 1931.)

white man is himself to do the primary work. It is a fact only if
one accepts a low standard of living or employs natives for the
manual labor. For decent or high standards the obstacles are
still too formidable.

The Matto Grosso of Brazil offers an illuminating contrast
between a pioneer area on the border of the tropics and a region of
normal settlement. A balance has long been maintained between
the natural environment of the Matto Grosso and the limits of
toleration endurable to man. A single long railway arm extends
from São Paulo west by north to the Paraguay River, and up the
Paraguay there is continued a transportation service by launches
to the head of navigation (p. 329). At Cuyabá there is reached
what may be called the very edge of civilization, government, and
modern life if we may indeed stretch the term that far. A few days'
travel, and one is at the edge of the wilderness; a week more, and
conditions are altogether primitive. Parts of the Gran Chaco of
southeastern Bolivia illustrate similar conditions. Yet in these
areas cattle are produced; they are driven to the railway; hides
and *charqui* are important items of transport. Men have established homes at distances covered by a week or a month of slow
cattle driving to the railroad or the river. Telegraph lines are widely
spaced and may be inaccessible. Mails may arrive twice a week, or
weekly, or biweekly. There is a natural limit to the transport
of heavy machinery, imposed in the first instance by the nature of
the roads and in the second instance by the necessity of transporting
any refined product over great distances under difficult conditions
to a railroad on which there are high freight rates and to an *entrepôt*
where there is competition with the same products produced elsewhere under more favorable conditions.

No pioneer area is a broad unbroken belt. It is, rather, a series
of scattered patches and strips loosely disposed in beltlike form
beyond the fringe of present settlement. Taking a world view we
see the pioneer lands in a rough zonal arrangement, each continent
having its share. A world map (Fig. 38) shows a belt in each
temperate zone and a large number of "spots" still in the pioneering
stage. It shows two similar zones of subtropical development of
which the southern has by far the larger extent, large enough to be
shown on even a small world map. The rain-forest belts of the
tropical zones have already been mentioned as a special case.

The "pioneer belts" map of the world includes only a little
land in the United States but much more in Canada—a broad belt

reaching from the prairie states eastward across northern Ontario
and parts of Quebec with their newly developing "clay belts."
In Asia it includes much territory on each side of the belt of settlement that has followed the Trans-Siberian railroad, expanding
northward to distant subarctic limits of agriculture and eastward

FIG. 45—View of Crown Hill "oasis," South Australia, 70 miles southwest of Lake Eyre. The
iron tank supplies the "oasis." This is surrounded by wire netting to keep out rabbits, emus,
and kangaroos. Inside this is a brushwood fence to keep out the sand drift. There is no permanent
settlement between this "station" and the Indian Ocean at La Grange—one thousand miles to
the northwest. (Photograph by Griffith Taylor, *Geogr. Rev.*, Vol. 8, 1919.)

to include most of the Amur country. Northern Manchuria and
Inner Mongolia continue the Asiatic belt and present a thousand-
mile front of pioneer land. Their arable sections are filling up at
so rapid a rate that their political and economic control involves
all adjacent sovereignties. When we learn that in the four years,
1924–1928, no less than two million Chinese immigrants are estimated to have settled permanently or semi-permanently in Manchuria we realize how fast this fecund people has pushed along the
political problems of our time in one of the largest pioneer belts in
the world. Chinese agricultural pioneers in large numbers are
crowding back the Mongolian nomads and creating "outside
the Wall" a new set of political conditions and forging social and
economic changes whose bearings we cannot yet see.

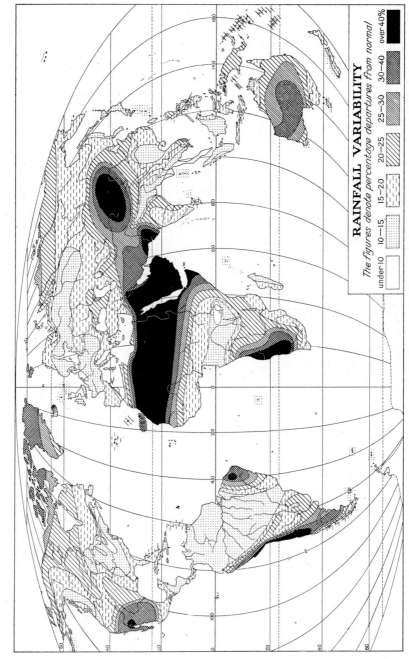

FIG. 46—World map of rainfall variability.   Based on Erwin Biel: Die Veränderlichkeit der Jahressumme des Niederschlags auf der Erde, *Geographischer Jahres-bericht aus Österreich*, Vol. 14–15, 1929, Plate 21.

To the Australian politician the whole interior of that continent is capable of development up to the level of the United States. The hard fact remains that no amount of ardor can increase the rainfall. The semiarid and arid parts of the interior of Australia will not yield to aspiration merely. Its climate takes no account of votes. It has also been found that huge appropriations will not work magic. Money cannot guarantee clouds and rain!

To conquer the pioneer areas on the semiarid fringe of the interior of Australia requires the expenditure of vast sums on railways, public works, and water supplies; but to be successful they must be works that are established by painful experiment. Each region must have its own laboratory for the study of the science of settlement. The British Empire Settlement Act after the war sought to push settlers into the pioneer lands. Western Australia became a focus of activity. The assisted settlers, working in groups, cleared the land, fenced it, put houses upon it, elected members of the group to have first chance to buy the land which the group had cleared. Many did not want to purchase but chose rather to continue upon the government payroll. Others tried farming for a time and then failed. On the one side the politician may claim success as he counts population; on the other, the economist sees failure as he studies the cost of the enterprise.

An Australian economist deplores the rapid growth of cities in the Commonwealth. Australia has the largest number of large cities, in proportion to the whole population, of all countries in the world. Even with the artificial stimuli of vast sums spent on railways, roads, land resumption, assisted immigration, and advances to settlers, there were but ninety thousand more people engaged in agriculture in the Commonwealth in 1921 than in 1891. "Decaying rural towns are dotted all over the map of eastern Australia."

This looks as if pioneering were a real problem to Australia's six millions. There is the land, but the "invitation" lacks something which government is asked to supply. Too many Australians look upon their realm as a place to acquire the means to retire to the city. Land requires a lifetime of study if its possibilities are to be realized, and how much greater the need for study if it is land of the experimental type at the pioneer fringe. It will not do its best for those who skin it and run away to enjoy the proceeds elsewhere.

The pioneer lands of Africa lie in two broad divisions on the

north and south of the tropics. They have a quite special interest
because their development depends upon the use of native labor.
Moreover they are, in the main, marginal to the tropics. Adaptations of ordinary agricultural practice are wide, and the boundaries
of the land capable of white development or management are
affected by cool highlands and the likeliest outlets for railways
and river boats. We have included in our map of pioneer belts
a section of Africa, south of the equator, that lies above 3280
feet (1000 meters); and lower territories in the Sudan and on the
northern edge of the Sahara carry specialization of crops even
further. Political sovereignty is exercised in such special forms—
colonies, mandates, independent states, British dominion states,
protectorates—that both political and social questions of varied
sort impinge upon settlement. The mandated territories have been
responsible for critical reviews of the problems of other territories
and peoples, and, as we shall see later on, almost all of Africa has
been thrown into the crucible of experiment.

The remaining pioneer lands of the world are mostly in regions
of deficient and less reliable rainfall. Their occupation ought
therefore to give great stimulus to studies in long-range weather
forecasting—or better long-range "climatic trends." Whatever
the difficulties, science will converge its resources upon the problem
of long-range forecasting with increasing intensity. There is
too much at stake for it to be otherwise. The polar regions may
furnish clues;[1] sunspots are being studied from this standpoint;
tree rings have yielded evidence that seems pertinent; and the
record of the rise and fall of inland lakes and the changing character
of their deposits are believed to have diagnostic value. Some
striking forecasts have already been made for southern California,
India, and Argentina. When the day of more reliable correlations
and forecasts shall have come the remaining pioneer lands will be
the chief beneficiaries of the new knowledge. Their occupation
will be less hazardous when we know "the times and seasons."
Science cannot change the rainfall; but if it can foretell it, even
approximately, it will provide the essential fact upon which relief
in years of drought and types of land use will chiefly depend.

One of the most useful of recent world maps is Figure 46. It
shows the *variability* of rainfall. It might also be called a world
map of relative rainfall *dependability*. "Inches of rainfall" is only
a statistical expression. It means little or nothing from the stand-

[1] Isaiah Bowman: Polar Exploration, *Science*, Vol. 72, 1930, pp. 439–449.

point of plant and animal functioning, crops, human life, future development. A geographer must know how reliable is the rainfall from year to year and how it is distributed in relation to the growing season of crops. Biel's map is of special interest from the pioneering point of view. If the map were also to show the seasons of heaviest and lightest rainfall its value would be greatly increased. Climatic data require interpretation in terms of possible crops. Like so-called economic data their value lies in their relation to human systems of culture which have their own complex modes of origin and distribution.

CHAPTER SIX

RAILWAYS AS PIONEERS

But, gentlemen, the great desideratum *is railway* communication
—Lord Strathcona

ONE of the first engineers to visit the western border of the copper country of the Belgian Congo is said to have required for his transport and sustenance 5000 native carriers organized as a sort of flying wedge. An enterprise of such scope can be supported only if the man is an expert engineer and the resourceful company that sent him believes the copper deposit to be rich. Evidently his business was more important than that of the man who wrings a living from the earth. A white inhabitant trying to get his produce *out* by native carriers would be bankrupt. This means that there is an *effective economic limit* to which a farmer and even a miner, for that matter, can transport a commodity. What that limit may be depends on the scale of the productive operation, the state of the roads, the means of transport, the cost of labor, and the market value of the product. Time changes each of these values. For example, the mines of Peru and Bolivia are now largely tied to railroads; but until 1892 the silver and tin of far-famed Potosí were transported by pack train and mule cart to the Pacific seaboard over 500 miles away at incredible cost. Perhaps the record is held by Serrania de Guadalupe in southern Bolivia from which in 1884 metals were sent by pack train to Rosario distant 1375 miles.

The end of a new railway line at the frontier of settlement is one of the most engaging places in the world. As a focus of interest for the settler it is far more important, as a rule, than any of the stations along the way. That is because a railway line, once built, temporarily settles certain things about land values and transport that "freeze" the economic situation. For a long time after a skeleton system of transport is provided there may be little change in the general situation of the pioneer, for it takes close settlement to bring roads and markets into a really improved state. The end of the railway in a region of active pioneering is an area of wild speculation. The rails may be extended now or later, may go this way or that, a town will spring up here and not there, and every settler feels that his choice of a location is in the path of progress. This means so rapid an increase of capital value, if he is right, that he is willing to endure all manner of hardship for a time and rest his case upon the hazard of his guess.

Two widely contrasted instances are St. Louis in 1846 as described by Parkman in "The Oregon Trail," and the town of Embarcación, Argentina, in 1913. In Parkman's first chapter, entitled "The Frontier," he writes, "Not only were emigrants from every part of the country preparing for the journey to Oregon and California, but an unusual number of traders were making ready their wagons and outfits for Santa Fé. The hotels were crowded, and the gun-smiths and saddlers were kept constantly at work in providing arms and equipments for the different parties of travellers. Steam-boats were leaving the levee and passing up the Missouri, crowded with passengers on their way to the frontier." This was the great western movement, starting from the end of the railway.

The railway to Embarcación in northeastern Argentina at the border of the Chaco country was completed in 1912, and I visited the place the next year. The builders had followed the string of settlements, on or near the piedmont border, as well as the new sugar estates dependent upon irrigation from the mountain streams and upon the Chaco labor supply. Mataco Indians had been attracted by the rewards of a season's labor in the form of brandy, mules or horses, and cotton cloth. From the end of the railway a trail led for hundreds of miles along the foot of the mountains through a string of scattered settlements that extend right to Santa Cruz de la Sierra (Fig. 222, p. 319). There were oil prospects ahead, and iron piping and well-drilling machinery lay about the railway yards. It was estimated that the northward-flowing commerce of the little station amounted to 12,000 tons a year. Only remoteness from the communities of closer settlement had prevented the whole mountain border from becoming a fertile zone of ranches and farms or haciendas.

To the end of the new railway came large herds of long-horned, big-boned, half-wild cattle gathered by the ranchmen and Indians of the Chaco during the season, February to March. After March, water is too scarce and the watering places too far apart for cattle driving, and there is little grass. The gaucho, herding cattle in the scrub, is a picturesque figure still with his *guardamontes* of stiff, tough cowhide to protect him from the thorny scrub. Jerked beef and rice make up the principal elements of his diet. At night he

FIG. 47—Sign post forty-five miles west of Burns, Oregon. (V. M. Tanner, Yellowstone Cut-Off Association.)

sleeps on the trail or at stations that at best are widely spaced in his vast domain. Ranching and farming, the oil fields' trade with the farthermost towns of the mountain border, new sugar estates, a beginning in quebracho cutting, the erection of a few new buildings, arriving and departing pack trains—these were the outstanding features of life, and they lent a color and interest to the place that was not equaled by any other town I saw in Argentina.

What the end of the railway means to the settler depends upon the settler himself as well as the region. If there is active settlement all about, it is but a line connecting him with the outer world. If he is introspective and homesick, and if the settlement is neither active nor hopeful, it may remind him of the joys left behind and thus dim the prospects ahead. Much of the history of settlement is related to railway building.

It is only in a simple society that life in the modern world can be maintained acceptably at great distances from the railway. Even so, production must be highly specialized, labor costs low, and land cheap. The hacienda of South America is described on a later page as the type of self-contained community that can exist at a great distance from the railway and assure the owner of the land a comfortable living and even a sort of rude luxury.

In a land of ordinary farm owners or independent managers or lessees, distance from the market may become an all-important matter. Specialization may exist in as true a sense as in the case of the hacienda or plantation; but it is a free choice, not an extreme necessity. Wheat growing is practicable on a commercial scale only within fifteen to thirty miles of a railway, and the latter figure is never exceeded except where new land provides an inducement. The independent farmer will not accept so low a standard of living as the peon of a hacienda or the black man on a plantation;

which means that the market or the railway to it must be nearer in the case of the farmer of the United States. The peon may still weave his own woolen textiles, accept a hut as a home, eat the plainest fare, and have no social life that bears comparison with a modern farmer.

The efficiency and success of modern farming depend in large part on good transport. This is not obvious at once. It is only as we see the working of the whole economic machine that we realize how closely related are good roads and motor cars to the prices paid at the local market. The whole transport and marketing system of the United States has a degree of flexibility that tends to equalize prices. There is no shortage of food anywhere in the United States from lack of the facilities of transport, though there is shortage in many places for lack of means to employ the facilities. In

Fig. 48—Wireless station, Churchill, Manitoba. (Nat. Resources Intell. Service, Dept. of the Interior, Canada.)

Mexico, before the railway extensions of 1880, the price of corn was so high in one province that people starved after a year of drought while in another province there was overproduction. It was found that a whole nation in the Mexican environment could not be fed and its business made prosperous by a transport system based on the carrying capacity of the mule and the burro.

Every modern state and not a few of the larger states of the past have held good roads and better transport to be almost their first concern. The British can do what the Romans could not do in the way of governing distant territories, largely because of the greater speed of transport and communications. There is a limit beyond which imperial affairs cannot be supported by man and animal transport. The machine-driven ship and plane and the wireless and cable immeasurably increase the range of control. In the United States the wide use of the motor has compelled the reconstruction of the entire road system of the country with such a

Fig. 49—The Pas, Manitoba, looking north. A pioneer town recently become a railway center. (H. A. Innis, *Geogr. Rev.*, Vol. 20, 1930. Photograph from Royal Canadian Air Force.)

change in ease of transport and in social life as to effect an economic revolution within the lifetime of a single generation. The type of our civilization is based on the good road.

A few years ago I drove through a section of eastern Connecticut along country roads that led across the course of the east-west traffic. The region lay between two main metaled roads about fifteen miles apart. As one left the main road one turned into a narrower crossroad that had a rough but oiled surface. In a short distance that gave way to a graveled road, then a common dirt road, and finally a rutty track that was interrupted by mudholes and boulders. After a few miles of this sort of going the road bettered again, and in reverse order the approach was made to the next main highway on the north. The striking thing about it was the change from the modern to the old-fashioned in the way of houses, fences, and barns, the layout of the fields, and the type of cultivation, in the direction of the poor roads. The only un-

FIG. 50—Hudson Bay Railway crossing the Nelson River at Manitou Rapids. Looking southwest. (H. A. Innis, *Geogr. Rev.*, Vol. 20, 1930. Photograph from Royal Canadian Air Force.)

inhabited houses were along the bad roads. For this the roads
were not alone responsible but distance to market also and especially
the absence of schools. Even the bad-road district had once
supported a thriving community; and not only what it had been
but what it had come down to showed the change in point of view
between the pre-motor and the present type of community life.

The pioneer of today comes out of a motor community. Before
he occupies new land he knows the market price of the products
he can expect to sell and the sort of economy that he must follow
if he is to realize the advantages of cheap land with all its virgin
fertility unimpaired. He can no more think of doing without a
railway or a motor road for long than he can think of himself as a
wilderness hunter in search of food. It is for this reason that the
railway plays such a large part in modern pioneering in spite of
the extreme cases of isolated settlements far from its path. In
the Peace River district of the Canadian Northwest the farmers

have gone a hundred miles from railhead in some cases; but they expect the rails to follow them, and economics and politics both will see that this is done. Nor will they have long to wait. This means that the front of the wave will get the most desirable land and show the widest margin between original cost and later value, except where chance and man-made opportunity may conspire to place a town on the railway. Close settlement comes later and always means a good system of roads and a railway near by. We shall now see what experience and expert opinion have shown to be the *effective economic distance* to a railway in a normal community.

The only detailed study of this sort that I have found in the United States was made in the period 1901 to 1912, the pre-motor era, so far as agriculture is concerned, by the Kansas City Southern, a railroad a thousand miles long extending from Kansas City to the Gulf of Mexico at Port Arthur, Texas. While the patronage of the road was drawn from a belt thirty miles wide, or fifteen miles on each side of it, the significant freight on which the road really depended for its livelihood (in 1901–1912) was drawn from a belt ten miles wide. A comparison was made between five counties closely associated with the road and five in its neighborhood that had no rail facilities. Between 1900 and 1920 the rail counties increased nearly 65 per cent in population while the railless counties decreased more than 5 per cent. The increase in the value of farm property in the one case was 50 per cent greater than in the other. The wide use of the motor car and the extension of the ordinary roads will change these figures no doubt, but they will not lessen the moral of good transport.

How far motor roads may take the place of railways in some pioneer communities is well shown in the Uintah Basin of eastern Utah. Here is a two-county community with a population of 17,000. Vernal, Roosevelt, and Duchesne are the principal town centers. Some traffic goes from Vernal to Craig, Colorado, 100 miles distant. The high rates on a narrow-gauge railway from Watson, 45 miles south and east of Vernal, and its unfavorable market destinations have drawn traffic westward, to Salt Lake City, 180 miles from Vernal, and to Ogden, at a still greater distance! Live cattle and other products are trucked over the graded and well-graveled roads. Mail comes from Price, 90 miles southwest of Vernal (airline distance). The annual Uintah Basin Conference draws two-thirds of the population and provides the means for wide consultation on road and school locations and the best use to make of the limited

FIG. 51

FIG. 52

FIG. 51—An Alaskan wagon road. Valdez-Fairbanks highway in the Chugach Mountains. (Photograph by A. H. Brooks, *Geogr. Rev.*, Vol. 15, 1925.)

FIG. 52—A railroad on Kenai Peninsula, October 20, 1918. (Photograph by Alaskan Engineering Commission.)

number of marketable products—wool, livestock, alfalfa seed, honey, cheese, and butter—that will stand the high transport rates which tend to "eat up the profits."

There is perhaps no better example anywhere of the importance of good transport to pioneer enterprise than in Southern Rhodesia today. An admirable report upon the railways in relation to

FIG. 53—A Red River cart brigade. The Red River carts were used in the pre-railroad days for transportation across the Great Plains from Fort Garry (Winnipeg) to Battleford and Edmonton. (F. J. Alcock, *Geogr. Rev.*, Vol. 10, 1920. Photograph by G. M. Dawson.)

mining and settlement was made in 1925. For political reasons in part, and in part to serve the mines, a railway system came into being that provided one mile of line to every 75 square miles of land, or one mile to every 6½ adult European males. The comparable figure for adult males in relation to railway mileage in the United States is about 460, about 100 to 200 for the various sections of Australia, about 350 for France. If the service of the road had been cheap enough no other new country in the world would have been so well supplied with railways. As it is, the rates are so high that settlement is retarded.

General Hammond found[1] that exportable grain crops would not bear more than 15 miles of ox-wagon transport when rail transport costs must be added. Cotton, tobacco, and dairy products that have a higher selling price and greater margin of profit can bear the cost of a 25-mile haul. With better roads he thinks this distance can be extended. For the present the government classifies its land on the basis of distance from the railway, all within 25 miles of the railway being called "farm land" as distinct from the "ranch land" that lies within the 25-mile and 50-mile strips parallel to the

[1] F. D. Hammond: Report on the Railway System of Southern Rhodesia, Salisbury, 1925.

railway. These great distances are explained by the cheap labor supply, the low cost of the land, and the specialized production.

Specialization is well illustrated by some of the pioneer districts of British Columbia where in recent years the effects of uneconomic distance from the railway were ameliorated when the settler learned cheese making and began to produce honey by utilizing

FIG. 54—Coward Springs depot, showing the fortnightly train proceeding north to Oodnadatta. The railway has been built for more than thirty years, but practically no settlement has resulted. The line is now completed to Alice Springs, Figure 128. (Griffith Taylor, *Geogr. Rev.*, Vol. 16. 1926.)

the wild fireweed blossoms. In the one-crop cereal type of farming as in the wheat belt of Western Australia, the limits are far more narrowly set. The government surveys the land, for prospective settlers, for a distance of only 12 miles, since 10 miles is about the effective economic limit of haul. Light railways have been built into the new wheat-producing country in order to provide quick and cheap facilities. When it comes to wool transport, 50 to 75 miles are readily covered, and in a few places in the United States the limit reaches 100 miles. Two hundred miles are believed to be the limit in Australia. The reader may wish to turn to pages 228 and 318 for a description of similar cases from southern Africa and South America.

In Siberia the low standard of living and the peasant's cheap time, lengthen the distance that land may be occupied on either side of rails. The farmer is there tied to the railway only in a limited sense and in areas of close settlement. In the more open type of settlement he has extended his operations over 100 miles from the railway, aided in winter by the snow cover which affords a natural road. Argentina shows a dependence upon rails that is perhaps as striking as any to be found in the world today. The pampa in the modern grain-growing period of Argentine development has been cropped only so far as the rails have been accessible by a 15-mile haul. The railway net and the edge of settlement have shown a continuing and close relation to each other.

For the vital relation of railroads to pioneering look at the railway net and the edge of the settlement today. The essential parts of the maps of the continents with respect to settlement are shown on pages 147, 175, 203, 257, 304. If we could see the maps grow by ten-year periods we should find that during the past thirty years the track extensions have been mainly in the less densely settled parts of the world. The United States passed the peak in 1916, and both the United States and Europe have had declining percentages of the world's total for two or three decades. It is the newer parts of the earth that attract the railway builders. For it is there that *the railway is the forerunner of development, the pre-pioneer, the base line of agriculture.*

Sometimes the railway lags behind the settler but not for long. The government is too eager to catch up with taxable land and increase its production. No government can afford to ignore the development of its resources. When more land is occupied by a farming population, the demands upon the cities increase, land values rise, industries expand. To intrinsic values and assets is added the indispensable asset of hope: tomorrow will be better than today; the tone of business is good; new capital is invested. The phenomenon is familiar to all Americans who have sprung from any part of the expanding West. The sense of greatness invades the consciousness of even the poorest. There is also the feeling that our own kind of people ought to occupy the lands of which we are possessed. Believing in ourselves, we want our descendants to inherit the earth. This is true of most of the newer communities of men in the world today.

Leaders may see even farther. Vacant land can be a source of political danger. It may attract another kind of people who also wish more land. The empty lands of the world are politically of two classes, active and passive. It is the business of government leaders not to permit any land that they might control to be politically passive. It is a source of power once its potentialities of settlement are realized. It not only helps the controlling national power but it keeps out political and social undesirables. A white Australian policy has definite, even if distant, political objectives, but it also has social objectives of the highest order. Not the land alone or its resources but that land as a theater for the working out of social and political ideals is at the roots of the policy.

Such are the motives that impel the railway builders as agents of business and empire in the newer lands. The railway has even been a pioneer of politics and modern development at the present-day pioneer fringe of some of the oldest lands and civilizations. The double rôle of the railway in economics and politics is well shown in Russian Central Asia (the Trans-Caspian country). There the growth of cotton and dried fruits has produced a need for cheaper transport. New irrigation works have been undertaken, the grasslands of the steppe have been invaded by the Russian colonist farmer, and railway building, particularly the "Turk-Sib" enterprise (page 259), has supplied the transport facilities that give life to the whole economic scheme. At the same time it serves to extend Russian political power in the buffer state of Afghanistan and to offset the growing political interest of Great Britain in northern India. It was not primarily for the economic service it could give that the Trans-Siberian railway was thrown eastward to the Pacific but to consolidate an empire. Colonization and pioneering have radiated from the railway in all the favorable centers of home making. Most of its branch lines have been built primarily as economic outlets to market and to serve the far-wandering colonist who, coming from old Russia, has here found an outlet at last for that land hunger that he was never able to satisfy at home.

CHAPTER SEVEN

SCIENCE PLAYS A PART

Our science is a drop, our ignorance a sea.
—WILLIAM JAMES

SCIENCE is like the pioneer in making things happen instead of waiting for things to happen. Every scientific truth goes pioneering. While man's culture may rise superior to his environment, it is equally true that the force of new ideas and the pressure of living have required man to rise superior to his prevailing culture. He measurably conquers his environment with the tools or the techniques at his command and every now and then improves both of them. He finds, for example, that grass grows best in regions where it is most difficult to cure, so he decides that he will not accept the handicap of poor grass in a good climate, or of good grass in a poor climate, but checkmate the climate by *artificially* curing grass wherever it grows best, and thus provide his stock with green feed the year round. Where deep snow blockades him for months at a time in winter he still pursues his economic objectives by inventing machines that to some degree conquer snow. When navigation demanded the refinement of an instrument for measuring longitude, the creative faculties of scientific men were stimulated by a government that offered a commanding prize. For over a century the "Royal Commissioners Constituting the Board of Longitude" remained in existence at London, continued the search for a perfected chronometer, and disbursed public money to the extent of a half million dollars.

The dry border of the pioneer lands of every continent offers science an especially wide field of inquiry and experiment. The engineer sees the physical job—the dam to be built, the canals for water distribution, the installation that will provide electric current—the harnessing of power, in short. If he is more than a technician he will look at the economic returns also; and, if not, he will be brought back to realities by the economist or the hard facts of existence quickly realized by the farmers who use his beautifully organized but possibly uneconomical plant.

The magic wrought by irrigation in the classic civilizations of the Near East has led us to a wrong conclusion about its use in a civilization of quite another type and upon our frontiers of settlement today. When one looks at an export list instead of at the standard of living of the people who make the list possible, one is struck with the productivity of an irrigated soil. But if the welfare of a people is the first consideration the story is quite a different one. We háve been led into thinking that engineering skill can transform the deserts of the world into productive gardens for the benefit of all concerned. The job can be done if there is no question of paying the piper. A city could be built at the South Pole or an artificial rain-provoking mountain range constructed in the Sahara, but it wouldn't pay to do either of these things. Between what is physically possible and what is commercially possible there may be a wide gulf. Nature has a way of taking heavy toll for man's conditional conquests. Man can throw a railway across a mountain range, but every ton of freight that he carries across the mountain takes so much more coal because of the heavy grades. The price of the coal is the toll that man pays to the mountain.

It is precisely the same with irrigation. We have had an admirable laboratory test in the United States. The Reclamation Service has been in existence for twenty-eight years. It has done constructive work in providing water for valley floors and bench lands in selected places in the arid West. It has developed irrigation projects where water has been stored and where the settler has been invited to come in under terms regarded as generous. The government has thus tackled directly the problem of the population capacity of the land. Yet what has been the result? In twenty-eight years how many people have we actually taken care of? The total farming population upon the twenty-four national irrigation projects of the West after twenty years of government aid and generosity was but 140,000, a population equal to that of the city of Long Beach, California, or Tulsa, Oklahoma. Irrigation alone will not solve questions of general overpopulation or the much deplored cityward movement. It is easy to see that a quite modest improvement of agricultural practice in settled communities will accomplish much more for the increase of agricultural production and the support of population than all the millions that have been poured out upon the government-built irrigation works of the West in a quarter of a century.

In the same period the population of the irrigated lands of the eleven western states and of the pastoral lands connected therewith has grown much more rapidly because unassisted irrigation

FIG. 55

FIG. 56

FIG. 57

FIG. 55—Cleared land and ringbarked trees in group settlement, Western Australia.

FIG. 56—Scrub roller for clearing, Peel Estate, Western Australia.

FIG. 57—Government excavator purchased for Peel Estate, Western Australia. (Photographs from Agent General for Western Australia, London.)

and development takes the line of greatest economic advantage. If it pays, it's done, and not otherwise. This means that only the best prospects are selected for development. The twenty-four government irrigation projects include land that private enterprise could not attempt to improve. Government is trying to do the economically impossible. The crisis was reached several years ago when it was time for returns to be reckoned with. The settler could not meet his payments. We hear no more about "homes for freemen": the man on a government irrigation project is really in bondage not to government as he supposes but to economic law of which even a rich government has sooner or later to take account.

Yet if we were to import Egyptians they would make our government reclamation schemes work because they would accept a standard of living unthinkably low for us. Irrigation must offer men the same advantages that they can win elsewhere if it is to attract settlers to the arid lands. Fine dams and aqueducts, rain and river gauges, and a picture of smiling verdure will not avail if the economic set-up is wrong. How much do people have to pay for the land? What will the soil return under an accustomed system of culture? What is the standard of living that must be accepted? These are the questions that are asked of the reclamation projects, by the prospective settler, and they are the same questions that he asks of the pioneer belts. Farming is not an exact science anywhere, and there will always be room for judgment as to what it is best to do or where it is best to go. Reclamation will progress if it makes an appeal to settlers that gives them the same wide chance to succeed that low capital values and virgin fertility afford him in the pioneer lands. When we lock the settler tightly within the con-

FIG. 58

FIG. 59

FIG. 60

FIG. 58—Oxen plowing, Island of Orleans, Quebec. (Canadian National Railways.)

FIG. 59—Homemade root drag, Peace River, Alberta. (Canadian National Railways.)

FIG. 60—Combining wheat, 38 miles northwest of Jordan, Montana.

fines of a five per cent system and leave no room for the *unusual opportunity* he will turn his back on the government-assisted project and strike out for the untamed lands on his own responsibility or try a new experiment with the latest idea in machine cultivation.

An open mind and an active imagination are necessary today in framing or understanding settlement policies that take account of economic trends. Doubtless these qualities were always needed; but in our times there are so many new instruments of power come suddenly into use whose ultimate effects no man can foresee—least of all the people who use them—that political and social intelligence are far outrun. The web of commerce was beginning to be so tightly drawn that a self-contained life was a mark of isolation and insignificance for any country, when radio came along to give men and causes such widened scope as we had not dreamed of. The net of airways is growing so fast that in a few years we shall expect to be able to reach any part of the earth by airplane, and we shall be surprised if any country is so benighted as not to have an air service. The sky and the sea have become new realms for the exercise of power. Since man asks so much more of nature, said Lord Bryce, he is obliged to study her more closely; and he regarded the progress of the "sciences of nature" as one of the three changes in the modern world "of the utmost consequence for the writing of history."

As new conceptions are imported into human relationships the relationships themselves become new and the march of humanity is deflected from its earlier course. At the turn of the road in olden times stood the emotional prophet to warn and forecast in mystic terms. Nowadays it becomes the test of science to look a little way into the future: the business cycle, short-range (miscalled long-range) weather forecasting, the effect of farm practices on soil fertility and past that to the social aftermath—these are among the possibly predictable things that affect man's mastery of himself and his power to "frustrate" nature, as Slosson terms it. It is in this spirit that we contemplate the pioneer lands of the world. We no longer look upon pioneering as a mere outward thrust of a virile stock, for all stocks have lost their old-time pioneering virility. Or, if the virility is still there, to exercise it in the old way would be foolish and even suicidal.

Man never conquered his spot of earth merely for the joy of conquest. He was after something of far more importance to him—a better future living for his family and greater opportunities

for his children. The conquest itself was incidental. And if he can
get those things today without the terrible effort of the past why
should he not do so?   Old-time pioneering meant the kind of
extreme physical toil that it is precisely the aim of science nowadays
to reduce. Unless the man upon the land is to become a clod,
a peasant, a serf, he must have a margin of time and strength in
which to develop and release spiritual energies that play upon his
life and outlook.

Spirit counts today as never before; pioneering is not a purely
business question. Pioneers are "luck-hunters," "believers in
luck . . . out yonder." Many of the older pioneers went out
into new territory because they didn't fit into the scheme of things
at home; the modern pioneer asks about the scheme of settlement
and estimates his fitness for it before he leaves home. The answer
to this inquiry is not found in a table of statistics! Sometimes
it is found in the community church. Religious communities
have been especially active in the settlement of Canada for the
past hundred years—not merely the narrower sects such as the
Hutterians, Dukhobors, and Mennonites, but the churches with
a larger following such as Methodists and Presbyterians who, in
the church flock, find a social unit that means a piece of home set
down in the wilderness to make it tolerable. Many a New England
outpost of settlement was bound by the same bonds. The names
of many New England pastors have become historic not merely
because they preached to but also because they led their flocks.
Religion and the community idea together kept many a frontier
settlement going until wider relations were established. The
wanderings and hardships of Israel have many counterparts along
the pioneer trail. The Bible was the textbook of life among the
pioneers of the Middle West.

Time was that the religious community found its haven on the
frontier because society was so narrow a thing that all the *mores*
could be transferred *en bloc*. The peculiarities of each sect set them
off from the rest of the world and stimulated the enforcement
of ancient custom. The policy was to get away from the rest of
humanity and to be "not of this world." To do that today requires
a return to the primitive life in some distant wilderness. For
material culture reaches out to the very border of the settled
communities, and no man can shut his eyes to the advantages of it.
The older generation could live on religion, the younger will not.
The consequence is that the sects of Canada, for example, have

had to look far afield; and Mexico, Paraguay, and South Africa have become the last fields of community experimentation on a religious basis.

Rural free delivery and the cream separator with all that they implied did more to widen pioneer horizons in the period antedating the radio and the motor car than all the other forces that play upon rural communities put together. They killed for all time

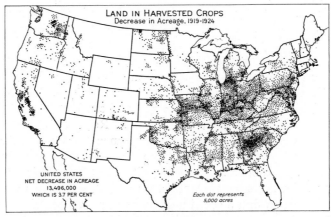

FIG. 61—The decrease in acreage of crops between 1919 and 1924 was general in most of the eastern, originally-forested portion of the United States, in general less fertile than the prairie and plains land and in parts too hilly to be well adapted to the use of modern farm machinery. With rising wages and increasing taxes it has become increasingly difficult to farm some of these eastern lands profitably. Scale approximately 1 : 50,000,000. (Bureau of Agricultural Economics, U. S. Department of Agriculture.)

the pioneer inheritance of the Middle West so far as self-sufficiency and isolation were concerned, and they were the deathblow to the narrower concepts of community living. Rural free delivery took the newspaper everywhere, and the cream separator provided a means for securing a steady cash income which greatly elevated the standard of living.

Who can gauge the willingness of a people to experiment? Who can reduce that willingness to statistics? Here the policy maker finds the going roughest. In taking account of the future population of the United States, and the means to sustain it, and in seeing the relation of western marginal lands to population problems we quite mistake Americans if we suppose that they will become rooted to place. There are many indices, the ones most commonly employed being the drift to the cities and the regional changes in farm acreages

under crops. Changes in dietary habits and the increasing use of
power on the farm have also had powerful effects upon the regional
movement of population. A tractor may not be any cheaper than
a horse, but it eats oil and gas, not hay; which means that the hay
may go into dairy products or the soil may be used for cereals
rather than grass. The combined effect is to increase production
of food crops and lower their price to the point where fewer and

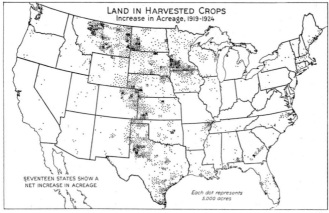

FIG. 62—The increase in crop acreage harvested in 1924, as compared with 1919,
was mostly in the level, or gently rolling portions of the United States, where,
despite the subhumid to semiarid climate and low prices for farm products, the use
of modern machinery, by increasing the area a man can cultivate, has made crop
production profitable on low-priced land. (Bureau of Agricultural Economics,
U. S. Department of Agriculture.)

fewer people will attempt to grow them for a livelihood. With
the amazing increase in the sizes of our cities and the decline of
rural population to less than a third of the total, with increasing
export of manufactured wares, it is astonishing that farm production has increased still faster. The crisis in agriculture is largely
due to the revolutionary *improvements* in agricultural methods.

We might suppose that farms would be abandoned in every region
and that lessening acreages of used land would be the immediate
result. Turn to the two maps, Figures 61 and 62, and see in the
one case the general *decrease* throughout the East in the acreage
of land in harvested crops and at the same time the *increase* in
such acreages on the semiarid border of the Great Plains where
the terrain is well suited to the use of machinery adapted to large-
scale farming. If the movement had been local in the five-year
period which the maps represent, it would be of little interest; but

it affected a whole chain of states from Canada to the Mexican border and indicates a wholesale experimentation that one would scarcely have looked for in communities so long established.

This general willingness to experiment is not based upon a definite forecast of economic success. The farmer does not *know* that he will succeed; he only *thinks* he will. What makes him think so is his common sense plus the general trends of the market and his neighbor's success. What he hears about he would like to try if he thinks he can make a go of it. In widening circles the successful thing becomes known until something like a mass movement results that can then be statistically analyzed and shown to be a good or a bad thing. When an agricultural crisis comes the data are generally available that enable one to say *why it came;* but few there be that can also analyze the figures to the point of showing the way out of the difficulty; and, even if science tries its hand, the farmer is likely to have to find his own remedy instead of taking the prescribed one. He will generally find it through further experimentation.

It has been calculated that even if our population reaches 200 millions we shall need to till but an additional 15 per cent of the land available for crops and not now so used. This would include land now undrained or unirrigated as well as plowable land in pasture and unimproved land in forest or brush. If we do not need to cultivate this unused land when our density of population has become so great, why are we concerned about the pioneer lands not yet subdued? From a purely American standpoint we are interested in them scientifically because they represent the last great advance of the race upon the fringe of inhabitable territory and we want science to help show whether or not it can be done economically. Again, the food production of other lands than our own interests us enormously because transport is now so flexible a thing (and credits and exchange so much more flexible) that what is grown economically elsewhere need not be grown here uneconomically.

New land is in truth irresistible. In a period when increasing acreages of land were being abandoned in the United States, many western farmers were migrating northward to take up cheap land in the Canadian Northwest. But this is after all a very natural movement in view of common customs and language and the general similarity of most elements of culture. It is hardly more than migration from one state to another. Canadians in search of cheap land and a better future would hardly come to the United

States. The strongly marked movements of Canadians into the United States have taken place chiefly in the East. That is because maritime Canada is a poor land in comparison with the eastern part of the United States. The pull of our largest cities has proved irresistible to those with special gifts or training no less than to those who seek employment in the mills.

In the Canadian Northwest settlement has been of two varieties, a first advance, rapid and extreme, which might be compared with a prospector's first examination of a mineral field, and a second advance in closer communities that has been the sure forerunner of full development. The second stage is one that generally takes place at a much slower pace, though it, too, may be rapid in places. More commonly it is an advancing fringe. Land is occupied because it is just over there. No change in the culture system need be made. The tillage is the same, the machinery required is the same, the crops are the same as those already known. If changes are required at all, they are moderate. The old friends are near by and accessible. Such a movement asks no questions of the statistician and the economist. It relies upon its own judgment. It would scarcely look at a soil map. And it certainly looks to no far horizons for opportunities that are or may be better than these. *This* is the bird in the hand. Such an advance is taking place wherever pioneer lands are available and in spite of a world-wide depression in agriculture, difficulties of transport, and great distances to market.

Science attempts to follow more closely than hitherto the lines of experiment and to generalize for the many the experience gained by the few. Best of all, it can bring together from widely scattered fields and put into readable and attractive form the experience of people in all of the pioneer lands where experimentation is going on. And it can reach back into history and analyze the causes of failure and success. It can make its findings known through the radio and the newspaper and by organizations like the Grange and the farmers coöperatives. *Government has too long been content to produce a bulletin and call the matter settled.* The time is coming when a wholly new conception of government will drive executives to get their results much more effectively to the ultimate consumer.

Science has still another function—it can recommend the national measures that affect settlement and the settler's welfare *in the long run and in a way that is invisible to him.* No intelligent immigration policy can be framed by a country having unsettled potential farm

FIG. 63—Seeding operations, Rockyford, Alberta. (Canadian National Railways.)

land of good quality without its knowing under what conditions people can be induced to go upon the land.   No country wants immigration to its cities, for there the newcomer either undercuts the wage earner already on the spot or increases the number of unemployed. People are wanted for primary production of the kinds that require hard physical labor which most people are inclined to evade.   There is an almost universal preference for the softer life of the city. A thorough study of its newer lands is required of every new country in order to gauge the extent to which Europeans may be admitted and how they are to be distributed. A constant interplay is required between immigration and other national policies that affect our social organization in city and country.

Every government with a frontier is faced with the necessity of backing up its own settlers, its pioneers.   Every government has a policy in relation to such persons and to the lands they occupy. These things are no longer isolated phenomena, nor can each continent or country individually solve its own problems of land division or land settlement.   The world community is now sensitive to happenings in its distant and separate parts.   The interna-

FIG. 64—Irrigation channel, Makeri Farm, Lusaka, Northern Rhodesia. (H. C. Darby.)

FIG. 65—Seeding on the "Giant Farm," east of Rostov, Russia. (From C. F. Marbut, *Geogr. Rev.*, Vol. 21, 1931.)

tional trade in two leading textiles, wool and cotton, reveals this sensitiveness in a remarkable way. The two are closely related to each other, and the conditions under which they are produced affect the welfare of the most widely separated communities. The agricultural policies of the United States during the next twenty-five years will develop not only in accordance with the demands of our own cities and with the use made of our own lands but in response to what happens in Canada, Siberia, and Australia. And we shall constantly want better knowledge as to what happens there. Economic laws will oblige us to know, whether we want to or not.

The effect of an invention that becomes a new instrument of power in agriculture is felt in many parts of the world, not merely in the land of its origin; for the agents of distribution carry it to the most distant fields in which there are culture systems capable of using it or willing to use it. When it is put to work upon the land, its cost and the cost of labor and the cost of land and the cost of transportation and the standard of living of the producer and the capacity of the buyer to buy—all these elements make an equation

FIG. 66—Southeastern corner of reclaimed portion of Tule Lake floor, California, looking west.

whose factors are of world origin, not of local origin merely. The
full development of any local community in time drives it to consider
its world relations.

Men no longer live in measurably self-contained units. Their
paths now converge. What we have said of wool and cotton as
horizontally extended world enterprises is also true of a multitude of
other commodities; in fact, all those in the billion- and half-billion-
dollar class, besides many others of lesser degree. Our economic
realms overlap. The solution of the problems resulting from this
overlapping calls for no end of ingenuity.

See what is happening in New England, for example. In 1920,
New England spent about $800,000,000 outside its own territory
to buy food; it consumed over a billion dollars' worth in all.[1] As
compared with fifty years ago, New England has seven million
fewer acres of food-producing land and four million more inhabitants
to feed. Such a process calls for ever fresh study and for continuing
and even accelerated adaptations. Today New England would
live under paralyzing handicaps but for an excellent educational
system, cheap sea food, a considerable amount of water power,
and unusual advantages of position.

We see the bearing of pioneer areas upon world commerce perhaps most clearly in the case of grazing products. The shrinkage
of the world's pasture lands was almost as rapid as land settlement
in the nineteenth century. The trend of prices of meat and hides
has been generally upward. It is doubtful if we have come to the
end of the process although cattle are raised in larger numbers upon
lands of "close settlement" than upon primary grazing regions. But
there is a limit to cattle raising upon close-settled lands, and the
limit is fixed not by the taste of humans for meat but by economic
law. A beast is a wasteful means of transforming vegetable life
into human food. With growing density of population the route
from the soil to the table must be shortened. Less meat and more
vegetables are inexorably demanded. It is in the pioneer areas,
where man is living in scattered farming communities which inter-
sperse the range land, that we see a temporary means for slowing
down, though not stopping, the rise in the prices of meat and hides.

It looks, at first sight, as if it would be simple enough to achieve
the intelligent occupation of undeveloped pioneer lands if the
demand for pastoral products is increasing; but, unfortunately
for so simple and beneficent a result, the qualities of men them-

[1] A. W. Gilbert: The Food Supply of New England, New York, 1924, p. 206.

selves have changed. Humanity is not the same today as it was yesterday. This is true of the prospective settler no less than of the upper classes within the confines of the towns. There is also the effect of intensive machine tillage with no traction animals to feed and a growing use of commercial fertilizers which together seem to have put an end to the need for new land in this generation. The grazing lands of the United States would inevitably increase in extent as the tilled acres diminish were it not for the difference in capital and tax structures in the newer and older counties. Hence the paradox that land which is best adapted to range purposes is temporarily cultivated in years of heavier rainfall while permanently better farming land farther east lies idle for want of tenants.

In succeeding chapters the nature of existing pioneer lands will be described in greater detail, and we shall then return to the regional applications of many of the principles here sketched in outline only.

PART TWO

REGIONAL EXAMPLES

CHAPTER EIGHT

WESTERN ZONES OF EXPERIMENT IN THE UNITED STATES

They have learned when to hustle and when to wait without losing courage.
—E. O. Wooton, *Settlers' Progress* . . .

Central and Southeastern Oregon

IN central Oregon is a famous road that crosses the "High Desert" and the lower lands that border it—in all, 135 miles of highway that runs with a determined air through the sage from Bend to Burns. Between Bend and the High Desert, sage and juniper border it, the latter in a distant view looking like a cool forest of evergreens (Fig. 72). Some sections of the road traverse unwooded hilly country. Most of the land is mantled with a light volcanic ash, which accentuates the desertic appearance where the sage is thin. In a few of the larger valleys there are irrigated fields. Along the High Desert road or within sight of it are 70 houses and shanties, of which only 19 were occupied in August, 1930. The doorless and windowless dwellings that are deserted (Fig. 67) are mostly of the type which are included in the "improvements" required by law to be made on homesteaders' plots and mark the places where settlers came in for a few years before the World War and tried to turn sage brush country into grainfields and ranches.

Some of the buildings have been overturned by the wind. The wire has been removed from the fence posts. Gates are warped out of shape or hang on the verge of collapse. The land has returned to its wild state except where good sites have made it possible for farmer ranchers to hold on. "I wouldn't give a nickel for a whole section of it," said the owner of one plot, who manages to live by selling goods on painfully long credit to his hard-driven neighbors. The history of the High Desert boom settlements—in a region that was called "the last homestead frontier in America" as late as 1925—is one of substantial failure.

The railway builders lost no time in stimulating the coming of settlers into a region where most of the land is unsuited for farming of any kind and gain-seeking land locators did their full share after the settlers arrived. The passage of the enlarged homestead act of 1909 was followed by the rapid spread of settlement in the Great Basin region, and this was further stimulated by a dry-farming boom that spread over much of the arid and semiarid sections of the West before and after the World War, largely in response to cheap land and the high price of wheat.

The annual rainfall of the High Desert of central and eastern Oregon is from 8 to 12 inches, with as much as 16 inches at long

FIG. 67—Abandoned house and farm buildings, High Desert, Oregon.

intervals as in 1922. The records of the Weather Bureau and the land studies of the Geological Survey reveal a short growing season. Crops are likely to be damaged by frost, the last spring frost occurring half the time in the month of June. The settlers came in a time of good seasons: after the peak of settlement, 1912–1917, precipitation was above normal in four out of six years and only slightly below normal in the other two years. If the land were productive under tillage it would have been demonstrated then. But the crops for even this favorable five-year period were below the normal for successful dry farming. Abandonment of the area was already in train when the World War came and drew off the young men who composed the greater part of the new population. That proved to be the finishing touch, and the High Desert reverted to sage except where the large size of the holdings and the better location of some of the cultivated tracts permitted a farming-ranching type of occupation to succeed.

Stepping across the outer limit of possibilities to experiment with land is characteristic of every region where the marvels of dry farming and the recurrence of wet years bring temporary and local success. The story gets about that money is easy to make on cheap land. Superficially a poor farm may look much like a good one. Experimentation with crops and tillage methods is the key to occupation of any sort. It runs right through the history of the semiarid West. And it is small wonder that there seems to be no

FIG. 68—Two miles north of boundary between Jefferson and Deschutes counties, Oregon, at a point three-fifths of the way from Bend to Madras, where the Washington-Oregon wheat belt has its southern termination. A map of the region may be found on page 105.

limit to land occupation when so much has already been done that once appeared to be impossible. The settlers were justified in believing the land good for dry farming, seeing what a dry-farming technique had done in sagebrush country in Washington and Montana. They could not be expected to know that the summers were drier than in other treeless regions that produced grain. Snow-capped peaks were on the western horizon. The main streams ran full. On the slopes of the Cascades and spreading out over the higher border of the adjacent plains were magnificent stands of western yellow pine. Explorers had reported the surfaces of basins and uplands covered with bunch grass "as thick as a meadow."

Settlers "poured" into central Oregon long before there was a railroad. The first comers of the seventies were stockmen. The "desert" east of the wooded eastern flanks and fringe of higher piedmont that borders the Cascades (Fig. 74) was long a sheep and cattle pasture. Bands of sheep and herds of cattle were driven

eastward of the mountains to winter in the comparatively warmer
basins of the desert. In summer, as the lower pastures became hot
and dry, they were returned to the higher valleys.[1] A range war
was in full swing at the turn of the century in the country east of
Prineville and was marked by the slaughter of sheep by cattlemen and the lynching of several sheepmen in the town.   Down

Fig. 69—Topographic cross section of the country east of the Cascade Mountains in the vicinity
of Bend, central Oregon.

to 1885 there was still little permanent settlement in the Bend
country outside of the scattered ranching communities.

By 1903 the growing settlements at Prineville and Bend gave sub-
stance to talk about a railroad, which came to Bend only after eight
more years of waiting. On June 12, 1903, the first automobile
reached Lakeview, Ore., on its transcontinental journey to New
York. It had taken eleven days to come from San Francisco!

There was a doctor at Prineville, but that was thirty miles away
for the people of Bend; and there were no motor cars or motor roads
at that time, no telephone to Prineville, no bridge across the
Deschutes River which runs through Bend. "No one dares to get
sick," said one observer, who thought that the coming of a doctor
would mean a 100 per cent increase in sick calls as folks became
ailment-conscious! Silver Lake asserted, albeit inaccurately, that
its 180 miles from the nearest railway put it farther from rails than
any other post office in the country. Southeastern Oregon is still
described by transport experts as the largest undeveloped triangle
of railless territory in the United States (Fig. 70). Not everyone
wants modern transport. One rancher boasted to me that he was
born 280 miles from a railway and that it was becoming impossible
to realize his ambition of dying at some point more distant still!

It is a land of winter rain; and when there is exceptionally heavy
rain in summer there is an epidemic of hopefulness. All the talk of
the early days was about rain. The dryness of the winter and spring
of 1908 led to the poorest crop prospect in six successive seasons, but

[1] The general shift of stock between summer and winter grazing grounds is known as "transhumance." It is a feature of human occupation throughout the Great Basin. For a map of seasonal grazing regions in Nevada see the *Geogr. Rev.*, Vol. 16, 1926, p. 488. For a study of transhumance in Utah see Langdon White: Transhumance in the Sheep Industry of the Salt Lake
Region, *Econ. Geogr.*, Vol. 2, 1926, pp. 414–425.

"the recent rains promise an average crop and the farmers are jubilant," said the *Bend Bulletin*, whose back numbers are filled with news of settlement in progress. Everybody was holding on until the railroad came, when the land would increase in value. "Nothing else would have induced them to leave comfortable homes in older settled sections and move into a new country so far removed from a railroad," says a sympathetic contributor. The reasoning seems circular. It is the gambler complaining because he doesn't always win. True, the coming of the railway would save 15 cents a bushel on grain transport by substituting rail haulage for mule- and horse-drawn freighters (see frontispiece). A great increase in acreage would follow cheaper transport, and did, but not always was there a crop to harvest.

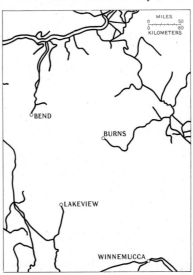

FIG. 70—Remoteness from railways of settlements in central and southeastern Oregon.

The stage roads provided travelers the opportunity of scanning the country for good sites. By 1905 many settlers had drifted into the Bend-Prineville "desert" where not a farm "nor a drop of water" (running water) had been seen two years before. They were self-styled pioneers "invading the wilderness" and "making promising homes." The juniper was cleared off and made into firewood and fence posts, the stumps uprooted and burned, the land cleared of stones, leveled, and plowed. Desert, juniper, sagebrush, experimentation—yet the stream continued. The first regular railway train came into Bend on the night of October 31, 1911. Three years after that, in 1914, ensued the greatest settlement activity in the history of central Oregon. Thirteen carloads of "immigrants' movables" arrived in the month of March alone. They represented fifteen families from Oregon, Washington, and Idaho. In the same year 15,000 sheep arrived in 65 cars from Coleman, 60 miles to the north. They were on their way to the summer grazing ranges in the mountains and came from their winter quarters in the lower country to the east and north. The transport of sheep by rail between summer and winter feeding grounds is now a practice of considerable extent in the Great Basin country.

Southeastern Oregon proclaimed itself "the greatest free-land opening for the homesteader left in the West"; and by 1910 it was available in 320-acre units—rolling land with a cover of sage and bunch grass. Settlers were enthusiastic about life in a 10 by 12

FIG. 71—The road from Bend to Burns. Characteristic High Desert country.

cabin, wheat outside the door, and domestic water 14 to 20 feet down in the lower sites near the streams. Late in 1910 and early in 1911, in a period of three months, thirty homesteaders' cabins were built within a radius of ten miles of Bend, most of them towards the southeast. "From every prominent hill one can see the clearing work being carried on." Settlers came by motor car, horse team, hack, stage, on horseback, and afoot from the nearest railway station 100 miles away. It wasn't the Klondike "rush" it was pictured to be—that is the booster's note; but it was a movement by scores and by hundreds. It didn't double the wheat output of Oregon, but it did widely extend the limits of unprofitable wheat production.

Most of the entrymen were unmarried. Many of them came from Seattle—city men and women who saw here a chance to make a beginning. By the first of May, 1911, 300 land filings on 96,000 acres were reported in Crook County, which then included Deschutes, and the wave had spread from the lower country right over the High Desert. By the spring of 1912 a note of caution had crept in. Farmers were warned not to depend on one crop or to attempt to cultivate too much. Though the railway had come to Bend, heavy teaming was necessary to get merchandise out into the country and the grain crops back to the railway. It cost 25 cents a mile to haul a ton of farm produce over an ordinary unimproved road. There was much talk of the rates by this route and that, so much a pound or a ton. In July, 1912, it was asserted that the motor truck run to Burns from Bend was "the longest in the country." The crops were good that year, and men clung to the fact that settlers had been in the country southeast of Bend for 40 years.

This was a second wave of pioneering; the first wave came forty

FIG. 72—View from Pilot Butte, Oregon, looking west over the town of Bend to the Cascade Mountains.

years earlier. The first settlers of southeastern Oregon were young men who had come from the east and south in two- and four-horse wagons, women and children, two and three weeks on the road. The settlers of the Bend region were a backwash from the Willamette Valley region. Having established themselves upon the better agricultural land west of the Cascades they came back over the mountains to take advantage of the fine pasture for sheep and cattle. Everything had to be freighted for long distances over poor roads. Freighting for the first isolated and distant communities of southeastern Oregon was a picturesque business—wool, hides, grain to Portland by freight wagon, in summer right over the mountains, in winter down the Columbia gorge.

It was hard on the women when the men were off freighting to distant points or out on the range for several weeks at a time. "Our women didn't mind," said my informant; "because that was the kind of life everybody lived," echoed his wife. "We had such remedies as pioneers always have"—which meant that they had next to nothing. The climate is healthful. Epidemics were unknown because of isolated living. "We had to shoot somebody to start a cemetery," said one of the oldest of the Burns pioneers. They

FIG. 73

FIG. 74

FIG. 75

FIG. 73—Sheep ranch 16 miles north of Pasco, Washington, showing "blowy" soils of the permanent range country west of the wheat belt.

FIG. 74—Summer pasture in forest openings, Cascade Mountains, Oregon.

FIG. 75—Typical juniper and sage composition in the lower country between Bend and the High Desert, Oregon.

thought of themselves not in a heroic way but as simple folks "looking for a place to make a home, get along, and grow up with the country." All of the older settlers still living are personalities; their saliencies have not been smoothed away by custom.

An enthusiastic settler of 1911 said, "Mark my words, this homestead country of yours will make one of the finest grain regions in the West." But by 1914 the people of Bend began to call the region "semiarid." By 1923 there was much putting forward of irrigation as the solution of agricultural development. The farmers began to look to the streams for salvation. There is heavy snowfall in the mountains and the Deschutes River is fairly regular in its flow. The homesteading talk had nearly died out. A county agriculturist was pointing to the realities of the situation. "Colonization" was the word in 1930 when I interviewed half a hundred residents along a thousand-mile route. The Oregon State Chamber of Commerce has appointed a man to promote state colonization.

Six years ago the territory tributary to Bend was called a "pioneer country, whose development has not yet been stabilized." [2] What had been a pioneer country in 1875 was still pioneer country. Bend might be prosperous because of its lumber mills and tributary trade areas, but the key to successful living on the land had not yet been found. One observer said, "I have seen many sorts of desperation, but none like that of the men who attempted to make a home out of 350 acres of High Desert sage." The sage plains of the southeastern portion of the state are not worthless territory, but the attempt to settle them has drawn much narrower limits to cultivation than the settlers of this twentieth century were long willing to believe.

It is sheep and cattle pasture except as farms can be located in moister localities, or a crop brought to maturity in years of heavier rainfall or on lowland patches and belts made fruitful by the application of irrigation water. Even as ranch country it has its drawbacks. The winter of 1921 was disastrous

[2] *Bend Bulletin*, Feb. 12, 1925.

FIG. 76

FIG. 77

FIG. 76—The basin of Goose Lake, near Lakeview, Oregon, the lake having completely disappeared in the past fifteen years.

FIG. 77—The road of the forty-niners across the floor of Goose Lake basin revealed for the first time when Goose Lake recently disappeared. (From V. M. Tanner, Yellowstone Cut-Off Association.)

for sheep. Deep snow is rare, but when it comes the sheep owner has too little stored hay in hand. In the severe winter of 1925, in the vicinity of Sisters, 13 per cent of the cattle died. A Fort Rock rancher lost 20 head in one day. The drought had cut down the winter capacity of the ranges, and there was little stored feed. Many cattle were "trailed" into California and Mexico, to be returned after the spring growth got started. The scarcity of pasture may make access to ungrazed free range a matter of life and death to the local farmer-rancher. That is why he wants the transient sheepman kept out. A sheriff can demand that the transient pay taxes on the spot, and he can attach the flock unless the tax claim is quieted. The pasture is sufficient if only the transient sheepmen will stay out. "If they eat us out we'll have to go back into the hills, and they might as well go back because they do nothing but drive sheep around," says the permanent inhabitant.

There were four steps in the occupation of the central Oregon region. The first was pre-railroad. The farming-ranching combination succeeded then in spite of the great distances from ranch to railroad because the land was cheap and the price of grain or of livestock sufficiently high. Cattle and sheep could be grazed widely and walked to railway shipping points. The second period was marked by the spread of dry farming just before and just after the railway came to Bend in 1911. The third stage was marked by the failure of dry farming except in the best locations and the best years and by the rather exact adaptation of farming and ranching to the local possibilities of soil, irrigation, and accessible mountain pastures. When the two big lumber companies arrived in 1915, with production in 1916, they inaugurated a fourth stage, in which the lumber industry offset the losses of the homesteaders, steadied the industrial and business life of the town of Bend, and greatly enlarged the extent of tributary industries. The lumber industry also helped carry agriculture to advanced sites in locally favorable districts.

That Bend did not decline in sympathy with the failure of badly located homesteaders was due to the relief offered by irrigation and more recently by the lumber industry. The merchant has not depended upon the dry-land farmer alone. The fortnightly pay roll of $150,000 at the lumber mills means prosperous shops. Good roads have brought larger tributary areas into relation with the town. A state highway program was set up in 1917. There were many expensive miles to build. The system is not yet completed, and

$150,000,000 has already been spent on the theory that good roads mean economic efficiency in operation and will pay. The national treasury has supplied a portion of the cost of the federal aid network of the state: where the per mile cost of a road in the federal aid system runs in excess of $30,000 the state supplies the excess. Forest highways have still further increased the mileage of improved roads. The local interest in road construction is shown by the willingness of the counties to vote the necessary bond issues that have provided the funds required for state coöperation and to make the tax levies required to build a system of market roads. Few are willing to say that the country is now saturated with good roads. When the cost of the service on road bonds is balanced ultimately against the income from permanent resources of farm land, ranch land, and timber, there may be another story to tell.

The Bend country is a borderland between the wheat-growing districts of north-central Oregon and the desert basins of the southeastern part of the state, western Idaho, northern Nevada, and northeastern California. The line of wheat cultivation is sharply drawn two miles north of the Jefferson-Deschutes county line. It is topography and soil, not rainfall, that here divides wheat and sage (Fig. 68). Northward are the long rolling slopes and uplands that run from Spokane southwestward to and beyond the Columbia. Volcanic débris—ash and lapilli, not the finer wind-carried loessial soils of more northerly localities—covers the more southerly country, which is minutely rough and has a soil that is light and in places stony. Even where trees grow in ash the soil may be unsuitable for farming. The trees depend on soil water that is derived from winter snow and rain, and there may be sufficient ground water for deeply penetrating tree roots where there is too little surface moisture for the shallow-rooted grain crops. The farther south one goes in the Great Basin the more marked becomes the summer dryness. Therefore the wheat acreages would naturally fall off as one goes south in central Oregon. But the ash cover and its minutely rough surface have given the limit of growth a sharp definition visible in the field from many a hilltop.

The basin plains of southeastern Oregon have singularly little wind. Irrigation through the recovery of ground water by windmills is therefore impossible. Pumping power must be supplied by internal-combustion engines. The absence of frequent strong winds is a boon in other respects. When the winter temperature falls below zero the unsheltered stock of the open ranges would be killed if the wind blew strongly. A vigorous wind would blow the light soil away. In the Pasco region of Washington, north of the Columbia gorge, the spring wind is in places strong enough to blow away the surface of a farm (Fig. 73). Cultivation must proceed cautiously lest the wind be given a chance. A windiness like that of the High Plains of Texas would mean the blow-out of the whole of southeastern Oregon. As it is, the roadways are hollowed along the tracks by the removal of the dusty constituents of the road material, and sand is sometimes blown into the yards and houses from the trampled bare spots about the ranch buildings.

In northeastern California an advance of wheat farming took place similar to that in central Oregon. Bieber trucked its produce 100 miles westward to the railway at Redding until the summer of 1931, when rails provided an easier outlet (Fig. 78). Settlers came first in the seventies. The eighties and nineties witnessed a wide search for ranch sites and farms. No grain was grown then, only alfalfa for winter feeding of stock. Here and there the sites were too advanced, and better houses were built than were justified by the poor pasture. The too distant sites were uneconomical. On others water was scarce for stock on the range. Most of the houses are ill-kept huts, and sheds are the rule, not barns—these are the ranch-building types in the pasture tracts of the forest far from the main highways of northeastern California and in the sage plains of the basins. Once Modoc County had a great grain production; later it became celebrated for its horses. At Adin a flour mill was once kept busy night and day. The mill has been idle for ten years. Little wheat is now raised in the valley. Flour has long been trucked in from the west. Farther south are mountain-border valleys that still raise grain. Ranching is a less troublesome business. "Now people ride around too much and don't want to work the land," said one critical old-timer who thus explained the decline in wheat production.

The farther one travels from the bases of the mountains that are scattered through the Great Basin the more open is the growth of sage and bunch grass, the latter giving out entirely in many places beyond the piedmont fringes. The basin floors are desert country— bare in summer, light green in spring when the grasses appear after the light rains, brown in winter in tracts where the grass has cured on the stalk. The cultivated places always mean irrigation. Wherever there is a gain in altitude on the slopes of the ranges it is possible to find sites at long intervals where sub-irrigation makes farming

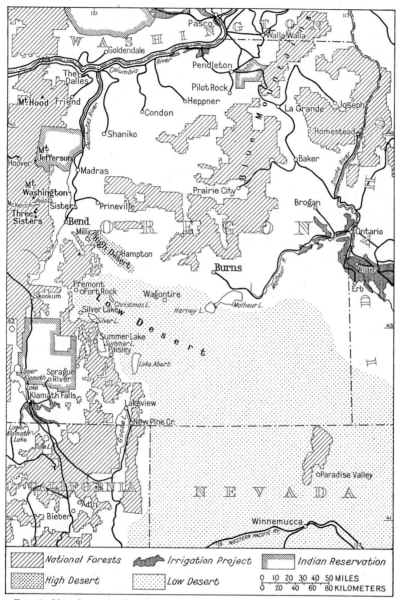

Fig. 78—Map of central and southeastern Oregon and adjacent regions, showing the location of places mentioned in the accompanying text.

The large extent of national forest is characteristic in the wooded parts of the Great Basin. The conservation policies, adopted nearly thirty years ago, led to a new type of coöperation between the national government and the local communities in the use of water and pasture and in the development of road-building programs.

possible. In any event, a "farm" is only an adjunct to a ranch: it is the cultivated part. In general, its grainfields are cut for "hay," not harvested for grain.

If there is forest at the higher levels there is summer pasture and the stream flow is steadier. The conservation of a forest is here not a mark of sentimentality for trees or a desire to conserve timber in fear of a wood famine. It is a mode of regulating streams, of keeping the soil intact where it is thin or likely to be overgrazed by hungry bands of sheep always making their heaviest drafts in dry years. The regular summer dryness means a dry forest litter and acute danger from forest fires, which are frequent and widespread. Nowhere in the West is the need for a scientific knowledge of natural resources more plainly indicated. Timber, grass, water, and soil are related parts of the natural environment, and no man can use one of them unwisely without doing possibly irreparable damage to the others.

Settlement ventured far in the High Desert between Bend and Burns but still farther in the Low Desert that includes Fort Rock Valley and Christmas Lake Valley (Fig. 78). There are about twenty-five houses between Silver Lake and Fort Rock. Not a single one is inhabited. If the house is not boarded up the windows have all been broken or the place is in ruins. The sheds have not been in use for a long time. The yards are unkempt. Sagebrush is all about. A third of the houses in the town of Silver Lake are unoccupied and the windows broken. There are no sidewalks. Heavy dust lies everywhere. Sage grows right up to the back yards. The town boasts a good high school and grade school with five teachers and about eighty pupils. Some of the parents move into the village when winter sets in and stay until spring. When the town was first built supplies were brought in and produce shipped out a month's journey to The Dalles on the Columbia. When the railroad reached Shaniko the haul to rails was cut in half. Things were then thought better; and they were thought excellent when rails reached Bend, 70 miles away in an airline. The roads are unimproved prairie tracks, but the big highways creep nearer.

Everyone talks about the present "dry cycle," the rain famine of the last two years. Those that are left tell of discouraged neighbors who have moved away. At least the snows of winter are as light as the rains, and that pleases the sheep herders; but the dry-farming crops need a moist ground, and it is winter snow and rain that supply it. Every dry-land farmer, whether in Oregon or Montana,

FIG. 79

FIG. 80

FIG. 81

FIG. 79—Burns, Oregon, a railway terminus at the eastern border of the railless triangle, Fig. 70.
FIG. 80—Main street of Silver Lake, Oregon, one of the oldest settlements of the desert country.
FIG. 81—Range country with scattered ranches and farms between the forested mountain slopes and the dry basin floors of northeastern California. The locality is 20 miles north of Bieber.

wants plenty of snow. Though the sage country looks hopeless, the ground water is so near the surface that it can be recovered easily; and at one point there is irrigation from shallow wells served by Diesel engines. Between Fort Rock and the eastern border of the Deschutes National Forest in a distance of ten miles there are 15 uninhabited and 2 inhabited houses on or quite near the road that runs through the driest and worst part of the valley. There are perhaps twice that number of houses on the hilly border of the plain, but they were too far away for me to see (August, 1930) whether they were occupied or empty. In the midst of the plain lies Fremont, once an occupied hamlet and now wholly abandoned (Fig. 24). Fort Rock has but two or three occupied houses besides the combined post office and general store. In all of the ranch yards there are windmills if the house is occupied, and half of those unoccupied have this lingering sign of the hopeful homesteader.

Southeastern Oregon was occupied before the Indians were driven out more than half a century ago. Experimentation has been going on steadily ever since. It is in progress today. The improved road and the motor car have changed the outlook and made it possible for some ranch owners to live in town and abandon their country shacks. Not every empty house means desertion of the homestead. No combination of farming and ranching works to the full satis- faction of the owner. Rails and improved highways may be nearer, but the "dry cycle" has broken up many a working combination of ranch and farm land, turned the owner back to experimentation or driven him out, and given the last touch of desolation despite the better roads and schools. The steady industry is grazing. The migrating flocks or "bands" again overrun many an unfenced field. Burns shipped out a big crop of wheat in 1925; in 1929–1930 it had to import even its chicken feed.

It is clear that the region is not going to the dogs when it is dry, nor must the climate be thought changed permanently for the better when it is wet. The oldest settlers got along because there was no thought about standards of living or of what it was economic or uneconomic to do. Everyone was working hard, but no one talked about hard work. The distances were great between settlement and railway, and the transport troubles were incessant. But anyone who lived on the frontier had to make long hauls and endure isolation and hard work or leave the country. Doctors' visits and amuse- ments were rarer than rain. If a railway came within fifty miles it seemed as if "everything had been brought right to the door."

Most settlers were of the sort that believed it "better to go to heaven in rags than to hell in embroidery," and they lost no opportunity to console themselves with the homeliest of philosophies, religious and social.

Agriculture is now narrowly confined. The recovery of the ground water is possible only for stock and domestic use in the High Desert though it is near the surface in the Low Desert and capable of recovery, at least on a scale to support gardens. Wells are too costly to sink in much of the High Desert region. The depth to water may run from 400 to 1000 feet. The cost of construction of a single well and installing equipment is about $2000. This means that a gallon of water is more expensive than a gallon of gasoline. The High Desert bands of sheep must be trailed by water carriers in dry years. The town of Imperial once boomed on the border of the High Desert. Thousands of dollars were spent and many persons ruined before the craze for lots subsided. The site is now a sheep and cattle pasture.

The failure of the farmers who cultivated land better suited for permanent range was not restricted to a few districts in Oregon. Montana and several other states had a like experience in their drier sections. At the end of 1916 Congress recognized the type of marginal land that had been the scene of failure and corrected the national settlement policy by passing "the stock-raising homestead act." This provided a 640-acre stock-raising homestead on lands "chiefly valuable for grazing and raising forage crops, [and which] do not contain merchantable timber, are not susceptible of irrigation from any known source of water supply, and are of such character that 640 acres are reasonably required for the support of a family." The government reserves lands within the scope of the act that are required for public watering places and driveways for stock. Within four months after the law had been enacted there were 60,000 gross filings embracing an area of some 24,000,000 acres.[3] This was the second time that the homestead unit was enlarged. The original homestead act of 1862 provided for a 160-acre unit, the law of 1909 provided for a 320-acre unit which is still operative, with local exceptions, in sections having a higher grade of land than that envisaged by the law of 1909.[4] As important

[3] Report of the Commissioner of the General Land Office, Department of the Interior, 1917, pp. 29–31.

[4] S. V. Proudfit: Public Land System of the United States, Historical Outline, General Land Office, Department of the Interior, 1923; and Milton Conover: The General Land Office, Its History, Activities and Organization, *Service Monographs of the United States Government No. 13*, Institute for Government Research, Baltimore, 1923.

as the restrictive effect of the homestead laws upon the original occupation of the land is the size of the farm unit, region by region, that has since come into being by the purchase of land in the free market.

"A desire to better our condition in some other place" is the entry in the Oregon Pioneer Association's records that explains the restless thrust of population into the untried fringe of settlement throughout the West.   If one were to contour the difficulties of settlement, central and southeastern Oregon would be a Himalaya on the human map of the United States.   How artificial seem the social problems of the cities, how helpless the population, by contrast to the social problems of the isolated settler and his enforced resourcefulness!   He does not know whether his crop will mature or shrivel up, or his cattle and sheep freeze on the range, or the transient bands of sheep eat up his best available pastures, or whether a railroad and an improved highway will ever come nearer to his home.

Those that survive the droughts and stick, keeping their courage, look upon themselves as the real inhabitants.   To them the comers-and-goers are mere adventurers.   A lowering standard of living may not be recognized.   A hundred of the schools of eastern Oregon have less than five children each.   The burden of government is heavier as people move out.   The apparatus of civilization wears out in a declining community.   The shanty never becomes a home.   There is a Heartbreak House in every section of "the homesteaded dry," marking the defeat of high hopes and sincere purpose not shared by the adventurers, the speculators, the transients.

When dry farming crept down off the wheat-belt hills of Oregon, out of the safe zone to the edge of the juniper and into desert sage it was the look of the land and past experience that set the venture afoot and the development policies of railways and land companies confirmed it.   The fact that stock could eat as hay the unthreshed, undeveloped grain saved the farmer-rancher from the full effects of his experiment.   Now it is all acknowledged "desert." Definitions have no place in this conviction, only experience with stock and wheat and the contrast to the wheatlands farther north that everybody knows about.   Stability of a sort is now at hand—by defeat in the incorrigible desert, by success through ranching, irrigation, and the highest type of dry farming upon proved land. The worth of the land has been discovered section by section.   The zone of experiment has been narrowed.

The Border Type of Settlement

It is frequently said that there is no longer an American "frontier." The preceding account of central and eastern Oregon belies the assertion. Central Montana has a like story to tell. The erroneous idea of a vanished frontier is due to the misconstruction of a statement in the report of the United States Bureau of the Census for 1890: "Up to and including 1880 the country had a frontier of settlement, but at present the unsettled area has been so broken into by isolated bodies of settlement that there can hardly be said to be a frontier line. In the discussion of its extent and its westward movement it can not, therefore, any longer have a place in the census reports."[5] In other words, the rather definite "line" that marked the border of advancing settlement was said no longer to have that marked continuity long displayed by it. Quite wrongly, later commentators have taken this to mean that frontier conditions had passed and that the years immediately preceding 1890 marked the end of pioneering. As a matter of fact, the frontier type of living is still the rule, not in one community but in scores of communities, not in isolated districts but throughout two thousand-mile belts of territory, one of them along the borders of the Great Basin, the other on the plains and uplands east of the Rockies.

Wherever the land was new the settler had to embark upon a life of experimentation. To experiment is occasionally to fail, but it is also true that one way to learn is to fail. A frontier or pioneering people could not survive if it refused to experiment. Instead of doing the same thing in much the same way from year to year, stabilizing its life, and adopting a settled agricultural practice, the frontier community is in a state of unsettlement. With unending change in strongly accented climatic and economic conditions an entire region may not be able to cease experimentation. The pioneering type of life then becomes not a stage of development but an ultimate result. Pioneering in America has had its great dramatic episodes because the westward movement took settlers into a succession of new and untried environments.

New tools, new seeds, and new farming practices were the ultimate means of conquest of the western plains. The advancing wave of settlement, though turned back again and again, at last

[5] Compendium of the Eleventh Census: 1890, Part I: Population, Washington, 1892, p. xlviii. It was also alleged in the same report that the country west of the 99th meridian had a rainfall "insufficient for the needs of agriculture, and irrigation is necessary for the cultivation of the soil" (p. lviii).

overcame every obstacle but climate.   A parched earth will not yield fruit.   If water cannot be got from an irrigation ditch the landowner is at the mercy of the weather.   And the farther west settlement has gone in the central Great Plains the deeper its penetration into the region of smaller and less reliable rainfall. The grasslands of the western border of the plains region are in the grip of a general law that the drier the climate the less depend-able is the rainfall.   Now at last the grain grower has reached the ultimate border of the dry-farming region.   Almost the last of the available farm land has been plowed, though a little of it here and there still has its original sod cover.   In some districts dry farming has even exceeded the economically possible limit of crop growth taking both good and bad years into account.

The marginal belts of light rainfall, where farming is barely pos-sible, are the regions of greatest agricultural insecurity.   Good and bad crop years alternate year by year or by groups of years, and so far they have been unpredictable.   How far one can go in reaping the bounty of the land in wet years and yet escape the penalties of recurrent drought is the perennial question of the dry-farming and farming-ranching country of the West.   The homesteaders of one period go in and, after trial and defeat, let the land grow up again to sage brush.   In common with the whole "troop of living creatures," they have felt the remorselessness of drought.   "This is our earth, most friendly earth and fair," was written for quite another rainfall zone.   The second generation of homesteaders in dry-farming country comes in with a new agricultural technique and, with some guiding experience from tenacious old-timers, it may succeed where the earlier generation failed.   All goes well until dry years and a drop in the market price of wheat and cattle compel a change in the size of holdings or a change in the balance between grain and stock or both, and after an exodus from the poorer or drier soils the region once more comes into a state of temporary stability.   Like all marginal areas, the western dry-farming and ranching communities are the first to feel depressions in the eco-nomic system of which they are a part.

The permanent border type of land and people is as definite in its expression as the corn-belt type or the cotton-belt type.   Wide and profound shifts in the border of settlement or in the density of population or in the systems of tillage or in the outlook are character-istics of the type.   This was never so apparent as today, with the rapid extension of wheat cultivation following the high prices that prevailed after the World War. The western border of the wheat country had a striking increase of crop land in contrast to the diminishing acreages farther east. The increase has been maintained in the face of a declining market, the lower price of wheat stimulating production instead of halting it, a process paralleled in Australia in the past few years. A thoroughgoing machine technique applied to virgin soil held in large units purchased at low prices, does not shrink because the market price of wheat is low. It beats the game, at least in selected regions, by employing more intensively the tools and stimulating the very conditions that brought about the crisis! The measure of profit is the cost per bushel not the yield per acre. Cheap land, low taxes, and small labor cost through the use of big machinery explains the map, Figure 82.

We take our agricultural machine technique for granted, whatever its depressive effects upon prices through overproduction. But when positively inevitable drought strikes the western fringe of the dry belt, government and private agencies are asked to give relief to farmer-ranchers who have chosen to live where one must gamble heavily on winning. Agriculture and business alike involve risks everywhere and at nearly all times. It is the degree of risk that matters in deciding whether a region can be cultivated successfully, that is permanently. From December 1, 1929, to June 1, 1930, 292 families in Valley County, Montana, which lies astride the Great Northern Railway, obtained Red Cross relief. In Garfield County, Montana, from 750 to 1000 families, or four-fifths of the total population, are requesting aid for the winter of 1931–1932. Twenty-eight of the fifty-five counties of Montana have applied for Red Cross relief. They have fair names, some of those dry-land counties—Golden Valley, Treasure, Prairie, Rosebud.

It is not the first time that the western fringe of settlement has known "social chaos and economic ruin," to borrow Webb's phrase.[6] To cross the line between woodland and plains required a change of technique, always a perilous thing. "Through invention and much experiment, new weapons were adopted, . . . new institutions were evolved or old ones modified . . . " Farms grew in size because they could and had to. The big farm machine was the answer to drought, and it could be applied because the topography was on a big scale; and trees, stumps, stones, and close-set gullies were absent from the uplands. Hot, withering

[6] W. P. Webb: The Great Plains and the Industrial Revolution, in "The Trans-Mississippi West," Boulder, Col., 1930, pp. 309–339; reference on p. 314.

FIG. 82—Map of the drier western part of the Great Plains, including the High Plains and the Edwards Plateau.

winds and repeated plagues of grasshoppers were answered by "better luck next year."

Experiment did not stop when a way had been found to make the soil yield a crop in years of light rainfall. Twenty inches of annual precipitation were once thought a requirement. It was soon discovered that much less would do if it were conserved by tillage—summer fallow, light surface cultivation to permit the capture of the rain and break up the capillary tubes that facilitate the evaporation of ground water. These practices soon became the commonplaces of dry-land farming. Two additional steps pushed the line of cultivation much farther and out to its present extreme limits: (1) the higher development of the big tractor-drawn farm machine, and (2) the storage of feed for stock that enabled the land-owner to emphasize the ranching element in dry years in alternation with the farming emphasis in wet (i.e. less dry) years.

THE HIGH PLAINS

The High Plains region was Indian country until 1874–1875, when the "native Americans" were at last moved to reservations to make room for the land-hungry whites. The next year cattlemen from other parts of Texas and from Colorado and Kansas began to move their herds into the high uplands of the panhandle of Texas and similar country farther north. The year 1881–1882 was known as the cattle-boom year, after which profits fell. Grazing was of the open type without winter shelter and without the interruption of barbed wire. The scattered homesteaders had been bought out or driven out in many places, and consolidation of landholding by purchase made it possible to gather immense acreages into a single ranch, some of the ranches running from a million to three million acres. This proved to be a temporary expedient. By 1887 incoming farmers were crowding the ranchers.

Almost at the beginning of settlement there came a series of extremely dry years. The first big settlers' movement into the upland country began and ended so abruptly, the penalties were so heavy, the climate was considered to be of such extreme desert dryness that there was a total collapse of the inward movement and a heavy emigration. Permanent depopulation was thought an established fact. By 1896 the drought had continued for four consecutive seasons. The event reached the proportions of disaster in Kansas, but the High Plains region of Texas was also involved. Johnson,[7] who had been studying the region for a number of years for the U. S. Geological Survey, called the High Plains definitely nonagricultural "because a supply of water for irrigation is not obtainable." Even where irrigation was thought possible he concluded that it was economically impracticable. He could see no means by which the upland region could have its precipitation "pieced out and be reclaimed for general agriculture." He thought that reclamation could only be effective through wells so spaced as fully to utilize the natural pasture and permit uniform grazing over the whole area. The windmill was the agency by which the ground water was to be made available.

It needed only a few years of normal rainfall to prove the agricultural worth of the High Plains and start a new settlers' movement that ended in complete occupation. Between 1900 and 1910 a fresh attack was made upon the inviting pastures and farms that a series of relatively wet years had made seem habitable to the folk who had acquired a better knowledge of dry farming in the meantime. By 1910 the thirty-two counties that compose the panhandle of Texas had a population of 123,684 in contrast to a population of 27,892 ten years earlier. By 1920 their population had increased to 163,000. This was the land that experts had declared with confidence could never be used except for pastoral purposes. The returning farmer found that he could pick up land cheaply from the

[7] W. D. Johnson: The High Plains and Their Utilization. *U. S. Geol. Survey, 21st Ann. Rept.,* 1899–1900, Part IV, pp. 609–741; *22nd Ann. Rept.,* 1900–1901, Part IV, pp. 637–669.

large ranchers, put machinery upon it, and trouble himself very
little as to the yield per acre if only he had acres enough. In almost
no part of the High Plains is the water-bearing sand so far below
the surface that a windmill will not recover it and permit grazing
over wide domains of which it had often been said that water lay so
deep that "it's about as far down as it is across."

The settler has in effect classified the land by a process of trial
and error. After the cattleman had ranged widely over the region
the farmer tried his luck. When the two interests got into a state of
adjustment the ranchman no longer pastured his cattle upon the
best sites to the injury of the settler. In short, the ranchman
became a farmer in part and the farmer a ranchman in part. The
old conflict of interests has gone. Each type of land is given the
efficient thing to do. Running water, ranch land, farms, and wells
are functioning as they should. A balanced production has made
its effect felt in the growth of substantial towns on the upland
prairies. It is a good land to look at, and the plainsman finds it a
good land to live in. The type of life is still open and free. The
pioneer quality remains in the people. The bronzed cattle veteran
is still here—the old timer, the first settler. It will take several
generations before the type is modified or the memory lost of the
long struggle that was required to establish agriculture.

Johnson's description of the High Plains is a classic, but his
forecast of the type of successful land use falls far short of the actualities today. When I visited the region in 1921 and again in 1930
I could scarcely believe that it was the country he described. After
crossing the "breaks of the plains"—the steep and ragged scarp
several hundred feet high that constitutes the eastern border of
the upland—one comes suddenly upon a new land laid out high in the
air. The country is nearly flat with only a shallow depression here
and there whose outlet is generally blocked by a low bank that
collects surface run-off in an earthen "tank." Windmills dot the
landscape. One "raises" a town by its windmills long before
the houses are visible, in the same way that one descries a ship at
sea. Water is in many cases the principal topic of conversation.
At one dinner table a traveler remarked how terrible is the wind,
the incessant wind that fills the air with dust, irritates the eyes,
and drums monotonously upon the ears. "I would not talk that
way about the wind," replied an old settler, "it is our best friend."
He went on: "I remember in the early days when we came into
this country what a terrible thing it was to have no water, how

FIG. 83

FIG. 84

FIG. 85

FIG. 83—Detail of upland and slopes of Niobrara Valley, Nebraska, looking west across the dry bed of Big Cottonwood Creek. Little irrigated land, the rest permanent range country.

FIG. 84—Ensemble of ranch buildings, pasture, cultivated patches, unfenced road, and gently rolling topography characteristic of the range country about Chadron, Nebraska, and northward to the Black Hills and Big Badlands. Two-thirds of the visible landscape is in grass.

FIG. 85—Sublette, Kansas, a characteristic High Plains town whose buildings have more relief than the topography.

difficult to build the first well, how deep the wells were, and how hard the labor of pumping water for ourselves and the stock. When the first windmills came in our anxiety was ended."

"One of the greatest difficulties frequently met by farmers is the scanty or delayed spring rainfall, which makes seed germination very uncertain or so late as to give too short a growing season." This is the conclusion of a government expert[8] with respect to the part of the High Plains that projects into New Mexico (Fig. 82). In this western portion, where the altitude runs slightly above 4000 feet, the annual rainfall is about 12 inches with possible departures of 6 and 7 inches in any given year. The lowest annual rainfall of record is 7 inches, and the highest nearly 36 inches. The elevation is so great as to cause a short growing season, and when a late spring is combined with a lack of moisture the crop yield becomes uncertain. The favorable seasons of 1900 and 1902 followed the building of the Pecos Valley Railroad and attracted settlers even from distant points. Some of them moved out again in 1903 because of the unfavorable weather of that year. Then for a period of four years settlement again progressed rapidly owing to the greater rainfall. There was a considerable exodus in 1910 at the height of a drought that lasted until 1912. Some of those who had left the region returned after the drought. New settlers came in. Almost no crops were raised in 1918, and the succeeding heavy snows of winter and the low temperatures resulted in the death of many range cattle from cold and hunger. On top of that came the decline in cattle prices, which "put out of business all of the larger cattle ranchers who had remained in the region."

The wet and dry periods had taught the farmers how to get along. They have experimented with the different sorghums and from them obtain crops in almost any year. They have learned how to have in sight at all times a two-year supply of forage for farm animals instead of importing expensive feed in dry years. A windmill supplies water sufficient to irrigate a small garden. Surplus stock can always be sold to pay the taxes. Having weathered the droughts of 1910 and 1918, they have learned how to meet the next one "which is sure to come." Practically all of the farmers of the western border of the High Plains, as reported by Wooton, have determined to stay; and many of them believe they are doing as well as in other localities they have tried, if not better.

[8] E. O. Wooton: Settlers' Progress in Dry-Land Farming in Eastern New Mexico, *U. S. Dept. of Agric., Circular No. 4,* 1927, pp. 4–5.

Acreage and type of cultivation have been adjusted to rainfall and crop yield. The size of the farms runs from 500 to 700 acres, with a fourth to a half of the farm in crops. Cotton is grown on some of the land part of the time. But for its low market price it would today be a more substantial part of the farmer's economy in spite of the high percentage of failures due to the short growing season and the recurrent drought. The use of large machinery is the rule. Tractors are common. Most of the farmers are satisfied with their locations. In two counties that were intensively studied in 1927 the farm owners reported that they were in good condition financially. Only a few were carrying debts amounting to as much as 40 per cent of the valuation of their property.

I have been describing the western portion of the High Plains. Farther east they decline in elevation to 3000 feet along the crest of the "breaks" in Texas. The rainfall increases to an average of 20 to 24 inches, some years having half that amount, others 50 per cent more. Here also the farmer has learned to provide himself with stored feed for the poor years. The farmer is also a rancher, as farther west. By means of cattle the poorer lands are used; that is the breaks on the borders of the area and along the deeper stream courses, the sandy areas where wheat does less well in wet years than on the heavier soils and better in dry years, the low, gullied valley borders covered with sand blown out of the river bottoms, as along part of the Red River. But every farmer is looking for crops which he can sell for cash. While cattle are supplementary to farming and enable a farmer to survive the years of drought, but the owner betters himself materially only as he produces crops for the market. The acreages of the farms run about the same as in eastern New Mexico—500 to 700 acres, though farms of 1000 acres and more are not uncommon.

THE EDWARDS PLATEAU

South of the High Plains of Texas is the semiarid upland known as the Edwards Plateau. The rainfall is lighter than farther north, and the topography more broken. There is a greater variety of soils and vegetation, and mixed farming and ranching are the rule. Here the great economic questions are how far can ranch land be turned into farms and what is the size of the ranching units. The region is in an experimental stage, the balance between farming and ranching being in a state of change. The improvement of the

FIG. 86

FIG. 88

FIG. 87

FIG. 86—Farmhouse and barns in the valley of Spring Creek, five miles north of Imperial, Nebraska.

FIG. 87—Typical farm buildings on grain-growing portion of High Plains in the western panhandle of Oklahoma, south of Liberal, Kansas. About thirty farm buildings are usually visible from one point in a circle of country 10 to 15 miles in diameter.

FIG. 88—Typical slopes of broad shallow valleys of the High Plains of central western Kansas, with farm land to the valley floor (Smokey Hill River) and widely spaced ranch or farm buildings on sky line.

livestock tends to increase the value of the land and thus forces the landowner to use it more intensively if he wishes to keep the proper balance between land, labor, and capital. But if all the tillable land is put under cultivation too rapidly, or too extensively, production exceeds the amount required for an emergency food supply for livestock and the surplus cannot be marketed economically. Another difficulty in the use of range land is the distance from market. The range country is now completely fenced. In the days of unfenced range the cattle slowly grazed their way to market, whereas they must now be driven for many miles through narrow lanes or through other men's pastures at a cost.

When Youngblood[9] studied the region ten years ago he found the ranches tending to become too small, as people without ranching experience were tempted by its apparent cheapness. Men who came from a region of ordinary farms that ran from 80 to 160 acres in size could not adjust themselves to the idea that permanent ranching country required units ranging from 2500 to more than 12,000 acres. Like the High Plains farther north, the Edwards Plateau depends upon an artificial water supply for the maintenance of livestock. The cost of drilling deep wells, installing windmills and storage facilities, and providing upkeep constitutes a large part of the current expense. Only by having large holdings and credit facilities has it been possible for Texas to utilize its vast extent of grazing land, which forms about three-fourths of the total area of the state.

Modern ranching has become a permanent business, and the development of economic and social institutions and customs suitable to a widely spaced ranching people has been a first requirement. Good roads and the motor car have enabled the communities of the Edwards Plateau region to organize on a broader basis. Schools and churches at scattered points have been made more accessible. Intercommunication is made easier by the wide extension of the telephone system. It is noteworthy that a high proportion of the sons of ranchmen go into the ranching business. Its outdoor type of life attracts young men in contrast to the conditions found in most farming communities.

The Central and Northern Great Plains

North of the High Plains of Texas the upland prairie continues across the western panhandle of Oklahoma, the eastern part of

[9] B. Youngblood and A. B. Cox: An Economic Study of a Typical Ranching Area on the Edwards Plateau of Texas, *Texas Agric. Exper. Sta. Bull. No. 297*, 1922.

Colorado, and western Kansas, fading out and changing in character in western Nebraska. Wyoming and Montana carry the general type of grassy upland northward to the international boundary. In all this vast territory dry farming has been the key to permanent occupation, and settlement has continued steadily since 1900. At many places it was in full swing down to 1931. Though there was a drought in 1930 in the central plains, the rainfall of western Kansas and adjacent parts of Colorado and Oklahoma was above normal. "Give us two more years of good rainfall," said the farmers, "and we shall have our land paid for."

So long as wheat could be sold at $1.50 a bushel a man might pay for his land with three good crops. He was then ready to add a second farm. He could do these things because he left the "belt of oppressive taxes" in eastern Kansas, Nebraska, and the Dakotas and had good luck with wheat in the virgin grass country. The land was low-priced because the cattlemen became discouraged as their holdings were taxed at a higher level. Cattle prices declined. It grew more and more difficult to manage the herds upon scattered holdings. "We came out here because we had to live," said one man in 1930, who had established himself in five years upon his own farm now fully paid for, fenced, and otherwise improved. He had been unable to make headway in the older community 400 miles farther east, from which he came, because the interest on the mortgage took what was left of his income after he had paid his taxes, three-fourths of which were spent on roads and schools. Of course the tax assessor in dry-farming regions in process of rapid development is not long in raising the tax rate, for better schools and roads are bound to come in; but the rise lags behind land occupation; and in those few years, with good growing seasons, the farmer establishes himself. The test of efficiency in local government comes when the first efforts must be made to keep the cost of roads and schools at a lower level than the increase of population. Good roads and good schools are demanded, but they need not be the best to be good enough. The highest possible standard of living is hardly appropriate for marginal country.

Jordan Country

At the northern end of the marginal country of the plains in central Montana the rainfall is so light and uncertain as to make farming exceptionally hazardous. To illustrate the conditions of

living in this belt of territory the communities of a restricted area,
Garfield County, lying between the Missouri and Yellowstone
rivers (Fig. 91), will be taken. It has a population of 4250, or
roughly 850 families, of which 250 live in Jordan, the county seat
(Fig. 89). They are scattered over 5000 square miles of country—an
area greater than that of Con-
necticut. Though there is cultivation of the land, to some
extent, by almost all settlers,
the population reached an average of one to the square mile as
late as 1920 only to fall below
this figure in 1930 when there
was a decline of over a thousand.
This is less than half that (two
to the square mile) which was
taken by the Census Bureau as
the minimum for "settled"
country whose nearly continuous
border was so long "the frontier": "All the region outside
[west of] this line may be re-
garded as practically unsettled country   .   .   ."[10]   There is

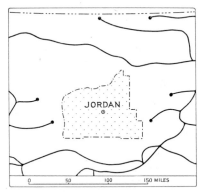

FIG. 89—The railless condition of the Jordan country midway between the Great Northern on the north and the Northern Pacific and the Chicago, Milwaukee & St. Paul railways on the south.

not a mile of telegraph or telephone line or railway in the whole
of Garfield County. The universal means of communication is
the motor car operating upon 600 miles of graded prairie road
when not driven pell-mell across sage brush flats or even across
gullies to distant ridge crests. A radio transmitter was in working
order for a few months in 1930; the radio receiver permits these
isolated folk to hear the world.

   It is 92 miles from Jordan northward to Glasgow on the Great
Northern Railway (Milk River Valley), and 94 miles southward
to Miles City on the Northern Pacific Railway (Yellowstone River
Valley). Both these railways lie far outside the borders of Garfield
County (Fig. 89). A railway, 120 to 150 miles long, east to
west, would cut midway through the best farming country and lift
the handicap of distance. For those who live in the northern half
of the region the project for a "federal-aid" bridge across the
Missouri River which would give access to the Great Northern
Railway is of even greater concern.

[10] Statistics of the Population of the United States at the Tenth Census, 1883, p. xxiv.

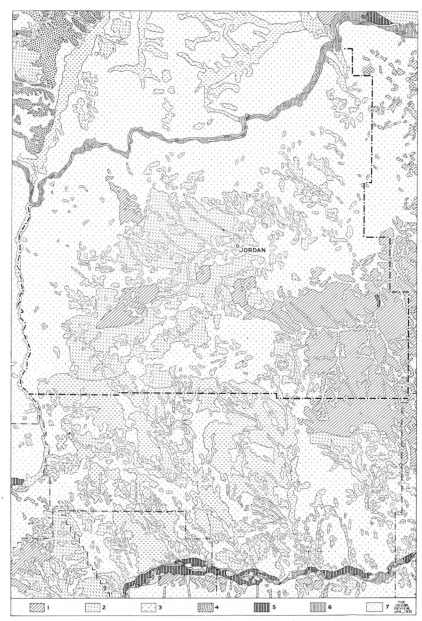

FIG. 90—Land classification map of the Jordan country based on the U. S. Geological Survey's land classification maps of the Northern Great Plains (scale 1 : 500,000). The scale of the map is 1 : 1,135,-000. Numbers have reference: 1, farming-grazing land (crop failures in dry years); 2, grazing-forage land (grain crop failures except in good years); 3, grazing land (tillage unsuccessful because of poor soil or very low rainfall); 4, stony land; 5, irrigated land; 6, Missouri River bottom land; 7, nontillable grazing land.

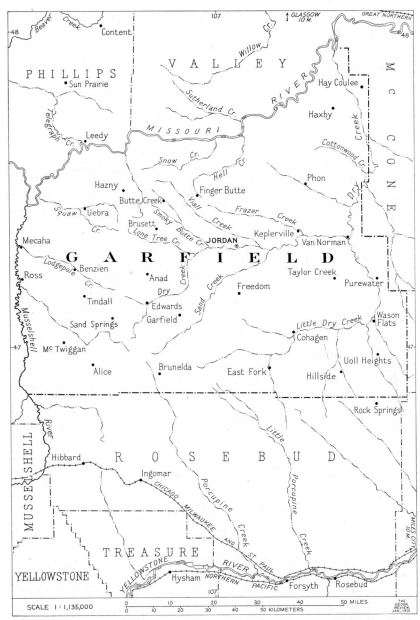

FIG. 91—Location map of the Jordan country, the area shown in Figure 90. All of the localities in Garfield County marked on the U. S. Geological Survey's land classification map are shown here. The county, which has an area of 5000 square miles, recorded a population of 4252 and 1077 farms at the 1930 census.

The plains portion of the Jordan country (Fig. 90) is marked by long slopes leading down to dry valleys occupied either by small rivulets or by the gravel-strewn beds of wet-weather streams. Only at intervals of ten or fifteen miles is there cultivation in spots here and there, with clusters of farms occupying favorable stretches of valley floor or bench land or stretching far up the slopes where soil and moisture are favorable. Rolling plains extend northward

Fig. 92—Panorama with Figure 93. The ridge crests in the background are ten to fifteen miles from the camera.

to the Missouri River or westward to the Musselshell, and at the valley borders the surface drops off in deeply dissected "breaks" that make a wild and tumbled five-to-twenty-mile border to the plains. Instead of the sweeping lines of the plains and the impression of vast distances, the "breaks" present a chaotic aspect.

The flood plain of the Missouri is marked by cottonwoods and a good deal of wild shrubby growth, including willows, wild rose, buck brush, and bullberry thickets. Big Dry Creek (Fig. 91) is bordered by a scattered growth of cottonwood. Juniper and cedar look startlingly misplaced in the "breaks" along the Missouri and the Musselshell, for they are found *below* the plains level as well as on a few buttes that rise above that level. Under the noonday sun the color contrasts are not particularly striking, but at the time of sunrise or sunset the fields of deep-green corn and light-purple flax stand out clearly from the dun-colored grama grass that forms the prevailing ground cover.

The deep perspectives and the tremendously long sweeping lines of the valley slopes that rise to crests ten or fifteen miles away make the landscape seem to engulf the scattered human habitations (Fig. 92). The log shack or the sod house or even the more pretentious cottage of the prosperous rancher is an almost undiscernible speck in a wilderness of grass or tangled watercourses or buttes and terraces that make up the rough "breaks" on the valley borders.

Though most of the short grasses of the Jordan country are locally given the collective name of "buffalo grass," the dominant types are more precisely described as grama grass, western needle grass, wire grass, and niggerwool. Grama grass is normally but a few inches in height and forms a uniform ground cover in favored places and gives the semblance of a well kept meadow. One sees it to best advantage in the hollows where the snow drifts during

FIG. 93—Composition of slopes near Rock Springs, Montana. Panorama with Figure 92.

the winter. The greener patches stand out prominently in the landscape, and in the dry season they are often signalized by grazing herds. Grama and needle grass are to be found upon the best soils; and, as one runs into the poorer soils, black sage and salt sage become more abundant, as well as prickly pear and greasewood. It is estimated that twenty-five head of stock can be pastured to the square mile of grazing country.[11] This means that some sort of grain crop must be raised if a family is to secure a living upon even twice a 160-acre unit of mixed farming and grazing land. From 75 to 100 head of stock are required to support an ordinary family at an acceptable standard of living. The equivalent of the "increase" of such a herd can be sold off each year to pay the taxes and purchase the family supplies. The size of the herd may fall to 50 or 60 head if there is a fairly well kept garden and if some grain is grown. If the number of animals drops to 25 it means that much more grain must be grown and that either a larger garden must be kept or, as is often the case, the head of the family must be absent for a part of the year earning sufficient money elsewhere to keep the family in food and clothing.

Upon the poorer land with a rough topography, light soil, and steep slopes the drainage is quick and the ground water lies deep. There the acreages must be still larger, for sagebrush, salt sage, shad scale, and greasewood make their claims upon the ground

[11] Land Classification of the Northern Great Plains . . . U. S. Geol. Survey, 1929.

water, and the edible grass may be quite scattered and thin. Ingomar, in Rosebud County (Figs. 91 and 102), is in the center of such
a region. About the town is a vast plain of desolation with intervals
as great as ten miles between grainfields, and there is not a drop
of water in the village itself except what is hauled in by the railroad

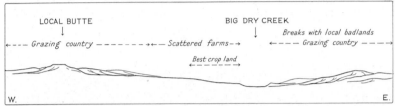

FIG. 94—Topographic profile in relation to land use, looking north from a point fifteen miles south
of the Missouri River crossing north of Haxby. A cereal crop in a region of light rainfall requires
large-scale farm machinery, and this in turn requires a smooth topography in detail as well as in
general outline. The distribution of smooth-contoured slopes in the grassland country is a limiting
condition of wheat cultivation (without irrigation) from central western Texas northward to
Canada.

and sold at 50 cents a barrel if it is brought to the house or given
away if one goes to the railway station for it. The grasses are
nutritious, but they are so thin that a ranch of a thousand acres
may be required to maintain a decent standard of living.

Up to 1917 the homesteader (who first came in numbers in 1913)
was out on holiday, so to speak. There was a fair chance for everyone, and the whole of the grazing country seemed about to become
a prosperous farming belt. The succeeding dry years resulted in
the almost wholesale abandonment of farms with a corresponding
effect upon the few scattered towns. Ingomar, for example, while
it ships grain, hauled for distances of twenty to seventy miles from
the western half of Garfield County, is also a substantial wool-
producing center, though one would suppose from the two huge
grain elevators that dominate the town that grain growing is still
a primary interest of the immediate vicinity.

The region is not one that is capable of full agricultural development in the sense of using all of the arable land for grain. If "average" acreages of wheat are sown in a given year there may be no
crop, and the whole growth must be cut as "hay." But the difficulty is that there is not sufficient stock to make full use of such
stored feed, with the consequence that it goes to waste. It cannot
be sold because practically everybody in the region is in the same
situation.

The rancher himself must do the guessing year by year as to

what constitutes arability, and when he guesses he must take into
account the possible increase of his flocks and herds and the extent
of land that he can cultivate with equipment in hand.   He must
stake his labor and money upon a rainfall that may vary as much
as fifty per cent from the normal in any one year and is pretty

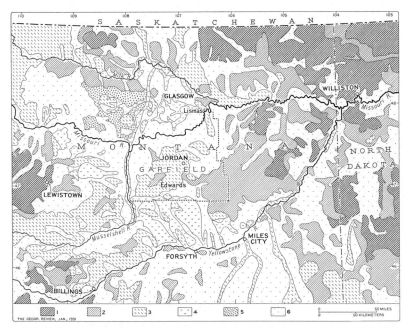

FIG. 95—The general setting of the Jordan country in Garfield County and the land classification of northeastern Montana and adjacent parts of North Dakota.   The nearest "big" towns
with the population reported for the 1930 census are: Glasgow (2216), Miles City (7175), Lewistown (5358), Billings (16,380), and Williston (4965).   Compare with the railway map, Figure 89.
Land classification is based on the U. S. Geological Survey's maps of the Northern Great Plains.
Numbers have reference: 1, farming land; 2, farming-grazing land; 3, grazing-forage land; 4, grazing
land; 5, stony land; 6, nontillable grazing land.   Compare Figure 90.   Scale 1 : 4,700,000.   Note
the fading out of the best farming land in the left-central part of the map westward of the North
Dakota line and its reappearance in the higher country near the mountain border west of Billings
and Lewistown.

certain to vary as much as twenty to twenty-five per cent in five-
year periods.   One may find examples of such guessing in every
neighborhood.   Only a few farms in the Jordan country had thresh-
able wheat in 1930, that is a crop running eight or ten bushels to
the acre.   The crop in 1931 was almost a complete failure.   Since
it costs $2.50 an acre to "combine" it, that is cut and thresh it,
and since it costs on the average 35 cents a bushel to haul it to
market (50 to 100 miles), the whole of the proceeds of a light crop

may go into the harvesting and marketing and nothing at all be left for seed, taxes, and labor.

Of course this means resorting to special crop methods wherever practicable. Flax yields exceptionally well if grown on new ground. Three or four bushels to the acre is a fair crop in a dry year, the

FIG. 96—Hereford cattle seem to be best suited to the grazing conditions of the short-grass country. It is seldom that any other breed is seen. (Photograph from the Great Northern Railway.)

haulage charge is less, and it fetches from $2.00 to $2.50 a bushel. In years of heavier rainfall it pays extremely well and is seeded right into newly plowed ground—plow, disk, and seeder being attached in series behind a gas tractor. The first crop of corn on newly turned natural prairie sod is astonishingly large even in the driest of years on account of the stored moisture in the soil and its freedom from weeds. On approaching such a field, especially in time of drought, one is certain that it must have irrigation in view of the contrast between it and the scattered and stunted growth of corn on the weed-choked older cropped ground.

With motor transport subsidiary to an east-west railway through the Jordan country there is no reason why diversified farming should not greatly reduce the present crop hazards. The "diversities" would include cream and hogs and poultry as well as a better adjustment of sheep and cattle to the respective areas where they will thrive best. These products are not all equally dependent upon rainfall, and it is drought that establishes the present danger line.

The time has nearly passed when one can follow the cattle business exclusively. "The cattle business is no longer a business but a disease," said one discouraged rancher. He was referring to large-scale operations conducted upon scattered holdings of grass. Continuous acreages of large extent are difficult to find if one is in the market to buy, and they are difficult to hold because of the increasing value of land and the rising level of taxes. It takes an investment of $150,000

FIG. 97—Sheep grazing on the "short grass" of the Jordan country in a region of smooth-contoured topography. (Photograph from the Great Northern Railway.)

to $200,000 in cattle to enable a man to make $10,000 or $15,000 a year, for the cost of labor is high and the cost of posts, wire, tank equipment, and the like is constantly increasing. A bad season, that may come in any year, may require the sale of substantial portions of a herd at the bottom of the market. The recent slump in the price of meat has cut the value of many herds in two, and at such a time the creditor bank calls no man brother.

The length and severity of the winter is a matter of great importance to the stockman. If his ranch includes a considerable extent of "breaks" his cattle may find shelter from the occasional blizzard, and the broken nature of the ground makes the grass accessible to stock. If the farm ranch includes only flat or gently rolling land the snow may lie rather evenly upon it and the stock be unable to pasture afield. Normally the period of winter feeding is half the year, the remaining half alone being available for sheep and cattle grazing at considerable distances from the stored feed of the valleys.

The man who depends on sheep grazing for a living must have not only a much larger holding of land but is kept very busy looking after his flocks, or "bands" as they are called. He employs sheep herders, but their business is to see that the flock is protected, that the salt is put out, and that bedding grounds are well selected—not to do the manual labor of farm or corral. The farmer must provide the hay, arrange for labor to distribute it on the feeding grounds, and provide the water supply. Cold and snow require constant watchfulness lest the flocks stray too far as they drift down the wind and thus get caught in snow-drifted places and perish. When the bands of sheep are not brought in for steady winter feeding they must be herded along the "breaks."

I was surprised to discover in so many communities of the dry-farming ranching country that hospitality is reserved for the stranger rather than the neighbor. It seemed, in some communities, as if there were very few men who had not a hard word for some neighboring landowner. If this had been the case in one community it could be called a local bad habit, but I found it in Oregon as well as Kansas and in Nebraska as well as Montana. I found men quite ready to talk about it. They were all quick to say that it was difficult to get a community to work together. The condition has grown out of an almost uniform pioneering experience. We are accustomed to extolling the good qualities of the pioneer. Here is one of the weeds in his garden.

When there was plenty of free range a neighboring cattleman was too far away to be a rival. As soon as the range became restricted and there were smaller holdings by title, it was generally because the farmers had come in and run fences around their homesteads. At once quarrels began; and down to two years ago they were still active in western Kansas in the region between the Arkansas and the South Platte, as they are active now in spots in the Jordan country. The small cattle owner is generally one cause of the difficulty today. He owns too small a farm to keep stock and allows his cattle and sheep to graze on land from which the owner is absent or cuts the wire fences of larger landowners, permitting his stock to feed on a tract grown to natural grass and reserved for winter feeding. Now the sense of proprietorship is as strong as the struggle to get established was hard. All reveal with large gesture the sense of earned possessions.

The clash most frequently comes over the use of the remaining free range or that which is "free" by neglect of the owner. One gets from free range what one has not earned except in the sense that one stuck to the fight and was there to take the free range as a privilege. The homesteader, as opposed to the earlier pioneer, is often an adventurer, a speculator. He wishes to hold until permanent settlers have come in and then sell at a profit. In the eyes of the old-timer he has few "rights" and should have no privileges. The old-timer feels that he has earned the privilege (he would call it a right) to pasture exclusively *his* cattle upon free range (where there is accessible water) as he has always done. The law slants his way because it stipulates that cattle and horses (but not sheep) may be grazed free upon unfenced homesteaded land which the owner has proved up but left temporarily until he can sell it. There is much of this land in Montana as well as in Idaho and Oregon.

The wide dispersal of the population in the Jordan country with but one town of sufficient size to support a doctor in all the great stretch of country between the Missouri and the Yellowstone, including areas far outside of Garfield County, means that there is a distinct group of hazards relating to public health. One doctor to 5000 square miles of territory, to take Garfield County alone, means that everyone must take chances on anything in the way of illness and accident. The striking thing is that this high risk does not drive people out, though it definitely keeps out some who would otherwise come in. The common answer to questions of health is, "We never get sick out here." It is true that epidemics are rare and local on account of the isolation and the dry climate.

The roads have been so well laid out and they are kept in such good repair that in fine weather one may travel almost anywhere at a speed of forty or forty-five miles an hour. A visit in fair weather deceives one into believing that the roads have made life much safer; and indeed they have, though only in the period of good weather. With rain and snow upon it, the gumbo or sticky clay of the road surface becomes so slippery that the speed is cut down to ten or fifteen miles an hour and even to the point of impassability with motor cars. Drifted snow presents an additional special problem.

The condition in the Jordan country before the use of automobiles became general is well described in a government publication, "Maternity Care and the Welfare of Young Children in a Homesteading County in Montana."[12] Down to about 1900, neighbors were some fifty miles apart in the Jordan country. With the opening of the region to homesteaders (the most rapid influx of settlers was in 1913) most of the land was taken up. Road building became the first requisite for the communication of neighbor with

---

[12] *U. S. Dept. of Labor, Children's Bur. Publ. No. 34*, Washington, 1919.

FIG. 98

FIG. 99

FIG. 98—The line of trees on the right marks the course of the "Big Dry," a creek tributary to the Missouri River. An inch and a half from the left-hand margin of the photograph is an isolated group of farm buildings, and the lighter patches to left and right are grainfields.

FIG. 99—Panoramic view of Jordan, Montana, in the valley of the "Big Dry" (creek). Supplies are obtained chiefly by motor truck from Miles City on the Yellowstone, 94 miles away.

neighbor and more particularly for reaching the markets far to the north and the south.   But the roads were prairie roads for the most part.   Down to 1917 there were but seventy miles of made road. While at the present time it is doubtful if more than a half dozen families are without some sort of motor vehicle, only one family in eight had automobiles in 1917.   Flooded creeks and the absence of graded roads meant that families were cut off for days from even their immediate neighbors.   Mails were sometimes delayed a week at a time, and the parcel post for months.   As one woman remarked of the receipt of packages from mail order houses, "People have Christmas till Easter."   Winter underwear ordered in the autumn reached one family in the spring.

"The whole area is young and struggling," and if this be true of the ordinary conditions of life one might suppose that women would be loath to follow their husbands into a country that obviously tries the strength of men.   The single physician in the county says that half of the maternity cases are unattended by a doctor and the mortality rate is high.   There is one hospital in the county, at Jordan.   Montana has an infant mortality rate that is one of the highest in the Union.   There is scattered midwife assistance, and in not a few cases the mother attends herself or is attended by her husband.   The women lead an outdoor life and for that reason are strong and make astonishingly little complaint about their hard situation: "The women make no fuss about things."

It is the mothers who take the keenest interest in the establishment of schools.   "The hardest thing is no schooling," said one. The schoolhouses are small one-room shacks.   A new schoolhouse is shown in Figure 10.   The greatest difficulty is the problem of securing teachers to live for eight or nine months at a time practically without social contacts except those afforded by half a dozen families living in small shacks in isolated districts.   In 1917, seven out of ten families lives in houses of one or two rooms.   In more than half of the houses there were three persons to occupy each sleeping room.   The log house, sod house, tar-paper house, and dugout were the prevailing types.   Only about half the houses were screened.   In recent years conditions have been substantially improved through the steady construction of screening, of frame houses of larger size, and of domestic conveniences in so far as these can be introduced in the absence of electric current or water power or local generators.   One natural advantage possessed by the region is stressed on every hand: "We could not live here if it were not for

FIG. 100

FIG. 101

FIG. 102

FIG. 100—Sheep herder's wagon at crest of ridge in midst of bedding ground in local "breaks" north of Forsyth, Montana.
FIG. 101—The single dwelling, store, and post office combined, at Haxby, Montana.
FIG. 102—Main street of Ingomar, Montana.

ferry crossing. Th[
formed into season[

The West is still
200,000,000 acres i[
railroads that may
provide new outlets
here and there that
Directly after the v[
total mileage of rail
to the East. The
was extended to [
road to triangles o[
tana have been ma[
lating effects upon [
distances to econo[
of the Cascades to
Pacific via Bieber,

If the standards
in the pre-motor er[
motor competition[
relatively low grad[
be taken of buildin[
in the bold style of
extremely cautious
the face of a rate
above an extremel[
in case of loss. Th[
tional rôle of wes[
building by railwa[
and there where t[
by settlers. Pass[
car and the almos[
states.

It is probable t[
only about half a[
management. Su[
definitely set up t[
years. When the
merely that there i[
represented by a [
him to dispose of

FIG. 103

FIG. 104

FIG. 105

FIG. 103—Ferry across the Missouri River at Lismas, south of Glasgow, on the way to Jordan.
FIG. 104—In the dry-farming country the acreage harvested in one year is matched by acreage in fallow for the following year, as on this farm near Glasgow, Montana. (Photograph from the Great Northern Railway.)
FIG. 105—Field of corn southeast of Edwards near southern boundary of Garfield County.

the coal.''
and is con
One see
addition o
replaceme
ment of t
and corral
trees and
the highw
vicinity of
Everyone
still furth
marvelou
at least
grazing t
important
The wh
gasoline.
gas were
roads or
seeding a
limited ti
miles of
but four
With a
breezes, a
land of p
to pay hi
family m
He may
be requir
The Jo
all comm
(Fig. 95)
between
In summ
winter ar
with thir
routing o
increasin
requiring

may have been assembling, or breeding, up to what he considers to be a safe carrying level for his land. If the natural forage is poor and the grain crop a failure either for threshing or for hay, the owner may be set back in his plans not for the year immediately following the drought but for four or five years. It takes that interval of time for him to build up his flocks and herds again. But it may be and often is precisely in that period that the rainfall is heavier and the forage good if only he had the stock to make use of it.

If three or four dry years succeed each other there is also a marked deteriorative effect upon grain. This requires the settler either to sow poor grain or to import expensive grain for seed. Obviously the economic and natural conditions that surround him call for the application of *an equalizing process* if he is to remain upon the land and not be defeated with each recurrence of dry years. That equalizing process must be government, since business operates to the personal advantage of those that engage in it. County, state, or nation must supply the equalizing process. Average conditions or average years mean nothing in such a climatic and economic set-up. Nor must it be supposed that the benefits of good years will enable the persistent farmer to meet successfully the bad years. In the first place, science is yet unable to tell him with assurance when the bad years will come. Long-range forecasts of weather conditions are not yet available. Therefore he cannot be prepared for the bad years. If he is conservative by nature he has no place in the dry-farming country. He can only reap the advantages of wetter years by supposing that every year will be wet.

The attention of the national government has been so sharply concentrated upon irrigation in the dry West that the public is little informed on the much more significant work that is being done in the way of intensive experiment in type areas and in the making of land classification studies. There is acute present need for the special qualities of statesmanship in land use. This statesmanship is something over and above the technical studies of the day. It has to take account, among critical factors, of the attitudes of men as well as the soil types and the variability of rainfall.

The matter becomes clearer if we look at the specific obligations of a state that desires to achieve the full exploitation of its resources. If the technology of the day is in advance of the experience of the people of a given region the state must step in to make the technology known. For it can do collectively what the individual or the small community cannot do. It can apply to a given problem all the technology that is available. The ideal state would not only do this but would then carry out policies of economic exploitation more precisely adapted to the fundamental conditions that underlie successful living. Naturally this requires standards as to what successful living is, that is, not only what man can do in the abstract but what men can do and what they ought to do in the concrete, natural region by natural region. This means, furthermore, that the state must import technology from the outside, for no state has had the experience of all the world. Russia and Brazil and China and Japan are also in the picture. Their experiences flow through books and maps and men. To take this point of view is to say that *the technologist is a creator of power, but the state must create or encourage the creation of the channels through which that power flows.*

Political action is traditionally far behind either the statesmanship or the technology of the day. To the extent that we intend to use all of the resources of our land the statesmanship of science must be insisted upon, that is, that special process by which we trace the applications of power to their consequences. We are here face to face with two distinct kinds of criticism and conflict, the one having to do with ideal statements of policy with respect to specific elements, like soils or forests or minerals, the other having to do with the regional composition of resources and conditions and powers in a way that is feasible. Our machinery at the present time includes nation, state, and county as the three principal means by which a subdivision of power is sought that has its ultimate result in the way in which people make a living from the land. Naturally, the coördination of these three agencies is not ideal. The thing works loosely and approximately. It is still a question whether the state can do more than this without creating an overhead of expense that could not be supported by a land of meager resources.

We need, for one thing, to have an exact study of the advances and retreats of population in wet and dry years in regions of pioneer settlement. We need to know how extensive they are, how severe the conditions that create them, and how they affect permanent occupation. The old advances and retreats of population as a series of dry years succeeded a series of wet years is now no longer so important in the dry West as the sudden contraction of credit, the forced sale of livestock, the squeezing out of the marginal farmer and rancher who ought to be maintained upon the land if we are to use the abundance of nature even upon his poor acres in a series of wet years. We need to know, further, what intensity of production is required in various lines to warrant highway and railway extensions and farm aid on any specified scale. We need to study regional trends of land occupation, limiting distances from railways and highways for various combinations of crop and stock.

The sense of neighborhood becomes an important factor in the development of new land. People do not live in a table of statistics but in communities. New counties are organized when there is an awareness on the part of a group of people of their community relationships. People in the West live by counties or "countries," not by states, for few state functions impinge directly upon the life of a community, as in the case of roads and schools. A county has a neighborhood stamp. This is not, primarily, a matter of political evolution but of economic evolution.

In both the range land and the dry-farming country of the dry western border of the Great Plains it is the standard of living that people have in mind in talking about current prices and the crop of the year. As one man put it, "Everybody wants everything." That is because they know about everything. The radio and the motor car have made that knowing easy. The radio brings the world to the interior of every shack and every dugout as well as every first-class modern home. It is constantly suggesting things to people who never knew about them before. The motor car operates in the reverse direction, taking people out to the towns. "Going to town" is the one diversion in the Plains country. It may be deplorable but it is natural that everybody wants everything. We are informed by current economic philosophy that this is a good thing for the country as a whole. There will be more buyers of goods, hence more prosperous industries, and so on in a circle. In times of drought all living standards go by the board. The present drought has brought living down to mere subsistence for the majority of families in each community of the stricken region.

If the local tax rate squeezes out all the profits, it will defeat the scheme of large holdings upon which successful occupation depends. On the other hand, if the best economic use of any given holding is not made, the landowner will be unable to pay his proportional share of taxes and will thus reduce the capacity of the community in which he lives to construct roads, maintain public health measures, support a county agent, and provide schooling. "A humane society would use scientific method, and intelligence with its best equipment, to bring about human consequences" (John Dewey).

CHAPTER NINE

THE CANADIAN FRINGE OF SETTLEMENT

And so we were at the beginning of things.
—F. W. GODSAL, *Old Times*

THE Canadian pioneer of the north country may not know what an "isotherm" is, but he has a genius for following it. The result is that we may no longer think of Canada as a narrow strip of fertile soil that got left out of the original United States, to use the phrase of the jingo of a hundred years ago. Canada got her westing in the last decades of the nineteenth century; her northing is an affair of this century, and the process is even yet in full swing. The settled country is no longer a strip but a belt widening toward the north. "A small and proud people," Canadians wish no sympathy from the rich and powerful if it implies that they have done the unexpected and come to amount to something after all. Many things have contributed to the increased dignity and elevated status of Canada among the nations, but perhaps none can be said to outrank in influence the discovery by Canadians themselves of the importance of *following the isotherms*. Thereby, in part, Canada has doubled its wheat crop since the World War, which is something that no other country in the world has done. The fact is of first importance in forecasting the Canada of that future with which the nation builder must be preoccupied. It is one of the tendencies that led the late Sir Wilfrid Laurier to say, with pardonable exaggeration, "the twentieth century belongs to Canada."

The map (Fig. 106) will make the theory of isotherms simple. The lines upon it connect places having the same mean temperature for July. They show the general pattern of the temperature belts of summer. The winter does not matter so much, for the Canadian soil is then dormant. Stefansson points out that Montana probably has a lower absolute minimum in winter than the North Pole; but one might reply that this is the fault of the North Pole and not of Montana. Arctic conditions are imported into our northern plains and Canada in winter and, on top of that, the vast interior of the continent has its own special way of cooling off like all large land masses in the so-called "temperate" zone—a zone that Mark Jefferson wisely says had better be called "inclement." We shall not stop to explain the process of land cooling and heating beyond saying that the interior of a land mass tends to be colder in winter and warmer in summer than the border of it where the sea exerts an equalizing influence. Earth warms more quickly and cools more quickly than water. In a rough way, it may be said that the greater the area of that earth the greater the effect. Therefore the larger

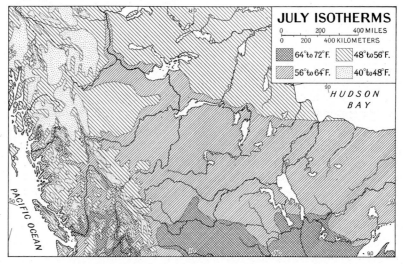

FIG. 106—Actual temperatures for July from map of North America by Unstead and Taylor in Philips' Comparative Wall Atlases. Compare the distribution of forests, Figure 107, and of the main types of farming, Figure 108.

the continental interior the more extreme are the summer and winter temperatures.

If we look at the map of Canada, Figures 107 and 108, we see that both the forest belt and the grain belt of Canada are tilted up on the left, or west, and for a long time it was a question as to how far one could count on the tilting to carry grain growing along the eastern foot of the Rocky Mountains, northwestward toward the Yukon. Both the temperature and rainfall conditions of the prairie provinces contribute in a most fortunate manner to the habitability of a wide belt of country east of the Rockies.[1] The favorable seasonal distribution of rainfall is shown in Figure 111 (p. 151).

[1] The physical conditions are well summarized by Helge Nelson: The Interior Colonization in Canada at the Present Day, and Its Natural Conditions, *Geografiska Annaler*, Vol. 5, 1923, pp. 244–308.

THE LAURENTIAN HIGHLAND SETTLEMENTS

It is the northward trend of present Canadian development that promises to lift at least a part of the great burden which Canada has borne because of the wide separation of her eastern and western farm lands by the so-called Laurentian Shield, or Laurentian Highlands (Fig. 109). Here topography cuts athwart the isotherms so broadly as to make the highlands "the major

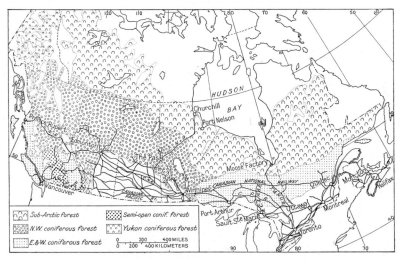

Fig. 107—Forest belts and railway net of Canada from map of vegetation and forest cover of the National Development Bureau, Ottawa, 1930.

geographical fact" of Canadian life. Only a small part of eastern Canada has good farming land—local tracts in the Maritime Provinces, strips of land broadening westward along the St. Lawrence, and the wide peninsula of southern Ontario. Between these fertile plains of the east and the prairie provinces of the west is an arm of the Laurentian Highlands 1500 miles across from Georgian Bay to the Red River Valley. This barrier, sometimes called "the bridge," is on the whole adverse to settlement. Mackintosh calls it "the great traffic desert" of Canada.[2] There is almost no local revenue for railways in the barrier, while the fixed expenses and operating costs are enormous. Traffic is light across the bridge and largely one way in character; and the presence of the Great Lakes brings water transportation into competition

[2] W. A. Mackintosh: The Laurentian Plateau in Canadian Economic Development, *Econ. Geogr.*, Vol. 2, 1926, pp. 537–549; reference on p. 544.

with the railways in the carriage of bulky goods during the season
of navigation.

Canada has reached her present stature only after two periods
of economic starvation; a first period lasting through the first half

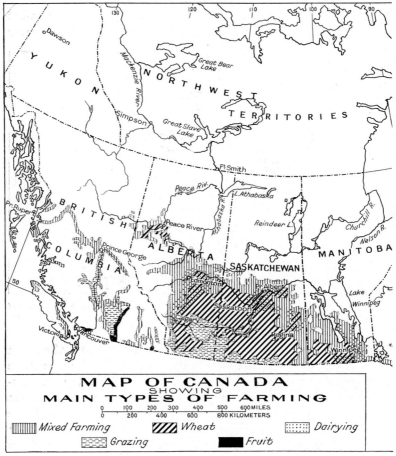

FIG. 108-A—Types of farming in western Canada. For forests and railways see Figure 107.

of the nineteenth century when she lacked a great export staple
that could be economically transported to European markets,
and a second period in the second half of the nineteenth century
when her westerly expanding settlements came up to the Laurentian
barrier on the north and west. It was only after 1900 that the
increased pressure of population in eastern Canada and the demands

of the world market gave the needed impetus to the attempt to turn the natural resources of the Canadian prairies into economic realities. Three collateral developments are chiefly responsible for the full realization of the agricultural possibilities of the prairie

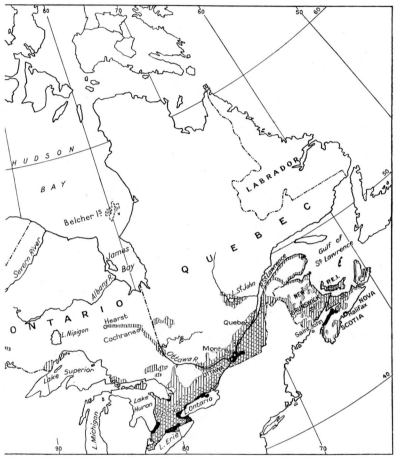

FIG. 108-B—Types of farming in eastern Canada. (From map by Natural Resources Intelligence Service, Canada.)

country: the rapid extension of branch railways, the perfecting of strains of early maturing wheat, and improved or adapted types of dry farming. The new strains of wheat alone cut off about a month from the average growing period of spring sowings, thus greatly extending the area of the potential wheat-growing country.

It is a sign of the rapid northward development of Canada that it was deemed expedient to build three great transcontinental lines. The first one, the Canadian Pacific, was built largely for political reasons as a means for bringing British Columbia into the Canadian federation scheme in 1871.[3] The other lines were built over a period ending just before the World War. The Grand Trunk Railway undertook to build the Grand Trunk Pacific from Winnipeg to Prince Rupert. The Dominion government undertook to build the National Transcontinental Railway from Moncton, New Brunswick, via Quebec to Winnipeg and to lease the line to the Grand Trunk Pacific at 4 per cent of the cost, the latter to operate the railroad. The third transcontinental was the Canadian Northern, privately built with generous government guarantees. The present Canadian National comprises the Grand Trunk Railway, the Grand Trunk Pacific, the National Transcontinental, the Canadian Northern, and the old Intercolonial.

The rail systems are fulfilling two main purposes: they make possible the wider exploitation of minerals and forests in the Laurentian Highlands, and they furnish additional communicating links between Atlantic ports and the rapidly expanding grain fields of northern Alberta and Saskatchewan (Fig. 107). The completion of the Hudson Bay Railway to Fort Churchill in 1929 represents a fourth enterprise designed to give stimulus to mineral and grain production and provide a cheaper means of water carriage to European markets.

It took time for the idea to win acceptance that the Laurentian Highlands could not be conquered through agriculture. Lumber and grain prices were high in the '50s and '60s, and settlement followed the lumber industry upon which it depended for prosperity. The government was therefore not averse to the building of colonization roads into the Laurentian country north of Lake Ontario and into the country between Georgian Bay and Lake Huron. But when the lumber industry declined after 1873, "the settlers found themselves stranded and marketless."[4] The settlers' crops of oats and potatoes could no longer be sold at good prices to the lumber camps for winter supplies, and the soil was too light to stand rainwash after the protective cover of the forest had been cut away. The colonization roads became lumbermen's trails in spite of the grants of free land along them. The barrier of the Laurentian

[3] For the relation of the Canadian Pacific to land settlement see J. T. Culliton: National Problems of Canada (McGill Univ. Econ. Studies No. 9), Montreal, 1928, pp. 65–75.
[4] Ibid., p. 541.

Highlands became a boundary of settlement. Today there are population densities of 50 to 75 to the square mile on the one side and less than one to the square mile on the other. In the hard environment of the Highlands there was left "a notorious rural slum," the most shiftless and incompetent elements of the population being left isolated and social conditions devoluting as agricul-

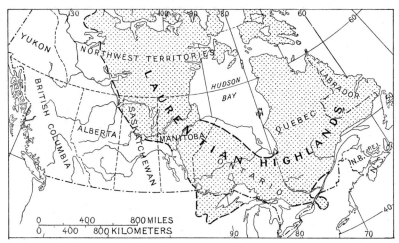

FIG. 109—The Laurentian Highlands (Canadian Shield) from map by the Natural Resources Intelligence Service of Canada.

ture failed. "A considerable number [of farms in the Trent region of Ontario] that ought to be abandoned remain occupied by those who lack the means and energy to move, thus forming a poverty-stricken community. A far-reaching policy for the management of this region must include a plan for the removal of this *degenerating* population."[5]

The "practice of pseudo-settlement,"[6] as the spread of population to the Laurentian Highlands is called, whether for agriculture or for the "skinning" of the land of its timber and pulpwood, has been hastened by the pressure of population in Quebec, by the discovery of clay beds in local basins extending east and west about 350 miles from near the western border of the province of Quebec to the Algoma District of Ontario and bearing the collective name of "Northern Clay Belt," and by the attraction of the lumber

[5] C. D. Howe and J. H. White: Trent Watershed Survey, Commission of Conservation, Toronto, 1913, p. 5.
[6] A. R. M. Lower: The Assault on the Laurentian Barrier, 1850–1870, *Canadian Hist. Rev.*, Vol. 10, 1929, pp. 294–307.

camps that provide labor for a part of the year. The French-
Canadian has led the way in forest pioneering, first harvesting the
pulpwood and then growing hay and vegetables and supplying dairy
products to the mining camps and towns. The so-called Algoma
Central and Hudson Bay Railway was built to make mines, forests,
and clay soils available. The government-built and operated

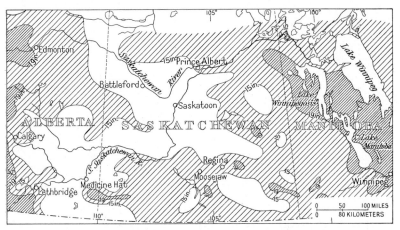

FIG. 110—Normal total precipitation for the year from map by the Meteorological Service of
Canada. The grain belt receives from 13 to 19 inches annually, according to position. A narrow
central belt of light precipitation is notable. Compare with Figure 111.

Temiscaming and Northern Ontario Railway, a colonization road,
was expected to reach tidewater at Moose Factory by the end of
1931. The Quebec government has a parallel scheme for a railway to
James Bay cutting through the clay belt and tapping mineral
deposits several hundred miles north of Montreal.[7]

It is natural that the lumbermen should first welcome the settler
whose frontier farm provides commodities which would otherwise
have to be brought in from a distance. Thus the two industries of
pioneer farming and timber cutting "accompanied each other further
and further into the wilderness." But the lumberman has not welcomed wholesale settlement, believing it to do more harm than good.
There have not been wanting political and other leaders who think
otherwise—that "trees should not stand in the way of men."
These have tried to push agricultural development to the limit.

By 1875 the assault upon the highland barrier fell off in Ontario;
but in Quebec, owing to the steady pressure of rural population

[7] H. S. Patton, Canada's Advance to Hudson Bay, *Econ. Geogr.*, Vol. 5, 1929, pp. 215–235;
reference on pp. 222–225.

in the restricted belt along the St. Lawrence, it went on with
disastrous effects. "I have never seen more burnt and devastated
woods than in the colonization district of East Canada."[8] Millions
of acres of forest have been ruined with relatively little addition
to permanently cultivable lands. With the rapid growth of the
pulp and paper industry of the twentieth century, settlement toward

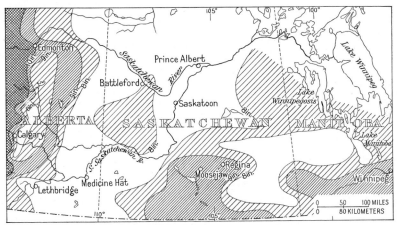

FIG. 111—Normal precipitation for the months of April, May, June, and July. Throughout
the grain belt slightly more than half the normal annual precipitation falls in a period of 122 days.
Compare with Figure 110. Compiled and generalized by the author from the records of the Meteorological Service of Canada.

the north received fresh impetus, and the Clay Belt has constituted
an anchorage ground that will hold the settler permanently to his
northern location.

Spectacular mineral developments in nickel, gold, and silver
in the Sudbury (1883), Cobalt (1903), and Porcupine (1909)
regions, besides several others, have stimulated railroad building
and settlement in their vicinity. The mines have drawn the
pioneer border northward in the same manner that the forests
did in an earlier epoch and to a less extent today. We may expect
that further exploration of the Laurentian Highlands will disclose
other valuable mineral deposits and that settlement will be drawn
eventually into all the available places, however distant. But
there is lacking coal,[9] the one mineral that would best lead to
permanent occupation of the territory, and its place is not properly

[8] Helge Nelson, *op. cit.*, p. 273.

[9] There is a considerable body of lignite on the Temiscaming and Northern Ontario Railway
north of Cochrane, which will be of substantial local use.

taken by water power, of which there is an abundance almost
everywhere in the Laurentian country. The power resources would
be used chiefly by the railways and the pulp and paper industry,
the latter already consuming about one-fourth of all of the electric
power used in manufacturing in Canada. The requirements of
the mining industry call for widely extended but relatively small
power developments. Only general industrial development that
goes hand in hand with dense settlement could make efficient use
of the abundant water power of the Canadian North Country.
Such general development it seems impossbile to bring about.
Continuous agricultural lands and a favorable position with respect
to large cities and world trade routes would seem to be among
the indispensable requirements of dense settlement which the
Laurentian country cannot fulfill.

THE WESTERN PRAIRIES

Syria has its Fertile Crescent only because there is a desert behind
it. What desert connotation have Canadian writers had in mind
in calling the territory between the North Saskatchewan and the
49th parallel the Fertile Belt? It was reported by both fur traders
and early cattlemen that the prairies were unsuited for agriculture.
The severe winters had almost established a tradition of frozen
soil a foot or two beneath the surface and of grassy plains adapted
by nature for the buffalo and antelope and their successors, the
herds of the ranchers. The northern woods that bounded the
prairies were clearly no place for settlement, and beyond them were
Barren Grounds and tundra.

With fuller exploration and the ups and downs of settlers' experiences to guide the scientist, quite different concepts came to rule
thought and action. We now know that even Fort Simpson is
not too far north to permit the growth of vegetables, while from
south-central Alberta the too-frequent droughts have driven settlers
to abandon agriculture for grazing and local irrigation. The
prairies and the country north of them are in truth a diversified
country about which accurate generalizations are not easily made.
A series of good crop years tempts both settlers and writers to
predict cultivation in the most distant situations. A series of
dry years invites equally extreme predictions of restriction of
settlement. The cereal crop of 1931 was the third in succession
to be affected by drought, as in the dry-farming sections of the

United States, and the wheat crop was little more than half that of 1930. But this does not mean depopulation. It is only the immemorial hazard of the weather. Agriculture in most countries has periodically to struggle with the time when there is "no rain in the earth."

The great need of agriculture on all the climatic margins of the world is for solid information about rainfall variability in the growing season. Cereal plants are shallow-rooted and moisture near the surface is the first requirement. Variability of snowfall is also important in the dry-farming lands of Montana and Alberta because what the chinook winds leave is available for ground water. In Canada especially the meltwater is held near the surface by the frozen subsoil of early spring long enough to provide a moist seed bed. It is

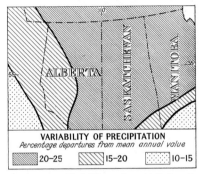

FIG. 112—Variability of precipitation in the prairie provinces of Canada. (After Biel.)

this refinement of observation on critical elements and seasons of precipitation that we need rather than figures of annual rainfall, which are often almost meaningless. An old plains farmer once remarked to me, "Annual rainfall? We have no such thing as an annual rainfall here! Once in a long while it rains."

Rainfall variability is greatest where the precipitation is lightest, as a general rule. In Figure 46 the rainfall variability of the world is shown. The deserts have the worst of it. A year may pass without more than a few worthless showers, while the next year may have so great a rainfall as to support a luxuriant growth of grass. Now it happens that certain very large grain-growing regions are in the climatic belt where rainfall is neither so heavy as on the central plains and Atlantic slope of the United States and Canada nor so light as in the desert. The rainfall variability of such grain-growing regions is likewise between these two extremes. The crops are astonishingly heavy in wet years, alarmingly light in very dry years. The greatest rainfall variability in the settled part of Canada is in the grain lands of Saskatchewan and eastern Alberta (Fig. 112).

It has been argued that it does not pay to raise even cattle in Montana and the drier sections of Alberta, and that equally it will not pay to raise grain as far north as northern Saskatchewan and the Great Slave Lake region even if it be possible to do so. It is one of the purposes of an investigation now in progress in Canada to determine the suitability of lands for given purposes. A Canadian committee on pioneer problems, working under the supervision of the American Geographical Society of New York, is engaged in a comprehensive field study of settlement. Its purpose is not merely to ascertain where settlers may now find unoccupied land suitable for settlement but rather to find where the best adaptations to the natural environment have been made, where failure or maladjustment can be recognized, and what shifts in location and agricultural practice will mean greater security in land occupation and a higher standard of living. Social problems also engage the attention of the committee, for this is a feature of land occupation now become as important as climate and agricultural success. Men and women to an increasing degree require the company of their kind. The radio is a boon on a far distant location, but it also keeps the isolated individual reminded of what he is missing in the settlements and towns. The required apparatus of civilization is now so complex that new settlement is not the simple problem it once was. School and church and hospital, good roads, a local library, and convenient shipping points are now looked upon as necessities, not merely desirable additions.

There will always be an incentive to carry crop production to the extreme limit of possibilities. Even a "cow country" has towns; and they require fresh vegetables, and the herds need winter feeding. Mining centers in the Laurentian Highlands induce land-minded individuals to see a living in small tracts of land near by where produce for the miners can be grown profitably. The lumberman of the highlands has also carried the farmer along with him, as we have already seen (page 150). The tin can is an efficient and indispensable container, but it costs to move it. Fresh vegetables have advantages that need no extolling. Finally, the farmer on the fringe of possibilities has this permanent advantage, that his land is cheap, even if its location is less desirable, and he can still make a living by accepting lower standards. To carry this to extremes would mean "a marginal people upon a marginal land," and possibly deterioration; but we still lack acceptable measurements and criteria. Individual experimentation is not yet ended. It is well to draw conclusions as to desirable social standards and to disseminate them, but a working acceptance will be extremely difficult to achieve.

When agricultural settlement began in the Canadian section of the Red River Valley, about 120 years ago, the lightly wooded uplands were the first parts of the back country to be occupied. Down to 1875 settlements clung to the river banks where transport

FIG. 113—Farm in the Kapuskasing district, Ontario. (Canadian National Railways.)

was least difficult, or they sought out "the semi-wooded districts" where homes were placed in the midst of clusters of trees. Pembina Mountain and Turtle Mountain were settled before the fertility of the soil of the untimbered valley floors was proved. The soil of the Red River Valley is a deep rich loam. The first crops to be ventured were abundant. No one dreamed that the grassy prairies of the wide uplands on the northwest were suitable for grain. "The early homesteaders shunned the high, treeless prairies."[10]

It took something more than good land to bring agriculture and permanent occupation to the prairies. The Hudson's Bay Company had territories which were not transferred to the Dominion until 1870 and then after long negotiation and a special act of the British Parliament. Within a few years after the transfer population flowed into the territories of the Northwest, and the process received stimulation from the fact that British Columbia entered the Dominion in 1871 and that by 1885 the Canadian Pacific Railway, assisted by subsidies and land grants, was completed to the Pacific coast. By 1870 it had also become known that cattle could be wintered upon the ranges without shelter and, after great losses, it was also learned that a certain amount of preparation

[10] J. W. Dafoe: Economic History of the Prairie Provinces, 1870-1913, in "Canada and Its Provinces," Vol. 20, Toronto, 1914, pp. 283-328; reference on p. 295.

for winter feeding was desirable and in the most severe winters indispensable. In the last two decades of the nineteenth century the cattle business spread throughout the whole prairie country, attracted by the same luxuriant growth of buffalo grass and other nutritious wild grasses that had been the support of the American cattlemen who rapidly displaced the Plains Indians after the Civil War.

The cattle business in Canada went through the same vicissitudes that marked the industry in the United States. When the snow was unusually deep or a surface crust formed, the cattle could not reach the grass below and thousands of them died. The winter of 1886–1887 was notably severe. Many cattle and horses perished from prairie fires in 1901, and no small number of shacks and corrals of ranchers and settlers were burned. The great round-ups were also times of dispute between rival ranchers over unbranded stock, the larger ones dominating the situation. From 1898 onward there was an increase in the outcry against "piratical American herds" that were driven by large cattle owners from the United States into Canada.[11]

After twenty-five years of growing prosperity the ranching industry so far declined that it was said that it had been "killed." The ranching interests contended that the Canadian Pacific Railway and the Dominion government were responsible for the decline. The railway was interested in local freights as a source of revenue, and grain meant more to it than cattle. It became the great champion of immigration, its agents traveling through eastern Canada, United States, Great Britain, and the continent of Europe "proclaiming the charms of the West and the fortunes to be found there."[12] The government naturally took the same position because political leaders thought of greatness in terms of population. The actual curtailment of the operations of stockmen followed naturally. Both large and small leases were terminated in those parts of the territories that were most suitable for farming. Homesteaders were allowed to settle upon the land; the price of grazing rights was increased; wire fences interfered with cattle drives and the access of range cattle to the lowlands in the winter time; there was continuous quarreling between ranchers and homesteaders. The system of maintaining vast herds upon cheap grazing land, which had been developed in the United States, quickly

[11] C. M. MacInnes: In the Shadow of the Rockies, London, 1930, p. 226.
[12] Ibid., p. 241.

came to an end in Canada as barbed wire cut up the territory and
led to overcrowding. By 1900 the mileage of fences had become
so extensive that round-ups were unnecessary and the day of the
big rancher had passed.

The government at first made the usual mistake of thinking
in terms of eastern acreages when the practice of homesteading

FIG. 114—Grand Prairie, a young grain-belt town south of the Peace River country of central-
western Alberta. (Canadian National Railways.)

was begun. A like period of experimentation and adjustment took
place in Canada that had been made familiar by experience in the
United States. The large grants to colonization companies, railways, and other corporations hindered development by encouraging
speculation through waiting for settlement to crowd about the
borders of the company holdings. It was at last recognized that
cattle ranching and farming were the right and left hands of any
successful system of land occupation in diversified tracts where
neither the one nor the other use of the land could be successfully
carried out alone. Local irrigation in the drier parts of Alberta
in 1885 received serious attention as the abundant rainfall of
the earlier part of the decade was succeeded by drought. New
varieties of wheat including winter wheat were introduced as suited
to drought conditions on the one hand and to maturity in a short
growing season on the other. But if there were difficulties in
settling the country there were also advantages. The absence
of forest meant easy cultivation and low capital cost for a new
farm.

If life upon the prairie seemed at first strange and isolated with

FIG. 115

FIG. 116

FIG. 117

FIG. 115—The old house of whitewashed clay in contrast to the modern home now being erected. Ukrainian settlement north of Winnipeg.

FIG. 116—Home and truck garden of new Canadians, Ukrainian settlement north of Winnipeg.

FIG. 117—Ruthenian home east of Edmonton, Vegreville, Alberta. (Photographs from Canadian National Railways.)

its vast horizons and its long distances between settlements, it was also true that the land quickly filled up. Growing railway lines brought supplies from outside, and the general trend of industry and transportation was toward delivery of products at continually lowering prices. Pioneering in much of the prairie country was an event of one generation, if we think of pioneering in terms of hardship, absence of near neighbors, scarcity of doctors, and life in primitive shacks. The advance of settlement has gone on continuously and is even now in progress, but it is pioneering of another variety. If it is not civilization advancing in full panoply it is at least an attempt to carry civilization right to the frontier or persuade government to make up social and economic deficiencies.

The railway builders speeded up the pioneering process by throwing out tributary lines into the likeliest agricultural zones under exploitation by grain farmers. They were held back by none of the inhibitions and ignorances that led some of the earliest writers and officials to regard all but a small part of western Canada as an Arctic outpost whose productive capacity was limited to furs. If Canada was to realize her ambition to possess herself in the twentieth century she had to have rails, and the government set to work to build its transcontinental lines so rapidly as really to exceed the needs of the time. Eighteen thousand miles in fifteen years were added, a rate equaled by no other country in the world. Three million immigrants were absorbed by Canada in that period and settlers along the

FIG. 118—Farmhouse, Peace River country, Alberta. (Canadian National Railways.)

lines under construction found employment in railway building for the otherwise unproductive part of the farm year.

The railway played a double rôle: it was a pioneer of settlement, and it steadied the economy of the settlers. It is true that the drop in the price of wheat in 1912, just as the new railways neared completion, resulted in the southward migration of many settlers; but the post-war years have seen settlement catching up with the railways until the production of the grainfields has mounted to the point where the Canadian National may not much longer be called the "white elephant of Dominion politics" and the Hudson Bay Railway is thought a present-day economic necessity. While the belt of settled land in the prairie country has been widening, the growth of industrial plants in Manitoba, Saskatchewan, and Alberta has kept pace with the more extensive cultivation of the land. From 1919 to 1927 the capital investments in industry in these three provinces increased by 137 per cent. In 1927 alone the gross value of manufacturing production increased 6.8 per cent. The region is steadily working its way toward the goal of an adequate degree of self-sufficiency.

The prairie provinces of Canada are by no means a one-crop

FIG. 119—The beacon of the prairies: grain elevator at Wawanesa, Saskatchewan. (Canadian National Railways.)

region, with such extreme penalties to be exacted by nature in the dry or cold years that wide depopulation will follow. Chiefly as a result of the lower wheat prices since the World War, and of the wide education of the farmers, the idea of diversified farming has taken firm hold locally with great effects in farm economy and the steadiness of life. The egg, poultry, and vegetable businesses have become established. The prairie country has entered upon an intensive stage of development. The extensive type of farming is now undergoing the same change that took place in the United States in the pre-war period. Even the northerly settlements of the Peace River Valley have accepted the principle of diversification on account of the narrower margin of safety owing to late spring and early autumn frosts.

The period of mass immigration from overseas ended with the Golden Age of railway building in Canada. The same critical questions are now put to European emigrants as the United States has asked since the World War. Canada wants the best that Europe affords, and she wants people who take to the land. Her cities have their own problems of unemployment to deal with, their labor union groups to•satisfy, their standards of public health to elevate, and they want no new city populations from Europe to increase their social and political problems. They want people who clearly hear "the invitation of the land" and are not afraid of hard work. So far have they gone in the application of the principle of restrictive immigration that they are as critical of United Kingdom immigrants as they are of others, to the increased perplexity of the British cabinet in anxious search of an eclectic remedy for unemployment.

A specific study of immigration and settlement in Saskatchewan goes so far as to recommend "That homesteading be discontinued and that the remaining Crown lands where immediately available for agriculture be sold (a) to residents of the province, (b) to other Canadians, (c) to British settlers, (d) to other immigrants."[13] The problem of the Canadianization of European immigrants, especially those who live in more or less solid blocks of population speaking the same language already presents itself to both Canadian society and government on a large scale.[14] This lends exceptional interest to studies on the limits of settlement and the soundness of communities already established that have passed through their first cycle of social and economic change.[15]

FIG. 120—Men laying steel at a mile a day during below-zero weather on the Churchill extension, Hudson Bay Railway. (Canadian National Railways.)

How extraordinary is the cycle of change that has swept Canada into its present advanced position with respect to immigration and the development of her new lands on the north! As late as 1896 it was deemed necessary to "stimulate" the coming of settlers. The number of immigrants from the United States into the Canadian Northwest being small (too small to show in the census statistics), the Lieutenant Governor of Manitoba placed advertisements in thousands of American newspapers and weeklies, arranged exhibits at American fairs, and appointed agents in key cities. The effects were immediate. In the following year, 2500 Americans crossed into Canada; in 1900 there were reported 13,500; and in 1913 the number of active, experienced Americans that came looking for cheap land had risen to a total of 139,000 for a single year; and they brought, on the average, capital to the amount of a thousand dollars each. The social and economic aspects of life

[13] Report of the Saskatchewan Royal Commission on Immigration and Settlement, Regina, 1930, p. 15.

[14] Walter Murray: Continental Europeans in Western Canada, *Queen's Quarterly*, 1931, pp. 63–75.

[15] See, especially, R. W. Murchie and H. C. Grant: Unused Lands of Manitoba, Department of Agriculture and Immigration, Winnipeg, 1926.

FIG. 121—The Pas, a "modernized pioneer town" on the Saskatchewan River (Fig. 124).
Founded in 1910, it had a population estimated at 4000 in 1928. (H. A. Innis, *Geogr. Rev.*, Vol. 20, 1930.)

in western Canada underwent a corresponding change as the land filled up. All was wheat in the first flush of settlement, and the wives of American migrants complained that the absence of the fruit orchard and the poultry yard worked hardship for them, that the social amenities were so scant it seemed as if the sod-house days of early Kansas were being lived over again. But diversified farming has alleviated the lot of most settlers, and coöperative marketing in grain has at least temporarily benefited the farmer.

Toward the close of the World War, the Canada Wheat Board developed the idea of coöperative marketing in order to satisfy the farmers who were of the opinion that they were the victims of the grain merchants and the elevator companies that operated through the Winnipeg Grain Exchange. The war over, the Wheat Board was besought to remain in existence; and in 1923 the three prairie provinces began a campaign for the organization of a wheat pool. Alberta took the lead and in that year marketed about half its wheat under contracts with the farmers. The following year Saskatchewan and Manitoba organized similar wheat pools, and soon the three pools secured a single federal charter. In practice the pool has proved politically and economically difficult in the face of growing stocks and high world production.

With railway systems extending their lines throughout the grain lands, and with coöperative grain-selling and social improvements, the pioneer on the northern margin of settlement has at his command the forces of the complex civilization from which he came. The customary hardships of the man on the fringe are now largely reduced, and great distances to market and low standards of social living are such temporary handicaps that the advance of settlers into the border may be expected to continue until the last frontier of Canada has been occupied.

FIG. 122—On the frontier of large-scale lumbering operations at The Pas, northern Manitoba. (H. A. Innis, *Geogr. Rev.*, Vol. 20, 1930.)

The northernmost invasion now in full swing in Canada is that of the Peace River Valley,[16] with its 73,000 square miles of good farming land almost all of it north of the parallel of 55° which corresponds with the northern tip of Scotland. There is a vigor in the Peace community that reflects the hopeful spirit which pioneers always bring to the conquest of new land. In 1911 there were less than 2000 persons in the valley even if we include traders, missionaries, and Indians. A hard journey of two or three weeks was then necessary to reach it. In 1916 the railway came. By 1921 there was a population of 20,000; by 1931, over 60,000.

The rush of settlement in the Peace River region has carried the homesteader fifty to sixty miles beyond the railway; and it is the business of the railway "to follow the settlers," to use the local expression. New towns have sprung up occasionally in a single summer season and at least one older town, Waterhole, was said to have been transported on huge sleds over the snow to a new site four miles away, changing its name to Fairview in the process. With the building of better roads, motor trucks shortened the time between settlements and railway, bringing farms formerly several days' hauling time from the railway to within a few hours. Fifty dollars an acre is not an uncommon price to pay for new land. There is still land available for homesteading, but most of it is remote from the railway and covered with poplar or willow brush that requires great labor to clear away. Undiscouraged by these conditions, homesteaders are still going in.

The use of varieties of wheat that mature rapidly has permitted cultivation to escape from the restricted lands of the valley floor, to which it was at first confined, and spread out on the upland soils of far wider extent. Spring wheat is the principal crop, with

[16] F. H. Kitto: The Peace River Country, Natural Resources Intelligence Service, Ottawa, 1928; and J. M. Imrie: The Valley of the Peace, *Canadian Geogr. Journ.*, Vol. 2, 1931, pp. 463–476.

oats and barley in second and third place. Mixed farming and ranching came in very quickly because if the oats do not mature or if the wheat is damaged by frost the crop can be fed to livestock. Hog-raising and dairying have offered their meed of salvation in untimely years. The severity of the winter climate and the fact that the grasses do not cure on the stalk as they do farther south, makes winter feeding of livestock necessary for part of the season— three tons per head is the requirement—though stabling and stall-feeding are not yet practiced.

Just as pastoral land at the margin of a desert has periods of drought that greatly restrict the usefulness of the pastures, so the pastoral land beyond the grain-growing border of the Peace River Valley has its periods of extreme frost and heavy snows, when the rancher is obliged to feed his stock for a longer period. Under the burden of extreme conditions the settler of limited means may trap to increase his income, or he may "work out in his spare time," or keep bees, or engage in fur farming. The farmer can sometimes turn to woodcutting and supply the market for fuel, railway ties, mine props, posts, and poles, for most of the Peace River region bears local stands of merchantable white spruce. If there is grain to export it is sensitive to the railway freight rates, and the area of production reflects market and transport conditions rather closely.

On the social side of life it is noteworthy that the Peace River district is well supplied with community halls where there are musical festivals, motion pictures, and other forms of community entertainment, The fact that there is a high percentage of English-speaking people makes it easier to organize the community than it would be if the population were cosmopolitan as parts of the pioneer fringe of Manitoba.

THE SUB-ARCTIC FRINGE

The North West Territories of Canada (Fig. 123) are said to represent the largest extent of land under the administration of a single Commissioner—over 1,300,000 square miles and a total white population of 1000 souls in addition to 7000 Eskimos and 4000 Indians. Of arable lands there are only small tracts in the Mackenzie Valley. These are restricted by climatic conditions to southerly locations. Along the Slave River cereals, hay, potatoes, and vegetables could be produced. The southern shores of Great Slave Lake are similarly suited to agriculture. The lower Hay

River and the Liard also come within the range of the agricultural belt of western Canada. In general these tracts have a forest growth that involves heavy expense for clearing. Surface boulders increase the difficulty of agricultural occupation.[17] Without a railway they can have only the most limited exploitation.

The risks from frost increase toward the north, and there are years in which the local crops suffer from drought; for northern Canada is a land of light precipitation, so light that in the latitude of Utah it would be semiarid. Only the growing of quite early-maturing varieties of cereals and vegetables will increase the chance of success upon the locally arable soils of the North West Territories.

FIG. 123—The North West Territories, from map by the North West Territories and Yukon Branch of the Department of the Interior, Canada, 1930.

Frost alone does not mark the border of the outer zone of settlement. Beyond the grainfields are the pastures. The Arctic or sub-Arctic prairies will carry settlement as far north as grass grows. There can be no doubt of this. There is a question, however, how dense that settlement will be. The pastures are of wide extent, but they will support only a thin population, like all other pastoral regions. The country of leadership, concentrated power, industry, and trade will lie to the south where cereal farming permits a dense population that requires the services of the prairie cities now in the stage of exuberant growth. There are really two pioneer fringes to most of the land still available for settlement. The first represents the farming border, and the second the pastoral border. Both the dry and the cold areas show a fading of grass cover and an increase in climatic severities away from the farm border. Which means that the grazing industry is either subsidiary to farming or supplementary to it. It has its own economic laws, its definite practices, its possibilities of well-being; but these are all enhanced in their effect if there is a tie-up of the region to the areas of closer settlement behind.

The moss-covered plains of sub-Arctic Canada suitable as ranges for caribou or reindeer are of vast extent. Domestic cattle, if sheltered through the coldest weather and protected from flies

[17] F. H. Kitto: The North West Territories, 1930, Department of the Interior, North West Territories and Yukon Branch, Ottawa, 1930, pp. 33 and 70.

during the summer months "thrive on grazing lands about the settlements,"[18] of the Mackenzie district. To utilize the grazing possibilities there is needed expert supervision of herds and the careful selection of animals and ranges. A special investigation of pastoral possibilities in the extreme north country on both sides of the Mackenzie River has shown a thick, soft carpet of moss and lichens with limited stands of willows and other dwarf trees of the tundra, forming thickets in sheltered places. The best development of lichens of the type known as "reindeer moss" is obtained in the open woods some distance south of the continental timber line where the ground is covered with so-called moss almost to the exclusion of other kinds of plant life. From the dead lower branches of the stunted trees black and gray types of moss hang in great profusion. Extensive winter ranges of this sort are found south of the Eskimo Lakes and attain their greatest perfection in the Great Bear Lake district. Forty acres per head is considered sufficient for the year-round grazing of reindeer in the hinterland near the edge of the forest and toward the coast where succulent grasses and sedges are found. From the Alaska-Yukon boundary to the west side of Franklin Bay (nearly 1000 miles) are ranges estimated to have a carrying capacity of at least 250,000 head.[19]

The airplane, like the railway, has become an agent of pioneering. It has the advantage of low initial costs, an almost free choice of routes, and great flexibility of schedule, and is thus ideal for remote localities which have neither the goods nor the passengers to support the expensive initial costs and necessary carrying charges of either motor road or railway. It was only a few years ago that north-bound travelers relied upon the flatboat service on the Mackenzie while now even in winter there is a weekly *airplane* service on that river from Waterways to Fort Simpson. Canada's pioneer fringe was glaciated in the last Ice Age, and an infinity of lakes and expanded stream courses make natural landing fields everywhere for seaplanes in summer and skid equipment in winter. Caches of food are established at intervals. It is the aim of the companies, though receiving no subsidy from government, to "link scattered communities and annihilate distance," and they have shown that there are sound commercial possibilities behind the purpose.

[18] *Ibid.*, p. 72.

[19] A. E. Porsild: Reindeer Grazing in Northwest Canada: Report of an Investigation of Pastoral Possibilities in the Area from the Alaska-Yukon Boundary to Coppermine River, Department of the Interior, North West Territories and Yukon Branch, Ottawa, 1929, p. 40.

The Hudson Bay Railway running from The Pas in western Manitoba to Churchill on the west shore of Hudson Bay was completed in 1929 after a third of a century of discussion and exploration of the navigation possibilities of Hudson Bay and Hudson Strait and the waste of over six millions of dollars in

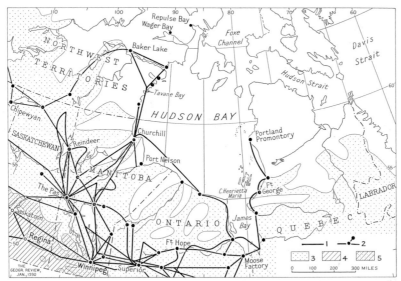

FIG. 124—Map illustrating importance of the airplane in northern Canada and the significance of The Pas as an air base. The broad character of the vegetational cover of the country is also indicated. Numbers have reference: 1, commercial air flights in 1928 from "Report on Civil Aviation for the Year 1928" (Ottawa, 1929); 2, gasoline caches; 3, forested area; 4, prairie; 5, transitional zone.

trying to make a more southerly location, Fort Nelson on Hudson Bay, suitable for the fairly large number of ocean-going vessels that the port must accommodate in a short shipping season running probably from late June until mid-November.

It is believed that the new line will act as a stabilizer in the export of wheat and provide western Canada and the wheat pool a weapon in freeing themselves of control by eastern monopolistic interests.[20] There is no doubt that the presence of the railway will stimulate agriculture in the northern prairie regions and bring about a hastened extension of settlement to the limit of cereal lands. The service of the line will tend to relieve congestion of eastern wheat channels and thus eliminate the heavy costs of summer peak-load operation. It is also expected to provide a

[20] Harold A. Innis: The Hudson Bay Railway, *Geogr. Rev.*, Vol. 20, 1930, p. 14.

cheaper outlet for other farm products including cattle. How far these uses will make it possible to secure an adequate return on the heavy capital investment in elevators, railway tracks, and loading facilities no one can say. The mineral resources are expected to supply the principal tributary streams of freight of immediate importance.

There is little doubt that the road offers an active stimulating influence to the mining industry and permits the safer extension of an airplane service already well developed in the prospecting field. There are also large traffic possibilities in timber. The railway runs across the lake region of Canada where an intricate maze of connecting rivers and lakes provide the readiest possible access to growing timber on banks and shores. The presence of the timber is an added advantage in mining.

Motor boat and airplane, rather than the motor car, are the most probable means of transport in the lake-dotted country of the Hudson Bay Railway, though advances have been made in winter transport by tractor that seem to show great possibilities in contrast with summer transport when there is much interruption and deflection of traffic by portages. Innis[21] thinks that the airplane is at a distinct disadvantage with respect to the tractor, since the latter may be adapted to sled travel in the Barren Grounds, thus providing "an efficient transport weapon in the attack on the Canadian Arctic." He sees distinct economic realities in the reindeer industry, the fishing industry, and the fur trade.

In no other part of Canada do we see the railway taking such an advanced position as an agent of pioneering as along the Hudson Bay route. The line has leaped forward under government subvention and enterprise until it is now several hundred miles ahead of the settler. From the standpoint of local traffic and the help it would provide to income account it would be desirable to have the line running through more promising territory. On the scientific side, and disregarding income for the road, it will be most interesting to see how far the presence of the railway and its auxiliary transport services in the air, on motor roads, and by navigable streams will offer inducements sufficiently strong to attract men to the region. It is not venturing far into the field of prophecy to say that the local resources of soil, forests, and minerals will be rapidly and, it may be, profitably developed and the pioneer fringe carried northward to positions well within the Barren Grounds.

[21] *Ibid.*, pp. 26–27.

CHAPTER TEN

THE PROSPECT IN AUSTRALIA

This fifth part of the earth.
—GEORGE HOWE SYDNEY, *Ode to the Kangaroo*

IT has been said that the two qualities of the human mind that most greatly distinguish men from animals are memory and hope. It is also true that men prefer to remember the joy rather than the sadness of life, while hope leads them to expect that happy experiences will come again. In a dry land hope and belief are widely entertained in a period of wet years that human occupation has ameliorated the climate, and the illusion may be fostered by improved methods of cultivation. The introduction of dry farming, deep-rooted alfalfa, drought-resisting grains, railroads, motor roads, and labor-saving machines has made the semiarid western United States a conquerable land. The dry-land settler is able to feed his hope with the fruits of experience.

If it is desired to locate the pioneer lands of Australia one needs to know what the rain gauge and the wet-bulb thermometer have to tell. The whole continent has been called "the victim of climate." Lord Bryce once said that the government in making leases to Australian settlers was not really leasing land but rainfall. In arid lands the driest years may have no rain, and cultivation and grazing may become absolutely impossible over wide areas that in wet years will pay liberally almost anywhere. As the farmer migrates into the belts of uncertain rainfall he has to *take chances with the rain*, and the border of close settlement will lie along the belt that experiment shows is likely to have more good years than bad. Beyond such a belt in the direction of growing aridity no surplus can be accumulated to meet the drain of bad years.

A single shower of wide extent after a dry spell in Kansas and Nebraska was often called a million-dollar rain. That was in the earlier years. Now it would have to be called a billion-dollar rain. At Vallenar in the Huasco Valley of Chile, a hundred miles south of Copiapó, no rain had fallen for three years previous to 1913, and, when one day great masses of black clouds came rolling up from the south, rain was confidently predicted and telegrams were sent to absent owners at Santiago to announce that it *might* rain! A single shower benefits pastures and fields and brightens the outlook of thousands of people. Neighbors forget long-standing quarrels over water rights. Two showers bring a year of plenty, and three or four showers make the year memorable.

Great variation in the amount of rainfall from year to year is the salient feature of dry-land climates. In the terrible seven-year drought at the turn of the century the whole continent of Australia was affected. By 1902, 15,000,000 sheep had died and 1,500,000 cattle. In New South Wales 20,000,000 sheep were left after losses and enforced sales, out of 60,000,000 five years before. The Bishop of Riverina compared his diocese to "a great Sahara."[1] Thereabouts water was carted for the fields from five miles away. Wheat production throughout the continent fell off to a third of the normal amount. So much of the land had a subnormal rainfall that the drought was a blow to the prosperity of the entire Commonwealth. When the rains came again "the forces of life" quickly produced a marvelous recuperation. After the great Australian drought that ended in 1902–1903 grain production increased from 500 to 600 per cent, and in three years the number of cattle and horses doubled.

A desert by definition is "a region of deficient rainfall with a sparse and specialized plant and animal life." A desert in most imaginations is a flat, sandy plain without a spear of grass or a tree or a wild animal of any sort. A desert in Australian politics is something hot and plantless that exists somewhere in the world but not in Australia.

The controversial element in the popular discussion of deserts comes of the common habit of simplifying conceptions. That is why every traveler is surprised when he first comes upon waving grass in the desert or a herd of antelope or cattle or a bit of woodland on an otherwise desert mountain flank. The politician says, "You belittle the country by calling it desert; there are people living there, and surely there is room for many more." Well, there are from two to three million people living in the Sahara and on its desert border, and no one denies that the Sahara is a desert. There is room for many more people in the semiarid interior of Australia and in the Sahara too.

From the political point of view it may be desirable to praise

---

[1] Sir John Eliot: A Preliminary Investigation of the More Important Features of the Meteorology of Southern Asia, the Indian Ocean and Neighboring Countries during the Period 1892–1902, *Indian Meteorol. Memoirs*, Vol. 16, Part II, Calcutta, 1903–1905, p. 248.

undeveloped country even if it will support few people. Better
the Arab saying, "Never praise your locust until you have eaten
him." Even while the settler is admiring his crop after a year of
rain, nature is conspiring to thwart him at the next sowing. That
is the peculiar mark of a climatically "unfavorable" or dry-land

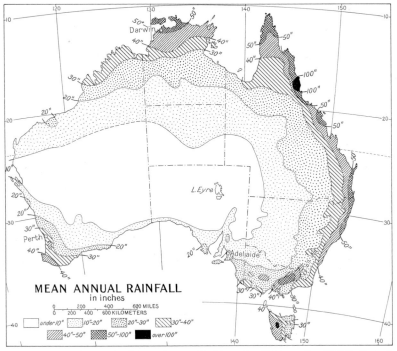

FIG. 125—The rainfall belts of Australia generalized from the official records. (Griffith Taylor.)

type of country—its rainfall has wide variations from year to
year. The Coast Range of Peru has heavy showers and luxuriant
pasture in wet years and only local showers in dry years. "How
often are you prosperous?" I asked a west-coast farmer. "Segun
el temporal y la Providencia" (that depends on the weather and
on Providence), he replied, pointing to the green hills and the gray
mist. If a traveler were to visit the Coast Range of Peru in a wet
year only, he would gain as erroneous an idea of its climate and its
capacity for stock and people as he would if he came only in those
extremely dry years in which there is a desperate hunt for pasture.

"The Dead Heart of Australia," by Professor Gregory of Glasgow, was published in 1906, and the author is often referred to today

as the originator of the "desert libel."   Instead of abating with
time, the controversy has increased.   Has Australia a desert and,
if so, is it patriotic to mention it?   No one questions the existence
of vast arable lands in Australia.   Differences arise over the question
how much is arable.   Where is the line of aridity to be drawn?

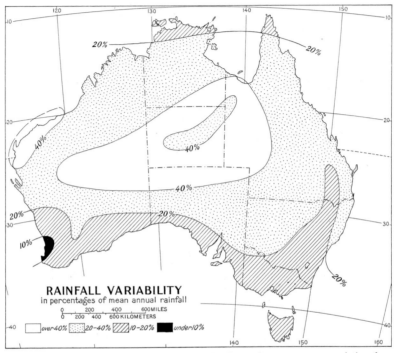

Fig. 126—The rainfall variability of Australia.   The figures denote percentage variations from
the mean annual rainfall in the period 1891–1910.   (Griffith Taylor.)

When one reads that there are seven or eight thousand camels in
Australia (introduced in 1846), and that they are still almost
indispensable in some regions, it appears that not all of Australia
can be a land of green fields and flowers.   Camels are not found in
Ohio or Kansas, and they are no longer used in Arizona, though
they were once experimented with in that state.   It is asserted that
some parts of Australia would have remained useless had camels not
been available for transport.   Australia is a land of great wealth.
The sun and the rain have blessed it, in parts.   Other parts are
cursed by a torrid sun and an all too cloudless heaven from which
dependable rains rarely fall.

Happily, the controversy among Australians over the "desert" of Australia has been responsible in part for an intensive study of agricultural possibilities, so that now one can define rather accurately the limits of pioneering in the vast interior of that continent. Two uninhabited areas half a million square miles in extent are

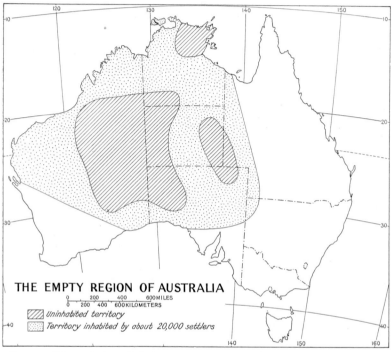

THE EMPTY REGION OF AUSTRALIA

0   200   400   600 MILES
0 200 400 600 KILOMETERS

Uninhabited territory

Territory inhabited by about 20,000 settlers

FIG. 127—"Economic Australia," the unshaded area of the map, has more than 99 per cent of the population.   (Griffith Taylor.)

known (combined in Fig. 127). In those two areas, so far as could be learned by Professor Griffith Taylor, formerly of the University of Sydney and now of the University of Chicago, at the time he made his report upon the subject in 1926 there was no white inhabitant and not a single head of stock. In addition to those wholly empty spaces there are others with almost no population. Roughly speaking, inhabited Australia includes 46 per cent of the area of the continent, and uninhabited Australia about 54 per cent. Put in another way, it can be said that 42 per cent of Australia is arid, or that 20 per cent is almost useless for stock and 22 per cent is fair pastoral country except in drought years. About 21 per cent

is fair temperate farming country, though from this must be sub-
tracted the rugged mountain areas. Only 13 per cent of the continent receives over 20 inches of rain (Fig. 125).

There is an enormous territory in Australia in which the conditions of life are distinctly marginal. As a continent in a state of

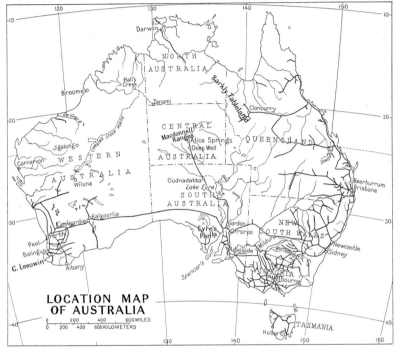

FIG. 128—General location map of Australia, showing places mentioned in the accompanying
text. Until its division in 1926 Northern Territory comprised both North and Central Australia.

active pioneering, Australia leads the world. Every step taken
in the development of its latent resources is on the road of experiment. Results are forged in the fires of controversy, by trial and
error. After the World War the discussion raged afresh. The
Commonwealth government put at the disposal of the newly
created Council for Scientific and Industrial Research sufficient
funds to undertake a thorough study of the resources of the continent
with the object of determining which of them is in greatest need
of development and how balanced production, a denser population,
and an approach to the political and social goal of *a white man's
continent* could best be achieved.

There is one feature of Australian pioneer life on the frontier that sets the continent apart from all other pioneering lands wherever situated: the enormous extent of territory unrelieved by mountains or streams, except at long intervals, within a given climatic zone. What this means may be understood by a com-

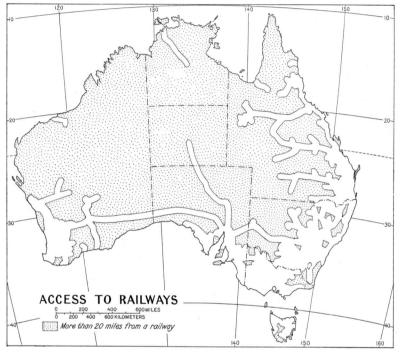

ACCESS TO RAILWAYS

More than 20 miles from a railway

Fig. 129—Conspicuous in the Australian railway scheme are (1) the east-west transcontinental line; (2) the north-south transcontinental project, still incomplete; (3) the Cloncurry line in Queensland to the border of the Barkly Tableland; and (4) the recent extension of the Westralian lines into new wheat-growing areas and group-settlement dairy country.

parison with conditions in the United States. Fortunately, our arid West is bordered by cordillera; and block mountains are strewn throughout the Great Basin. Each mountain range acts as a rain-making machine; and the larger ranges, like the Wasatch and Sierra Nevada Mountains on either side of the Great Basin and the Humboldt Mountains within it, are partly covered with forests and their borders nicked by watercourses that enable ranches and farms to be established. There is a *variety* of physical conditions and anything but uniformity in the manner in which the natural resources have been developed.

Were lofty mountains to traverse central Australia their flanks would be covered with forests, running streams would descend from them, and millions of people would by this time have made homes about their borders. Instead, the continent has its highest elevations near the east coast, and between them and the sea is a belt of

Fig. 130—Bullock teams carrying wool to railway station, New South Wales. (Commissioner for Australia in U. S. A.)

heavier and more dependable rains where there are the greatest possibilities for agricultural development and where there is the densest population. Here Professor Taylor believes 20 millions of people could engage in agriculture and manufacture before serious congestion would arise; and here he believes money should be spent for intensive development rather than wasted upon fanciful schemes for turning permanent pasture into farm land or reclaiming the hopeless interior shown as uninhabited in Figure 127.

How different would be the history of the Australian people if the first explorers had realized their hope of finding a better land behind the coastal zone! Eyre in 1839 followed up a broad valley that he believed would lead him to fertile highlands in the interior. Instead of realizing his dream he came to rocky and barren hills without the least sign of grass or water. Instead of a future home for prosperous settlers he looked out upon a dismal landscape convinced that he had reached a vast and dreary desert.

Until 1860 the Lake Eyre district was considered a barren and dangerous desert. An expedition then reached it in an exceptionally good season. Lakes and meadows were reported. Cattlemen were not long in coming in. "Its history since has been a series of periods of promise and hope followed by bitter failure and ruin. It is a tantalizing, fascinating region. In its good seasons its

FIG. 131—Kalgoorlie now has only 11,000 population, whereas in 1911 it had 26,000. It is on the desert margin, where formerly was only bare soil or scattered growth of small trees and shrubs now displaced by gardens and attractive dwellings. The water supply is piped from the Helena River over a distance of more than 300 miles. (Commissioner for Australia in U. S. A.)

hundreds of miles of knee-deep grasses lure men to their destruction. Once they have come under the spell of its vast spaces they cannot leave it. The waving grassy plains change to a burning stony desert, the stock cease breeding and gradually die out, the sand drifts over the pitiful fences and stockyards no longer used, its yellow, glaring ridges slowly approach and engulf the homestead, and yet men hang on."[2]

Australia is fundamentally unlike the United States in the vastly greater proportion of desert to densely settled country. In short, Australia has a bigger problem with far fewer people and resources with which to meet it. Man's struggle with his environment is here carried very much further than anything experienced in the arid lands of the United States. The rainfall belts of Australia are disposed in concentric fashion, as shown in Figure 125. There is a bit of country on the north and another on the southwest that

[2] C. T. Madigan: Lake Eyre, South Australia, *Geogr. Journ.*, Vol. 76, 1930, pp. 215–240.

are better favored than the interior. A wider and longer strip of territory with a more reliable rainfall is located on the east and southeast. But it is not enough to study the annual rainfall. Its seasonal occurrence and reliability are matters of first consequence. Reliability is shown in Figure 126, whose concentric belts are broadly in sympathy with the belts of total rainfall.

In a recent report of the Governor of South Australia *a single page* contains references to three drought-relief acts, one to water supplied to farmers, and another to a concession in railway rates to farmers with starving stock. New South Wales has more than seven hundred watering places. Western Australia maintains two thousand miles of stock routes built with government aid. The stock routes themselves vary in carrying power according to the seasons. Some of the wells dry up and remain dry for several years in succession. On long drives whole herds of cattle may be lost entirely. At the time of Taylor's visit to the De Grey River, which flows only at long intervals, he found one of its tributaries had not run for nine years, although ground water at fifty feet was not difficult to obtain.

Many pastoral tracts are so isolated that the cattle they support must be driven from two to five months over improved stock routes to market. In January, 1931, 60,000 cattle were reported in a drive from Northern Territory southward almost across the continent. In the drive of 1921, 73,000 head made the journey, taking two years and following a course made possible by rains that brought grass into being and filled the water holes. In some localities large areas of roofage have been constructed to gather the rain water. In the Barkly Tableland, water may be obtained in many cases at depths of one hundred to two hundred feet, and future settlement will depend largely upon the cost of sinking and equipping wells, which now runs from \$2500 to \$5000 each. One well makes available the pasture within a radius of eight miles—the limit to which cattle may graze from a single source of water. Most of the grazing land is occupied by cattle, because the high labor costs and the difficulty of transporting the wool have driven out the sheepmen, cattle being able to travel many times farther than sheep to reach a market.

The Australian pioneer has pushed into almost every part of the continent. There are special reasons why population has gone so far toward the limit of its possibilities in searching out the habitable lands of the interior. The prospector has been an active explorer and pioneer. The mineral deposits of Kalgoorlie and Coolgardie in southwestern Australia drew settlers far beyond the possibilities of ordinary settlement. When gold was discovered in New South Wales (1851) a "rush" ensued that almost depopulated parts of the country. Many farmers abandoned their land, crews left their ships, sheep remained unsheared. In many instances government officers deserted their posts. Between 1852 and 1861 nearly a half billion dollars' worth of gold was recovered from the two chief mining centers.

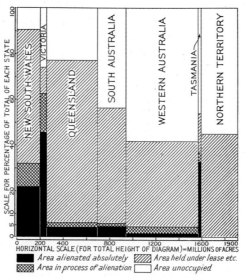

FIG. 132—Note the high percentage of land held on lease. (Year Book of the Commonwealth of Australia, 1930.)

Almost every part of Australia has had its day of gold excitement, its rush of mining pioneers. Yet as a basis for permanent settlement the mines of Australia are no more enduring than those of other parts of the world. It has been calculated that in the non-agricultural mining fields of the continent there are probably not more than 120,000 inhabitants. In southern Africa the mines attracted the railroads, and the number of permanent settlers increased rapidly. Neither a mine nor a railroad can create opportunities; they only help to bring the natural opportunities of the soil to realization. If the environment is not favorable, population is limited to the needs of the mines; and when these are exhausted the country returns to wilderness.

In a pioneer land limited to grazing, all the conditions of life become highly specialized, and society is primitive in the extreme. If such territory be of wide extent, a rather definite social type results. Sir Hubert Wilkins has the following to say of his countrymen of the distant interior stations. I quote from his "Undiscovered Australia" (1929): ". . . In many of the districts visited we found the living conditions, even in places where much better could have been afforded, to be of the lowest type, apparently from choice. There are, of course, some magnificent homes on some of the Australian stations, but these are few and far between. The Australian settler generally expects his sojourn in the country to be temporary. . . ." Wilkins was disappointed, as an Australian, to find that so many able-bodied men "retired" from productive work with only just enough money for a bare existence. "In most cases there is no pride in holdings or in homesteads. The 'near enough,' 'it'll do for me' slogan has been so thoroughly ingrained into the people during their temporary sojourn in the country that they cannot overcome it when in retirement . . . ."

The coastal part of northwestern Australia provides a picture of one of the most experimental of the pioneer fringes of that extraordinary continent. So far as the land is concerned, it is habitable pastoral country. There is grass for a hundred to a hundred and fifty miles inland. Wells can be sunk to serve the needs of cattle stations. To encourage the pastoral industry the Westralian Land Law permits an individual to acquire as much as ten thousand acres, and beyond this he can lease as much as a million acres on annual payments at two and a half dollars per ten thousand acres![3] Western Australia has two hundred and forty-five ranches of more than one hundred thousand acres each, and some stations that represent an amalgamation of interests have more than a million acres. While most of the leases will expire in 1932, some of them will run to 1948. It is doubtful if the lessees will have any difficulty in renewing their leases, for a larger population seems improbable and only this will make it necessary to limit the size of the holdings. On some of the large stations the feed is so poor that ten to fifty acres are required to support one sheep.

Inland from the coastal zone of northwestern Australia the climate is drier, and the question of stock routes to the coast, of wells and pasture becomes more acute. The population of the Westralian desert that can be economically supported by cattle raising is not likely to exceed twenty persons for each million acres, or a thousand to two thousand persons for the entire desert region of the state. In his account of field work carried out in 1924[4] Clapp concludes that "no white person *will* live in the Northwest of Australia unless forced to do so in order to earn a living."

When the magic of irrigation was invoked to reclaim the arid

[3] F. G. Clapp: In the Northwest of the Australian Desert, *Geogr. Rev.*, Vol. 16, 1926, pp. 206–231; reference on p. 230.
[4] *Ibid.*, p. 231.

FIG. 133

FIG. 134

FIG. 135

FIG. 133—Soldier settlement at Beerburrum, North Coast Line, about 40 miles in an air line north of Brisbane, Queensland. (Commissioner for Australia in U. S. A.)

FIG. 134—A settler's home, Mildura, Victoria, maintained by irrigation from the Murray River in an area having a yearly rainfall of 11 inches. (Commissioner for Australia in U. S. A.)

FIG. 135—Making a home in the bush, Springfield, northeastern Tasmania. (Commissioner for Australia in U. S. A.)

lands of the western United States, Major Powell, later director
of the United States Geological Survey, in his famous report on the
"Arid Lands of the West" was quick to see the severe limitations
unless there were substantial streams to provide the water. He
liked to say that all of the artesian water of the Dakotas would
not irrigate a single county. It has been calculated that under

FIG. 136—Settler's home, with first crop of cotton, Dawson Valley, Queensland. (Commissioner for Australia in U. S. A.)

the best of circumstances, and discounting evaporation and soakage,
only 1/300 of the western districts of Australia could be irrigated
by artesian waters. The figure is still further restricted if account
be taken of saline artesian water not suitable for irrigation. A
calculation of the use of irrigation water in the Transvaal shows
that a million cubic feet are required for the irrigation of eight
acres. The riverless parts of Australia are of little agricultural
moment. Their ground waters, soakages, and artesian sources
combined can be of much greater value as a support for the livestock industry.

It is a wise government that spends public funds on schemes
that represent not the outer limits of possibility but the probable
and attainable limits of possibility in the way of reclamation and
amelioration. Schemes for the defeat of nature too often end in the
defeat of man. We must bow nature out: we cannot kick her
downstairs. In a region of climatic extremes fundamental research
may tell how far nature can be frustrated. It should be possible
to apply natural laws to the processes of climate and tell what the

climate and weather are going to be at least in the immediate
future. So many factors affect rainfall and temperature, and some
of them are so inconstant, that meteorological forecast can never
be expected to be an exact science. Man can never hope to forecast
storms as exactly as the astronomer computes the future position
of a comet or a planet. Yet even now the short-period forecast

FIG. 137—Settler's home, Murrumbidgee Irrigation Area, one of the principal irrigation areas
in Australia, with a rainfall of about 15 inches. (Commissioner for Australia in U. S. A.)

of the weather is of practical benefit. Even if we are not told when
to raise an umbrella, we are usefully warned when it is wise to carry
one. If we could go as far as that in long-range forecasts we should
be able to provide safeguards in years of drought.

It is a well-known fact in climatology that a series of dry years
suceeds a series of wet years so that the curve of rainfall is likely
to show either an ascending or a descending trend that will probably
continue *for a time*. Were it possible to show these trends in
advance, to discover the laws that govern the irregular occurrence of wet and dry alternations, it would pay the Australian
Commonwealth many thousands per cent to invest government
funds in equipping and maintaining all the stations necessary to
secure the observational data. The menace that now hangs over
Australia, dark as a war cloud, would be diminished in this way,
and the fuller use of the land achieved. Instead of taking chances
with the rains, farmers and ranchmen would adjust their operations
to the rains. *Man would not ask more of the earth; he would simply
inquire of the earth what she intends to do.*

If the rainfall probability were forecast, how would a knowledge of it benefit Australia? For one thing, in years of greater rain the impounded waters of the drainage basins could be conserved. In years of lighter rainfall, stock could be driven to better-favored sections before the drought effects reached their peak; or it could be sold off to the limit set by the diminished carrying capacity of the ranges. Forecast is not merely telling what is going to happen in the way of rainfall and temperature. Once there has actually fallen a given amount of rain, it is possible in a growing number of places to estimate its effect. To do this is to provide a useful warning to farmer or pastoralist. An instance is the wool clip of Australia. So long as the climatic data were expressed in *averages for large districts* there was relatively little value in the correlation of rainfall and wool production. But when a record for a long period, 1893–1926, became available for a station near the center of the Western District of Victoria "some quite remarkable correlations" were disclosed. By taking the acreage of an estate (variable), the total number of sheep carried (a reflection of the grazing capacity of the pastures which varied little from one sheep per acre), the number of sheep shorn, and the weight of the clip in pounds, it was possible to make a correlation with rainfall.[5]

It was found that the critical rainfall period is January and February, eight months before shearing. The correlation is valid even if sheep are hand-fed with grain in the subsequent dry season. Over the western half of Victoria the number of sheep that one acre of pasture will support is equal to 4 per cent of the number of inches of annual rainfall, e.g., 25 inches per annum will support one sheep per acre; 15 inches will support three sheep to five acres; and 12½ inches, one sheep to three acres. A head of cattle is equal to six sheep in reckoning the carrying capacity of pastoral land, and a horse equals 10 sheep. A hilly country has much lower carrying capacity than a plains country. Below 12 inches the variability of the seasons, that is "the coefficient of dispersion" or departures from the normal, is so great that the carrying capacity is less than that of an average season.

In like manner the wheat and rainfall correlation of Australia supplies the basis for forecasting economic conditions during the following calendar year. It is not the amount of the rainfall during the year but rather the amount that falls in the critical period

[5] Due account was taken of the improvement of the pastures and of breeding. See Henry Barkley: Forecasting a Wool Clip, *Pastoral Rev.*, Vol. 37, 1927, pp. 759–761; also *idem*, Forecasting Economic Conditions in Australia, *Econ. Record*, Vol. 2, 1926, pp. 161–173.

before the wheat plant flowers. For the west-coast region this is June, and for northern Victoria it is the last of August. The latter region, lying in the center of the eastern Australian wheat belt, seems to provide a key to the whole Australian wheat yield, even if we take both total yield and bushels per acre into account. The spring rainfall of the northern district of Victoria Barkley calls "the magic key to the situation" because its close correlation with some branches of primary production enables a forecast to be made of economic conditions during the following calendar year. He concludes: "As an early index to the wheat yield it should serve to check undue speculation, to indicate our jute requirements and the necessary shipping space, in addition to forecasting a large part of the national income from exports. As an indicator of prospective prices both agricultural and general, it shows the probable trend of the volume of business and banking, and is very intimately associated with the purchasing power of money, the cost of living and the value of the effective wage."[6]

The Central Part of the Continent

The reports of the official administrators picture the difficulties confronting the settlement of the arid lands that comprise so large a part of the interior. Those for North Australia, Central Australia, and South Australia deal with the whole central block of the continent, a strip 1500 miles long and 600 miles wide, or nearly a million square miles (Fig. 128). Land occupation, whether for grazing or farming, is a hazardous enterprise throughout this whole vast tract. Settlement has met the challenge of drought courageously. There is no region with a similar climatic handicap where men can claim greater tenacity of purpose. The price of conditional success is heavy. Some Australians believe it to be too heavy in view of undeveloped possibilities elsewhere in Australia.

The net result of one hundred years of experiment in trying to settle North Australia is that it refuses to be settled in the sense of being self-supporting. If you were to become a resident of Northern Territory you would find yourself one of 3000 white persons, and you would very soon learn that your community is not self-supporting but is almost entirely dependent financially upon the federal government. You would discover a paralyzing public debt of nearly $40,000,000 and a total revenue from all

[6] Henry Barkley: Forecasting Economic Conditions in Australia, *Econ. Record*, Vol. 2, 1926, pp. 161–173.

sources of $300,000, or less than 1 per cent of the debt. Growing at its present rate, the debt would rightly seem to you to be inextinguishable. You might well ask yourself if it were not better for the government to provide every white man, woman, and child in the Territory with an income sufficient for maintenance in institutions, free of cost, for the rest of their lives, give up this painful experiment on an incorrigible frontier, and let the land revert to wilderness.[7]

It was here in 1918 that government practically disintegrated. A Commonwealth cruiser put into the port of Darwin, and military authority was substituted for civil process for a time. The labor unions maintained that workers should be paid increased wages because they had to live in a distant territory and endure uncommon hardships, among which they underlined the abnormally high cost of living. Mr. Justice Powers in November, 1924, spoke of the "disadvantages necessarily suffered by those living at Darwin, which all but residents who have been there for a long time recognize. . . . " He thought that special consideration could be given only for "isolation." In his award on the issues in dispute he called attention to "relief work" that provided white settlers a rate of pay so high that the wages for one or two days' work would support a whole family for a week. Both single and married men have at times refused to leave Darwin, even at the expense of the government, when offered a free passage to the south where higher wages and better living conditions could be secured.

Young men cannot be expected to go to such a land, and Sir George Buchanan concludes that it is obvious that "if the young pioneer is to be paid a special isolation allowance over and above the very high basic wage obtaining in the Northern Territory, all attempts to develop that country had better be abandoned." The best of the pastoral lands are held in large areas on long leases, and the pastoral industry is not in a flourishing condition. There is so large a number of aboriginals in and about Darwin that they furnish an adequate supply of cheap labor. Chinese and colored population exceeds the European population, and the Chinese are increasing more rapidly than the Europeans. In the period 1911 to 1924 the white population increased by 200 only. Ninety-five per cent of the men are not married and do not intend to marry, and generally speaking the men are old or near middle age. There

---

[7] If this picture seems overdrawn, see Sir George Buchanan: Northern Territory Development and Administration, *Commonwealth of Australia Parliament, 1925 [Publ.] No. 48,* [Melbourne], 1925, p. 5.

is a marked absence of the young men that characterize an active pioneering community.

The introduction to an official bulletin refers to rainless periods and says that the truth lies between the extremes of opinion, on the one hand that it is desert and on the other that it is a paradise. The author finds isolation affecting every phase of the pastoral industry, lack of communication causing such personal inconvenience that the settlement of white women in the country is not only difficult but involves actual risk to themselves and their families. Medical attendance is impossible in the interior "and medical comforts well-nigh unobtainable in a place which only receives a fortnightly mail, limited to a three-pounds parcel's post."[8] Thus runs the description of the Macdonnell region in the heart of Central Australia. Time had provided an ample test of the vitality of the settlements after their establishment more than sixty years before. The belt of high country that includes the Macdonnell Range is 400 miles long and 20 to 50 miles wide, with an elevation more than 4000 feet above sea level.

An official report on Northern Territory endorses everything said in its favor as a white man's country: the northern half "is *never* subject to drought as are the other states of the Commonwealth," and that this part of Australia, though situated in the tropics, is not really tropical in nature because, except in very few places, "there is no such thing as the tropical jungle."[9] The report concludes that the author would be wanting in duty and patriotism if he did not urge settlers to "lose no time in availing yourselves of the wonderful offer now before you." Many students of Northern Territory speak of its isolation and its long distance from market, but this investigator believes that "when the railway is made Darwin will be the front door to the Australian continent."

Here is a franker and more disinterested opinion by Lieutenant Colonel Sir Henry Galway given in a discussion of Michael Terry's paper "From East to West Across Northern Australia."[10] "It [Northern Territory] really is the 'white elephant' of Australia. It is all very fine to talk about its beauty and richness. You will find that ninety-nine people out a of hundred, nay, more than that, 999 out of 1000, who crack up the Northern Territory, have never

---

[8] T. E. Day: Report and Plans of Explorations in Central Australia, *Northern Territory Bull.* No. 20, December, 1916, Department of Home Affairs and Territories, Melbourne, p. 20.

[9] Robert Williams: Report . . . on Behalf of the Welsh Settlers of Patagonia, *Northern Territory Bull. No. 9,* September, 1913, Department of External Affairs, Melbourne.

[10] *Geogr. Journ.,* Vol. 64, 1924, pp. 21–37; discussion, pp. 37–43.

been there! They crack it up from Sydney, Melbourne, Adelaide, Brisbane, and Perth. . . . They do not go there; they tell other people to go!"

Sir Henry went on to say that the tropics could not be developed with white labor, a conclusion that he had reached after thirty years in the tropics. The white man is not fitted to do manual labor there, nor can he breed and bring up children under tropical conditions.

Sir Hugh Denison, former High Commissioner for Australia in the United States, added, in the discussion of Terry's paper, that he had been in the Northern Territory and thought that the class of emigrants going out to Australia today was not composed of the enterprising young fellows who were not afraid to open up these "wide places." He added: "There is too much government spoon feeding, and that is the sort of thing that is killing the opening up of a wonderful country such as Australia."

In Northern Territory the period 1870–1889 is described as one of "delusive booms," marked by exciting episodes, "the telegraph, gold mines, plantations, railways, Chinese, and stock."[11] An offer was made to Japan, and promptly declined, to send settlers to the Northern Territory. In 1881 huge plantation schemes were devised, "agricultural" land taken up in large blocks, and range land in still larger blocks. There were efforts to effect close settlement in the coastal zone. In 1888 the great schemes failed. "National sentiment barred the door to cheap coloured labor." In the late nineties came "the gold-mining tragedy" which drove out much capital.

The idea of basing economic welfare upon the advantage of position as the northern gateway and on coastal plantations ended in "a complete fiasco," says Price, "agriculture failed, the railway [to the interior] became a losing proposition." "It seemed that Nature had designed the Northern Territory to be 'a monstrous harlequinade.' "[12] The natural difficulties had proved to be serious. Money in too large amounts had been spent upon the wrong geographical areas. "The coast is both a threshold and a barrier," thinks Price; and most significant in one proposed plan of redemption by leasing is the suggestion that the region be freed of its "national ideals and burdens."

How much "spoon feeding" should be done, how much sub-

[11] A. G. Price: The History and Problems of the Northern Territory, Australia, Adelaide, 1930, p. 15.
[12] Ibid., p. 33.

sidizing of the settler, is the eternal question on the rim of settlement in Australia. We may agree that government aid is vital in the development of a new territory, but how much aid and in what form it should be given can hardly be determined except by experimentation. Dr. H. Priestley of Sydney University found no physical degeneration of children of the third generation in northern Queensland, but he thinks that the women have a very hard time in the tropics. The men get out to their work, but the women have to stay in crude and inconvenient homes with very little assistance, and the result is that "a woman 32 years of age, after having lived under conditions that exist at Broome or Darwin, and having borne a couple of children, is as old as a woman of 50 in South Australia." If women have to live under impossible conditions, and if they are an essential factor in the development of a white Australia, it is doubtful if the tropical portions of Australia can ever become white.[13]

Dr. Priestley thinks that the mental factor is peculiarly important and cannot be measured in figures. Concentrated mental work is not possible in the tropics except by spells, and mental development in a new country cannot be ignored. A hot climate and the nature of the employment available impose upon parents the necessity of separation from their children and also the separation of husbands from wives, the women being kept elsewhere in Australia. Almost all the women express a longing for a cooler climate, and all persons who can afford to do so send their children for a part of their education to a school in a cooler climate, from which they return in so much better health as to put in contrast the disadvantages of the boys and girls who cannot get away. This is a great social drawback, if a settled population is desired.

All phases of development here have their starting point in climate. Government officials are clear that the Northern Territory is primarily a stock country and that any railway policy must be considered in relation to the stock industry. The Barkly Tableland in the southeastern part of the Northern Territory is thought capable of supporting 14,000,000 sheep; but further development is impossible in the absence of railways, for sheep, unlike cattle, cannot be driven long distances to the railway or from one drinking place to another. The Barkly Tableland is therefore peculiarly suited to railway pioneering as a basis of pastoral development. But the government must take the initiative. No possible com-

---

[13] Buchanan, *op. cit.*, p. 19.
See also G. L. Wood: The Settlement of Northern Australia, *Econ. Record*, Vol. 1, 1926, pp. 1–19.

bination of private interests could finance a railway to tap the resources of this upland region now in a low state of development. Nor can any pastoral country become fully developed when drinking places for stock are locally from fifty to one hundred miles apart. One observes in the report on the pastoral industry in the Official Yearbook of the Commonwealth of Australia for 1930 that the total number of cattle in Northern Territory by the end of 1928 was 768,750, of sheep 7635.

How does the government of such an isolated region manage to survive? The admitted difficulties are appalling. In Sir George Buchanan's report of 1925 he speaks of the deplorable effects of divided control, with bitterness and friction between the various government departments. He frankly admits that until the Territory can afford to do so, interest and sinking fund on a special development loan for the construction of capital works could not be paid except by the federal government. He attaches great importance to the office of administrator, since the incumbent must be responsible for "the social fabric in Darwin." He recommended "substantial tropical allowances" for officials sent to the Northern Territory with the opportunity of being transferred if they are assigned to service in the Northern Territory, instead of depending upon volunteers, since otherwise a man would be "banished to the Northern Territory for life," hardly the phrase to induce settlers to come.

The opinion of Sir Hubert Wilkins is in consonance with the earlier quotations. In "Undiscovered Australia" he reaches the following conclusions: "Although the [Northern] Territory holds much fertile land and is watered by many navigable streams, the distances, not only within the Territory, but also from the central markets, are so great as to make economic development most difficult." He adds: "Without doubt white men can work in the Northern Territory, and, indeed, in any country where the conditions are not really tropical either in vegetation or in climate; but whether they will work is another question . . . even with the most efficient and scientific equipment it is exceedingly doubtful if much progress is feasible in the Northern Territory without the introduction of coloured labour. The White Australia policy is a wonderful idea for the people of to-day, but with it a very long time must elapse before Australia is populated to its carrying capacity."

Wilkins found little unoccupied country east of Darwin suitable for stock. Though the region is not fully stocked, some of the station owners feel obliged to shoot many of the older cattle "to make room for the growing ones that may mature at a time when they may be sold at a profit."

CENTRAL AUSTRALIA

The first report of the administrator of a new government in a pioneer area should prove a document of absorbing interest, and such is the report of the administrator of Central Australia for 1927.[14] If North Australia, whose government problems are beyond the power of the handful of white persons that constitute its "population," cannot manage its own affairs, how can it expect to administer a territory lying hundreds of miles to the south in the heart of the continent? At least, so the still smaller handful of people in Central Australia regard the matter. A new territory was formed (Fig. 128). Local government was welcomed by the small isolated settlements of the interior. On the economic side, the building of the railway from Oodnadatta to Alice Springs "has given the people of these parts fresh heart." The administrator made his tour of inspection of the settled area with camel transport. He found surface waters practically absent, the country for miles in the vicinity of the wells was denuded of fodder, and where he did encounter pasture it was useless because too far removed from existing waters. Settlers were shifting their stock farther west, and heavy mortality among the stock was feared.

In the past it had been sought to encourage settlement by renting vast areas in Central Australia at extremely small rates to influential companies. The administrator thinks this method of encouraging settlement has been proved a failure. He adds: "If Central Australia is to take its place as an inland colony, a vigorous policy of water conservation must be carried out. If the stocking conditions are to be insisted on, then the carrying capacity of the lands must be increased."

The administrator thought the needs of the region could be summed up in two words, railway and water. The whole grazing industry would be stimulated if more watering places were provided so that sheep as well as cattle could be kept, sheep requiring from eight to ten times the number of watering places that are required for larger livestock.

[14] Report of the Government Resident [of Central Australia] for the Period 1st March, 1927, to 30th June, 1927, Commonwealth of Australia, Canberra.

The disadvantages of the country are the absence of permanent water, isolation, heavy transport charges, and severely dry climate. These are so great as to outweigh the lure of low rentals and to make it necessary for government to undertake an extensive well-sinking program. Otherwise the natural surface waters will be used to their full limit, the accessible ranges will not have a resting period, and excellent pasture far from existing waters will not be used.

FIG. 138—Oodnadatta, South Australia. The railroad was built to Oodnadatta in 1891; the section from Oodnadatta to Alice Springs was completed in 1929. (Commissioner for Australia in U. S. A.)

"The fifty miles dry stage between Alice Springs and Deep Well has always been a handicap to droving. Repeated efforts to locate water on the route between these two points have proved futile."

Consider the hardships of the pioneer at a distant station through the absence of medical attendance. The report of the administrator is eloquent on the subject:

"The great disadvantage is the absence of a medical officer in Central Australia. The hostel established by the Australian Inland Mission is greatly appreciated and availed of. Although the nursing sisters are highly capable in their profession, the presence of a doctor in the district would naturally be more reassuring to settlers, especially the womenfolk, and would certainly be more conducive to settlement. It is hoped that, with the early growth of the population around Alice Springs, the Government will see its way clear to appoint a medical officer for Central Australia. At present the nearest medical assistance is at Oodnadatta—a distance of 331 miles."

We are here considering a territory 236,000 square miles in extent (about the size of Texas), with a population of 411 persons, having

under their care livestock numbering nearly 120,000 head.   The
rainfall for twelve months ending June 30, 1927, was 6.84 inches;
the highest rainfall recorded from 1917 to 1927 was 28 inches (1920),
the average, 12.46 inches.   The administrator assumed his duties
in a time of drought and saw the worst aspects of the country at
the beginning of his term.   Even the branding of the cattle had
to be delayed because the horses were too poor to work, particularly

FIG. 139—Typical arid pastoral country on the tropic in Western Australia near Jigalong.   There
is no settlement east of this point for 700 miles.   Spinifex in foreground, mulga by the car.   Rainfall
10 inches.   (Griffith Taylor, *Geogr. Rev.*, Vol. 16, 1926.)

in the area around Alice Springs, where most of the settlements are
established.   Fortunately, a light rain had fallen in the country
between Alice Springs and Oodnadatta, so that the stock could
be driven to railhead for transport.   But, good forage not being
available on account of the drought, the cattle were in poor condition
when they reached the market.

Sometime in the near future there will be a different story from
this interesting laboratory of experiment on the margin of habitable
Australia.   It will be when the years of rainfall come in a group
as they did from 1920 to 1923.   Then there will be a great burst of
development, and those that have hung on will prosper greatly.

South Australia

One has constantly to fall back upon official statistics and
statements lest the degree of aridity of the Australian interior
seem to be exaggerated.   If we turn to the Annual Report of the
Department of Lands and Survey for 1925 and 1926, published by
the government of South Australia, we shall get a notion of the
meaning of drought conditions on the pioneer fringe.   In that gov-

ernment alone the amount advanced to applicants for drought relief under the Act of 1914 was about three and three-quarters millions of dollars. Drought-relief acts succeeded one another in 1919, 1923, and 1926. The Act of 1926 was made necessary by a drought so severe that the settlers in several districts could not keep their dairy stock, put in a crop, or continue on the land without assistance.

All of this had to be done as an emergency measure, and Parliament was asked to validate the action taken by the administrators. Water had to be carried by rail for the use of settlers in various parts of Eyre's Peninsula (Fig. 140). The railway department charged "drought rates," the settler undertaking to refund a part of the difference between these and normal rates "when able to meet the liability." There were delivered 2,690,266 gallons of water under this arrangement.

The following paragraph from the report referred to pictures the drought effects of 1926, not in Northern Territory or Central Australia, but in South Australia. Rain sheds and tanks to the number of 52 were erected during the year 1925–1926, making a total of 386 that were completed down to June 30, 1925, for settlers on Eyre's Peninsula and the west coast. Here is a characteristic entry:

CONCESSION IN RAILAGE OF STARVING STOCK, FODDER, ETC. Owing to drought conditions, arrangements were made with the railway authorities (Commonwealth and State) to carry by rail starving stock for agistment, fodder, super, and seed-wheat from the 1st March, 1926, at 50 per cent. of the usual rates for settlers beyond Gordon, the balance of the railage charges being debited to the Lands and Survey Department. It was also decided that, owing to the disastrous fires in the Mount Pleasant district, similar concessions would apply in that locality.

Subsequently it was decided to extend the concession to Orroroo and other stations north thereof.

The settlers were required to furnish declarations showing that the starving stock were only being shifted for the purpose of taking them to feed to save their lives, and not for the purpose of sale, that the stock were the applicants' sole property, and that the fodder was for the sole use of feeding the applicants' starving stock; also that the super and seed-wheat would be used entirely and solely for seeding purposes during 1926 on land held by the applicants.

Settlement in South Australia is rather closely limited to the southern part of the territory, population swinging up the east side of Spencer's Gulf but becoming much more scattered on the west side as droughts are there more frequent and severe in their effects and the climate changes gradually to the more extreme type that characterizes Central Australia.

The history of the settlements of South Australia parallels that of most dry-land borders. Good seasons brought in settlers and they prospered so greatly that land values were placed too high by government. The squatters were refused the right to purchase at public sales, and there was much abandonment of pastoral land (1861–1864).[15] The drought of 1864–1869 almost destroyed the salt bush and gave the land "the fearful appearance of desolation." In a year sheep perished to the number of a quarter million, and the cost of hauling water increased fourfold. New farming methods, a better knowledge of the country, and a recognition of a practical limit to cultivation had steadied both agriculture and grazing by the end of the century.

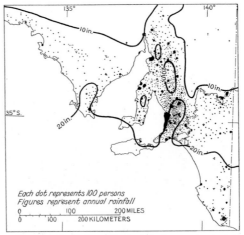

Each dot represents 100 persons
Figures represent annual rainfall

FIG. 140—South Australia, from the human standpoint, is a narrow coastal belt about Spencer's Gulf. Eyre's Peninsula is on the west side. (Charles Fenner.)

The southern territory illustrates admirably the advances and retreats of population that mark a new country. These are not the result of rainfall changes merely. World economics often plays a decisive rôle. New settlement is experimental everywhere, and highly so in a region of light and uncertain rainfall. "Whenever one travels throughout the older settled districts of the Australian States, one may occasionally note the presence of ruined houses, old wells, neglected orchards, solitary chimneys, disused roads, and other similar evidences of human culture in localities where at the present time homes are rare.

"In some cases enquiry reveals this somewhat depressing feature to be a part of the ebb and flow of population that is continually taking place—often associated with the fact that families grow up, the young people move away, the old people die, the farm is bought and used for less intensive agriculture, and the home is no longer occupied. In other cases, agricultural districts have thrived because of the nearness of markets provided by mining towns, and

15 S. H. Roberts: History of Australian Land Settlement (1788–1920), Melbourne, 1924, p. 254.

with the closing of the mines there has been a natural falling off in the farm values of the neighbourhood, with consequent emigration."[16]

South Australia's half million population keeps pushing into the drier areas beyond the 10-inch rainfall line, but the limited success of the effort is indicated by the fact that for nearly twenty years no new counties have been opened up. Good years have a cumulative effect because they come in groups. Some of the counties that were opened fifty years ago outside the 8-inch winter rainfall line have either no agricultural production or so little that they are disregarded by the government statistician. Within the 10-inch rainfall line are almost all of the railways and towns, the area so

FIG. 141—Wool teams, Carnarvon, Western Australia, a port on the Gascoyne River serving a large number of sheep and cattle stations just south of the tropic. (Commissioner for Australia in U. S. A.)

defined providing access to rails or ports on coast or river at distances no greater than twenty miles.

WESTERN AUSTRALIA

Western Australia contains almost a million square miles of land, the equal of the United States west of the Rockies. Within the area enclosed by the ten-inch rainfall line, which may be called the "line of settlement," the land is uninhabited desert. This leaves grazing land marginal to the coast on the north and an agricultural triangle on the southwest (Fig. 125). One should not be deceived by the large extent of desert and semiarid country into thinking that the southwestern territory having more than 10 inches of rainfall a year is insignificant either in area or productivity. Be-

[16] Charles Fenner: A Geographical Enquiry into the Growth, Distribution, and Movement of Population in South Australia, 1836–1927, *Trans. and Proc. Royal Soc. of South Australia*, Vol. 53, 1929, pp. 79–145; reference on p. 138. This paper contains a most interesting study on well-being which is summarized in a "prosperity graph" that relates population changes to the principal factors believed to have an effect.

tween Cape Leeuwin and Albany, southeast of Perth, there is a well-timbered and relatively wet strip. The best forests grow where the rainfall is 30 or 40 inches a year. From this district timber is exported, much of the original woods having been cut down "to make way for dairies and orchards."[17] Here are the main railway lines, the areas of close settlement, the largest towns.

The advance of the wheat farmer into the back country of south-western Australia, in places to the 10-inch rainfall line, could not have been carried so far if it had not been for the adoption of scientific methods of cultivation which include dry farming, crop rotation, artificial fertilizers, drought- and disease-resisting wheats, and labor-saving machinery.[18] These have contributed, as in

FIG. 142—Settlers at the post office in one of the group settlements of Western Australia. (Agent General for Western Australia.)

America, to the advance of cultivation along much of the dry interior border of the coastal belts of Australia. The limit of cultivation has not yet been reached, but it is a fluctuating limit in any case and will depend upon economics no less than rainfall and better methods of cultivation. A small effect upon pastoral settlement has been brought about recently by the recovery of ground water in areas once regarded as useless desert, thus extending the wide pastoral belt in a manner analogous to the widening of the agricultural belt.

Western Australia has apparently not yet reached the point of overextension of settlement which proved so disastrous in South Australia (p. 195). Down to 1908 the state was still importing a certain amount of flour to meet the demands of its people, and during the World War there was a decline in total wheat production in the territory.[19] In the last ten years land surveys have been

[17] Griffith Taylor: Australia: A Geography Reader, Chicago, 1931, p. 257.

[18] W. H. Wynne: The Development of Public Land Policy in Australia, Reprint from *Journ. of Land and Public Utility Economics*, October, 1926, and February, 1927.

[19] H. P. Colebatch: Westralian Wheat Lands, *United Empire*, Vol. 17 (N. S.), 1926, pp. 660–662.

widely extended to meet the needs of settlers, and railway lines have been built into the most promising areas with much tributary mileage of light railways for grain transport. The latter are built at a cost of about $7500 per mile, or about a fourth of the cost of construction and equipment of standard railway lines. Farms are located up to ten miles from the railway, "the recognized economic distance." A hundred miles of railway increases the population by about 24,000 persons when the corresponding town population increase is added to the new farm population.

The advancing settlers have learned to utilize to good effect the regular winter rains and the less reliable and lighter rains of summer. The ground is prepared so as to receive and store a maximum of moisture. In this way the total available soil moisture for each harvest season is increased perhaps 30 per cent above the normal amount.[20] It is believed that still further improvements may push wheat growing even beyond the ten-inch rainfall line in exceptionally favorable places. The active advance of the wheat farmer has provided a quantity of new data that on further study will permit closer estimates of the probable extent of wheat land yet to be developed. Five years ago there was still believed to be available 25 million acres of unimproved land suitable for wheat.[21]

Under the British Empire Settlement Act of 1922 group settlement was taken up in Western Australia; but after several years of experimentation and the introduction of some hundreds of settlers, chiefly in the timbered southwestern districts, the scheme fell in abeyance because it was found that it cost more to make a farm than it was worth, and in some cases the excess was as much as 50 per cent.[22] A total of forty-five million dollars has already been spent on the scheme, "and a large part of this may have to be charged off as loss."[23] This is believed to be too heavy and permanent a load on the community, an unprofitable expenditure, "a mortgage on future prosperity." In return for this enormous sum the state had added by January, 1930, only 1696 new settlers, or a total population of 7483 on land aggregating 392,444 acres. "It is certainly development—at a price."[24] On the largest government

[20] Results of Rainfall Observation Made in Western Australia, Bureau of Meteorology, Melbourne, 1929.

[21] Colebatch, op. cit.

[22] P. D. Phillips and G. L. Wood, edits.: The Peopling of Australia (Pacific Relations Series, No. 1), Melbourne, 1928, p. 99.

[23] Report of the British Economic Mission to Australia, Dominions Office, London, 1929.

[24] Gordon Taylor: The Development of Group Settlement in Western Australia, Econ. Record, Vol. 6, 1930, pp. 28–43.

unit, the Peel Estate, each location cost $17,500 in return for which there were sown only 118 acres besides 130 acres in pasture. "The country was experimental, the development largely experimental— the administration was blindly groping in the dark," said one of the government leaders in extenuation of the loss.[25]

The experts now believe that government should have restricted its sphere of experiment and left more to private enterprise. Western Australia has reached the point, in added population and extended wheat acreages and dairy farms of the group settlement region, where the government is bound to take account of social and economic conditions tolerable to settlers of the best type. Mere acreage, or the filling up of empty space, in itself means nothing. The welfare of the individual as a member of a new community has now become the basis of judgment. This is read from experience with group settlers: "One of the worst features of the Group Settlement system was the degree to which settlers tended to drift away from the groups. Original settlers were replaced by new and less experienced settlers, and they in their turn gave up and others took their places . . . up to the end of April, 1925, about one-third of the settlers had left the groups."[26]

Western Australia at last realizes that its objective should not be mere numbers of people upon the land or total acreage under the plow, but rather the best way in which to build communities that are economically and socially sound and that contribute to the welfare of the state as a whole. Dependent or subsidized communities maintained upon an uncertain fringe of settlement are only a source of weakness. In these respects Western Australia is one of the most interesting experimental zones upon any pioneer fringe of settlement today.

[25] *Ibid.*, p. 42.
[26] *Ibid.*, p. 32.

CHAPTER ELEVEN

THE WHITE MAN'S LANDS OF
SOUTHERN AFRICA

So huge the all-mastering thought that drove.
—RUDYARD KIPLING, *The Burial*

IN a quite practical sense the dreamer is the doer. This would not be true in the long run if men were not moved by idealistic purpose as well as by profit and loss. The biologists have a convenient word, "saltation," to express the jumps made every now and then in contrast to the more orderly sequences of evolution. This is also the way of mankind and the processes that we call civilization. The dreamer and the prophet have hurried men along by insisting every now and then on the long look ahead, by jumping rather than crawling forward. They lead men by the power of visions. They drive them by the fury of their beliefs. It is sometimes said that such men anticipate destiny. They do more than that, they create it! From the "Story of a South African Farm": "The glory of a dream is this,—that it despises facts, and makes its own."

Among the men who have not been content with what lies on this side of "the rim of the known world," there is one, Cecil Rhodes, who has molded destiny and cut the pattern of life for most of southern Africa. About the council tables of empire men take account of him as truly as if he now sat among them, for the force of his ideas projects the personality of the man in lengthening stature down the generations. He created a breed of his own stuff that has assumed the right to control southern Africa as a white man's country, making no apology for the application of that "right" because they believe themselves the heirs of a civilization that is equal to the task of exercising power over both white and black and holding the scales of justice evenly at the same time.

We need not for the moment inquire too closely as to the wisdom of their scheme of things nor as to the manner of its administration; the main thing is to recognize that there is a scheme and that to it men in large numbers bring so high a degree of devotion and intelligence that they make it work. The edge of settlement in southern Africa cannot be understood except in the light of this scheme. The pioneers of Northern and Southern Rhodesia, for example, do not have the outlook of those in the western prairie lands of Canada, the Far West of America, or the fringe of settlement in Australia. They come among large native populations as masters. They supply the capital and the organizing skill, but they do not propose to do more than a small part of the manual labor of the fields, the mines, and the ranches. Their government first of all guards the rights of the white men who bring the machinery and the ideas of modern life.

The most striking feature of the geography of southern Africa[1] is the large extent of uplands on the summits and about the borders of which the white man finds it tolerable to live and work (Fig. 143). Were the interior uplands not accessible by rail the great distances that separate some of them from the coast would make white occupation impracticable except in periods when commodity prices are high. Fortunately all are in process of being tied to the ocean by lengthening trade routes—railways and waterways provide access from Egypt, from the coasts of Tanganyika and Kenya Colony, from the Union of South Africa, and from Portuguese territory facing the south Atlantic and Indian oceans. The upland areas were long removed from the sphere of white action; but the white now has full political control, and his economic machinery is being extended everywhere. This means a standing invitation to men with capital to invest in land and mines and to be traders and transporters of imports and exports and managers of black labor that is capable of producing valuable raw materials.

It was long thought that only the northern and southern extremities of Africa would support white colonization: Northern or Lower Egypt, Libya, Morocco, Algeria, and Tunisia have more than a million white settlers; and there are about a million seven hundred thousand whites, chiefly of Dutch and British blood, in the Union of South Africa. Aside from these two great belts, white settlers in the past have been scattered about the margins of the continent and at strategic trade centers in the interior. The uplands of tropical Africa have introduced a third type of region of significance in the future of the white settler because there is black labor near at hand and the uplands are accessible to adjacent valleys in which tropical agriculture may be extended profitably.

---

[1] The term "southern Africa" includes not merely the Union of South Africa but all the territory south of the eighth parallel south as shown in Figure 146, page 203. The use of this term avoids the frequent repetition of the names of regional or political divisions.

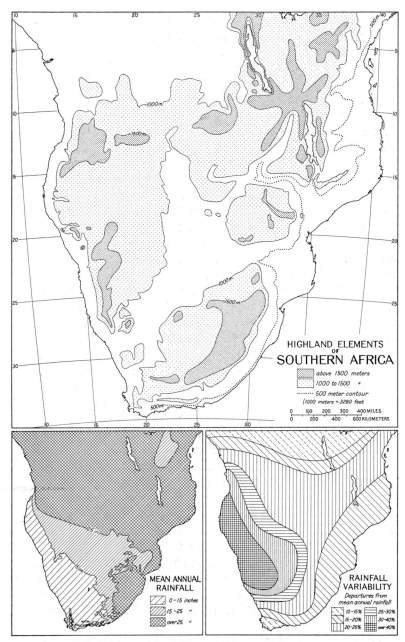

FIGS. 143–145

FIG. 143—(top) Highland elements of southern Africa as outlined by the 1000-meter (3280-foot) and 1500-meter contours.   For a note on sources for Figures 143, 144, 145, 147 see page 204.
FIG. 144—(lower left) Mean annual rainfall.   FIG. 145—(lower right) Rainfall variability.

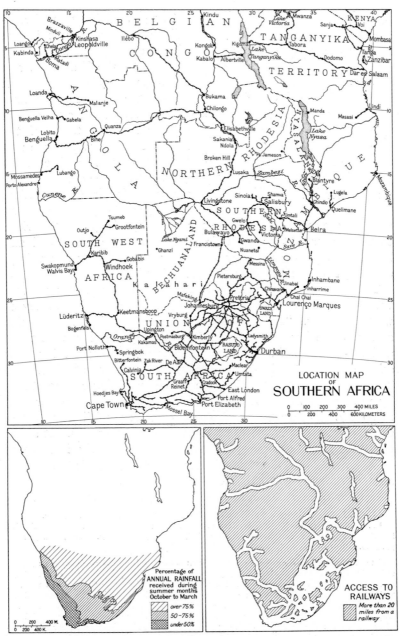

FIGS. 146–148

FIG. 146—(top) General location map of southern Africa.
FIG. 147—(lower left) The summer rainfall of the southernmost part of Africa.
FIG. 148—(lower right) Access to railways in southern Africa.

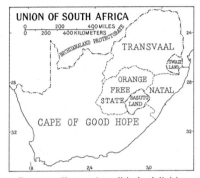

FIG. 149—Key to the political subdivisions, Union of South Africa.

The general increase of rain-fall from west to east in the higher country of the Orange Free State, the Transvaal, and Rhodesia has given settlement toward the north a strong east-erly trend. This, as has been said, is also the trend of the higher country, which the rain belts follow sympathetically (Fig. 144). The greater reliabil-ity of rainfall in this direction, as well as its greater absolute amount, are responsible for the extension of white population right to the border of the highlands on the east where a ragged and broken line of scarps, locally crested by mountains, marks a drop, generally in short distances, to subtropical levels.

The rainfall of the whole of southern Africa is subject to great variability. A knowledge of its times and seasons is the key to white conquest. "Africa challenges science to define, to determine and to guide her future" said Jan Hofmeyr, and the best use and conservation of water supplies are in his catalog of things that science must do for European settlers.[2] Plummer's studies in the Transvaal provide a clear picture of the increasing chances taken by the settler who moves away from the zones of greater rain reliability.[3] Figure 150 shows the amount of rainfall that may be expected to occur in the region in 75 out of 100 years. It shows the characteristic increase of rainfall with easterly increase of elevation and, when compared with Figure 145, reveals the increas-ing uncertainty of the rainfall toward the west.

In a wide view of rainfall distributions in southern Africa and

[2] Jan H. Hofmeyr: Africa and Science, II, *Science*, Vol. 70 (N.S.), 1929, pp. 294–299.

[3] F. E. Plummer: Rainfall and Farming in the Transvaal; Part I, A Preliminary Investigation into the Variability of the Rainfall of the Transvaal, *South African Geogr. Journ.*, Vol. 9, 1926, pp. 5–20.

Note on the sources for the maps on pages 202–203: Figure 143 is generalized from the 1 : 500,000 series of topographical maps compiled by the Surveyor General's Office, Windhoek, and printed at the Ordnance Survey, Southampton, 1927; and from the War Office (London) 1 : 2,000,000 Series, G.S.G.S. No. 2871, 1918–1929; Figure 144 is based on the map of Average Annual Rainfall (accompanying Rainfall Normals up to the end of 1925, Union of South Africa, Department of Irrigation, Meteorological Office, Cape Town, 1927); Figure 145 is reproduced from a part of Erwin Biel's world map: Die Veränderlichkeit der Jahressumme des Niederschlags auf der Erde, *Geographischer Jahresbericht aus Österreich*, Vol. 14–15, 1929, Plate 21; Figure 147 follows the map opposite page 336 of the Handbook for Farmers in South Africa, Department of Agriculture, Pretoria, 1929.

of the limiting values they set upon successful agriculture we see the critical basis of settlement today. Not the average rainfall over large areas but its local reliability is of importance in determining the limits of cultivation. From August to October there is little or no rain over the southeastern sector of Africa. This means that for crops grown in those months,

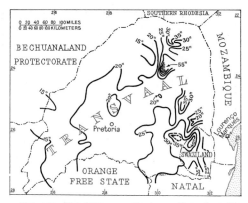

Fig. 150—The figures on the heavy lines show the amount of rainfall reasonably to be expected in each of 75 years per century. From Plummer, Pretoria, 1927 (see footnote, page 204).

and the months immediately succeeding, irrigation is indispensable over most of the region. When there is a swing of rainfall from a wet to a dry phase the effects are not local but widespread, and on the distant borders of settlement they have again and again been devastating. The climatic instability tends to retard settlement and the growth of white population.

In the Union of South Africa it is considered that the land lying between the rainfall lines, or isohyets, of 15 and 25 inches is semi-arid, the land with less than 15 inches arid (Fig. 144). One third of the Union has a rainfall of more than 25 inches a year. The better-favored lands have been rather fully occupied, and any addition to the cultivated land will be relatively small and in the direction of less rainfall and a specialized type of agricultural practice. Increase in the acreage of plowed land here means less productive land and a lower standard of living. Even now the principal crops of the Union are extremely low in average yield, maize yielding about one-third of a crop judged by American standards.[4] The soils are "desperately poor" in organic matter. The loessial type of soil familiar in many of the dry-farming areas of the United States seems to be absent.

Feeding stock during exceptionally dry summers makes an added drain upon production, a drain similar to that made upon the cattle industry in the drier parts of the western plains of the United States, where there is winter feeding on account of the cold.

[4] Sir Frederick Keeble: Soils and Fertilisers in South Africa, *Nature*, Vol. 126, 1930, pp. 417–420.

One good year in four or five is the most that can be expected by a farmer in the Union of South Africa. If he cannot use the prodigality of that year to help him over the leaner years he is not the type of settler best suited to the country.

In general, farming in the Union may be expected to become more intensive, the country breaking up into better demarcated regions in which ranching, diversified farming, and transitional farming practices will be the rule. In the direction of uncertainty of rainfall the size of the farms tends to be larger and occupation more unstable. This instability makes its special appeal to legislators, who number among them a large proportion of farmers; and the consequence is possibly "an over-expenditure of state funds to relieve the hardships of the sufferers."[5]

The stage of evolution to which the Union has come serves to emphasize the pioneer quality of development in the highlands farther north. The advance of settlement means the extension northward not only of a social or cultural system but also of a standard of living. Before looking at the northern uplands, region by region, brief reference will be made to the manner in which the modern push to the uplands came to be made.

The migratory habit of the early Dutch outpost settler in southern Africa carried him into nearly every corner of the habitable country. His characteristic way was to move to a new site, remain several years, and then move on again. He is to be found in the hinterland of Angola, or Portuguese West Africa; he has explored most of the border of the Kalahari; and he has gone far up into the highland areas and down into the subtropical valleys. Much of our knowledge about the possibilities of the country is based on his experiences. While he was a rough guide to settlement at one time, that is no longer true today. His problem was one of survival, while the white land settler of today is interested in the possibilities of a given region for commercial farming, that is the production of raw materials that he can export in order that he may import agricultural machinery and other material necessities and raise his type of living above the level of mere subsistence.

The first advance of settlement from the Cape was northeastward along the cooler and moister uplands of the Orange Free State and the Transvaal. Mixed ranching and farming was the rule. Transport was by ox team. The trader went even farther than the

[5] H. D. Leppan: The Agricultural Development of Arid and Semiarid Regions, Johannesburg, 1928, p. 266.

FIG. 151

FIG. 152

FIG. 153

FIG. 151—Wagons loaded with lucerne, Britstown, the Cape. (South African Railways.)

FIG. 152—Across the open veld modern roads have been built opening up much rich easily worked country for a new generation of farmers.   (South African Railways.)

FIG. 153—Cultivators at work, the Upper Karroo near Britstown, the Cape. A considerable area is here under irrigation.   (South African Railways.)

settler. Slow-moving ox-drawn wagons creaked their way right across the Kalahari from Walvis Bay to Lake Ngami from one water hole to another. Hunters brought back stories of wild game, including vast herds of eland and antelope, feeding upon grassland that could support cattle. Where settlement was densest or mineral wealth, chiefly gold, was abundant the railway came later. By the time the Boer War was over, after the turn of the century, young ex-service men had seen much and heard more about southern Africa as a land of cheap ranches in new territory that was the equal of any already occupied.

Soon began the wide search, the northward movement of settlers to Rhodesia, a movement still in progress. It has carried the pioneer fringe to the border of the Belgian Congo, to the interior highlands of Kenya, Tanganyika, and Nyasaland accessible by rail from the Indian coast, and opened up half a continent. The railway was the base line of the advance. Through Cecil Rhodes the British South Africa Company had come into being in 1889. It was originally designed to develop concessions obtained by him in Mashonaland and Matabeleland—a private trading enterprise on the company plan. Mineral wealth was the first attraction, and railways were built to suit the needs of the moment. The company paid little attention to settlement. The railways were not meant to be pioneers, however much they came to help land colonization.

White occupation is not limited to the shaded zones of Figure 143. Many lower situations have agglomerations of settlement. Some parts of the shaded zones cannot be effectively occupied *until bordering regions through which they are reached are supplied with roads and railways* and, in special cases, cleared of the menace of tropical diseases. Not all of the upland areas are free of malaria. The effect of the specific qualities of the upland climate, the wide daily range of temperature, and the slight seasonal variations remain to be studied before white colonization can advance with greater confidence.

The change in climatic conditions from north to south in southern Africa is diagrammatically shown in Figure 157. The tilted heavy line may be called *the line of tolerable temperatures*. It rises towards the equator and descends towards the pole. Some elevated tracts lie just above it or below it, and these diminish in number and area toward the equator. Southward there is an increase in the area of lands lying above the level of the line of tolerable tempera-

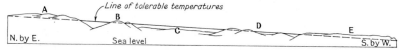

FIG. 157—Line of tolerable temperatures in relation to valley and highland elements in southern Africa: a sketch. A represents highlands of Tanganyika; C, Zambezi Valley; D, Southern Rhodesia, etc.

tures; and the entire countryside is capable of white occupation up to the limits set by rainfall, as on the borders of the Kalahari Desert. The whole of the upland of Southern Rhodesia can be occupied. Twenty-four per cent of its territory is above 4000 feet in altitude. The rapid growth of Salisbury, the center of a grazing and mining region, reflects this condition. Its population is 27,000, of which nearly 10,000 are whites, and its tributary areas are so extensive that its industry is in process of wide diversification.

A moment's reflection will make clear that some areas lying just below the line of tolerable temperatures will be occupied before those lying just above it, because the human system is capable of a certain amount of adaptation and endurance without serious loss of vitality. Some risk and discomfort will be accepted if there are compensating advantages. The nearness of a railway line generally leads to crop production in marginal areas that might otherwise remain unredeemed wilderness for an indefinite period. Nor is more than a fraction of the best land with the most favorable climate yet made available to settlement by railways and motor roads. There is an additional commercial incentive. It is not the regions of coolest climate but the tropical valleys and basins of Africa and the lower uplands that on the whole furnish the kind of goods most keenly desired by the countries of the temperate zone for food and industrial consumption. Coffee, cotton, cacao, rubber, palm oil, cane sugar, tobacco, and tropical and subtropical fruits in addition to minerals such as petroleum, gold, and copper, are among their primary needs.

The Transvaal may be taken as the type of rather fully settled country with quite limited areas available for new settlement. These areas may be termed a permanent frontier fringe with agriculture and stock raising subject to the hazards of repeated drought. One effect of the full occupation of the land has been an increase rather than a diminution in the size of the farms, as experience teaches the necessity for larger holdings. When the opposite takes place and farms are divided in families the line of poverty is passed, and this is one cause of the poor-white problem.

Southern Rhodesia is a step in the direction of experimental

FIG. 154

FIG. 155

FIG. 156

FIG. 154—Westphalia Estate, Tzaneen district, eastern scarp of the Drakensberg, altitude 2375 feet. Here is a thriving population of pioneer farmers. Citrus, tomatoes, groundnuts, and semitropical fruits flourish; sugar, tobacco, cotton give good results.

FIG. 155—Citrus farm, White River, Eastern Transvaal. A new orange-growing settlement, eastern border of scarp of the Drakensberg. Altitude a little over 3000 feet.

FIG. 156—Native location on the outskirts of Windhoek, South-West Africa. (Photographs from South African Railways.)

occupation.   Farming is here pushing out actively towards a border that is capable of further advance and far more intensive development.   Northern Rhodesia represents an almost pure pioneer community from the white man's standpoint.   The whole of it is a region of frontier settlement.   The railway from Livingstone to Broken Hill (Fig. 146) offered the first inducement, and now the country still farther north is provided with the incentive supplied by railway communication right across Northern Rhodesia into the copper country of the Belgian Congo.   The cooler uplands of Northern Rhodesia, the extent of native production, and the growth of ranches and plantations owned by white settlers have combined with the railway to form a productive agricultural area with an outlet close by in the Belgian Congo instead of almost impossibly long hauls southward to the Cape or northward and westward over the Benguella line to the Atlantic coast of Angola or southeastward across Southern Rhodesia to Beira on the Indian coast of Portuguese East Africa.

SOUTHERN RHODESIA

Southern Rhodesia illustrates the associated development of upland and lowland through the introduction of the white man's system of land use.   There are few tracts above 5000 feet (about 1500 meters, Fig. 158).   At this level the mean annual temperature is between 60° and 65° F.   Between 3500 and 4500 feet the mean annual temperature is between 65° and 75°.   Below 3000 feet subtropical temperatures are the rule.   It is in the 3500-to-4500-foot zone that there is a higher production of the things most desired in world markets and better able to stand the extremely high transport charges to the coast.   On either side of Southern Rhodesia are deep valley lowlands—the Limpopo on the south, the Zambezi on the north—where one may pass from temperate to tropic conditions with rather sharp dividing lines between.   Only on the valley floors is the climate tropical the year round.   Woodland covers about 60 per cent of the area.   On the upland agriculture can make its way: the average annual rainfall for two-thirds of the country is less than 30 inches; the east and northeast has over 30 inches with a maximum on the eastern border range (Umtali and Melsetter districts) of more than 50 inches.   The droughts that afflict South Africa so terribly are here less extreme and less frequent, and water is not difficult to obtain from wells.

There are nearly a million natives in Southern Rhodesia and a white population of 50,000. Plantation culture has here a field of the first importance. The natives can be cared for under their present cultural system on about 37 per cent of the territory, accord-

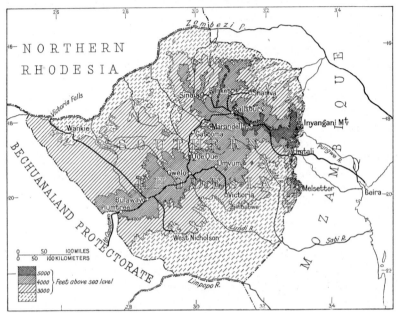

FIG. 158—Southern Rhodesia, from contour map by the Southern Rhodesia Geological Survey.

ing to the recent studies of the Commissioner of Lands, thus leaving about 62 per cent of the land area—of quite uneven value—for white occupation. The early settlers kept to the regions of high elevation, believing the low country unhealthful, and the first development of mining and farming was on the divides and plateaus between 3000 and 5000 feet.[6] The later expansion of cultivated land was outward and downward. Diversity in production is only beginning, the farmers still concerning themselves with cattle and export produce (rather than mixed farming) as they must because of the small requirements of the local market.

White immigration might be more rapid if it were not for the desire of the government of Southern Rhodesia to prevent the growth of the poor-white class. It admits no immigrant who does not have employment guaranteed him or £50 for his own use.

[6] A. C. Jennings: Irrigation and Water Supplies in Southern Rhodesia, *South African Journ. of Sci.*, Vol. 24, 1927, pp. 21-29.

The newly arrived immigrant finds it impossible to support himself by either skilled or unskilled labor until he has learned the types of cultivation best suited to the several climatic and crop zones of the country and has accumulated a little capital with which to become a landowner or an employer of black labor.[7] The government holds that the incoming farmer-settler should have a minimum capital of £2000. All classes agree that it is no place for a white man without capital. Trade unions are active in keeping up the standard of living of the white workingman, who falls in a class between the "native proletariat" and the "white aristocracy" that owns plantations and ranches.

A man with £2500 of capital will put £1000 into land and improvements and £1000 into labor, seed, and implements—£500 being regarded as not too much to be kept as a reserve in case of a bad crop year. With this division of his resources he may expect to set up a plantation, hire forty or fifty negroes, and have land enough to keep them economically employed. Aside from maize, which is exported to centers of consumption near by, the products of the land include tobacco, skins, and locally minerals, these three being shipped out of Africa. Since the World War there has been a steady effort in England to develop the whole of southern Africa by British people. It is expected that there will be a reciprocal consumption of African goods in England, owing to the nationality of the settlers and their tendency to buy at home. The shop windows of London reflect the effort; fruit and tobacco are most commonly in evidence. The fruit trade especially has grown with great rapidity.

It is obvious that white population is here in an exploitative relationship to the land and to the black. Foreign capital supplies the railways, the machinery for the mines, employment on the farms, and reserves for bad years; foreign brains organize the scheme of life and development; and foreign need furnishes the impetus. The black does the primary work. This is not meant to imply that the black is unfairly exploited, for it is brains and transport and the needs of white men elsewhere that make the other half of the circle. The question really is not, does the white man gain, but rather, does the black man gain also?

It is one of the most striking facts of African economy today

[7] Mention should here be made of the intelligent work of the Overseas Settlement Board at London and of the sturdy and enlightened efforts of the 1820 Memorial Settlers' Association which will become more widely known through *The 1820*, a journal which first appeared in 1929 and is aimed at promoting emigration to South Africa by collecting information and giving advice.

that labor is becoming more and more scarce in a continent hitherto thought crowded with blacks. In the next ten or fifteen years it will be necessary for all the governments concerned to give the most serious attention to the conservation of the supply of human labor. Very soon it will not be a question of land and minerals and crops of interest to white men, better means of exploitation, and the like, but, who will do the heavy labor required to get out ore, build railroads and wagon roads, drain the swamps, clear the land of brush, and plant and harvest the crops? The white man cannot or will not work in the fields. But if the black will do it the white will give him certain advantages, and the bargain seems on the whole a fair one. But what will happen when the black labor is fully employed and no more is available? Will not the black, who in more than one locality is "rapidly acquiring civilized ideas," realize that his labor has a higher market value and that he is an essential part of the scheme?

Thus we see Southern Rhodesia not as a colony of white farmers in which each owner toils upon his land as an independent freeman but a community based on a modernized form of the plantation system. The cooler uplands have permitted the white man to migrate towards the tropics. But distance from coastal ports and European markets compels him to produce the things that he can grow and transport with profit. He can do this (1) by falling back on the device of the isolated farmer far from the railway, that is obtain cheap land of wide extent; and (2) by employing a substantial number of cheap laborers. He must also practice *specialized production*, so that his land will yield the things that will stand high transport rates. Proud of his race and position, he has determined to hold to a specific social system with definite canons, and he insists that government shall aid him in maintaining it. In short, he wants to keep a ruling class of white men of an advanced social type with a keen sense of solidarity and with a settled determination that they and their kind are going to occupy the land and organize and control production through government.

Mining, in point of production and as a source of revenue to the government, to the British South Africa Company (as owner of mineral rights), and to the railways, is still the first industry; but before long agriculture will outstrip it. In the first place, agriculture directly supports a larger European population than do the mines, and it supports 95 per cent of the native population also. It brings in more new settlers and capital, and its poten-

FIG. 159

FIG. 160

FIG. 161

FIG. 159—Portion of 200-acre field of tobacco in the Umvukwes, to the east of Sinoia, Southern Rhodesia. (High Commissioner for Southern Rhodesia, London.)

FIG. 160—Farm near Umtali, mountainous eastern border of Southern Rhodesia. (Photograph by G. W. Marshall; courtesy High Commissioner for Southern Rhodesia, London.)

FIG. 161—Homestead and surroundings of the Rhodes Inyanga Estate of 100,000 acres, devoted to ranching (cattle and sheep) and fruit growing. (Photograph by G. W. Marshall; courtesy High Commissioner for Southern Rhodesia, London.)

tialities are obviously very great because of the large areas of fertile and undeveloped soil that enjoy a favorable climate. "The two industries are still largely inter-dependent for their greatest good, and on their joint well-being is based the prosperity of the Colony," says General Hammond,[8] who also thinks that "the time for aggressive development policy is most opportune when

Fig. 162—Settler's home, second stage, Southern Rhodesia. (Photograph by G. W. Marshall; courtesy High Commissioner for Southern Rhodesia, London.)

the unrest of the war, and heavy taxation in Great Britain and all the older countries, are driving men and money abroad."

The Rhodesian farming community regards all land within twenty-five miles of the railway on either side as "farm land" and all land from twenty-five to fifty miles from the railway as "ranch land." All land more than fifty miles from the railway is not of present practical importance to the land pioneer. It has been found that about half the strips of land in the "farm-land" zone have a sufficiently high altitude, rainfall, and fertility to guarantee good crop production. In the ranching strip the proportion of good and poor soils is about the same, but the good soils are richer and the climate more favorable for the growth of money crops, the railways having been built mostly on the less fertile watersheds. Only about three per cent of the land available for cultivation is so used, present production being principally pastoral with a very small profit per acre.

Ranching of the company type can be carried out on cheap land still available in large holdings. Darby has noted[9] the existence

[8] F. D. Hammond: Report on the Railway System of Southern Rhodesia, Salisbury, Rhodesia, 1925, Vol. 2, p. 31.
[9] H. C. Darby in "Pioneer Settlement," *Amer. Geogr. Soc. Special Publ. No. 14*, New York, 1932.

of 20,000- to 30,000-acre ranches up to 100 miles from the railway at an altitude of 2000 feet. He reports 100,000 head of cattle in one ranch at Nuanetsi. Another has 50,000 head. The natural tendency in the future will be for both farms and ranches to be smaller in area. About Gwelo farms of 6000 acres have been divided into 1000-acre tracts, and ranches of 60,000 acres have been halved.

FIG. 163—Avilion Farm, Mazabuka, Northern Rhodesia. (H. C. Darby.)

The farm products of Southern Rhodesia compete in the world markets under extraordinarily severe conditions. Salisbury is 1200 miles from the Cape; and, if railway and port elevator charges are added to the costs of steamship transport, any product reaches the world markets so loaded with charges that little is left for the original producer. General Hammond's report on Rhodesian railways concludes that no evidence could be found that naturally good land suitable for maize and within ten or fifteen miles of a railway was not being used. He thought that a drop in the rates would merely increase by four or five miles the width of the zone on each side of the railways from which it would pay to export maize, taking the cost of road transport at about one shilling a ton mile.

A lowering of the railway freight rates would mean a larger return to the farmers already growing maize and would stimulate them to grow more. It is thought, however, that the total result of such a lowering of the rates would not be great and that it would be better to develop the area devoted to maize culture along each side of new railways rather than to extend the width of the belt in which it is grown along the lines already established. It is shown that tobacco culture has increased, in spite of the high freight rate

FIG. 164—Ox team and wagon, Northern Rhodesia.   (H. C. Darby.)

on unmanufactured tobacco, but that the transport costs cut into the grower's profits so deeply that a reduction in the rates should be made.

If the demands of the agriculturists were met the rates would be so greatly lowered that the farmers would receive benefits at the expense of the mine owners.   Such benefits as the farmers already receive reflect everywhere the pioneer quality of both the country and the railways.   Besides the rebate on transport charges for cattle shipped overseas, a distinction is made between maize for export, local maize, and maize shipped to the Congo by the farmers of Northern Rhodesia.   Similar distinctions are made with respect to tobacco, dairy products, and eggs.   Each region and each product must be studied relatively in order that a fair compromise may be reached between the interests of the railways and those of independent mine owners and farmers.   Balanced production is the goal of these frontier communities whose leaders look forward to a day of substantial economic strength, but this takes little account of world economics or of regions where specific products may be more economically produced and delivered to the consumer.

FIG. 165—Road improvement in Southern Rhodesia: low-level bridge over a stream.   (High Commissioner for Southern Rhodesia, London.)

In appraising the value

FIG. 166—Plowing by oxen at Kalomo, Northern Rhodesia. (H. C. Darby.)

of railways to pioneer development in Northern and Southern
Rhodesia, one should clearly recognize that grain crops will not
bear more than about fifteen miles of ox-wagon transport, with
thirty miles as a limit, when the costs of rail transport must be
added. If the settler will grow cotton and tobacco, and ship dairy
products—all of which command a higher market price and yield
a greater margin of profit than grain crops—he may extend his occupation of the land to a distance of twenty-five miles from rail and
to even greater distances if he has good roads and motor
transport.

The status of the railways now assumes greater importance
because the opening of the Benguella Railway to Lobito across
Angola (Fig. 146) is expected to effect a substantial diversion of
traffic from the Belgian Congo to the west coast, and this traffic
will be permanently lost unless competitive transport conditions
are established in South-
ern Rhodesia. It is
difficult to see how this
can be done. Some pas-
senger traffic will also be
diverted to the new line.
Those going into the
Belgian Congo or North-
ern Rhodesia will save a
week of steamship travel
southward to the Cape
by taking the Benguella
Railway, and the long

FIG. 167—Camel transport for grain, Fort Victoria district. (High Commissioner for Southern Rhodesia,
London.)

railway journey north from the Cape is far more expensive than is the shorter route from Lobito.

In spite of their inland position and distance from the market the settlers of Southern Rhodesia contend that the soil is the best source of colonial wealth and point to the American railways as colonizers. They are the true "pioneers of mass land settlement." They would like to see a policy of national scope with a reasonable amount of advertising, assisted steamship passage, free transport for the settler and his family and effects, carriage of his market crop free or at a normal rate for a year or two, the gift of breeding stock and implements or at least their purchase on a deferred payment plan, and free grants of land or payment on easy terms with strict conditions of residence and improvement.

This looks like a list for a Christmas stocking and raises the question as to how far public assistance should go. All sorts of economically unsound projects can ride to success at the taxpayer's expense. With machine production extending its effects to so many parts of the world, the question to be put to any region is how well qualified is it to produce economically in comparison with other regions of its class. Land and labor and cost of haulage to market are all a part of the problem. The use of the machine on the land has come to the point where the world is in the midst of an agricultural revolution as profound in its effects as the industrial revolution beginning a century and a half ago. Like its counterpart in industry, this force now expending itself in agriculture will not reveal its modes in a year or ten years. The new communities of the pioneer fringe in southern Africa have their special problems and are involved also in a world problem common to the whole of agriculture.

The high standard of living and the rigid social standards of necessity set limits to white settlement in the pioneer fringe of southern Africa. To overcome the social disadvantages it is customary in both Northern and Southern Rhodesia and Nyasaland for white settlers to build their houses in groups four or five miles apart instead of scattering them as in the Union of South Africa. Costs of education are higher in the isolated country districts than in the city. Northern Rhodesia still has only primary schools, while in the case of Nyasaland education is in the hands of missionaries and private teachers. Nowhere else in the British Empire is the number of boarding scholars from country districts so large as in Northern Rhodesia. The isolation is hardest on the women, because of the scarcity of doctors, the hard work of running a household, and the necessity for "doing without." Children's diseases bring times of special anxiety. Neighbors are difficult of access in the wet season. ". . . at times we have the treacherous thought: 'Is it worth while?' But, glancing at our homes, here in the wilderness, there comes the thrill of achievement; the knowledge that where we white women are, with our children, civilization and higher moral standards must necessarily follow."[10]

NORTHERN RHODESIA

The area of Northern Rhodesia is 290,000 square miles, 11 per cent greater than Texas. There are three broad zones of territory. The western zone is plains country, evenly but thinly forested and having much swampland.[11] The central zone is a plateau 150 miles wide occupying the watershed between the Congo and Zambezi rivers. From 3000 feet in the south this section slopes upward toward the north and includes some country above the 5000-foot level. Here three-fourths of the mining and agricultural activities are carried on, and here most of the native population lives. There is a comparative scarcity of water, and the forests are patchy but thick. The eastern of the three zones includes the higher elevations of Figure 143, running west of the northern end of Lake Nyasa. It is a mountainous, dry, yet heavily wooded section with native villages concentrated in the deeper valleys and sunklands where two crops a year are raised in contrast to the single crop grown on the plateau.

With increase of altitude there is more rain and a longer rainy season, the rainfall of the central zone increasing from 20 to 50 inches from south to north and the rainy season from three months to five months. The temperature variations correspond to the changes in elevation, the central upland in the hottest months (October and November) having mean maxima around 85° in the 3500-to-4000-foot zone, while the Zambezi Valley stations show averages of 97°.

Crop growth is limited, except in irrigated areas, to the rainy season, so extremely dry is the rest of the year. The tsetse fly is widely distributed.[12] Native peoples number about 1,300,000,

[10] Muriel Drayton: The Farmer's Wife—in Kenya, *The Landmark* (London), February, 1931.

[11] Robert Murray-Hughes: The Geology of Part of North-Western Rhodesia, *Quart. Journ. Geol. Soc. of London*, Vol. 85, Part II, 1929, pp. 109–162; reference on p. 112.

[12] R. Bourne: Aerial Survey in Relation to the Economic Development of New Countries, etc., *Oxford Forestry Memoirs No. 9*, 1928, p. 11.

and of these 62,500 are employed in white-men's enterprises, 22,000 in the mines. The white population, now numbering 14,000, is increasing steadily chiefly in response to mining. Only about 6½ per cent of the total area is "alienated" to the companies, the whites, and the native reserves.[13] There is a small acreage in wheat, a much larger acreage in maize, and the beginnings of coffee culture. Maize for local consumption and for export to the Belgian Congo, besides vegetables and other food crops, occupies the greater part of the cultivated land. There are marked variations in annual rainfall, and the recurrence of dry years increases the hazard of farming and lowers the usefulness of the pastures, never in a state to support highly improved cattle during the whole of the year. Extra feeding in the height of the dry season seems to be required for improved stock, which commands a higher market price. The native has almost no means of getting his crops to market; and, if his production excess is to be used by the white or to feed native labor in the mines, the organization of transport is a first essential.

The rainfall variations and the unequal demand of the world market for the crops that may be exported are responsible for repeated expansions and contractions of the occupied land of Northern Rhodesia. The tobacco slump of 1929 reduced the settled area; and 1924 and 1925 were years of cotton failure, so that the cultivation of cotton was temporarily abandoned and the limits of cultivation still further reduced. "The settler in these lands has to make a great success of his farming even to make a livelihood at all."[14] Having to stand heavy transportation costs and to depend upon native labor, the settler tends to concentrate on a single crop. Good cotton and tobacco prices for a time tempted the white settler to depend too much on the plantation type of agriculture; and there is no Land Bank as in Southern Rhodesia to provide him with long-period loans at a low rate of interest when prices fall or the lean years of drought arrive.

White occupation of the upland has carried the problem of native rights as far as the Congo border. Native production alone is either wasteful or inefficient. The native has no means of transport to make any surplus production count in accessible markets. His production methods may improve, and he may be provided with roads to connect with the railway; but there still remains the

---

[13] Northern Rhodesia, Report for 1929, *Ann. Colonial Repts. No. 1516*, 1931, p. 7.
[14] H. C. Darby: Settlement in Northern Rhodesia, *Geogr. Rev.*, Vol. 21, 1931, pp. 559–573.

Fig. 168

Fig. 169

Fig. 170

Fig. 168—Araluen Farm, Kalomo, Northern Rhodesia.   Clearing bush, 1906–1907.
Fig. 169—Plowing by crude oil tractor, Chisamba, Northern Rhodesia.
Fig. 170—Mazabuka Research Station, Northern Rhodesia.   (Photographs from H. C. Darby.)

FIG. 171—Broken Hill, Northern Rhodesia. (Aircraft Operating Co., London.)

question of his rights in the land and the terms under which he may
be employed by the white. There is also the question of the areas
he may occupy, the native reserves. Only in so far as the white
man can engage in dairy farming and the production of wheat
and fruit can he become independent of native labor.

In spite of the difficulties of uncertain rainfall, heavy transport
costs, and the ups and downs of the world market, occupation
of the land has gone on rapidly under the stimulus of the railway
to the Congo via Broken Hill and the nearer market provided
by it. If the mine-railway stimulus is continued the population
will increase to the point of requiring good motor transport, and
this in turn will open up tracts now unavailable from lack of
animal transport, the tsetse fly keeping livestock down.

There are well-marked limits to the transport of maize by ox-

FIG. 172—Nkana Railway Bridge over Kafue River, Northern Rhodesia. Railroad extension opened in the summer of 1930. Smoke from bush fire in background. (Aircraft Operating Co., London.)

drawn wagons. The farmer with but one team of oxen is confined to a distance of ten miles from the railway, and even at that distance he can bring but one load a day to the railway. The larger and better-equipped plantations may haul as far as thirty miles. Products that command a higher price make still greater distances feasible; the tobacco of the Fort Jameson district of northeastern Rhodesia being brought by motor lorry to railhead in Nyasaland over a distance of three hundred miles. Wool may be transported from fifty up to two hundred miles. Wheat was considered transportable in Tanganyika at the prices of 1928 for a distance of seventy miles.[15] Unfortunately, the railway across Northern Rhodesia was located on the line of the watershed where building

[15] Tanganyika Territory, Land Development Survey, First Report, 1928–1929, Iringa Province.

costs were low rather than in the best agricultural areas, with the consequence that crop land and railway are not always accessible to each other. With the increased demands of the new markets at the mines there is a tendency to diversify farming and to stabilize agriculture through organization so that the mining companies may be assured of a steady supply from year to year.

From Broken Hill to the border of the Belgian Congo the aspect of the country down to 1927 was that of "a bush-covered wilderness, with a few lonely, widely-spaced villages, and here and there a copper prospect that created but little outside attention."[16] It was then that copper sulphides were discovered and a great new copper center began to boom: "towns are being hewn out of the virgin bush," says Bateman, "plants are being reared, and ramifying branch railways are being pushed out from the single line of steel. . . . "

It is an "open, park-like, bush country," a region of shallow stream depressions formed upon a flat plateau 4000 feet above sea level. Upon such a surface, road and railway building is simple. There is an excellent supply of ground water. The tsetse fly keeps out domestic animals. In May, 1931, the mills were started at the Roan Antelope Mine. The ore averages 3.81 per cent, and there appears to be a hundred million tons available. The equipment is designed ultimately to produce 45,000 tons annually.[17] It is hardly necessary to point to the probable effect of so huge a development upon land settlement once the full demands of the mines are felt.

There are two contrasting railway systems that are of special economic interest in their respective relations to pioneering, the Rhodesian system in southern Africa and the Alaska railway line in a territory of the United States. In the two Rhodesias privately owned companies have built railways to serve mining interests, not settlement; and in Alaska the railway is managed by the government in the interests of the whole population, although the mining industry supplies the larger part of the traffic, with foodstuffs running a close second. Both serve pioneer societies and must maintain a balance of interest between mines and settlers. In Rhodesia the settlers have taken the initiative in securing better rates. In Alaska the national government has taken the initiative

[16] Alan Bateman: The Rhodesian Copper Deposits, Reprint from *Canadian Mining and Metallurgical Bull.*, being part of *Trans. Inst. of Mining and Metallurgy*, 1930.
[17] *The African World*, No. 1494, Vol. 115, 1931, p. 346; No. 1496, p. 411.

in studying the needs of transport and in establishing agricultural experiment stations and other agencies that might discover or exploit the agricultural potentialities or at least make them known to prospective settlers.

The push given by railways to settlement in southern Africa throughout the period of white advance might lead one to the conclusion that they were always hailed with joy and encouraged by both shipper and government. As a matter of fact, there was competition from the first. In early days it was the oxcart that took away part of the business; today it is the motor lorry. At one time the competition of ox wagons was so severe as to lead to the imposition of special taxes on them and on neglected road

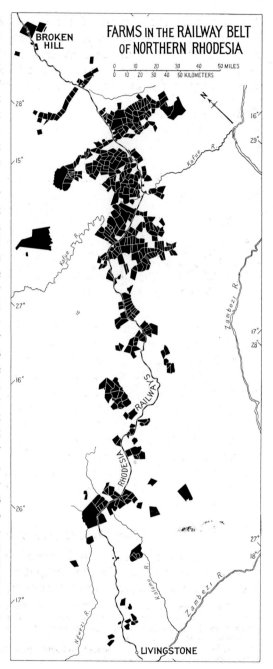

FIG. 173—Farms in the railway belt of Northern Rhodesia between Livingstone and Broken Hill according to H. C. Darby, *Geogr. Rev.*, Vol. 21, 1931.

construction in the interest of the railways.[18]   There was little
competition from ox wagons in Natal after 1895 in long-distance
transport, although their use continues for local transport and as
feeders for the railways.   Sayce writes[19] of eighty wagons employed in 1923 for transport between the cotton-growing Condover

Fig. 174—Tobacco barns, Macheke, southeast of Salisbury.   (Southern Rhodesia Publicity
Bureau.)

Estates and Boomlaager, the nearest railway station eighty miles
away.   The freight rates by rail were at first so high in some
instances as to paralyze the movement of goods.   The railways
of the Union of South Africa have now entered the field of road
transport.   In 1928 they had 198 services running over routes
aggregating nearly 9000 miles, carrying a million passengers and
100,000 tons of goods.[20]   The competition of private lines is greatest
in and between urban areas from which the motor transport of the
railways is excluded.   Another source of financial difficulty is the
fact that 5000 miles out of a total of 12,400 of the South African
Railways system are "branch lines of which the greater portion
do not even yet pay."[21]

THE NATIVE QUESTION

Up to this point we have barely mentioned the existence of the
native and his relation to white occupation.   The question of his
treatment, the wages paid him, the reserves to which he has been

[18] Railway Rates and Road Competition [South Africa], *The Round Table*, No. 77, 1929, p. 183.
[19] R. U. Sayce: The Transport Ox and the Ox-wagon in Natal, in "Studies in Regional Consciousness and Environment," Oxford, 1930, pp. 69–77; reference on p. 76.
[20] Article cited in footnote 18, p. 196.
[21] S. H. Frankel: Road and Rail Transport in South Africa, *South African Journ. of Sci.*, Vol.
26, 1929, pp. 958–971; reference on p. 964.

or is sought to be confined, and the quality of his economic and
social life under the stimulus of white association—all these are
the heart of domestic politics in southern Africa. They are questions viewed from two opposing angles by those who seek liberal
treatment and those who regard the black as less than human.
"In Church and State there is no equality between black and

FIG. 175—Zoa Tea Estate, south of Blantyre, Nyasaland. (H. C. Darby.)

white" announced the early constitutions of the Boer republics,
Transvaal and Orange Free State.

The opposition of moral and political forces has already had at
least one good result. It has called into being a series of studies
of deep import. It has shown how fundamental to the question
is the whole life of the native, his wasteful system of tillage, the
constant tendency in many sections to shift the tribal domain, to
exhaust the soil, burn grass and forest, allow the torrential rains
to erode a soil in most cases thin and none too fertile, and in general
to keep to a primitive type of agriculture that but "for the enormous
natural resources and recuperative power of the continent" would
by now have turned most of Africa into "a howling wilderness."[22]

The problem of settlement *is* the problem of the native to a
high degree, not merely a relating of population to rainfall belts,
uplands, and transport. The present writer has not avoided it
merely because it is complex in its relationships. The space available for its discussion is too limited in a book dealing primarily
with geographical data and points of view. There is a wealth of
reference and well-considered argument available. For the reader
who would get at the heart of the problem in the briefest time

[22] J. C. Smuts: Africa and Some World Problems, Oxford, 1930, p. 83.

FIG. 176—Sketch map of Nyasaland showing the situation of the Mlanje Mountains.

there will be special interest in the paper on "Native Labor in South Africa," by C. T. Loram, in a companion volume entitled "Pioneer Settlement."[23] A South African scholar who has made a profound study of the question there presents the problem in a judicial spirit.[24]

NYASALAND

A railway branch to Blantyre (Fig. 146) has tied the southern uplands of Nyasaland to the sea at Beira and furnished access to the Shire River and Lake Nyasa. Here is a girdle of highland about a navigable lake that is over three hundred miles long. The density of population is high in locally favored areas, but the production excess that might be created cannot be thought marketable until railways tap the more distant areas. Lake Nyasa is deep, but its shores are so steep as to make approach difficult from the highlands. A railway branch from the Tanganyika district has been proposed to reach the northern valleys. However, this is still a paper project.

The southern highland elements are of most immediate interest because of their accessibility. The Shire Highlands (Fig. 176) rise above 2000 feet elevation with local ridges and peaks, as in the Mlanje massif, rising to over 9000 feet.[25] There is a rainy

[23] Pioneer Settlement: a Series of Papers by Thirty Authors, edited by W. L. G. Joerg, *Amer. Geogr. Soc. Special Publ. No. 14*, 1932.

[24] For a more comprehensive treatment of the status of the native see R. L. Buell: The Native Problem in Africa, 2 vols., New York, 1928. The government's point of view on the treatment of the native is presented in Report of the Commission on Closer Union of the Dependencies in Eastern and Central Africa, London, 1929, pp. 35–85.

[25] Frank Dixey: The Mlanje Mountains of Nyasaland, *Geogr. Rev.*, Vol. 17, 1927, pp. 611–626.

season extending from the end of November to the end of March, the rest of the year being dry. The yearly rainfall is 40 to 50 inches, with higher values and a longer rainy season in the vicinity of the mountains, where there are also the only stands of really heavy timber. "The heavy rainfall is an economic asset to Nyasaland," says Dixey, "in that it has given rise to a valuable tea-growing industry." It also provides, in conjunction with the relief, potential sources of water power of considerable magnitude.

The uplands have a grassy cover; the ravines and gullies are densely wooded. As the grazing becomes more and more scanty in the lowlands, with the

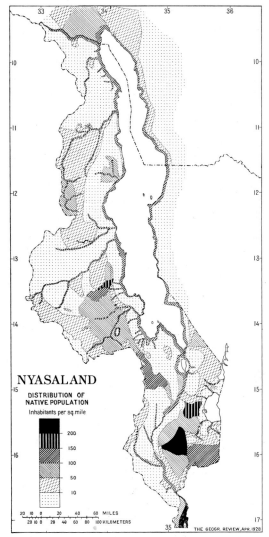

NYASALAND

DISTRIBUTION OF NATIVE POPULATION

Inhabitants per sq. mile

200
150
100
50
10

20 10 0   20   40   60 MILES
20 10 0 20 40 60 80 100 KILOMETERS

THE GEOGR. REVIEW, APR. 1928

FIG. 177—Map of Nyasaland showing distribution of native population according to the census of 1926.

advance of the dry season, August to December, cattle are driven to the uplands. Overgrazing, grass and bush fires, and the furrowing of wild pigs have led to a restriction of forest growth and to the advance of grasses of drought-resistant types. They have also led to deep gullying and rapid erosion of the shallow soil.

An important asset of the region is the large bauxite deposit of one of the plateau elements of the Mlanje Mountains, "the only one known on the eastern side of Africa that offers any possibility of commercial development."[26]   Ample water power is available, as required, for the reduction of the ore in producing aluminum.   There is also a native labor supply and a reasonably healthful climate.

The lower Shire Valley has the densest native population in Nyasaland, some parts having from 200 to 300 to the square mile (Fig. 177).   Of the European population of Nyasaland, 1656 in 1926, more than one-third live in the Blantyre district.   There are no native reserves as in Northern or Southern Rhodesia.   The northern Nyasaland plateau is sparsely populated and suffers depletion through the continuous migration of natives to Rhodesia and South Africa.[27]   The problems of population are intimately related to water supply, to the extension of native industries, and to the fly-infested areas near native villages.   They are problems of critical importance in white settlement if plantation agriculture is to be extended.   The natives are still too dependent upon surface streams where at moderate cost the ground water could be tapped and windmills installed.   This close association of village to stream marks the fact that good agricultural and grazing lands are not occupied only because water for domestic use is lacking.   The matter becomes critical in abnormally dry years.   "The people have frequently to walk miles from their villages to obtain [water] from the sandy beds of streams."

Cotton has been grown near Lake Nyasa, on the northwest; but tobacco is coming in now, and rice is grown locally.   Bananas are here the main food crop.   Millet, maize, and sweet potatoes are among the other crop possibilities.   The native sticks to the lake shore and the valley bottoms, disliking the thick mists and drizzling rains of the uplands, for which his ill-clad and ill-nourished condition unfit him.   An extreme limit of occupation is supplied by one of the tribes, which lives in the valleys and on the slopes of the Livingstone Mountains up to heights exceeding 8000 feet. Midway down the west coast of the lake (Angoniland) are upland tracts 3000 to 4000 feet above sea level, with a locally dense population, while the higher slopes of the Chongoni Mountains farther south are uninhabited.   The country between 4000 and 7000 feet

[26] *Ibid.*, p. 617.
[27] Frank Dixey: The Distribution of Population in Nyasaland, *Geogr. Rev.*, Vol. 18, 1928. pp. 274–290.

is considered suitable for white settlement, and the native would probably follow the white to the uplands as in Kenya and Tanganyika. Except in a few places the scarps of the Nyasaland uplands are too steep and dry to support population.[28]

THE SUBTROPICAL FRINGE

On the eastern border of the higher country of southern Africa there is a subtropical belt that is well above the coastal lowlands and has a native population that tempts the white planter. In a general way its eastern border is outlined by the 500-meter (1640-foot) contour shown in Figure 143.

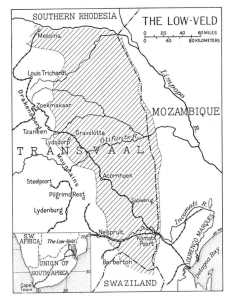

FIG. 178—The Low Veld, from J. Stevenson-Hamilton: The Low-Veld: Its Wild Life and Its People, London, 1929; with additional place names and locations from the War Office (London) 1 : 2,000,000 Series, No. 2871, G.S.G.S., 1918–1929.

Between that contour and the 1000-meter line of the lower of the two upland zones the white man tries his fortune in plantation culture, but so far with little success. The germ diseases and the insect pests have proved a serious environmental problem to the advancing colonist wherever he has sought to enter the lower climatic zone. The physician and the settler and a government willing to spend money on applied tropical medicine are a combination as yet hard to create.

The southeastern part of Africa is the most promising part of the country between the 500- and 1000-meter contours, as shown in Figure 143. The rains are far from being regular, but they are more reliable and substantial than farther north and the vegetation more useful for forage. The nearness of the inner mountain border to the coast makes the heavier rainfall of the mountain belt available for irrigation on the farms of the lower belt on the east. The rain belt lies between 2000 and 4000 feet above the sea.[29] Most

[28] For reference to a northeastern railway outlet still in the project stage see page 240.

[29] T. G. Caink: The Possibilities and Development of the Coastal Belt of South Africa, *South African Journ. of Sci.*, Vol. 16, 1919, pp. 211–225.

of the run-off does "very little service to the country," yet has great potential value. If properly controlled it would supply power as well as irrigation needs and provide water for urban centers on the coast. The water now going to waste would, if conserved, increase the areas of closer settlement and greatly hasten the day of a more balanced industrial development.

The portion of the subtropical belt form along the eastern border of the Transvaal is called the Low Veld country (Fig. 178). It is seventy miles east and west, three hundred north and south, and has a low-grade native population. Abandoned villages mark the collapse of hopes that drew in settlers from time to time. Eloquent on that score is the entry for Leydsdorp in the 1931 edition of the "South and East African Year Book and Guide": "A police post, telephone bureau, and hotel are all that remain of the old capital of the Low Veld pioneers." At 2375 feet elevation, only 175 feet higher than Leydsdorp, is the town of Tzaneen which "serves a thriving population of pioneer farmers" (Fig. 154). This is at the foot of the Drakensberg escarpment. Fertile valleys provide attractive but limited sites for high veld farmers who are not dismayed by high summer temperatures and the more than local prevalence of malaria. Probably not more than five hundred whites live in the Low Veld today.[30]

The two railway lines that cross the Low Veld have helped induce whites to go in. The bait of cheap production is always tempting when there is a good season. Some years are favored with a rainfall of 30 to 40 inches, and the natives are required to work free for ninety days in return for exemption from rent. When the rainfall diminishes to less than 10 inches, as in 1922, the whole land is a parched waste. The rain falls in deluges with a high rate of run-off and low efficiency for crop growth. Most of the natural vegetation is bush and dwarf forests, the latter growing principally in the Kruger National Park, which embraces the eastern half of the area. The Low Veld has too little altitude—600 feet on the east, 1500 along the foot of the Drakensberg escarpment—to bring it within the zone of cooler uplands.

Intermediate between the tropical lowlands adjacent to the coast and the cool mountain country of eastern Rhodesia (Melsetter region) is a belt with a humid climate but without oppressive heat. The whole of it to the mouth of the Sabi River is densely populated. Vegetation is luxuriant and water abundant. The

[30] J. Stevenson-Hamilton: The Low-Veld: Its Wild Life and Its People, London, 1929, p. 190.

manioc plant is cultivated everywhere, and upon it the natives depend for food when grain is not available. Cattle are scarce, principally on account of the prevalence of the tsetse fly in comparatively recent years. Near the coast are a few experimental cotton stations.[31] The white population has entered the upper border of this zone at a few places only.

West Coast Highlands

In the western half of southern Africa are uplands that run parallel with the coast and carry farming and ranching possibilities almost to the border of the Congo forest. The general conditions of rainfall and relief and access by rail and sea are shown on the maps, pages 202 and

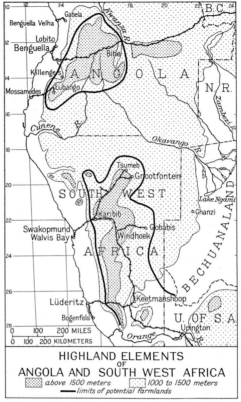

HIGHLAND ELEMENTS
OF
ANGOLA AND SOUTH WEST AFRICA

Fig. 179—The limits of the cultivated areas are adapted for South West Africa from Fritz Jaeger's Afrika, Leipzig, 1928, p. 364; for Angola from notes by T. A. Barns, Angolan Sketches, London, 1928. The contours are generalized from the 1 : 500,000 series of topographical maps compiled by the Surveyor General's Office, Windhoek, and printed at the Ordnance Survey, Southampton, 1927; and from the War Office (London) 1 : 2,000,000 Series, G.S.G.S. No. 2871, 1918–1929.

203. Prosperous farms are now in operation by Dutch, Portuguese, and foreign syndicates in Angola and by German and Dutch elements in South West Africa. The marked effect of elevation is well shown in Angola, where frost is common in the dry months. The higher moorland sections of the plateau are too cold and windy and have extremes of temperature too wide to furnish the best grazing country. Cattle do better on the "sweet veld" of

[31] H. de Laessoe: The Lundi and Sabi Rivers, *Proc. Rhodesia Scientific Assn.*, Vol. 6, Part II. 1906, pp. 118–138.

the drier lowlands. The whole upland, including its valleyed border, is suitable for further white settlement.

North of the Orange River in South West Africa (Namaqualand) there is a rainfall of less than 10 inches a year. The coastal region is arid, the interior semiarid with a rainfall sufficient to support a grassy steppe-like vegetation and to permit ranching and farming in the most favorable sites and seasons. Sheep may be grazed on the thorn-free grassy tracts, Keetmanshoop being the center of a marked recent expansion of the industry. In the central part of the highlands (Windhoek Plateau) the elevation is over 6500 feet, and the rainfall is from 12 to 20 inches a year. Here is excellent pasture, and cattle, horses, and sheep do well. The town of Windhoek has a population of 4600 whites and 10,000 natives. The region was the first to be developed in South West Africa.[32]

Toward the north the Windhoek Plateau declines to the thornbush upland of Herero Land. The elevation is still sufficient to permit agriculture where rainfall is most concentrated, the rest of the land being suitable in part for grazing.

The central interior of Angola consists of a highland belt 400 miles wide in places and having altitudes in excess of 4500 feet. The mean annual temperature is about 70° and the rainfall 45 to 50 inches, in contrast to the desert conditions of the coastal belt. The rains are fairly dependable, and there is a network of rivers flowing down to the lower country on each side.[33]

North of the line of the Benguella Railway there is reported to be farming country with small acreages in wheat, groundnuts, and potatoes. There is a considerable native population. Running streams are everywhere. A Portuguese farm is reported by Barns[34] having 300 acres of wheat as the principal crop and 100 acres in coffee, with bananas planted in rows as windbreaks. Cotton plantations have been established along the line of the railway, and cattle ranches are numerous. At lower elevations sugar and sisal plantations are found profitable.

Although the deep Cunene Valley is "a waterless waste," conditions of habitability improve northward with increasing elevation. In southern Angola open-grass country is the rule in contrast to the moister veldt of the more northerly and southerly plateau country. Native herds are prosperous everywhere. The center of the cattle country is Killenges, halfway between the Benguella

[32] Fritz Jaeger: Afrika, 3d edit., Leipzig, 1928, pp. 362–367.
[33] T. A. Barns: Angolan Sketches, London, 1928.
[34] Ibid., p. 116.

Railway and Lubango, the interior terminus of the short railway extending back of the coast at Mossamedes. Wheat is also reported south of the railway. Portuguese ranchers maintain large herds in the country south of Lubango, according to Barns, and export beef in casks to the islands of São Thomé and Principe and live animals to Matadi at the mouth of the Congo. Humpata, south of the Benguella Railway, is the center of an agricultural region containing about 140 square miles having an elevation of more than 6000 feet above sea level. It was originally settled by Boer families in 1881.

The government regulations in Angola require all able-bodied males between sixteen and forty-five to give service for hire or show cause why they should not do so. This has made it possible to complete the Benguella Railway and build a superb system of automobile roads and has enabled ranchers to secure native labor that has been trained for generations in the care and breeding of cattle. The government grants land in separate blocks of 12,500 acres for agricultural purposes or 125,000 acres for ranching. The applicant has first to survey his land and define its boundaries and position, and, after making a deposit of money in the Lands Department, he is given a permit to occupy for ten years with a small annual quitrent. In the case of an agricultural block the tenant must carry out development amounting to 200 times that of the yearly lease; that is, he must build houses, clear the land, purchase stock, plant trees, etc. The larger ranching blocks are governed by similar rules requiring the construction of a dipping tank and other improvements, and the majority of the Portuguese employees on a ranch must be given 100 to 300 hectares of land per family.[35]

THE KALAHARI BORDER

While extension of the grazing industry about the borders of the Kalahari is continually urged, limiting conditions are rather severe. Without boreholes the desert itself is practically uninhabitable. The rainfall is too light and too uncertain in its distribution both in locality and in time. Moreover, the local cattle market is too restricted to encourage ranching on a large scale. Only an export trade would make it worth while to develop cattle of acclimated breeds and invest money in the necessary plant and transport facilities. The government continues to prospect for water and has decided that Crown lands in the region shall not be

[35] *Ibid.*, pp. 183–184

alienated until more is known about the underground water supply.[36]

Probably the most isolated white settlement in southern Africa is Ghanzi (Fig. 179) east of the railway terminus at Gobabis. The original settlers, of British and Dutch stock, with the encouragement of Cecil Rhodes, began their long journey in 1894 with a halt of four years before their remote destination was reached in May, 1898. Only twenty-five of the original sixty families "took root." The population is now well over one hundred. The story of their hardships, including sickness, in traveling to the promised land and of isolation since then is one of the great epics of pioneering.[37] There is, even today, no telephone or telegraph and no electric installation. By 1929 a single motor car had visited the settlement, but no airplane had been seen. The elevation is 3800 feet, the climate is regarded as excellent, and the health conditions are good. A meteorological tower symbolizes the modern view of not putting everything up to Providence in a land of scanty rain. Cattle are held up in dry years by the absence of pasture and water along the stock routes to the Rand gold fields across the Kalahari. A favorite route to the north and east has been via Lake Ngami and Victoria Falls; but the tsetse fly has appeared, and a new track must be established if the Katanga market is to be retained.

An extreme instance of the spread of settlement into marginal country about the Kalahari border is to be found north of the Orange River, east and west of the Molopo tributary that comes in from the north. Here are the Gordonia and Mier settlements. North and south the tract is 250 miles in extent, east and west 200 miles. Though only parts of it are settled, and those parts sparsely, it is believed that the ranching industry may reach into the better-favored parts if boreholes are constructed to provide stock water. Almost the whole of Gordonia has been surveyed for occupation by farmers. In the Mier country irrigation is practiced locally, and after the rains "a good deal of wheat is grown."[38] The rainfall is probably not more than 11 inches even in the most favorable places. It is from 7 to 9 inches in localities where it has been measured. Most of the occupied farms are situated along the lower section of the Molopo River. Elsewhere there is only a little farming in the most favorable spots. The region is

[36] B. E. H. Clifford: Habitability of the Kalahari, Geogr. Journ., Vol. 77, 1931, pp. 355–357.
[37] The Great Ngami Trek, The Round Table, No. 65, 1926, pp. 81–101; and After the Great Ngami Trek, ibid., No. 74, 1929, pp. 325–341.
[38] A. L. Du Toit: The Mier Country, South African Geogr. Journ., Vol. 9, 1926, pp. 21–26.

below the 1000-meter contour, and the northwestern corner of it falls within the zone of greatest rainfall variability in Africa, a urther deterrent to settlement in that direction. While the conditions improve in a southward direction, the whole of the district as far as the Orange River has a high rainfall variability.

Irrigation as the basis of settlement in the western half of southern Africa is well illustrated by the colony at Kakamas on the Orange River. The colony was designed by its founder, the Dutch Reformed Church, to provide a place of settlement for men and women of the poor-white class. Several hundred carefully selected farmers have been installed on the Hartebeestpoort "communal" farm. When ability to carry on is shown, a man is given a six-acre plot of land to cultivate, a daily wage, and assistance from government in marketing the crop, from which the government recovers its wage outlay.[39]

One of the detached topographic units of southwestern Africa is Namaqualand south of the Orange River, between Calvinia and Springbok (Fig. 179). It lies north of the Cape zone of heavier winter rains and represents a transition region akin to the Gordonia and Mier districts—between the belt of normal agriculture and Kalahari dryness. There was no bad harvest in the region between 1896[40] and the time that a comparative report on the area was available twenty-three years later, in spite of the fact that the mean annual rainfall is less than 8 inches. It is extraordinary that wheat is grown successfully on land receiving no more than 6 inches of rain, probably a world record.

This record achievement is due to the very low cost of land and labor, the shallow and cheap cultivation—three-inch plowing is the rule—and to the skillful conservation of the soil moisture. Thin sowing contributes to the same end. Seven to ten pounds of wheat per acre is the rule. Thus each plant receives its due share of water. The harvest return is fifty to sixty times the quantity of seed that is sown. The extensive type of cultivation is carried to an amazing extreme. The net result is a high return per unit of capital invested—chiefly in land and seed. Marketing involves high transport costs, but railways have already made much of the wheat land available. The number of farmers is small on account

[39] F. J. van Reenen: Irrigation and Settlement of Irrigated Land in the Union of South Africa (continued), *Internatl. Rev. of Agric.*, Part II, *Monthly Bull. Agric. Economics and Sociology*, Vol. 21, No. 2, 1930, pp. 50 and 55.

[40] Report of the Departmental Committee on Wheat-growing, appointed by the Minister of Agriculture to enquire into the Conditions of Wheat-growing in the Union of South Africa, Cape Town, 1919, pp. 15-17.

of the vast acreages required per unit of ownership, but the limit is far from being reached: "there is room for a much larger number of settlers."[41]   Most of the land is essentially pastoral.   On the south is a part of the Calvinia district, which receives 75 per cent of its 12-inch annual rainfall in winter in the form of "soft protracted rain."   Cultivation is somewhat more intensive, plowing deeper, the sowing thicker and the yield twice as great.   The return per unit of seed is, however, only half as high.   The opening of the railway to Calvinia in 1914 brought into cultivation large additional areas.

I have confined this chapter to "southern Africa," but the pioneer lands of the continent are not limited to the southern section.   In addition to the North African zone of colonization now in process of occupation by both French and Italians, there is the Sudan borderland between the Sahara on the north and the tropical forest on the south.[42]   Finally, there are the highland areas of Uganda, Kenya, and Tanganyika, each distinctive as to population, continuity of highland areas, number of native population, and relation to the sea.   The white settler's country of Kenya is composed of large continuous areas, the Uganda country is occupied by the densest population of Central Africa, while the highlands of Tanganyika are broken by deep valleys, and the southwestern section has soils that tend to be shallow and easily eroded.   It is held on the basis of railway studies[43] that European settlement in the southwestern highland section of Tanganyika will be scattered at best and that only a small part of the land is of potential agricultural value.   The crops that may be grown in such a remote situation have little chance to compete in world markets.   It is concluded that a railway through the highland section connecting with Northern Rhodesia (Dodoma-Fife route) would not pay for an indefinite term of years and that a more southerly route to Manda, on the northeastern shores of Lake Nyasa, that could utilize the lake has a better chance of success. Under this plan feeders to ultimate centers of production on the highlands would provide rail outlets.

[41] *Ibid.*, p. 17.

[42] An economic appraisal of the region and the technical means for developing its resources are represented in "Le Sahara vaincu peut-il être dompté?   L'aménagement du Sahara," *Annales Acad. des Sci. Coloniales*, Vol. 4, 1929.   The specific rôle of the railways in the development of French territory is set forth in "Nos richesses soudanaises et la chemin de fer transsaharien," by Maurice Abadie, Paris, 1928.

[43] C. Gillman: Report on the Preliminary Surveys for a Railway Line to Open up the Southwest of Tanganyika Territory, London, 1929.

CHAPTER TWELVE

IMPRISONED SIBERIA

We must now widen our purview . . . East and West meet.
—J. F. BADDELEY, *Russia, Mongolia, China*

THE background of the Siberian pioneer is European Russia.
He is a part of that huge peasant population spread over
plains so vast that we describe them in continental or
world figures. Nansen thought Russia "a world still unborn,"
one whose melancholy echoes appear to come from "the unknown
depths of an alien existence." If this be true of "mighty Russia,"
what must be said of her colonizing peoples? Throw some millions
of settlers into the boundless steppes and along the forest belt of
northern Asia, put at their European border that Russia which
has always been ill-equipped with economic machinery, provide
a social organization that is at least as backward as that of the
villages from which it comes, change the weak political structure
of the Czar for the experimental scheme of the Soviets, and you
have Siberia today, locked into the innermost compartment of
Asia with continental distances to overcome before even the
seacoast is reached by her raw materials.

Siberia is like the Far West of America at the close of the Civil
War. It is a horse-cart, not a motor-car or railway community.
The total area of Siberia (Fig. 180) is nearly 5,000,000 square miles;
and the population, in round figures, is 18,000,000. The total
railway mileage of Asiatic Russia is about 10,000, with nearly 30 per
cent of it in Russian Central Asia. This is as if Canada were
restricted to the Canadian Pacific and a few feeders only. Everyone
who knew the American West before it was tamed with barbed wire
remembers the broad "tracks" that swept over the plains from
one settlement to the other. In the wet season they became
broader as the ruts deepened. Such bands in parts of Russia today
are from three to six miles wide, narrowing to a point only when
obliged to converge at a ford on the river bank or at the "crossing"
of a swamp or at a railway station. Tributary roads go cross-lots
over the prairie in direct lines. The tendency increases in the
winter time when streams furnish a temporary highway and
change the pattern of the roads, with the whole countryside under

deep snow and transport going any way it pleases. Every road-
building program is held back, in part, by the present convenience
of winter travel across country.

Excepting Manchuria, there is no place in the world where
pioneering settlement has gone forward on so vast a scale as in
Siberia. In 1896 a Russian official declared that the land open

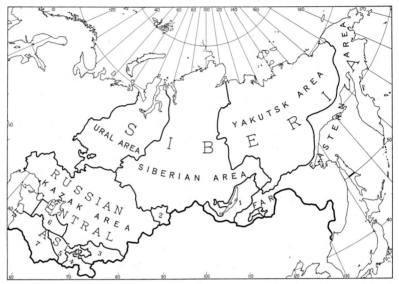

Fig. 180—The political divisions of Siberia and Russian Central Asia as the terms are employed
in the accompanying text. From map of the Union of Soviet Socialist Republics, showing Administrative Divisions as of January 10, 1930. Scale of original map is 1 : 15,000,000.

to colonization in Siberia would not accommodate more than
130,000 additional settlers. In the next eighteen years over three
million peasant migrants settled in western and central Siberia and
the Steppe Region. The migrants went "on horseback and sometimes even on foot with their children and baggage on a wheelbarrow."[1] What happened was that the peasant found a broad
belt of black earth (Fig. 182) like that which made the fertile cereal
lands of central-southern Russia in Europe. He traced it out in
the field along the course taken later on by the Trans-Siberian
railway. It was his peasant instinct and initiative that won the
land. Migration and colonization were not stabilized by government. Because of bad organization and dissatisfaction the casualties
were heavy: 15 to 30 per cent of the colonists returned.

[1] International Migrations, Vol. 2: Interpretations, New York, 1931, p. 558.

The land hunger of the Russian peasants could not be satisfied in Europe. Short-lived were all the relief measures that followed the abolition of serfdom (1859–1866). The population of the Empire doubled in the last fifty years of the nineteenth century. The Russian peasant was on the verge of starvation practically all of the time. In the six-year period, 1907–1913, from a quarter

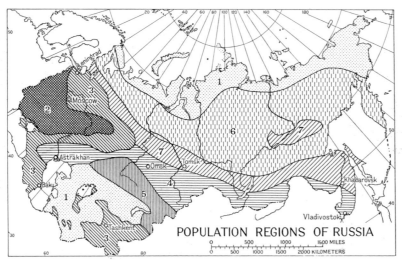

POPULATION REGIONS OF RUSSIA

FIG. 181—Population regions of Russia. Numbers have reference: 1, areas not suited to agriculture (tundra and desert); 2, areas with rural overpopulation; 3, fully occupied areas with no excess of population; 4, relatively densely populated areas with possibilities for additional settlement; 5, sparsely populated areas; 6, part of the *taiga* belt unsuited to agriculture; 7, southern border of the *taiga* belt suited to agriculture. (From Paul Czechowicz: Russland: Die innere Kolonisation in den Jahren 1923 bis 1928, *Wirtschaftsdienst*, Vol. 44, 1929, pp. 1908–1910.)

to three-quarters of a million of colonists annually went to Siberia, or 3,000,000 in all.[2] By 1907, however, reserves of land suitable for immediate settlement became harder to find. Road building and well drilling have never kept up with the front of the pioneering advance.

The World War all but halted migration. In 1917 only three thousand colonists crossed the Urals. After the war, the flow of population began once more, though it almost ceased again when the break-up of the large estates in Russia offered the peasant the chance to get land nearer home. In recent years the stream of colonization has swelled. The migrants are encouraged by a central colonization bureau at Moscow, by the technical studies of soil

[2] Arved Schultz: Sibirien, eine Landeskunde, Breslau, 1923, p. 14. The detailed composition of the population of Siberia and the Kirghiz realm in 1911 are given by Schultz, p. 164.

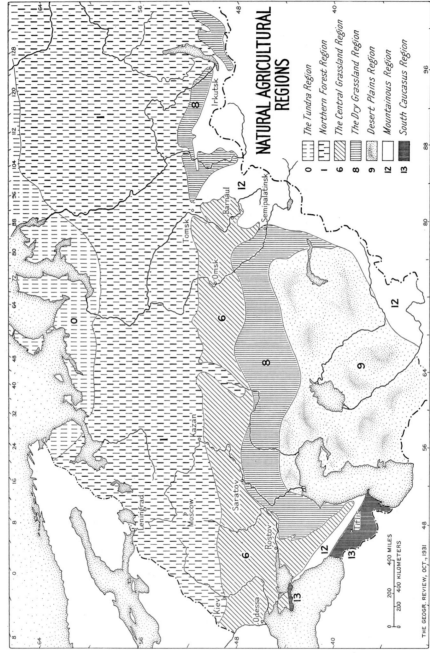

NATURAL AGRICULTURAL
REGIONS

0	*The Tundra Region*
1	*Northern Forest Region*
6	*The Central Grassland Region*
8	*The Dry Grassland Region*
9	*Desert Plains Region*
12	*Mountainous Region*
13	*South Caucasus Region*

THE GEOGR. REVIEW, OCT., 1931

0   200   400 MILES
0 200 400 KILOMETERS

Fig. 182.—The natural agricultural regions of Russia according to C. F. Marbut (Agriculture in the United States and Russia, *Geogr. Rev.*, Vol. 21, 1931, pp. 598–612). The grassland belt, numbers 6 and 8, covering an area of nearly a million square miles, is primarily a wheat region. The more northerly part (6) is the famous belt of chernozem soils, the more southerly part (8) corresponds largely with the belt of chestnut soils. The former soils are highly productive and are found in a rainfall zone where the annual precipitation ranges from 16 to 20 inches. The latter are lighter soils with a lower content of organic matter; as a rule they have a smaller rainfall average and more frequent crop failures.

and climate that have given the colonist the benefit of the rapidly developing science of soils, and by increased railway building now in progress.

The best lands have now been taken. The expense of settlement in the forest or steppe-forest belt (north of the black-earth steppe) is much greater than in the black-earth region. Unoccupied rich soils are a condition of the past. The complaint is now made that the productivity of the soil is diminishing. Only in the neighborhood of the larger towns or the railways are the farmers inclined to practice the three-field culture system, to rotate crops, and to fertilize the soil. Elsewhere the farmer depends on the natural fertility of the land aided by a system of fallowing with crop on the poorer soils in alternate years or at longer intervals of two to fifteen years on the better soils according to quality.[3]

The future depends upon the wider use of machine tillage, the growth of industrial plant in the cities, and the creation of markets nearer than those that fringe the coasts of the Pacific and the Atlantic. Town population—an element in the achievement of a self-contained life—is already assembling, although nine-tenths of the population is still rural and settlements are mostly of the village type with a single street, the log huts of the settlers strung out on both sides of it and the aspect primitive.

Among Siberian cities the record for growth since the Russian Revolution of 1917 is held by Novo-Sibirsk, the principal administrative center of Siberia and its largest railway and waterway junction. It is on the bank of the Ob in the center of the black-earth region. Its site was covered by a pine forest as late as 1895.[4] In 1926 its inhabitants numbered 120,600, an increase of 2310 per cent since 1897! In general, the cities of colonizing Siberia grow more rapidly than those of Russia in Europe, but of cities having more than 100,000 there are still only five (census of 1926) with Omsk, the largest, having a population of over 161,000. Siberia's neighbors are in general in a low state of economic development and do not stimulate city growth.

We commonly think that Peter the Great gave Russia imperial stature by his "western policy" whereby the power of the Muscovite drove forward to the shores of the Baltic. But this vigorous ruler had also an "eastern policy," and it was in Siberia that the most conspicuous territorial gains were made. "Winning of the East"

[3] *Ibid.*, p. 175.

[4] B. Semenov-Tian-Shansky: Russia: Territory and Population, *Geogr. Rev.*, Vol. 18, 1928, pp. 616–640.

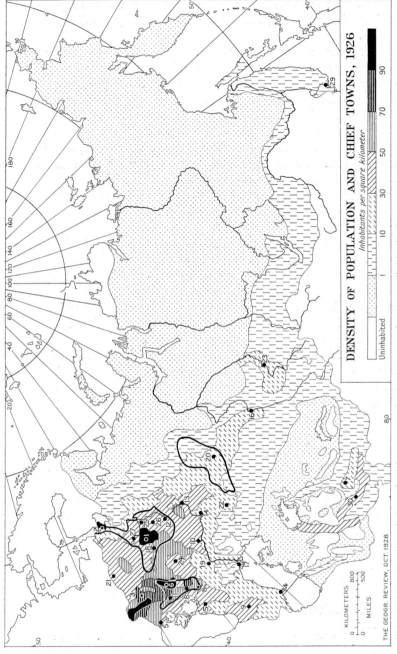

DENSITY OF POPULATION AND CHIEF TOWNS, 1926

Inhabitants per square kilometer

| Uninhabited | 1 | 10 | 30 | 50 | 70 | 90 |

THE GEOGR. REVIEW, OCT. 1928

FIG. 183—Density of population and chief towns according to the census of 1926, compiled by B. Semenov-Tian-Shansky. Towns with over 100,000 are shown by black dots numbered in order of size (see Table I in B. Semenov-Tian-Shansky: Russia: Territory and Population, *Geogr. Rev.*, Vol. 18, 1928, p. 635.) Number 16 represents Omsk; 20, Stalingrad; 22, Orenburg; 23, Novo-Sibirsk; 29, Vladivostok.   The heavy lines enclose the three regions having the greatest development of urban settlement.

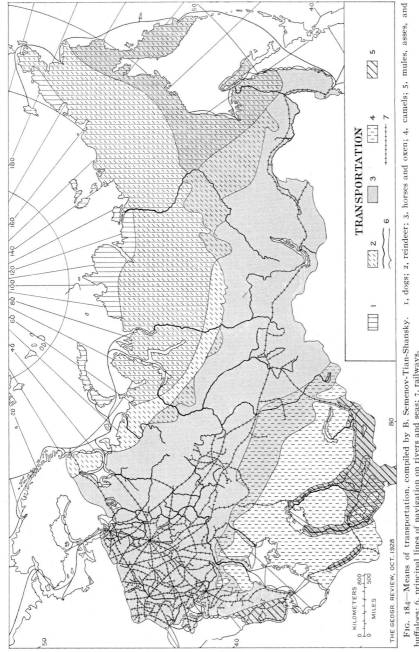

FIG. 184.—Means of transportation, compiled by B. Semenov-Tian-Shansky. 1, dogs; 2, reindeer; 3, horses and oxen; 4, camels; 5, mules, asses, and buffaloes; 6, principal lines of navigation on rivers and seas; 7, railways.

it has been called in the pattern of America's phrase, "Winning of the West." Russian trappers and traders in pelts and wares had wandered over the length and breadth of Siberia in the century before Vitus Bering, at the imperial command, undertook his two great voyages of discovery (1725–1730 and 1733–1742) that were to carry him to the shores of North America and give Russia its

FIG. 135—A part of the city of Novo-Sibirsk. (Georg Cleinow: Neu-Sibirien, Berlin, 1928.)

Alaskan domain. This was the heroic age of discovery and settlement in Siberia. When western peoples were carrying the exotic products of the New World eastward across the Atlantic, successive land caravans were traversing the seven thousand miles of plain and mountain, desert, and grassland, to bring the teas and spices of Cathay to the trade marts of Russia. From the standpoint of traffic Siberia was then the Atlantic of the eastern world, with unlike cultures on its opposite sides.

Here was an immense stimulation of that association with the Far East that has continued into our own times with ever-increasing political significance. Russia's eastern orientation is not just a figure of speech or a recent outburst of ambition but a deep national impulse. It was not an affair of conquest merely but of trade and colonization. Tea was first imported from China in 1638; the Cossacks reached the Pacific coast in 1656. When Russia penetrated Siberia and established a chain of military posts it was to

break the power of the Mongol Tatar hordes forever and to substitute for the rule of the nomad a wide trade organization that
was the forerunner of settlement and the firm occupation of the
land.

The Russian pioneers in Siberia could never have been such
powerful agents of empire if they had not retained that community

FIG. 186—The village of Srosk on the Katun River, a tributary of the Ob. The town is near the
eastern end of the central grassland region. (Georg Cleinow: Neu-Sibirien, Berlin, 1928.)

organization which, more than any other one thing, characterizes
Russian life. To retain this in new country where a man must be
able to become farmer, tradesman, hunter, fisherman, or cattle
breeder, according to the circumstances of the place in which he
settles, is to show a power of adaptation that is the first essential
of successful pioneer life. The community organization has given
stability to the Russian colonizing movement in Siberia. It is
especially effective in an agricultural folk, and the bulk of Siberian
pioneering has been done by peasants from Russia. It was farm
colonization primarily, a thrust of Russian folk into the Siberian
cereal lands, that called for adaptations to climate, to a longer haul
to market, to larger acreages per farm, to a more varied farm
economy. The soil was still "black earth." There were Russian
life and people in neighboring villages of pioneers. The effect was
to maintain the Russian traditions of community life, so markedly

a feature of the social organization in Siberia today, while permitting the growth of new organizations peculiar to the region.

In the large features of life Siberia is a part of European Russia. Her economic imprisonment is still a reality, not a figure of speech. In detail, Siberia is like all frontier regions, a place where society is in more rapid evolution. The government at Moscow has recognized this feature. Cleinow,[5] writing in 1928, says he found no considerable town in which there was not a football field and a number of shooting clubs. In the Tomsk region there were 97 shooting clubs with 2075 members, besides 141 military associations with 2911 members. These are looked upon by the Soviet authorities as broader bases of indoctrination than the village communities since the village psychology and that of the landowner are not in harmony with the idea of the rule of the proletariat. In other words Moscow could dispense with or destroy the time-honored "soviet" of the local community, but it could not destroy the community spirit. The tempo of life is set by the younger generation of pioneers, those who came to Siberia after the turn of the century. It is they too who have made the greatest change in the landscape, the first wave of pioneers of the previous century having utilized the best districts, displacing their Tatar predecessors while mixing their blood to a notable degree with the indigenous elements unlike the more pure-blooded and more energetic communities of later origin.[6]

Cheap land is to the farmer what a new gold field is to the miner. News of it travels far and encourages the venturesome of many nationalities to wander to distant places. It would be an extraordinary pioneer land that drew but one kind of people. Three-fourths of the population of Siberia is made up of Great Russians or their descendants. This gives a decidedly Russian stamp to Siberian life. Culturally, *Siberia is a human peninsula of European Russia*. But the opportunities of a new land have also drawn other folk in considerable numbers, Germans, Poles, Letts, Estonians, Tatars, Kirghiz, Kalmucks, in scattered settlements in the west, and a large number of Mongols. Religious sects have furnished pioneer communities in some number. So the life is not exclusively Russian, and the new conditions everywhere have lent further variety. It cannot be said that there is any one Siberian type of land use. There are types as varied as the land

[5] Georg Cleinow: Neu-Sibirien, Berlin, 1928.
[6] Schultz, *op. cit.*, pp. 162–163.

itself. In a given string of villages it may happen that each is a law unto itself because of the variety of places and cultures from which the present population sprang.

To the pioneer, agriculture at first meant, and still means to a large degree, *food for domestic use.* It is therefore natural that

FIG. 187—A farm in the Ob Valley south of the main Trans-Siberian railway at Novo-Sibirsk. (Georg Cleinow: Neu-Sibirien, Berlin, 1928.)

"the size of the family was and is the measure of the wealth of a Siberian farmer."[7] Children are an asset, not a liability as in the poorer sections of a city population. The more primitive the life the more useful a child can be at an early age, if there is land to be tilled or stock to be herded, though quite the contrary if hunting and fishing are the means of livelihood. The two contrasted cases of Eskimo and Quechua Indians (those of northwestern Argentina) illustrate the principle. In the Arctic, children are so great a burden in a hunting economy that infanticide is sometimes practiced, and in the environment of northwestern Argentina children are so great an asset in a pastoral Indian economy that a girl is thought more marriageable if she can bring a *dot* in the form of two or three illegitimate children![8]

[7] Cleinow, *op. cit.*

[8] Éric Boman: Antiquités de la région Andine de la république Argentine et du désert d'Atacama, Paris, 1908, Vol. 2, p. 437.

In Siberia, as in most pioneer communities there is a high percentage of young married couples who seek independence in a new land. There is also much coöperation of neighbor with neighbor in the sowing and the harvest and in the use of machinery and tools, one man contributing a plow, the other a horse; one man furnishing capital in the way of draft animals and land, another furnishing field hands and time, the crop to be shared accordingly.

In the beginning of settlement in the Kusnetsk-Altai Province of Siberia the village community plan was carried to the point where almost the whole of the arable land that could be cultivated from one center was used before a new settlement came into being near by; and ranching was not an alternative source of livelihood because of the lack of capital and the danger from wild animals afield. If labor was required for public works or for a local industry, it had to be imported because every man already on the spot was anchored to his land. To induce labor to come, a message was sent to the home village in Russia and land offered rather than wage. This the employer could get through his influence with the government, and the newcomer was bound to him economically and politically through the device of advancing to him such provisions and tools as he required.

Naturally this meant that the freer spirits ranged more widely, giving up the security of community life for the hardships of the isolated settlement, gaining thereby also the freedom from that bondage to the large landowner that the latecomer to a settled village must endure in some measure. Many a corner of the remoter steppes and forests has its "squatter" or floating population that has sought to escape government and taxes and the handicap of lack of capital. The specific contribution of the squatter, as elsewhere in the world's pioneer lands, is that he explores the possibilities on the farther side of beyond, the "out-back" country; and, if he strike good tillable soil, a tolerable climate, and a practicable way to market, the less venturesome settlers of the border behind him are not long in finding it out. The squatter is an explorer as much as he is a settler. He leads a self-contained though primitive and experimental life. It is through him largely that we have learned the outer limits of the habitable lands of Russia.

The field of settlement is narrowed in central Siberia owing to the broken character of the country—mountain chains on the south, a rough topography throughout the central strip, and forest and tundra on the north. Here population groups in valley and basin are separated from each other. Native influences thin the stream of Russian blood and culture. Whereas the population of western Siberia is only 8 per cent native, it is here 25 per cent.[9] Central Siberia is like a long bridge of territory between the more fertile plains of the west and the belts of arable land that fringe the Manchurian border and extend to the Pacific coast. It presents but little scope.

The northern limits of agriculture in both Asiatic and European Russia are shown in Figure 188—not the ultimate limits but the probable effective limits judging by the distribution of farms today and the lay of the land. Each dot on the map represents 1000 sown hectares (2471 acres). Since farming rather than stock raising is the type of Siberian economy, we have a picture of both the land and the people in such a map of the sown acreage. If we compare Figure 183 with this map we see the close dependence of the densest population upon the black-earth belt of soils. But at the moment it is the departures from this belt that we are interested in. See how amazingly far to the north the farmers of both eastern and western Siberia have pushed cereal cultivation! In the Lena Valley they have almost touched the parallel of 65°; though even this is surpassed by the settlements about the White Sea in European Russia where cultivation has reached the Arctic Circle. This is better than anything that Alaska can show at the moment. Pockets of warm soil in sheltered locations in the Ob drainage basin on the west, and in the Lena Valley on the east, hint that scattered farming settlements may one day come into being probably as far north as the coniferous forest extends (Fig. 182).

The deeper valleys are warm oases protected from the cold by the surrounding heights. These are the northern outposts of agriculture for grass and the hardier cereals such as barley and special strains of cold-resistant wheat. Sixty miles north of Yakutsk there are years in which barley ripens in 71 days, wheat in 77, summer rye in 80.[10] The limiting line for garden vegetables probably runs close to the Arctic coast of Siberia, as in Alaska where experiments near the Arctic coast by members of the International Polar Expedition to Point Barrow, 1881–1883, showed a remarkable rate of growth for garden vegetables in the strong and continuous sunlight of the Arctic summer.

9 Schultz, *op. cit.*, p. 14.

10 W. P. von Poletika: Klima und Landwirtschaft Russlands, *Berichte über Landwirtschaft*, Vol. 9 (N S.), 1929, pp. 478–527.

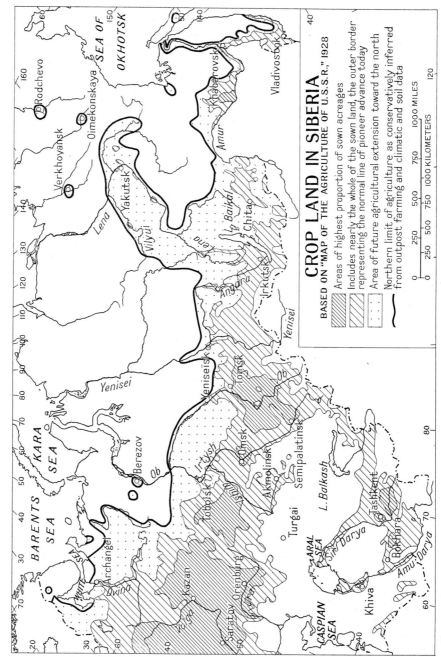

CROP LAND IN SIBERIA
BASED ON "MAP OF THE AGRICULTURE OF U.S.S.R.," 1928

Areas of highest proportion of sown acreages

Includes nearly the whole of the sown land, the outer border representing the normal line of pioneer advance today

Area of future agricultural extension toward the north

Northern limit of agriculture as conservatively inferred from outpost farming and climatic and soil data

0   250   500   750   1000 KILOMETERS

0   250   500   750   1000 MILES

FIG. 188—Crop land in Siberia. Generalized by the author from the dot distributions shown on "Map of the Agriculture of U.S.S.R.," Moscow, 1928.

The line upon our map (Fig. 188) therefore shows only the readily practicable northern limits of agriculture in Russia. It is a line that will long contain the cultivated agricultural land of Siberia, for there is still much room for improvement in cultivation methods on good soils not far from the neighborhood of the railway. While only about a third of the arable land is occupied at present this includes the best, and to realize the full advantages of arability rails must come first. The community organization of the settlers tends to hold them together, and the railway is the necessary condition of export. True, the effective economic distance within which the crop may be hauled to market is here greater than in America or the Argentine or Australia (p. 73), for the time of the owner and his beast have little value in the winter season and the snow cover offers a direct route to the railway station that makes the long haul possible. But beyond the fifty-mile zone the peasant pays for the long haul in a lower standard of living. His surplus is so small a part of the crop in any case that it takes but a small part of his time to market it if the hauling distance is not excessive.

Pioneering, like every other business, has its inevitable specialties of production and in Siberia it is wild honey, fur, butter, hides and skins, wool and hair. These are the exportable things that can stand higher transportation rates and supplement the grain or wood export or take their place altogether when distance from the railway becomes too great. They make the outer limits of agriculture wider than would otherwise be the case. They are responsible in part for the extreme northerly position of the line of agriculture shown in Figure 188. But for the special conditions of transport in Siberia they would have helped carry settlement to quite extraordinary limits, as we shall now see.

Though Russia has about one-sixth of the land surface of the globe it is her fate to be without the natural outlets required by a full use of the land. Under Peter the Great and his successors the need for warm-water ports was recognized, but the population of that time was a marginal one and distinctively European. Siberia was then tribal territory and unsafe for the settler or the traveler. It had not yet lost the tradition of the Mongol hordes. If the need for salt-water outlets and good lines of communication to them was so great that it became the preoccupation of the rulers of Russia for over two hundred years, what must it have been in the last twenty-five years with empty steppe in innermost Asia suddenly transformed into farmsteads by millions of settlers who have *only raw materials* to sell? It is the distinctive quality of the Siberian pioneer region that it has come to a standstill economically through lack of transport and available markets. The form of government has also played its part, the communist system being especially ill-adapted to land culture in a pioneer area. The settlers came for land, not to practice a social theory.

In European Russia the peasant was at first won to communism by the offer of free land as large estates and Crown lands were divided. His allegiance to the new land policy was shortlived when he found that he was not to own the land and that he was obliged to sell his surplus not in a free market but in one that was rigged against him. The authorities fixed the price of the crop and charged him many times the accustomed prices for the machine-made goods that he got in exchange. In Siberia the peasants had all the land they required, and there was no proletariat worth mentioning. The only things the Siberian peasant sees in communism are interruption of free trade, rising prices for goods that he must buy, and diminishing capital for the general services of transport and markets.

When the economic life of a country as large and populous as Siberia is brought to a standstill, the causes, at least, are not hard to find. They must lie in the trade conditions that government controls or influences, provided they do not spring from the artificialities of an actual war in progress. In 1927 the sown acreage of Siberia was only 7 per cent higher than in 1913, according to Cleinow, the number of horses was slightly less (Siberia is horse poor), the number of cattle 22 per cent more, and the quality of cattle and horses was becoming decidedly worse. If Siberia is to gain its old rate of progress two things are required, (1) a lifting of the trade barriers that now impede and in many cases completely prevent the flow of Russian raw materials into the markets of industrial countries that need them and in some cases would bid eagerly for them; and (2) the construction of an adequate network of railways and tributary motor roads that would keep the border of the tilled land advancing until it reaches the full limits of the agricultural zone.

Distance is so great a handicap to production in Siberia that railway outlets, west and east, will not serve to lighten the burden of transport costs. A self-contained economy is required, and the time for it is long overdue. Freight rates to distant markets are too high. A commercial liaison of unlike regions is one way out.

Subsidized transport is another so far as the need for outer markets continues in a balanced development of Siberian life. Until these measures are put into effect Siberia can be only an outlying colony of European Russia. The outlets are now choked to the world-encircling and commercially life-giving sea.

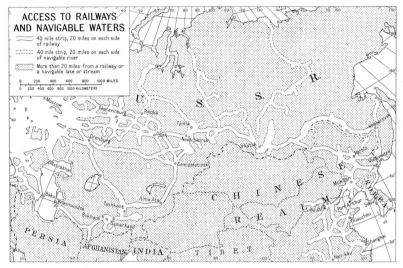

FIG. 189—Access to railways and navigable waters, Siberia.

Motor transport as an auxiliary to the railway is still unthinkable in Siberia because of the bad state of the unimproved roads. Were even a few surfaced roads available in each district it would mean a greatly augmented flow of marketable produce. Such a scheme will work only if the service of the railways is itself improved. At the present time traffic blockades are both numerous and costly. The whole transport problem, so vital to close settlement and the civilizing services of the towns that it supports, is the key to the further exploitation of the land and forest resources of Siberia. Otherwise, area may prove an element of weakness. Much has been made of the diverse wealth of Siberia; but forests, fisheries, and minerals may be so distant from centers of manufacturing, so difficult of access from commercial lanes and markets, as to be almost useless. Better internal transport would mean larger cities, and of these Siberia and indeed all Russia has still too few for the support of heavy industries. The many villages make but a small contribution to industry; their function is that of a local mart. Siberia has potential resources, but they cannot become wealth until their development is attacked by an effective economic organization. This in turn implies education and initiative and, above all, machinery so that one man's work will satisfy more than one man's need.

Faced with continuing foreign opposition to their export program in addition to the problem of excessive transport costs in the case of Siberia, Russian leaders have seen no way to open a new chapter in Siberian pioneer life other than by creating an economically self-contained unit. To do this there is required railway communication between two complementary trade areas that have long engaged the attention of Russian economists: western Siberia and the territory known as Russian Central Asia (Fig. 190) which includes former Russian Turkestan. The Siberian area produces grain chiefly, and southern Turkestan produces cotton and dried fruits for export. Russia as well as Siberia requires increasing quantities of cotton and cotton textiles, and the world sources are drawn upon with difficulty because of trade restrictions. Both France and Great Britain have begun cotton growing in their colonies on an enlarged scale with government support. Russia likewise asks, "Where are the cotton lands whose development will make us self-sufficient in cotton textiles?" The answer is Russian Central Asia. Both cotton and grain would then be sold with a minimum of transport costs, because their markets would be (in part) in adjacent regions. There is no reason, argues the Russian economist, why the manufacture of textiles might not be developed in the seats of production of raw cotton or at least in the to-be-created mills of western Siberia. This will help Siberian economy at the same time that it provides export of cotton goods to Mongolia and China where the demand is constantly increasing and where the political significance of Russian trade may become greater in proportion as it finds a way to supplant the textiles of the western industrialist.

The new Turkestan-Siberian or "Turk-Sib" railway, over eight hundred miles long, has a part to play in the advance of the settler. Scores of new communities have sprung up along the line. But it plays a far larger part in uniting a wheat belt and a cotton belt (Fig. 191). Opened to traffic on May 1, 1930, it is also expected to have an immediate influence upon timber production in the forests of western Siberia and in cotton growing in the Tashkent region. The inhabitants of Turkestan can now get forest products cheaply, and they can get their grain from Siberia at a price that enables them to devote themselves more intensively to cotton growing. Parallel with the building of the railroad, Moscow has made far-reaching plans for the extension of irrigated land, employing for this purpose an American, the former director of the Bureau

FIG. 190—The new railway net of Russian Central Asia, together with the limits of the coniferous forest and the boundaries of the political divisions.

of Reclamation at Washington. Cotton shipments from the United States to Russia dropped from $51,000,000 worth in 1927–1928 to $31,000,000 in 1928–1929. Still further decreases are anticipated with the rise of the cotton-growing industry in Turkestan. A school for cotton culture has been established at Tashkent, with a large student body of cotton experts and agrarian technicians. It is claimed by the government at Moscow that 50,000 peasants have been mobilized for work on the plantations at the "cotton front" in Russian Central Asia and that the proposed production has been realized.[11]

The linking of the cotton and wheat areas is made more practicable by freight tonnages in prospect along the line. The present trend of settlement in the drier steppe lands on the common border of Siberia and Russian Central Asia is toward the south. The Russian farmer has pushed forward the edge of the sown land so far as to alarm the Kirghiz nomads and require the making of an agreement with them, fixing the limits of the grazing lands that they may occupy. One would suppose that the aridity would long ago have stopped the farmer, who is here at the very edge of the dry steppe land. We see from Figure 191 how the border of agricultural settlement swings around the northern end of the Caspian Sea owing to the uncertain rains. This is the "famine belt" of Russia from which thousands fled in 1921–1922 before foreign relief could be organized on a large scale.

As a matter of sheer necessity, Russian farmers, like the farmers of Canada, the United States, and Australia, have adapted their tillage to the rainfall habit and the water-holding capacity of the soil. Each year they find themselves master of more land in a belt that was long thought too dry to grow crops. Because the aridity increases toward the south, there is a limit to the advance of settlement, but it was not reached at the 15-inch rainfall line and will probably not stop at the 10-inch line, where it now stands. Like the rainfall of the arid border of the Great Plains of the United States it is largely summer rain and therefore available to a high degree—under dry-farming methods of tillage—for shallow-rooted cereal crops.

The pioneer belt of southeastern Russia, southern Siberia, and Turkestan is represented in Figure 191.[12] The lines representing diminishing rainfall toward the south are of critical importance. The 16-inch rainfall line marks the northern border of the Dry Region. South of this line the high summer temperatures and the deficient rainfall frequently make it impossible to produce a crop. Three complete crop failures were recorded in 1891, 1906, and 1911 over a period of 20 years. During these two decades poor yields were noted ten times in Saratov and five times in Samara. This is another way of saying that in Saratov there were only five good crop years in a 20-year period. It is not always that the crop is

[11] *Journ. Royal Central Asian Soc.*, Vol. 18, 1931, p. 420.

[12] N. M. Tulaikov: Agriculture in the Dry Region of the U.S.S.R., *Econ. Geogr.*, Vol. 6, 1930, pp. 54–80.

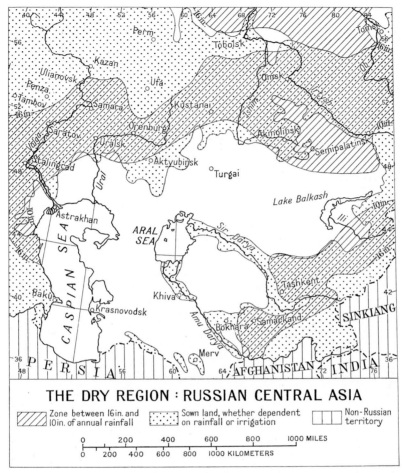

FIG. 191—The Dry Region, Russian Central Asia. While the sown lands are limited, in general, to the 10-inch rainfall line, they exceed the line in the more favorable sections, as south of Aktyubinsk. Irrigation accounts for extensions beyond the 10-inch line southeast of the Aral Sea. Data chiefly from Map of the Agriculture of U.S.S.R., Moscow, 1928.

proportional to the rainfall. In the province of Samara the lowest precipitation in the first decade of the century occurred in 1909; but the crop yields were high, the precipitation having fallen at the time when the crop could best use it.

As in all dry countries, there is a great difference in the quantity and time of the precipitation. If the rain falls during April, May, and June it benefits the crop most of all. If it comes in July or later its effect is smaller except in the case of corn. Of all crops spring wheat is most affected by the spring drought; and since spring wheat and other spring grains have been the main crops of the Volga area the spring droughts are particularly harmful. Millet and sugar beets benefit most from the rains of June and July. For corn and potatoes the critical rain period is in the forty days from July 10 to August 20. *The years that have a favorable rainfall,*

FIG. 192—Primeval forest and swamp in the Yenisei Valley northwest of the mountainous zone of central Siberia. (Luftschiffbau Zeppelin.)

that is heavy June rain so important for crops and grass, occur only 30 per cent of the time and unfavorable conditions 70 per cent.[13] The June rain, to be most favorable, should exceed 70 mm., or nearly 3 inches. The data are for southeastern Russia in Europe. Toward the east and south the rainfall régime becomes worse, the rain less reliable. The agricultural system is still rather archaic, which reinforces the extremes of climate and intensifies the effect of bad years and bad situations. Agriculture in the dry areas should be adapted to the rain habit, district by district.

Government experiment stations seek to reorganize agriculture in such a way as to bring the population closer to the land it works, to study the proper balance between field crops and livestock, to improve types of drought-resisting, high-yielding wheat, and to

[13] Von Poletika, *op. cit.*

discover and adapt plants that will utilize the precipitation during
their growing periods. In spite of low yields the wheat is richer in
protein than is the wheat of moister regions, as in our own dry-
farm wheat in the western Great Plains. In a region so near the
margin of cultivation the selection of seeds and soils and the
methods of cultivation are peculiarly critical. Some strains of

FIG. 193—Part of the great swamp region of northwestern Siberia, through which flow the Ob
and its lower tributaries. (Luftschiffbau Zeppelin.)

Russian soft spring wheat mature in spite of drought and produce
about 13 bushels an acre even when all other crops are a complete
failure. In a similar way several strains of quick-maturing and
cold-resisting spring wheat and oats have been evolved, thus
permitting the northward extension of the agricultural zone of
eastern Siberia.

If agriculture of a balanced type can be developed, closely
adapted in a technical sense to the complex natural conditions,
it is hoped to avoid all but the most severe effects of drought,
prevent the selling of stock during dry periods, and mitigate the
hardships that have afflicted settlers in the past. Paradoxically,
it is the favorable seasons that make such problems acute, for they
tempt men to go beyond the safe limits of settlement. The two
successive droughts of 1920 and 1921 in the Volga region followed

a number of favorable seasons. When the terrible effects of these years had passed there was an interval of only three years when the drought of 1924 again afflicted the greater part of that region.

In Siberia the best soils and the best forests lie adjacent to each other. The *taiga*, as the evergreen forest of Siberia is called, contains the largest single body of conifers in the world. This suggests the possibility of a better balanced economy for both farmer and lumberman. It means also an eventual world market for Siberian forest products. Politics cannot prevent this consummation because the world's supply of useful woods is diminishing. The ax is rapidly cutting back the forest border in the United States and in the most accessible parts of Canada. But the forest will not market itself. Railways are needed for lumber development as well as for the transport of grain in the black-earth belt. In Russia they can be built only by the state, and the investment is a long-term one. A railway requires from three to five years to build and at least as many more years to develop traffic to the point of self-support. Again, the European market is far distant, and logging operations are limited by the nature of the rivers.

In seeking an outlet for the commerce of western Siberia the northern routes have not been neglected, extraordinary as their approach may appear to be through an Arctic Sea. The Kara Sea route for the river-transported goods of the Siberian interior has been a theme of growing importance and preoccupation to leaders and led, through the past three decades, after three centuries of discredit. In 1927 all of the ships in the Kara Sea service made successful voyages, and three-fourths of them have succeeded even if we take the longer period since 1874. The Russo-Japanese War stimulated interest in the route, and the World War likewise. The explorations of Nordenskiöld and Amundsen and the work of the Russian Hydrographical Expedition that traced the northern coast line and discovered Northern Land (Nicholas II Land, or Leninland as it is now called)[14] gave added stimulus to the enterprise. Even Chinese tea, before the opening of the Trans-Siberian railway, could be carried down the Ob and shipped by the Kara Sea route more quickly and cheaply than over the long land route to Leningrad.

Studies of ice and weather—the distribution of the one, year by year, and the habits of the other—have helped greatly. Wireless

[14] N. A. Transehe: The Siberian Sea Road: The Work of the Russian Hydrographical Expedition to the Arctic 1910–1915, *Geogr. Rev.*, Vol. 15, 1925, pp. 367–398.

stations equipped with airplanes have been installed at the mouth of the Yenisei, west of the peninsula of Yalmal, and at the entrance to the straits south of Novaya Zemlya. From this point aviators reconnoiter the region and inform the boats of ice conditions and probable best courses. In the last few years this organization has enabled a number of boats to cross the Kara Sea safely. But the ice conditions themselves and the state of navigation on the rivers cannot be altered. The streams flow northward, and this means that their lower courses are not free of ice until late spring— April or May. On the upper Ob, Yenisei, Lena, and Amur rivers the navigation period is from 180 to 203 days in length, in the middle courses from 176 to 193 days, and on the lower courses from 152 to 175 days. At the mouths of the first three rivers the navigation period lasts about 90 days. All Siberian rivers have a great number of shallows, bars, and rapids, and their basins are isolated from one another. Navigation must be timed to make all haste when the rivers are free and full. The commerce is not sufficient to justify expensive works to correct the river courses or stabilize the discharge. River fleets must be built and operated in sizes and periods that are adjusted to the régime of the streams.

The river commerce of the past ten years shows exports of wood, wool, butter, hair, flax, hemp, oil cakes, and hides and imports of tea, metals, chemicals, paper, machinery, and tools. Official statistics (of moderate reliability) of exports by the Kara Sea route in the period 1925, 1926, 1927 give 340, 617, and 350 thousands of poods respectively, with imports of 466, 545, and 798. In 1928 the imports by that route were increased to $3,500,000. The exports amounted to $7,000,000. These figures represent but a thread of the whole stream of Siberian commerce and are significant in their bearing on the future course of settlement northward into the basins of these great rivers. They show no substantial promise for the millions of settlers that now conduct their main commercial relations by rail in the black-earth region.

The appearance of airplane and airship in the Arctic have raised the question whether the long Arctic coast of Siberia may not have a special commercial importance in the fast-coming day of commercial aviation and thus make a new and special pioneer zone along the border of the polar sea. More than a dozen air lines are now in operation in Russia and cover courses totaling more than ten thousand miles. It is expected that these services will be trebled by 1933. The advantage of the airplane lies in its small capital cost, its mobility, and the readiness with which it can reach isolated groups of settlers at irregular times when the demand for transport rises as products are got ready for the market. The demand for civil aviation will probably be greater rather than less if the present road and railroad building program is carried out. The government is alive to the necessity of improving all its transport services to equalize production and demand.

Siberia is well described as a land of the future. But in a sense this is because it must wait for the needs of the world to catch up with its production of raw materials or it must still devise the means of living a self-contained life in part complementary to that of Russian Central Asia. The world demand for butter, lumber, hides, skins, and furs is increasing. So too is the world demand for cereals, seeing that the world population is augmented annually by about twenty millions. But here comes machine production to increase the output per man upon the land and leave vast acreages to grow food for humans rather than work animals. This will affect the world market to the detriment of the Siberian grain that must be hauled long distances. While the tractor may work wonders in Siberia, as it has already done in America, the lack of capital on the part of the government will make this revolution a consummation of the future.

CHAPTER THIRTEEN

A MODERN INVASION

In that vast territory which bears the name of Tartary.
—FATHER D'ORLEANS, *History of the Two Tartar*
Conquerors of China

I. THE PIONEERS OF MONGOLIA

THE Chinese, turned pioneer, must hear far off the laughter of his gods as he carries his plow into the grasslands of his ancient conquerors, the Mongols. Once he feared the firebrand that might come out of this terrible country "beyond the Wall": his thousand-mile defense was then a veritable line of fate. Now it is he, patient agriculturist, and not the mounted horseman, that has broken through the wall, and the way lies north into nearly empty country, not south to the land of rich cities and plunder. The southern prairie fringe of Inner Mongolia is broken by the plow of the Chinese peasant, and a "horseman's paradise," as Buxton calls it, is being turned into a land of adobe villages. The Chinese of the Middle Kingdom call it the "Country of the Long Grass," and their pioneers are described as "eating up the prairie" at the rate of a mile a year northwest of Kalgan (Fig. 194) and elsewhere at the rate of two or three or even ten miles a year.

The Chinese penetration is not new except in the sense that it has been newly stimulated. Nearly three hundred years ago Chinese peasants began streaming through the defiles that lead up to the grassy border of the plateau of Mongolia. They bought the privilege of tilling the land from the Mongols. The Abbe Huc, in 1844, and Professor Berkey in 1927, have provided first-hand impressions. The Abbe reports a conversation with a displaced native Mongol:

"Your country is a fine country." The Mongol shook his head sadly and made no reply. "Brother," we proceeded, after a moment's silence, "the Land of Grass is still very extensive in the Kingdom of Gechekten. Would it not be better to cultivate your plains? What good are these bare lands to you? Would not fine crops of corn be preferable to mere grass?" He replied, with a

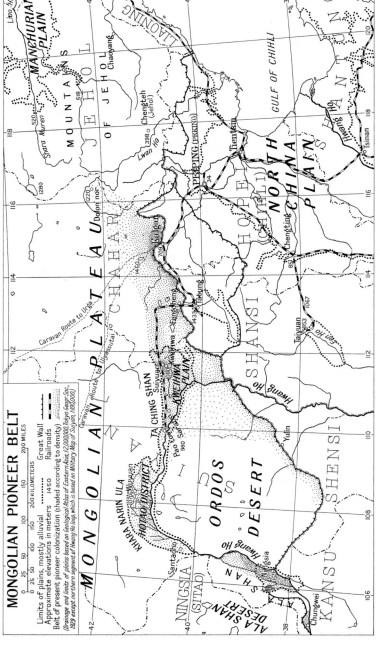

Fig. 194—The zone of active pioneering advance in Mongolia. (G. B. Cressey in Pioneer Settlement, *Amer. Geogr. Soc. Special Publication No. 14*, New York, 1932.)

tone of deep and settled conviction, "We Mongols are made for living in tents, and pasturing cattle. So long as we kept to that in the kingdom of Gechekten, we were rich and happy. Now, ever since the Mongols have set themselves to cultivating the land, and building houses, they have become poor. The Kitats [Kitat] (Chinese) have taken possession of the country; flocks, herds, lands, houses, all have passed into their hands."[1]

"Within a day's traverse," writes Professor Berkey,[2] eighty years after the journey of Abbe Huc, "the desert country gradually greened into the typical Mongolian grassland, and at about mile 725 the first cultivated fields of the encroaching Chinese came into view. From this point onward the occupants of the country are Chinese, and, except for travelers along the trail, one sees no Mongols. The outermost patches under cultivation are scattered, and clearly represent a pioneering experience; but within a very short distance there appear extensive, well-cultivated fields of grain with ripening barley, oats, flax, and millet. It is noted also that the soils look rich and heavily cover the rock floor. . . . For the first time in five months one could see cultivated plants being grown for food. The prosperity of this immediate country naturally suggests the possibility that a much greater portion of the Mongolian border might be adapted to the same purpose. . . . The limits of farming without special adaptation to arid conditions appear to be not far beyond the present zone of occupation. Within two days' journey in our mode of travel the bounds would surely be reached, and cultivation beyond would have to be confined to local areas of special favor, where irrigation could be practised. . . .

"It is most amazing that these arable lands have lain untilled, on the very borders of a land where the struggle for existence has been so severe for generations. With an example of great agricultural competence before them, even at their very doors, the Mongol owners of these tracts seem never once to have tested this quality. . . . "

The distribution of the arable land of Mongolia at the fringe of pioneer settlement has a critical relation to the Great Wall and to the historic movements across it. The map, Figure 194, shows that the Great Wall is not, as commonly described, the accurate mark of a well-defined climatic and physiographic boundary. It crosses

[1] Évariste Régis Huc and Joseph Gabet: Travels in Tartary, Thibet and China, 1844–1846, transl. by William Hazlitt (The Broadway Travellers), New York and London, 1928.
[2] Charles P. Berkey and Frederick K. Morris: Geology of Mongolia (Natural History of Central Asia, Vol. 2), American Museum of Natural History, New York, 1927, pp. 183–187.

many types of country, and, while taking advantage of topographic and drainage features, its loops and turns are very irregularly disposed from any standpoint. It faces the Ordos Desert in Kansu and Shensi, traverses broken ground and parallels river courses in stretches east and west of the Ordos country, and swings over high mountains northeast of Peking to cross a narrow plain before it reaches the sea near Shankaikwan, the village of "Under Heaven Number One Gate."

In tracing the course of the Great Wall fifteen years ago, Clapp[3] found that the sands of the Ordos Desert (part of the great Desert of Gobi) had covered what is here called the "First Frontier Wall," built about four hundred years ago. The true Great Wall is believed to lie a hundred miles farther north (near the Hwang-Ho, Fig. 194). The intervening region was once prosperous and thickly populated with Chinese, witness the numerous walled cities, buried or ruined highways, and the presence of a rich soil now covered with sand. Mile by mile the encroaching dunes and drifts of Gobi have driven relentlessly forward, engulfing the once fertile plain. When Clapp visited Changlopu, near Yulinfu, he found it beleaguered by sand dunes, and one had to climb over them to enter the city. Deforestation is chiefly responsible for this havoc to a once fertile plain. A forest belt, perhaps a mile wide, might stop the progress of the desert blight. The edge of settlement has here been withdrawn. Man is fleeing, not advancing.[4]

East of the Ordos country the climatic boundary, the line between desert and potential farm land, lies well to the north of the Great Wall. This means that the grazing is better the nearer one comes to the Wall from the Mongolian side. It means also that there were repeated attempts at colonization from south of the Wall by Chinese farmers and that the present attempt is only the last of a series, albeit the strongest. The present pioneer belt is an ancient zone of strife between these two opposing types, the nomad and the farmer, and the forces of nature have had a signal part to play in the drama. A part of the agricultural advance has been at the expense of forest as well as grazing land. The province of Shansi adjoins the Ordos country, and its forests have been progressively cut away for two centuries. Quoting Lowdermilk,[5] "Thousands

[3] F. G. Clapp: Along and Across the Great Wall of China, *Geogr. Rev.*, Vol. 9, 1920, pp. 221–249.

[4] Waldemar Haude: Siedlungsmöglichkeiten in Zentral- und Westchina . . . , *Zeitschr. Gesell. für Erdkunde zu Berlin*, 1931, pp. 192–202; reference on p. 197.

[5] W. C. Lowdermilk: Forestry in Denuded China, Reprinted from *Annals Amer. Acad. of Polit. and Soc. Sci.*, Vol. 152, 1930, p. 3. See also J. L. Buck: Chinese Farm Economy, Chicago, 1930, p. 144.

FIG. 195

FIG. 196

FIG. 195—The main street of Tsin pien, a town along the Great Wall in the southern part of the Ordos Desert.   (Photographs 195 and 196 by George B. Cressey.)

FIG. 196—Abandoned farmhouse and courtyard in northern Kansu just south of the Ordos Desert.   The roof timbers were taken along when the family moved elsewhere.

of cubic feet of good timber were found rotting beside oat fields in the mountains of Shansi in 1924 and 1925."

The rolling country northwest of Kalgan might be parts of Saskatchewan or central Montana. Kalgan is the commercial and military center of the region (in Mongol, *khalga* means "pass"). Here winds the Peking road that runs through the Nankow or Southern Pass where one crosses the Inner Wall. This is one of the most ancient and celebrated trade routes in existence—wool and furs coming down from Mongolia, tea and wares bound north-westward to destinations scattered in earlier times all the way to the Urals. Five subsidiary walls protect the pass and testify to the importance of the route, the trade, and the city. At the village of Chüyungkwan, near the Nankow Pass, the Imperial Road runs through a gate bearing religious inscriptions in six languages or characters—Sanskrit, Tibetan, Mongolian ("in Phag's-pa lama characters"), Turk-wigur, Hsi-hsia (Tangut), and Chinese.

The country northwest of Kalgan has its "yellow days," when the wind carries fine dust like a mist and sifts down over the land the loess from farther north. But there is no advance of sand dunes as in the Ordos country farther west. The climate is not favorable to the traditional rice culture. Toward the north and west is a land of diminishing rainfall. Wheat, millet, and oats, not rice, are the chief support of this modern invader of the land of the nomadic barbarian. By adapting his culture to the ways of the seasons there is no reason why the Chinese farmer may not advance like the dry farmer of our own West and at last reclaim the soil to the border of that No Man's Land—the Land of Grass, as the Abbe Huc called it[6]—that lies between China proper and the Desert of Gobi.

Where the Chinese colonist comes in, the land "retains almost nothing of its Mongolian character except the vigour of its air and the immense sweep of its distances," says Lattimore;[7] and he adds that it is not pressure of population that is responsible for the advance of the settlers but the desire of the provincial governments to collect taxes from settled Chinese rather than evasive nomad Mongols. To him, the best of the Mongol "civilization" is prefer-able to the lowest of the Chinese. He thinks that we had better keep our remaining pasture lands for the wool and meat and hides that they supply rather than put more land under the plow for the

[6] Huc and Gabet, *op. cit.*
[7] Owen Lattimore: The Desert Road to Turkestan, London, 1928, p. 35.

benefit of more Chinese who will live in the same state of misery once they have filled up the land.

The Chinese immigrant of Inner Mongolia is not always a farmer, and the plow is not everywhere the tool of conquest. A hundred and fifty miles *northeast* of Kalgan, in the Shangtu region, the Chinese farmers who have pushed into the "undulating grassy plains" are not simple agriculturists but horse and cattle breeders and dealers, "buying from the Mongols their stock, feeding them up for a brief period, and then reselling to the great cities on the plains of China."[8]

If the pioneers of the Mongolian fringe were to raise their standard of living they might breed a new type of Chinese who could perhaps lead the people into the way of a new social and economic order. Instead, they make use of the wider margin of safety which the new land affords by working less hard and by living less close to starvation. "His home is still squalid, his diseases just as multifarious, his leisure just as empty," says Lattimore. If the old vicious circle of large families and divided homesteads is maintained, the occupation of the pioneer lands will not change the economy of the Chinese people; it will but increase the area of their breeding grounds.

The Chinese make their living with the hoe, and they are anchored to the land in a double sense—the soil is the source of their livelihood, and in it rest the bones of their ancestors to whom they owe devotion. "Man belongs to the soil, not the soil to man . . . ," says Keyserling, speaking of the Chinese peasant, and adds "the inherited fields are . . . his history, his memory, his reminiscences." The Chinese are traditionally not colonizers, nor are they trained in the coöperative principle that is a prime essential in modern or at least in western civilization. Community building is a new experience for the Chinese, and it is a basic process in the occupation and economy of new land. Men create homes in a pioneer region, but they also create communities which render spiritual and material services that the home alone cannot supply. How were the settlers of the Mongolian pioneer zone led to plow and plant and live in a region so unsuited to the traditional culture of the Chinese?

It is a combination of farmer and trader that has turned the trick, with government aiding and abetting. The farmer builds the permanent home; the trader widens the field of view. When

[8] Lawrence Impey: Shangtu, the Summer Capital of Kublai Khan, *Geogr. Rev.*, Vol. 15, 1925, p. 586.

FIG. 197—Mongolian habitations. The farms are built of *kaoliang* stalks and covered with felt. (South Manchuria Railway Co.)

the Mongol nomads become sufficiently indebted to the traders, the Chinese officials and the traders combine to negotiate for the "sale" of a part of the Mongol lands; and this is at once thrown open to settlement. Bit by bit the edge of the grassland is thus eroded away from the domain of the Mongols, who already have a deficiency of winter pasture and whose herds, without shelter, are decimated in some seasons to the extent of one-third of the total number.[9] The process reminds us of the lands bought from the American Indians—in the small price paid and the seeming insignificance at first to the Mongol himself of the tract that he lets go. But the trader does this also—he provides a direct incentive to the

FIG. 198—Carts hauling stores to Han-nor-ba, Mongolia, 15 miles north of Kalgan on road to Urga. (F. G. Clapp: *Geogr. Rev.*, Vol. 9, 1920.)

[9] Serge M. Wolff: The People's Republic of Mongolia, *Contemporary Rev.*, Vol. 135, 1929, p. 366.

FIG. 199—Traffic on the Kalgan pass into Mongolia. (Paul Wilm: Wirtschaftsarten in der Mongolei, *Berichte über Landwirtschaft*, Vol. 7 (N.S.), 1928, pp. 266–313.)

farmer to produce a little more than is required to keep his family from starvation. By this means there is created a surplus that enters the currents of trade flowing between old China and the pioneer zone of Inner Mongolia.

It appears as if only the arid border of the Desert of Gobi will stop the organized Chinese advance. The Chinese government has established special colonization offices or reclamation bureaus whose business it is to facilitate the departure of the Mongols on friendly terms by the offer of money and new pasture grounds. Plenty of pasture can still be found in the remoter parts of Mongolia, and the Mongols themselves are decreasing in numbers. Moreover, the strip of pioneer land, while important from the standpoint of agriculture, is less important to the wide-ranging nomad. It is at

FIG. 200—A Chinese farmhouse group in Mongolia. (Paul Wilm.)

least 500 miles long from northeast to southwest, but its width is limited by dryness to a strip from 50 to 200 miles wide. Once the Mongols have retired from a given district it is the business of the official bureaus to distribute the land ($6.00 to $7.00 an acre) among Chinese families coming from the overcrowded districts of the south and sent by the provincial authorities to the centers of colonization where the division of the land is made and new farmsteads established.

A primitive mud "house" and a well are the first requirements of the new home. The land needs no clearing. A few tools, a few head of draft animals for the heavier tillage, a few pigs and chickens complete the farm equipment. The average size of the farms is about thirty acres, and the largest do not much exceed three hundred acres. To kill the native grasses the farmer sows rape as a first crop; after that oats are grown. In some districts this cereal occupies about half the cultivated land; in others, a third of it. Oats are grown for human food, not for animals, the grain being ground and the meal made into a kind of pastry and also into pancakes. Rape seed is second to oats in importance, occupying 10 to 15 per cent of the cultivated area. Each farmer has one or two fields of potatoes, and for the rest wheat, barley, and millet occupy the land.

The facts of agricultural production are given by Paul Wilm in the *Chinese Economic Journal*.[10] He notes that the tendency is for the land to pass into the hands of those who work it. Forty per cent of the colonized area is cultivated by the owners, and the rest by tenants. The highly important point is made that while large-scale farming would provide a higher standard of living for a small class of well-to-do landlords, such a system would support a smaller number of the poorer classes. Moreover, small farming is embedded in the traditions of the nation, and the well-being of the country as a whole cannot be studied on any other basis. To own the land they work is one of the deepest sentiments of the Chinese people.

We have already seen that almost every remaining pioneer land requires special adaptations of culture and crop, and it will be interesting to see how the rule works for the Chinese in the prairies of Mongolia. The climate is not friendly. The winter season is almost rainless as a rule, and the cold is so severe that, without an adequate snow cover, the sowing of either winter wheat or winter

[10] Paul Wilm: The Agricultural Methods of Chinese Colonists in Mongolia, *Chinese Econ. Journ.*, Vol. I, 1927, pp. 1023–1043.

barley is out of the question. The spring rains open the season of cultivation, and, as they arrive late (the first rains may not fall until June), the farmer is in an anxious state because the crop may not have time to ripen. July and August are the only "rainy" months of the year. A series of dry years may mean additional hazards to the crop, just as on the semiarid border of our own Great Plains or on the edge of the dry steppe country north and east of the Caspian Sea. It is possible that these recurrent seasons of drought were responsible for the retreat of the line of cultivation outside the Wall in centuries past. The plow of the pioneer occasionally turns up the relics of a former settlement, signs of an earlier advance of agricultural Chinese into the neutral zone between them and the roving pastoral Mongols.

If the light rains limit cultivation, the dry autumn also makes the harvest easy. There is no need for shelter; the grain is stored in open ricks; threshing is done by flail or a small stone roller; and the surplus crop is carried southeasterly in the direction of the larger towns, Kalgan for example. Some of the crop goes to the Mongols in exchange for cattle, skins, and wool. The Chinese stick to agriculture and will have nothing to do with cattle except in certain small districts where the grassland is not easily plowed. They also import dry dung from the Mongols. There is great need for imported fertilizers which, however, are too expensive for the settler to buy. In the course of six or eight years, says Wilm,[11] who has observed agricultural methods closely, the natural fertility is lost in large part and the crop yield falls off. The hoe must then be used more and more, and irrigation is no remedy except in a few favored places.

The farms of Mongolia have drawn in the migratory laborer. Two or three are employed on every farm. Most of them return to their homes in the south when the harvest is over. The need for them arises through the type of tillage employed. As soon as the plants are above ground they require hoeing to keep out the weeds and especially to make a surface mulch that breaks the capillary tubes near the surface and preserves the moisture in the subsoil. A larger acreage must be tilled to support a single family than is required in China proper. The corn, rice, sweet potatoes, groundnuts, cotton, and beans of the more southerly provinces are absent here. Besides oats, barley, millet, and potatoes the Mongolian farmer grows peas and beans and also buckwheat, for it requires only a

[11] Ibid.

short growing season. There is no second crop owing to the short interval between the spring rains and the autumn frosts.

In turning grassland into grainfields the Chinese are adding to the landscape a new feature, the adobe village, where formerly there were the yurts of the nomads. The Mongol village must

FIG. 201—Cultivated fields of Chinese farmers. (Photograph by R. C. Andrews, courtesy of American Museum of Natural History.)

follow the herds that move with the seasons, while the Chinese village is fixed. The latter is in many instances surrounded by a high wall as a protection against bandits and wild beasts as well as the weather. Where there is an inn the Chinese traveler enters; the Mongol, if he comes by, stays outside the wall. "Two types of habitations seem to be springing up: first the walled inn, and secondly what may be described as the walled hamlet. In the remoter valleys the villages are entirely open and trust to their dogs, as the Mongols do, for defence."[12]

Both Outer and Inner Mongolia belong to the distant marches of the old Chinese Empire, and the Chinese government of today has the same weak hold upon the peripheral regions as the former rulers had. No railways, wagon roads, canals, or navigable rivers connect these distant provinces with the eastern seats of population and trade. That being true of the Mongolian population of the grasslands, what will be the political effect of the invasion of the border by Chinese? While Buxton reports the settlers as too much engaged at the present time with the struggle entailed by their hard environment, to have any leisure for politics, it is hard to say what developments the future may bring forth.

[12] L. H. Dudley Buxton: Present Conditions in Inner Mongolia, *Geogr. Journ.*, Vol. 61, 1923, pp. 393–413; reference on p. 401.

The Mongolian nomad here comes into the story, because his numbers and position as well as his temperament make him susceptible to the influence of the ambassador that comes bearing the richest gifts. When the Chinese Revolution broke out in 1911 Russia began aggressive measures and then negotiations that

FIG. 202—Cattle on grassland in northern Manchuria. (South Manchuria Railway Co.)

resulted in Chinese recognition of the "autonomy" of Outer Mongolia, a recognition that was confirmed in 1915 by representatives of Russia, China, and Outer Mongolia. Russia thereby gained a privileged position while Chinese troops were not to be admitted into Outer Mongolia and *Chinese subjects were not allowed to colonize the land*. On the other hand Russians were allowed to move about freely in the territory, conduct any business they chose, export and import without the payment of taxes, and enter into agreements with the Mongolian government for the working of mineral and timber lands, fisheries, and the like. There were also special rights of pasturage.

While the Mongolian agreements were designed to turn Mongolia into a Russian province, the ties that bound Outer Mongolia to China for over two hundred years could not be set aside so lightly, and Chinese rather than Russian trade continued to flourish. With the growth of difficulties in Russia, following the Revolution of 1917, there ensued a wide restriction of Russian ambitions and power in the Far East, and the old order was reëstablished in Outer Mongolia by presidential decree in 1919. By the convention of 1924 Russia recognized Outer Mongolia as an integral part of the Republic of China and agreed to respect Chinese sovereignty there, at the same time withdrawing her own troops. Russia further agreed to relinquish the rights of extraterritoriality and consular jurisdiction, thus definitely renouncing her former special privileges and agreeing to the principle of reciprocity and equality. But Outer Mongolia was not a party to this agreement, and in the same year its chiefs declared their country independent and adopted a republican constitution which provides for a national parliament. Inner Mongolia alone remains Chinese.

Out of the present difficulty between China and Russia new questions will undoubtedly arise respecting Mongolia, for neither power has the strength to give stability to the forces at its command along the enormous distances of the common frontier. But the fight will take place in, and the settlement be guided by, the Manchurian not the Mongolian realm. It is to that region that we now turn for the study of the greatest folk movement in the world today and one that involves three powers—China, Japan, and Russia—in a struggle whose end will hardly be seen by our generation. The forces at work are vast, the realm wide, and the stake one of the richest anywhere remaining to be seized by political and military means.

II.   THE PIONEERS OF MANCHURIA

Folk movements have a way of confounding the prophet and the statesman. Consider the gathering of the tribes on the distant horizon of the highly organized Roman Empire, how little we know about it, how rude the organization until the Roman system was copied or adapted, how far-reaching the effects! In our day, and to an increasing degree, governments are exercising the creative faculty and bringing into play technical knowledge in order to produce mass reactions, "evoking new forces," as the business of government has been defined. So far as population is concerned, governments only deflect the flow or, at best, enlarge or diminish the scope of its movement: they rarely originate or stop it. Great Britain would like to double or treble the emigration of her island stock to the Dominions; but all her efforts have had diminishing effect in post-war years. Japan would greatly like to see her small farmers migrate to Manchuria and create there a cereal-growing colony analogous to the Canadian Northwest. Italy can persuade but a handful of her swarming millions to make their homes even in the comparatively attractive coastal regions of Cyrenaica and Tripolitania.

These stimulated movements do not succeed because the dynamics of migration has no necessary relation to government; it has to do with the native sense of the people, the intimate conditions of their lives for which there are few or no spokesmen, the limits of toleration among them for insufficient food or heavy work, news of the best places that kinsmen have found, their ability to raise cash for a journey to new lands, and many other homely things that are talked out by the individual fireside, not in a government office.

Why have the Chinese "burst like torrents upon Manchuria," to quote the phrase of a traveler? Because they have discovered the homely things, which they understand and in part create, in a new land where they can escape from a struggle for existence that is one of the most severe in China. Manchuria has seen less of revolutionary armies; the military draft is less common, in northern Manchuria at least; and the tax collector works rather more by rule than by guess as in China proper. There is plenty of work on new railways and ports, and plenty of good land to be had in a domain as large as France and Germany combined. It is estimated that the population of Manchuria has increased from some 15 millions in 1911 to some 25 millions at present, with Chinese constituting 90 to 95 per cent. In 1927 and 1928 Chinese immigrants numbered nearly a million, and over a million in 1929, though more returned in 1929.[13] As late as 1925 the percentage of women and children among the migrants was but 7; two years later it was 25. It is now a family movement, not merely a seasonal labor movement. While many thousands still return to the south for the winter, so many remain that Manchuria is now a Chinese country in aspect and culture, not merely a colony from which the newcomer escapes as soon as possible.

The junks of Chefoo bring their thousands to the southern shores of the Liaotung Peninsula; and from every port of the Shantung region the steamers leave, crowded to the rail. Coolie cargoes walk on and off the ship and save handling charges, says Young. Less than half can pay the reduced fares north. The rest must walk —men, women, and children— to Changchun and even Harbin with terrible sufferings on the way. Both Chinese and Japanese do what they can to prevent and allay distress. The present need is for a colonization policy directed by government since new land and willing labor are not enough to ensure success to the rice-growing Chinese turned northern farmers. Yet so strong is "the invitation of the land" that no amount of hardship (which increases with numbers, the facilities of charity being overtaxed) can stem the stream. It is a spontaneous outpouring of population into the richest and largest of the pioneer belts of eastern Asia, and for this reason alone it is of the greatest interest to every student of settlement as well as to statesmen of every power having interests in the Far East. The present rate of increase by migration is smaller possibly because of greater disorder in Manchuria and less in Shantung in the past few years.

One of the streams of greatest significance is directed down the lower Sungari (Fig. 213). This takes Chinese agricultural development right to the Amur, the Russian border. Forty per cent of the immigrants who entrain at Harbin detrain along the railway or go direct to Sungari settlements (100,000 to the Sungari in 1927).[14] The river serves as a highway for produce sent to Harbin and also supplies cheap transport for the immigrant.

If the old imperial government had not discouraged migration to Manchuria, China today would hold a less questionable title to the rich province that has attracted Russia and Japan and brought territorial problems to a focus in the Far East. Whether it was fear of Russia or the desire to maintain the imperial hunting grounds, the old dynasty laid heavy restrictions upon settlement in Manchuria, and not until the opening of the present century could the Chinese pioneer plant himself securely upon the land of northern Manchuria. Southern Manchuria has been open since the seventeenth century at least, and Chinese colonists have settled in increasing numbers there since the beginning of the Manchu Dynasty. For the whole of Manchuria it is estimated that about one half of the arable land is in crop, and the railway lines are sufficiently numerous to provide widely distributed shipping points. The railway mileage now exceeds 3700, with several hundred miles under construction, whereas there was not a mile of rail thirty-four years ago.

Assistance to new settlers has been provided by the Chinese government and by voluntary associations.[15] Housing and money-

[14] Young, op. cit., p. 302.
[15] Ibid.
    Idem: Economic Bases for New Railways in Manchuria, Chinese Econ. Journ., Vol. 1, 1927, pp. 324–335;
    Idem: Chinese Labor Migration to Manchuria, ibid., pp. 613–633.

Fig. 203

Fig. 204

Fig. 203—Winter scene, Sungari Valley.   (South Manchuria Railway Co.)
    Fig. 204—The plain of Southern Manchuria, near Mukden.   (P. M. Roxby: The Distribution of Population in China, *Geogr. Rev.*, Vol. 15, 1925.)

FIG. 205—Refugee immigrants from Shantung on deck of steamship bound for Manchuria. (South Manchuria Railway Co.)

lending facilities were supplied by a colonization association in 1913 on the ground that larger farm production would augment taxes. In 1922 the railway fares for women and children going north to Manchuria were reduced, and lower rates were again made effective in 1925 after an interruption owing to disorder. A proclamation issued in 1926 and posted in the provinces of Fengtien, Chihli, and Shantung invited emigrants to settle on new lands located near the confluence of the Sungari and the Amur rivers. Free land was offered to settlers who would break the sod and plant a crop. Housing would be furnished for the first year, and besides money for food there was offered the free use of agricultural implements. Not all the promises were kept, and many settlers found themselves stranded far from home. It sounds like Australia and New Zealand and the broken promises of the land companies of the United States and Canada in the heyday of pioneering with land titles often clouded and the seats of authority far away.

In western Manchuria the incoming Chinese settler displaces the Mongol as in Mongolia itself, where much the same grassy country runs for a thousand miles toward the west and south. The appropriation of territory follows the same general scheme that we have seen in operation in Inner Mongolia. Traders and officials "buy" the land, open it for settlement, and recoup on taxes and trade. In eastern Manchuria are the hunters, canoemen, and fishermen of the forested valleys of the Ussuri, Sungari, and Amur rivers; but they are relatively a feeble folk, and the pioneers have no difficulty in pushing them aside. Kirin is perhaps the most interesting of the provinces of Manchuria, for it possesses an unusually rich endowment of forests, mines, and fertile soil. It has just been tapped by the new Kirin-Tunhua Railway, completed by the Japanese in October, 1928. Starting from Kirin it will run to

the border of Chosen
(Korea) and thence
connect by rail with
the sea. The rail-
way has high stra-
tegic importance to
Japan in the assem-
bly of troops in
Manchuria, and the
new line will offer
an alternative route
to the eastern sea-
board that will
divert some of
the traffic of the

FIG. 206—Open storage of soy beans, Manchuria's leading export, Dairen wharf. (South Manchuria Railway Co.)

Chinese Eastern Railway—of which more in a later paragraph.

How have the millions already settled in the far corners of Manchuria managed to get their goods to the consumer? When there was not a mile of railway how did the Chinese settler reach his market in view of the strict limits of distance hauling in most pioneer regions? In the first place although his standard of living in this new land was higher than in the south, it was still so low that he could afford to spend a disproportionate amount of time on the road to market. In the second place, his production costs were very low, with new fertile land and cheap coolie labor from the hunger-stricken south. If he could not bring his millet to the port of Dairen he could feed it to pigs and haul their frozen carcasses in winter. His tobacco and hemp were of the nature of specialized products that every pioneer people is trying to find in order to have something that will stand the cost of the long haul to market. Skins were in the same class, and beans nearly so. In addition he was sometimes able to walk pigs and cattle to market.

We have, fortunately, a stirring account of the pre-railway traffic from an English observer who knew the region well— Alexander Hosie, whose book on Manchuria was published in 1901.[16] He found distance to be the greatest barrier to development—the long and expensive transport of grain by cart in winter, the only season in which the roads of the interior were fit for traffic. Most of the grain was fed to the pigs or used for the manufacture of spirits at the numerous distilleries scattered about the centers

[16] Alexander Hosie: Manchuria: Its People, Resources and Recent History, London, 1901.

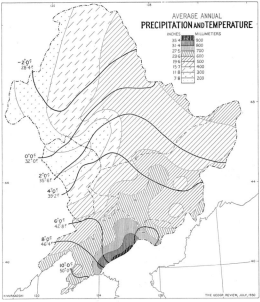

AVERAGE ANNUAL
PRECIPITATION AND TEMPERATURE

FIG. 207—Average annual rainfall and temperature, Manchuria. (The Manchurian distributional maps on this and succeeding pages are from Murakoshi and Trewartha: *Geogr. Rev.*, Vol. 20, 1930.)

of production. He had not seen anything in China that for its magnitude so impressed him with the vast trade of that country as the cart trains moving from north to south in Manchuria. "Until late in the afternoon, when, owing to a snowstorm, we had to abandon the possibility of making the city of K'aiyüan Hsien that night, we met at least a thousand carts heavily laden with the produce of the interior. . . . If we take the average team to have numbered five animals, we met some five thousand animals in one day. At one place where a difficult gully had to be crossed, there was at least one mile of carts, three deep, waiting their turn to pass it." Sheep, dog, and goat farming were then in vogue in much of northern Manchuria, the products being especially valuable in proportion to bulk and thus able to stand the cost of the long haul.

The railway has markedly changed the economics of farm production. In 1927 the soy bean was exported to an amount almost reaching four and a half millions of tons, and the soy bean and its products now constitute more than half the total export trade of Manchuria. The production has doubled in the last twelve years in response to the world market created by its excellence. Japan, China, the United States, Denmark, and other European countries all require increasing tonnages.

Carts were described as "the railway carriages" of Manchuria thirty years ago, and they still are for all that vast region far from the railways. Besides the smaller carts there are great open carts with teams of five to seven ponies or mules bringing the bulky products of the interior to the banks of the streams, there to await the opening of navigation in the spring after four to six months of blockade by ice. The heavier snowfall of the center and north permits the use of sleds in winter; but this condition affects only a small part of the total area of settlement, and the same may be said

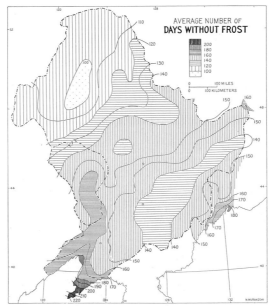

FIG. 208—Frost and the growing season, Manchuria.

of transport over the ice of the streams. When the waterways open, the products are carried by river barge, and the draft animals are then freed to work in the fields. Thousands of boats were in operation in Hosie's time, and "a forest of masts" appeared on the banks of the southerly streams where the great ports lie. This was the picture in summer; but in the autumn, generally in November, the boats disappeared into the interior "where they are drawn up and beached on the banks of the river [Liao] till the ensuing spring." Hosie estimated that 20,000 boats of seven to fourteen tons capacity, manned by crews of three to five men, were engaged in this carrying trade and that each boat made on an average eight trips during a season, bringing down grain, tobacco, beans, hemp, etc., and taking back salt, old iron, and general cargo.

In northern Manchuria today wheat is the chief crop, and there we find the largest area in China devoted to wheat cultivation. The accompanying maps of Manchuria[17] show some of the main agricultural elements. The maps Figures 207 and 208, giving

[17] Nobuo Murakoshi and G. T. Trewartha: Land Utilization Maps of Manchuria, *Geogr. Rev.*, Vol. 20, 1930, pp. 480–493.

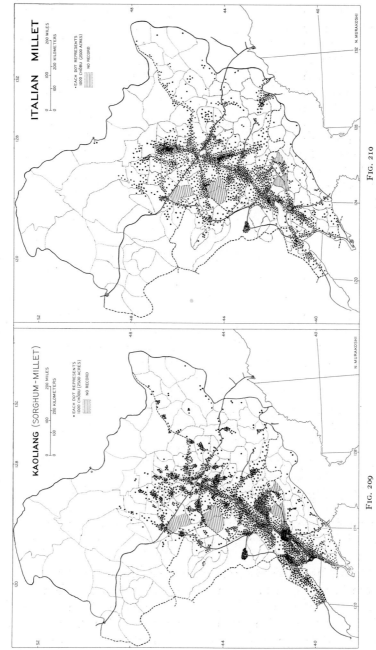

FIG. 210

FIG. 209

FIG. 209—For its best growth *kaoliang* (sorghum-millet) requires at least 150 days without killing frost; hence the crop reaches its greatest importance in southern Manchuria. It is to the south what beans and wheat are to the north. About the Gulf of Liaotung it occupies over 70 per cent of the cropped land and about Mukden over 50 per cent.

FIG. 210—Italian millet, being deep-rooted and tolerant of drought conditions, has its greatest relative importance in the semiarid western lands. The linear and radial pattern of distribution reveals the influence of railway communications (compare Fig. 213).

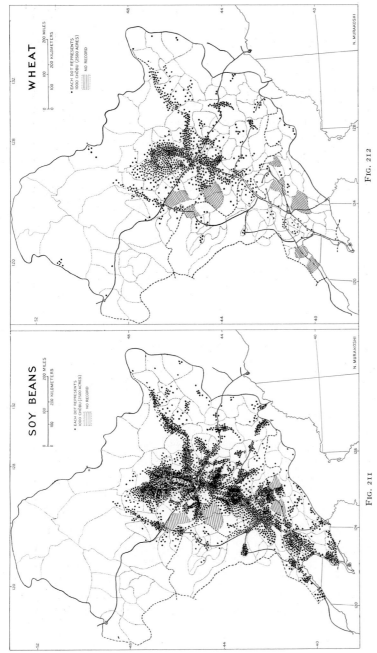

FIG. 211.—The soy bean crop reaches its greatest relative and absolute importance in the north, reflecting an ability to mature in a somewhat cooler climate with shorter frost-free season than is true of *kaoliang*. The beans grown in the north are reputed to be of higher quality, there being a progressive increase in their oil content with increasing latitude.

FIG. 212.—Wheat is emphatically a crop of the north, and on the far frontier where the total crop area is small it reaches its greatest relative importance. The competition of crops requiring a somewhat longer growing season is one reason for the lesser importance of wheat in the south. Eighty per cent of the crop is spring-sown. Rainfall throughout most of Manchuria is scant during spring and early summer, reaching a maximum in late summer and early autumn.

growing season and annual temperature suggest how restricted agricultural settlement will be in the northwestern section and throw light on the maps of the distribution of soy beans, millet, and wheat, all of which are grown in the better situations along the valleys and on the floors of the local basins.

Until the opening of the Chinese Eastern Railway the production of wheat, which had been carried on for several centuries, could play no great part in the life of the Manchurian peasant because he could not get it to the centers of consumption, the large cities in the south. The Russo-Japanese War increased production, for huge armies had to be fed. By 1917 Manchurian wheat was exported to Chosen (Korea), Japan, and other countries. The area of chief production lies in the watershed of the Sungari River and its tributaries and in latitude 43° to 50° N.

About 10 per cent of the area of northern Manchuria is sown to wheat yearly, according to the estimates of Skvortzov;[18] or 10.9 in 1927 for all Manchuria, according to Murakoshi and Trewartha.[19] The north Manchuria weather is fickle, and the most useful strains of wheat must therefore be somewhat resistant to both drought and cold. In 1926 Manchuria had the worst drought in twenty years.[20] Nineteen varieties of wheat are said to be grown, some of them especially robust and resistant to climatic extremes; and further seed selection and experimentation are urged.[21] Special tillage methods are employed. The narrow furrows are set in the direction of the prevailing southwest winds, which are so strong as otherwise to scatter the soil. The spring winds, called literally "yellow dust," come from the direction of the Mongolian plains and blow with great violence.

So important is the Chinese Eastern Railway today as an instrument in the colonization of northern Manchuria, and so acute is the political situation with respect to it at the moment, that the significance of this pioneer zone will be missed if one fails to take into account the special relations of this extraordinary railway line. Originally the Chinese Eastern Railway was a joint-stock company financed by private funds, and the whole of Manchuria was involved in the scheme of development set in train

[18] B. W. Skvortzov: Manchurian Wheat (abridged sketch), *Publ. Manchuria Research Soc., Commerc. and Indust. Sect., Ser. A, No. 18*, Harbin, China, 1927; reprinted from the *Manchuria Monitor*, Nos. 4 and 5, 1927.

[19] *Op. cit.*

[20] The Farmers Movement, Nanking, 1928, Vol. 1, Sect. 4.

[21] Skvortzov, *op. cit.*, p. 25.

by Czarist Russia. The zone of the railway had extraterritorial privileges, Russia having her own troops on the spot, her own police arrangements and courts. When, in 1898, the original concession was expanded to include a line from Harbin south to Port

Fig. 213—Map of Manchuria showing the provincial divisions and chief towns and railways. The important influence of the railways is clearly apparent in the crop distribution maps shown on preceding pages.

Arthur the first step was taken that led eventually to war with Japan (1904–1905). With the defeat of Russia, only northern Manchuria remained under Russian control, while Japan established a sphere of influence in southern Manchuria, served by the South Manchurian Railway. Thus came into existence the two opposing railway systems and corresponding national interests which are in active opposition today.

After a short period of Japanese control at the close of the World War, and of supervision by an Inter-Allied railway board, a new treaty between Russia and China was made in 1924, which declared the Chinese Eastern Railway to be a commercial, and not primarily a political enterprise. But the breakup of China was at hand, and it was not long before the Manchurian war lord made his own agreement with Russia and retained the right to redeem the Chinese Eastern Railway with Chinese capital at any time before the expiration of 60 years. Russia was to retain the general managership of the railway and thereafter listened only at convenient moments to the claims and demands of Chinese authority. The real issues are never lost sight of between Japan and Russia. On the part of Japan is the desire to pursue a policy in Manchuria and North China that will enable her to invest capital, develop resources, and if possible (though up to this time with no success) to settle her people. There are in all Manchuria less than 200,000 Japanese today. Japan gains what she sought in 1904: her railroads and ports prevent the emergence of Russia upon the shores of the Yellow Sea.

No less aware is Russian authority of the value of the Manchurian grainfields and the dense and pliable population of Chinese farmers. Eastern Siberia has a limited extent of grain-growing lands, and it would round out the Soviet domain in the east if Manchuria could be added and Soviet control exercised over a solid block of temperate-zone territory of large dimensions fronting a warm sea. We cannot expect such conditions to lead to stability. Manchuria is too far from China to be governed effectively by that power. Japan is too strongly entrenched, her investments in railroads, coal and iron mines, and forests are too heavy (calculated at a billion dollars in 1929), and the needs of her crowding industrial millions are too sharp, to permit the government to let go any commercial advantage on the mainland that would provide a substitute for emigration at home. She encourages Chinese immigration, for it means more freight for the South Manchuria Railway. This combination of political economy and strategic conditions lends high interest to the occupation of the region today by the millions pouring into it from China.

It has been urged that the Chinese may build railways too fast in Manchuria, owing to a spirit of enthusiasm. If they outrun agricultural development, rapid though it is, population will be wanting to create the supporting tonnages. It is an argument familiar to all Americans of the pioneering West: Shall the railway play pioneer and precede but entice the settler, or shall the settler be asked to take the risk of pioneering ahead of the railway? Judgment and opportunism and the strategy of the "higher command" in government or railway building will make the decision, and no small part will be played by the get-rich-quick real estate promoter, as active in Manchuria and Mongolia as he was once in Montana and Oregon and Kansas. How the thing works in the pioneering country of eastern Asia is well described in the China Year Book:

"The procedure usually followed is that the heads of government buy up large tracts of land in the sections in which they plan to build railways, and it is common to have the railway avoid the towns by several miles so as to force purchase of the lands lying between the towns and the railway lands, such lands having, of course, first been bought up by the authorities interested. By such means it is possible to gain large sums very rapidly, but the enthusiasm which the discovery of this new, and heretofore overlooked source of quick riches has begotten seems likely to lead to construction far more rapid and extensive than development is able to follow. Furthermore, one may also observe a tendency on the part of the management of new lines to try to make money too quickly by making freight rates considerably higher than the traffic can reasonably bear, causing the thrifty settler to revert to his old resource of transporting his goods by cart, and as a matter of fact, cart traffic may in Manchuria be operated so cheaply that in a number of instances it may be seen competing quite successfully along roads parallel with railways. This phenomenon has been witnessed along the C.E.R. line between Harbin and Changchun."[22]

Once arrived at his place of settlement or employment by a pioneer farmer, what prospect has he? How does he dig in? We have a recent account from a Chinese student, Tsao Lien-en:

"The migrant farmers on arriving in Manchuria are generally poor with a little belongings consisting of bedding and some clothes wrapped up in bundles which are carried on their backs. They have no cattle, no houses and no agricultural implements. . . . Some farmers come with small sums of money, but these are not enough

[22] The China Year Book, 1929–1930, p. 354.

to open unreclaimed lands. The crop season in Manchuria lasts from April to November, and during this short space of six months the hardy, industrious farmers build in the wild Manchurian plain a home, and make the wilderness productive of many cereals. . . . . When the fields are ploughed, and the seeds are sown, the farmers stay at home for four months to come out again in the autumn to reap the harvests, without taking extra care on the fields such as irrigating the farms or stripping off the weeds. . . . After the harvest season, which comes during the end of October and the beginning of November, the migrant farmers either return to their homes in Shantung or Chihli or settle down in Manchuria for some other work. The bitter Manchurian winter sets in in November, when a heavy cloak of white snow mantles all the farmyards, and all agricultural activities come to a halt. In winter some farmers are hired by timber contractors to fell trees in the timber concessions." [23]

"Land-hungry" is the term applied to the settlers of northern Manchuria. [24] The effect upon the individual who enters such a land is curiously at variance with general economic conditions. Pushing out the frontier in a given country tends to raise the standard of living on the spot only if the food supply of the migrant is the primary desideratum. This is China's case. A Chinese migrant is always a hungry person. You may depend upon that. In Manchuria his welfare depends little upon tillage and production elsewhere, because *his* land is new and fertile and he got it cheaply. In addition, a world market has been created for one of his special products, the soy bean.

Or take the common farm laborer. His day's wage may be ten times greater than it was in his home province in the south. The pioneer farmer lacks "hands," and he risks the loss of his labor through the attractive wages paid by technical enterprises connected with road and railway building, ports, factories, mines, and many other industrial enterprises now being supported by Chinese capital. These are the marks of a self-sustaining state rather than a dependency or a colony. The development of the rich resources available for agriculture, cattle raising, forest exploitation, and mining mean a higher standard of living. They mean also an advanced unit of China.

[23] Tsao Lien-en: The Method of Chinese Colonization in Manchuria, *Chinese Econ. Journ.*, Vol. 7, No. 2, August, 1930, pp. 831–852; reference on pp. 832–833.
[24] Hans Maier: Die Nordmandschurei als Kolonial- und Wirtschaftsgebiet, in "Koloniale Studien: Hans Meyer Festschrift," Berlin, 1928, pp. 253–271.

How will this advanced unit be regarded by Japan and Russia? Certainly neither will diminish its effort to keep its hold on trade. As a place of settlement for the Japanese, Manchuria has been proved impossible. There are not more than a quarter of a million Japanese in the province and they are town dwellers—artisans, merchants, engineers, railway and government officials. Japan has learned that "economic colonization" is a substitute for folk movement. She can make her yen migrate to Manchuria, and she can keep all her "rights" and ceaselessly guard against every form of encroachment upon them. She is the principal buyer in the Manchurian market, the exports to Japan having exceeded those to China since 1899.[25]

[25] *Ibid.*, p. 258.

CHAPTER FOURTEEN

SOUTH AMERICAN HINTERLANDS

Nothing is wanting . . . but a settlement here, and orders what to perform.
—CHRISTOPHER COLUMBUS, *Journal*

THE first burst of settlement into South America was one of the most extraordinary human events this earth has ever witnessed. It carried pioneers into places so remote that the closer settlements of today have not yet caught up with them. It carried European seeds and livestock everywhere. In a number of cases the first explorer of record, outrun by the native trader, found the people of a newly "discovered" region already in possession of European manufactured articles of light varieties. Only a self-contained manner of living with a minimum of imported wares made such wide deployment possible; and only by the use of cheap native labor did the white population create an endurable standard of living. As time went on, there came into existence two types of culture areas, the one near the sea or a railway or navigable stream by which the burden of transport was made light; the other in the back country, the remoter valleys, and the banks of distant streams. The latter type of settlement never lost the mark and the habit of pioneering. It also never lost its dependence upon cheap or free labor and cheap land. How this came about is not merely an interesting chapter in the history of Hispanic civilization; it is one of the basic conditions of the economic revolution that is running its course in South America today.

In the first place, government aided the planter in a distant valley by making the ownership of property in land the privilege of the whites. In the second place, local as well as national laws were enforced by the authorities on the spot pretty much as they pleased. It could not be otherwise in a country where the absence of all but a few roads and trails made the operations of even a small military expedition extremely arduous. While there are brilliant exceptions, both Spanish and Portuguese have a weak conception of efficiency in management. They are a negligent people. Personal feelings play a livelier and a more determining part than we can possibly conceive. That which is customary has the force of law, as one may test almost anywhere by appropriating the

principle and standing upon "the custom of the country." En-
croachments upon the rights of the Indian holders of the soil could
be made, under these conditions, with an impunity that shocks
every sense of justice. Thus we have the spectacle of the Indians
of Bolivia in some instances having to buy from avaricious whites
land held by Indians from time immemorial. Some tracts were
bought back several times over. Other tracts were bought by whites
with the stipulation that the Indian holders should be exempt
from certain taxes which under a later régime were again unjustly
levied. For protection against encroachment there have been cases
of a trusted Bolivian invited to become the patron of an entire
Indian group. To turn their lands over to him and become virtually
his serfs was preferable to an uncertain fate as nominal landowners.[1]

The peonage system, so widely practiced today in the Amazon
country, is nothing more or less than slavery of varying degrees
of hardship or mildness according to the instincts of the landowner
and the relative weakness of government authority. It is distinctly
a feature of the *interior* of South America. It means that the
landowner who has title to the soil enjoys also the right to the
part-time labor of the Indians who live upon his land, even though
the Indians have always lived there and regard the land as their
own. In some places where the community type of landholding
still persists among the natives there is a yearly allotment of community land among them by their own elders. In other places
the governor makes the allotment, a scene of extraordinary intensity
of interest to the participants, as I witnessed it at Anta, north of
Cuzco, in 1911. Intense, because upon the word of the governor
hung the welfare of the individual for another twelvemonth, the
land being of uneven quality. Besides his assignments of grazing
and arable lands the Indian may have the exclusive use of a plot
of ground, with possibly a garden and a corral, upon which his
hut stands. This focus of his life he regards as his own, and in
many instances it has come down to him from distant generations.
Yet he is not free, having to pay taxes or supply free labor, or both,
to the titular white or mestizo owner of the large estate on which
he and the fellow members of his community live. Local revolutions have again and again followed upon the attempt on the
part of the landowners to take more of the Indian lands than they

[1] G. M. McBride: Agrarian Indian Communities of Highland Bolivia, *Amer. Geogr. Soc.
Research Ser. No. 5*, 1921, pp. 10 and 17.

FIG. 214—San Martín de los Andes, Province of Neuquen, northern Patagonia. View from the hills overlooking the town, looking southwest toward the little bay of the eastern end of Lago Locar. (Bailey Willis: Northern Patagonia, New York, 1914. Photograph supplied by Ministerio de Obras Públicas, Buenos Aires.)

were entitled to or to remove Indian huts and corrals from their accustomed sites. Peru and Bolivia are among the countries that have witnessed the flowering of the system.

Thus, by the device of a privileged class, the plantation system of agriculture has survived even at great distances from the streams, from the markets of earlier times, and from the railways of today. The system has even supplied the planter with a better frontier life than he could possibly expect elsewhere, though as a rule what he gains in freedom and power he loses in comfort and social contacts. The plantation system has enabled him to use the most distant lands, and it has provided the government with larger and larger acreages of taxable property. In return for mineral or rubber concessions the government has often demanded a road and bridges and agreements to keep them in repair, each new highway or trail making possible the further exploitation of the soil in still more remote places or along the right of way. And so through the centuries a pioneer fringe has been maintained in sections of the interior of South America that could never have been settled at all under conditions of free labor and common rights in land.

The agricultural frontier of Brazil has been carried far into the wilderness by negroes and Indians, and by mestizos as well. Freemen and fugitives (both criminal and political) still form, as they have always formed, a thin fringe of populated land "beyond the habitual reach of the law" in the back country of every agricultural community. Though calling themselves settlers they are really squatters with shifting agriculture as their mode of life. The shift takes place naturally or through the compulsion of the man who has title to the land and who only awaits the creation of capital values to assert his ultimate rights. Some of the more restless settlers move on to new locations, others accept more or less willingly a feudal relation set up by the owner. The law of Brazil protects the squatter in the enjoyment of the buildings and crops that he has created, and he can no longer be driven from the land without remuneration. The frontier plantation, remote and feudal, can also be a means of protection to a serf. The lawless owner may himself represent the law to the ruder societies or individuals about him.

The background of the pioneer is an important part of his equipment. From what social and economic systems came the South American who now lives on the fringe of settlement? I have found throughout South America the definite assumption that aristocracy (and in most countries the church also) is a rational if not a necessary creation. In precisely its historical forms the aristocratic point of view was advocated in Spain down to the revolution of 1931. Church and State for centuries consolidated their power in the long struggle with the Moor. Soon after the closing of that chapter the exploitation of the New World came into full swing. The knightly cavalier no less than the soldier of fortune of lowly birth found here the means of realizing traditional cultural ideals which included, on the emotional side, religion and war. It happened that where there was gold and silver there was also an organized agricultural folk that was tied to the soil and had no place of refuge, no forests in which to hide, no untamed open plains. The conquerors became the overlords, that is, the aristocrats of New World society. They fastened themselves upon the native system, adapted or overturned it, and, working together closely, priest and cavalier became the cornerstones of a new order.

How natural in the distribution of rewards for this great conquest that large concessions should be made in lands so new and wide, to men so few! All the Spaniards could be lords or *caballeros* God had fixed a great gulf between the conqueror and the conquered of dark skins. Concessions and grants could be made generously. For every man there was, in a sense, a principality. Here went on with redoubled enthusiasm the contest between heathen and Christian. Here was war and Christianization, service to the church, and all of the spirited repetitions that appealed to the Spaniard as a reliving of the life of the heroic period.

With the land went the people upon it, including the right to their service upon the plantations, the right to expel them from the best soils on irrigable terraces and bottom lands. When the wars of liberation came, over a hundred years ago, they were directed against the representatives of the Crown who, among other shortcomings, sought to maintain strict social distinctions in a land where two and a half centuries had at least thrown a bridge across the gulf that once separated white and native. The mixture of blood had gone too far to enable the classes to remain rigorously apart. In addition, trade restrictions in South America worked hardships even greater than those imposed upon the American colonies. Thus a system admirably adapted to maintain that solidarity through which alone a handful of men was able to overrun a vast territory, at last became too rigid for the masses.

Helped by their geographical situation, their wide distribution over a difficult terrain, they were able to gain political freedom; but their culture could not be changed so easily. The plantation system persisted, the church maintained its sway. The forms of democracy were written into constitutions patterned after that of the United States, but the actualities of government closely resemble those seen in a land of privileged aristocracy. Said one of the Peruvian prefects after the revolution of 1911, when I asked him about national politics, "This telegraph key and that file of soldiers— they are the government of Peru."

Physical environment played a great part in this persistence of traits and institutions. A people is generally more flexible in its habits of thought in a new environment. Why has Hispanic America been the great exception? Wherever irrigation could be practiced the immemorial union was made between capital and labor, as in all societies that have developed in arid lands. In fact, irrigation without coöperation is unthinkable. It may be an enforced coöperation without other social or economic corollaries, but coöperation it must be since the control of water is the essence of life. Government in arid regions is built around that fact. This was true in places as far apart as Assyria and the Inca realm, just as it is true of Egypt today, and of central-northern Chile or Peru. The wide extent of land on which the regulated use of water controls cultivation is an outstanding feature of Hispanic America. Equally important is the organization of a plantation, with specialized production, export, and transportation. The whole thing depends upon coöperation, with brains at the top and much rough and heavy labor at the bottom. Moreover, to produce, transport, and sell requires that machines and facilities come into being. This involves capital, and capital in a new country is extremely hard to obtain. It is in the hands of a much smaller class than is the case in a long-established society.

The second half of the nineteenth century, the period in which most of the railroads were built, witnessed, curiously enough, a drawing-in of the limits of settlement in many remarkable instances, as men became tied to the new economic system of which the railroad was the symbol and in which *time* came to be more and more important. The speed of transportation now became a vital part of the process of moving goods and men. How different the colonial period! Even today the hacienda system makes possible the occupation of farm land far, far beyond the strict economic limits set by civilization in the United States. The United States has no class upon whose shoulders can be dropped so heavy a load as that which is dropped by the South American upon the lowest ranks of his society. He is intent upon maintaining the privileges and luxuries of a class: all is well if these privileges and luxuries are being enjoyed; all is wrong if they are taken away, no matter what the reason may be. In unbroken sequence the concepts that so long ruled Iberian life may be traced through the colonial period and the period of liberation in South America down to our own time.

In both the forest and the desert environment the hacienda works because it maintains those accustomed social and political forms that came into being more than a millennium ago and that by an extraordinary set of circumstances have been able to continue in the New World, as well as in the old, because they express certain basic human qualities—love of power, love of privilege, pride of caste, sheer human vanity, and that desire for gain which supports all the others.

What a different story might be told if the New World had been uninhabited and there had been no comparatively dense populations to exploit! But there stood the native, his strongest units living in the midst of an environment in which irrigation and organized coöperative living had been practiced as in the land of the Spanish conquerors. These circumstances made it easy to continue the traditions of the conquering race.

The farm or homestead system familiar to us is not without fitness for certain geographical situations. Southern Brazil, in so far as it is peopled by Germans, has a farm system because the settlers brought with them workable ideas of landownership and farming practices.[2] Farther north is São Paulo, where a single crop (coffee) requires a large labor supply in a short period of time, and here the small farm has no place. The production of sugar likewise requires operations on an extended scale, a substantial

[2] A description of the colonization of southern Brazil is not included here because it has largely run its course. Its history provides many illustrations of the difficulties of European pioneering in South America, not only at the beginnings of occupation but subsequently when the second generation had to take account of nationality in a country of different race. The matter may be pursued by the reader in three publications by Mark Jefferson: Peopling the Argentine Pampa, *Amer. Geogr. Soc. Research Ser. No. 16*, New York, 1926; Recent Colonization in Chile, *Amer. Geogr. Soc. Research Ser. No. 6*, New York, 1921; Pictures from Southern Brazil, *Geogr. Rev.*, Vol. 16, 1926, pp. 521–547. See also Jefferson: An American Colony in Brazil, *Geogr. Rev.*, Vol. 18, 1928, pp. 226–231. There is an extensive bibliography in German. Among recent items may be mentioned C. G. Cornelius: Die Deutschen im brasilianischen Wirtschaftsleben, Stuttgart, 1929; and Hundert Jahre Deutschtum in Rio Grande do Sul (1824–1924), Porto Alegre, 1924.

machine plant, and related works such as dams and irrigation canals if artificial watering is needed, as it is in many parts of Bolivia and Peru. A fifteen-acre plot provides the merest subsistence, while a one-hundred-acre or two-hundred-acre plot is a profitable economic unit.

The plantation system in South America persists in some places because it is economically best for all concerned, while in other places it is a device employed by the landowners for maintaining an essentially aristocratic system based upon land. Far and away the best case in point is Argentina, the best because it is a cereal-growing country, not one that specializes in tropical products. That it is an outgrown system is shown by the present efforts to avoid a cataclysm like that which came to Mexico before the land-tenure laws could be revised. Large landholdings became the rule when Argentina was primarily a pastoral country; they have persisted through the change into a cereal-growing system in which pastoral interests still bulk large. The large landowner really doesn't want to give the small landowner a chance. He wants to maintain his system as he found it. As Mark Jefferson[3] has put it, "Agriculture has here become the handmaid of stock raising." He finds that fully one-half the grain exported from the republic is an incident to cattle raising. Seeing that his once cheap (and in places worthless) land has increased in value and made a fortune for him, the owner has made up his mind not to part with any more of it. Says Jefferson, "He could get a lot of money for his land if he sold it, but what should he do with the money? . . . He might lose it; and wasn't the value of the land increasing every day? Better keep the land and let the gringo [foreigner, i. e. European immigrant] go on working for him."

Coupled with this state of things is the feeling that only members of the upper class are intelligent and responsible. In their view they own the land and govern the community in quite a proper sense. The peon has a station in life akin to that of the peasant in Europe, and the educated Argentine knows the culture and economic systems of Europe better by far than he knows the development of the really democratic systems of the New World that he thinks himself a part of. Little wonder, under such a system, that not all the good tillable land is by any means yet occupied. To the untilled acres must be added the economic loss sustained by a

[3] Mark Jefferson: Peopling the Argentine Pampa, *Amer. Geogr. Soc. Research Ser. No. 16*, New York, 1926, pp. 168–169.

Fig. 215—Access to railways in South America.   Cities of over 250,000 population are shown.

superficial cropping of the land. Thus the peopling of the Argentine pampa by small farmer-owners "that began so gallantly in the fifties . . . has practically come to an end" (Jefferson, in reference to the Esperanza district).

One of the most extraordinary features of South American life is the persistence of frontier conditions through the centuries since the Conquest. In spite of its phenomenal material prosperity it is still a continent of pioneer fringes. The tourist whose primary interest may be in cities or who spends a day or two in the tropical forest or travels only by rail will come back with the impression that the continent is making great strides and has "come of age." The spots he has visited are all he believes them to be, but he would see more deeply if he looked at the continent as a whole and particularly at the railways.

Those portions of South America that are more than twenty miles from the railway are shown in Figure 215. *All* the known railway lines are taken into account, not simply the principal ones. The surprising fact appears that, in proportion to the spread and number of the population, South America has the fewest railways among all the continents. The pampa of Argentina has a close network of railroads; and within a given area all the land is occupied by farmers and served by steam. There is another close network of rails that includes the coffee country of São Paulo and the region about Rio. Chile has her longitudinal line, but a *network* exists only in a few places, as in the nitrate country and the small central valley. Outside of the three regions just cited (in Chile, Argentina, and Brazil) there are only short lines running inland from coastal ports and serving individual valleys. Less than a fifth of the continent lies within twenty miles of a railway.

One may see what that means by turning to an American example. The best one is the Kansas City Southern, noted on page 70. It was there found, in the pre-motor era, that by far the greater part of the freight originated in a belt not more than five miles wide on each side of the railway. When a country fills up with people the spaces between the railways grow smaller as new lines are built between those first established, until the market haul is *reduced to an effective economic limit*. In South America the lack of railways has been offset in part by the wide use of "the flowing roads," the rivers. But the mere existence of a stream is not a guarantee of economical transport. On most of the South American rivers the means of transport are highly inefficient. Small boats with irregular sailings, or no fixed dates at all, are the rule in spite of a few excellent lines that provide real service.

We now see why frontier conditions have been maintained for so long a time in South America. The United States frontier of settlement, as officially recognized, was a line marking the outer border of country with a population density of two or more to the square mile. It began to be a broken and wavering belt by 1890,

Fig. 216—Grassy plateaus of Rio Grande do Sul, Brazil. (Mark Jefferson: Pictures from Southern Brazil, *Geogr. Rev.*, Vol. 16, 1926.)

though locally pioneer conditions have lasted down to the present.[4] The frontier type of life still persists in the interior of the United States. It represents the last stage in the advancement of agriculture into the dry-farming country of the western plains and remoter basins. Little good arable land has been left unoccupied. By contrast, Brazilian folk have barely reached the interior. With local exceptions Brazil, with over forty millions of population, is a fringe of civilization along the coast. This is due partly to the long resistance of the wild Indian, which still limits white penetration on a wide front. A second reason: the rainfall of the interior of Brazil comes mainly in a single season that is followed by drought, an alternation of extremes that renders the water supply for stock undependable and that reduces transport to primitive means. The greater part of the coastal plateau has a dense tropical forest on its seaward fringe. Only in southern Brazil is this wooded fringe really narrow, and here settlement has sought out the treeless plateau with gentle slopes and grassy cover: such is the interior of Rio Grande do Sul and Santa Catharina. The pioneer

[4] See chapter eight for a description of frontier communities in the United States today.

of North America has had no tropical forest to overcome; in a relative sense the Indian problem was soon settled. In addition, the frontier in North America had a climate suitable to cheap cereal production at a time when manufacturing Europe needed an oversea food supply for increasing numbers of city workmen. The last of the unsettled West was, as commonly expressed, treeless "prairie waiting for the plow"; and its soils are of extraordinary fertility. Every undeveloped grassland in South America has a special handicap not matched in North America.

The frontier stamp may be kept even by a large and growing town. There is a notable list of colorful towns of the frontier type in South America. Copiapó, in Chile, has kept its frontier quality to a degree not matched by the towns of North America, at least outside Mexico. The city of Copiapó attracted trade along the main north-south valley of Chile (Fig. 218). The mountain trails, running beside the converging tributaries of the Copiapó River, focus here. The town is a natural center of gravity for trade from the coast to inland points. In the earliest days it was an outpost of the conquering Inca rulers and for a time the southernmost outpost of the *conquistadores*. When the nitrate fields were opened rapidly in the last quarter of the nineteenth century, Copiapó was Chile's frontier town on the north. Its copper deposits, for a time the richest known, led to its development as one of the most advanced places in Chile. Here was the first opera house in Chile and the first railway, and here were schools and an organized social life. But with changing fortunes in mines, railways, and settlements Copiapó had to find a new orientation. Through it all, its trails kept their fame and their activity. North, south, east, and west the pack trains went to the dependent settlements and mines. Always there was a cattle business with the Argentine, for thus was imported meat for the workers in the copper mines and, later, the nitrate fields. Trails and pack trains, the professional *arriero* (muleteer), the saddlery, and the blacksmith shop—these are the unchanging elements of the frontier towns of South America. Try to get off the beaten track and you find that the pack train, the canoe, and the launch are almost the only means available in spite of stories of wide conquests by the cheap motor car.

Copiapó is indeed among the more fortunate towns of South America, for at least it has its railway. One can well imagine how unchanged is a town far from the railway and how like its early pioneer days it has remained. Several hundred miles north of Copiapó is the desert town of San Pedro de Atacama, now reached by a motor road (Fig. 234). Its service to tributary small towns has been little modified. It is one of the oldest settlements in South America. Through it has trickled a commerce between mountain and town. From their valley homes and upland pastures the shepherds come for their supplies of *chuño* (dried potatoes), chañar (nut-like seed pod with edible mealy interior), dried fruit, wheat, and flour. Their woolen ropes, besides the wool of sheep, llama, and alpaca, are given in return. Once the capital of a province, San Pedro de Atacama has been left in an eddy. The Antofagasta and Bolivia railroad to the north, the nitrate business nearer the coast, and the development of coastwise shipping have withdrawn earlier commercial advantages and left it an isolated tributary town with fixed frontier qualities.

THE SOUTHERN FRONTIER IN CHILE

Few of the countries of Hispanic America have had the system of large landholdings, or *latifundia*, so firmly established as Chile. In the province of Santiago, where the land has been highly developed, 51 family properties occupied three-quarters of the total area included in rural holdings in 1925. In the whole of Chile 2576 large owners held 20,300,000 hectares out of a total of 25,600,000 hectares in all rural properties. Most of the small farms are diminutive in size. For example, in Valparaiso 1517 rural properties embraced a total of but 2024 hectares.[5]

One might suppose that there would be harsh effects under such a system. The government has always been one of farm owners: "She has never had a president, I think, who did not have a farm and spend a part of his time on it. Her congress is made up chiefly of rich landlords. Social life is dominated by families whose proudest possession is an ancestral estate. All the élite have rural properties."[6] This means that the social and economic life as well as the political life of the country has been dominated by the *hacendado*. The land looks empty, says Jefferson, because the

---

[5] These figures are quoted by George M. McBride: The Agrarian Problem in Chile, *Geogr. Rev.*, Vol. 20, 1930, pp. 574–586, who has gathered them from *Anuario Estadíst. de la República de Chile*, Vol. 7, Agricultura, 1925–1926. It is also upon McBride that I have depended for most of the data on Chile, supplementing it with information gathered by Mark Jefferson: Recent Colonization in Chile, *Amer. Geogr. Soc. Research Ser. No. 6*, New York, 1921; and The Rainfall of Chile, *Amer. Geogr. Soc. Research Ser. No. 7*, New York, 1921. Besides many other minor sources, I have consulted A. R. Gonzalez: What the Ministry for Southern Territories Is Doing, *Chile: A Monthly Survey of Chilean Affairs*, March, 1930, pp. 104–107.

[6] McBride, *op. cit.*, p. 574.

country is held in large estates; and he describes the laborer, or
roto, as "landless, ignorant, wretched, and almost without hope."
But McBride sees in the tenant class a people not brought to a
state of abject poverty, as in Mexico, and a laboring class not
reduced to "abject servility" as in Peru.   He regards the rule
of the *hacendado* as a benevolent one in general and thinks the

FIG. 217—Cultivated lands bordering upon Lake Llanquihue where half a century ago was
dense forest.   (W. E. Rudolph: The New Territorial Divisions of Chile with Special Reference
to Chiloé, *Geogr. Rev.*, Vol. 19, 1929.)

patriarchal relation of rural employer and employee rather satis-
factory.   This means a certain acceptance on the part of the lower
of the two main classes of society of its status in the existing scheme
of things.   It also means that intensive agriculture has had its
development delayed and that the greater number of the Chilean
people have had no participation in government.   It means further
that fully half of the population is without property "and the
stimulus that is born of proprietorship."

Chile has been able to find room for her people, although it is
a land so narrow that any part of it may be crossed in an hour by
airplane from east to west and the northern portion is a desert
with capacity for but a limited population dependent upon local
water supplies and the development of the nitrate deposits.   The
southern part of the country is equally inhospitable owing to
excessive rainfall and a heavy growth of forest.   Only the restricted
central part of Chile is broadly favorable to agriculture.   Even
there the amount of land under cultivation is surprisingly small:
in Santiago province, 8 per cent of the surface; in Colchagua,
11 per cent; in Talca, 8 per cent; in Aconcagua, 4 per cent.[7]

[7] Official statistics for 1925, quoted by McBride, *op. cit.*, p. 576.

It has been fortunate for Chile that her population has not increased rapidly, that irrigation developments have gradually added new and very productive areas, and that the development of the nitrate fields on the north to supply a world demand has offered outlets for population that have had a stabilizing effect upon Chilean society. Now that the point of saturation of population density has been approached, government has concerned itself more and more with the development of industries, partly as an outlet for population, partly to become more nearly self-contained. Social legislation of an advanced character has been enacted, and the development of an agrarian program of wide scope has begun. One of the items in the program is the colonization of the remaining public lands.

Chile's most promising frontier is in the south. Exploration and mapping of the better sections are in progress as far south as the Strait of Magellan. Upon the grasslands of the extreme south a new type of property is being formed, the cattleman's homestead, a tract 1235 acres in extent being considered necessary for subsistence. Instead of granting leases to large companies, as in the past, the state is now renting or selling in small blocks directly to settlers. This is in the small Chilean section of Patagonia. Farther north colonization is most active in the "Frontera" (Fig. 218), and even the unoccupied sections of the Island of Chiloé are not overlooked despite the obstacle of dense timber and bamboo.

Hitherto the settlements of the southern provinces have been almost completely isolated during the rainy season. Jefferson, who visited the country in 1918, wrote that "in winter no through ticket can be bought from Santiago to points south of Valdivia. While wood is the main material for building, it is gradually being replaced in the more pretentious buildings at Puerto Montt and Valdivia by corrugated iron, as alone able to withstand the violence of the rain for any length of time."[8] In 1903 the Frontera was still almost uninterrupted forest, with few inhabitants other than Indians. Now large parts of it are cleared, fenced, and cultivated. The Indian is no longer in evidence in native dress. It is remindful of the transformation of eastern Oklahoma after its opening to white settlement. The signs of new settlement include the squatter, who, after he has actually occupied his land for a period of ten years and made reasonable improvements upon it, may secure title.

[8] Mark Jefferson: Recent Colonization in Chile, *Amer. Geogr. Soc. Research Ser. No. 6*, New York, 1921, pp. 16–17.

Seeing that 47,000 properties have their titles still in doubt, the heroic proportions of the job of straightening them out may be appreciated. To effect this a new ministry, the "Propiedad Austral" has been created.

We are witnessing today in the Frontera the last successful large-scale occupation of new land in Chile. It is the last chapter in a series that have been written around the colonization laws that date from 1868 down to the present time. The patronage of the government has been extended to new settlers who in past years have included both Chileans and Germans. Government even went so far as to forgive "obligations that turned out to be unreasonable." But the government never showed the same consideration to Chileans as it did to foreigners. The Frontera towns have been foreign in composition.

No one has yet calculated the extent of the pioneer zone of southern Chile, and no one can calculate it until the surveys now under way have been completed. The rainfall (Fig. 218) has increasing intensity toward the south. "For 900 miles the woods are so wet that it is impossible to set a fire for clearing without constant relighting, even when all the people of the countryside turn out to attempt it. In the southernmost islands the attempt would be quite hopeless."[9] No one knows the wettest places in Chile, for the rain gauge has not been established in the wettest districts in the mountains. Valdivia has 100 inches, and Casapangue has 160 inches; Reñihue has 200 inches.

[9] Mark Jefferson: The Rainfall of Chile, *Amer. Geogr. Soc. Research Ser. No. 7*, New York, 1921, p. 1.

FIG. 218—Rainfall map of Chile showing one of the limiting conditions of Chilean agriculture. Based on W. Knoche, *Zeitschr. Gesell. für Erdkunde zu Berlin*, 1929. For a corresponding map of Argentina see Figure 239.

Where the line of settlement ends will depend upon the value of the products that the settler can get from the soil and upon the limits of human tolerability with respect to rain and its consequences in muddy roads and shortened seasons of labor. The experience of hardy settlers on many frontiers shows that the limits of tolerability cannot be forecast. The Frontera is therefore a region of experimentation in a broad sense. Trees have to be felled, rain endured, and poor communications as well, and specialized production practiced. The environment is new and strange to the colonizing Chilean; and it can hardly appear as the best of earth to the German or French or Swiss immigrant. Government will improve some of the conditions, no doubt, as it has done in the past.[10]

Eastern Andean Valleys:[11] Valleys and Basins of Eastern Peru

To ride down from the cold uplands to the warm valleys of eastern Peru seems like entering paradise. If it were not for limited social contacts, the absence of medical skill, and the cruelly long haul to the plateau market towns, it would be the scene of a rush of settlement instead of a land where the pioneer creeps forward slowly. Each hacienda is a social oasis, as it is often a geographical oasis. Here are self-contained communities in all but the trade of specialized products that are exchanged for the products of the towns; and what the towns supply depends upon the size of the community—the larger places take a greater variety of wares. The tastes and wealth of the owner and the distance to market are other governing conditions of trade.

The ample layout of a South American hacienda, viewed from an artistic standpoint, is wholly suited to the large scale of the surrounding landscape in the mountainous sections of the continent. Whether it lies on the floor of a mile-deep canyon or in a broader valley carved out of softer rock, or spreads its acres over the radiating alluvial fans at the mouth of a tributary stream, its elements form a perfect composition. Gardens and fields in lighter and darker greens form a pleasing contrast to the untamed land all about, the scrub or *monte* (woodland) of the drier valley pockets (Figs. 220 and 238).

[10] For reference to the Chilean portion of the Patagonian region see page 345.

[11] The type of country described under Eastern Andean Valleys runs northward from western Argentina to the Caribbean in Colombia and Venezuela. Figure 38, page 50. To avoid the repetition of details I have confined the text mainly to examples in Peru and Ecuador.

The life of the eastern border haciendas is not without pleasures for those in control. The young people ride to neighboring haciendas on special social occasions; there are hunting parties now and then; the weeks and months spent in the nearest large town mean a round of pleasures which are the more enjoyed because of the long isolation. The planter himself is a sort of patriarch, guardian of the morals and peace of the community, a man who is ready enough

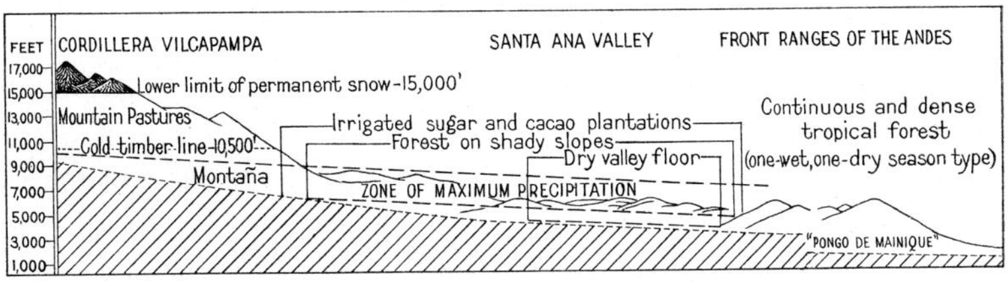

FIG. 219—Climatic cross section from the crest of the Cordillera Vilcapampa down the eastern mountain valleys of Peru to the tropical plains.

to use the instruments of the law if these are available and properly subservient to him; otherwise he will create his own instruments on the spot, sure of himself because of his economic and political power. The family includes many relatives of various degrees of kinship, and there is a division of labor that more or less closely corresponds to the dignity of place within the family. Everyone has his definite tasks, and the white population is as busy as the peon class. The spacious patio, the long low buildings, the gardens round about, and the regularity and order of the cultivated fields make an unforgettable picture of apparent prosperity and comfort.

The trend of tropical agriculture in these distant frontier haciendas would normally be toward a varied production which would make better economic use of the scanty labor supply. But distance and the pack-train mode of transportation lay heavy servitudes upon the border planter, and he must turn to the best means at hand. Only by importing labor can he manage to survive. He must have an agent in the towns of the plateau to gather men and send them down on a contract basis. For the rest he depends upon the scattered labor native to the hacienda itself.

The planter depends largely upon brandy production. His product has an evil effect upon the Indian population and benefits only the few whites that make up the management. Practically all of the brandy manufactured in the eastern valleys of Peru is consumed in the country. What the valley populations do not take is sent to the plateau, where it is the chief cause of vicious conduct. Though the planters, one and all, complain bitterly of the drunken habits of the laborers, they themselves put into their hands the means of debauchery. The peon is the ultimate consumer of the product that must be marketed by the planter if he is to live. Deplorable is the effect upon the greatest single asset of the country, the strong native stock too often disregarded by both planter and concessionnaire.

FIG. 220—A hacienda on a terraced alluvial fan in the Santa Ana section of the Urubamba Valley, eastern Peru.

Naturally there have been ups and downs in settlement so distant and precarious. The Spanish occupation of the eastern valleys was early and extensive, a sixteenth century wide-ranging exploitation of the land that has not been surpassed since that day. The later eighteenth and early nineteenth centuries saw a quite general retreat of the border of civilization. Native "rebellions" have been frequent throughout the history of the eastern valleys, too remote to be well protected.

The eastern fringe of the Andes all the way from Colombia to northeastern Argentina repeats the cultivation pattern of eastern Peru, with variations due to good forage in Bolivia (see p. 320), to flat playas in Peru with abundant water for irrigation, and to restrictions of scope in eastern Ecuador where the valley floors are narrower and the descents steeper than farther south. Cheap land is the bait that draws the planter. In those hundreds of miles of mountain border there is abundant water for irrigation, and there is a choice of altitudes to suit any desired type of production. In some places there are graded trails built at government expense, and it is possible to collect labor if there are plateau towns near. For the man with small capital and a large family, what better prospect than to settle at the margin and give his sons and daughters occupation on the land—not labor in the fields but the management of labor, thus maintaining the traditional form of aristocracy.

The eastern valleys have climates suited to every taste. The inviting hills are within reach if the lower elevations prove irksome in the hot season. There is woodland near by, and a sawmill is one of the necessities of each plantation. Below lies the forest, the home of wild Indians and of those semi-civilized tribes that are in contact with the white man rarely for more than a brief labor season, more often for trade or barter.

The hopeful spirit of the growing frontier is not infrequently in the air—the talk of lands beyond, the forecast of abounding prosperity when the railroad comes nearer or the government trail is finished to this or that point. Some of the men who make up this frontier society are among the most enterprising in the land; others sense only the slowness of heralded prosperity. The best are men of great solidity of character who manage the community, assemble machinery and labor, maintain social contacts with distant neighbors in the interest of the young people, and help sons to locate and settle the farther reaches of the valley where there are still good lands to be found cheap.

EASTERN ANDEAN VALLEYS: THE ORIENTE OF ECUADOR

In Ecuador the border valleys facing east are narrow and steep, like those that run down to the plains northeast of Cochabamba in Bolivia. Remote from the main plateau markets, such valleys have had very little development. They will remain outposts so long as there are no modern transportation facilities. The trails are still indescribably bad. There is also a deficiency of labor, which, in some places at least, causes local feuds to arise: "there being not enough Indians to go round." The existing settlements are small and far apart. The coffee, cotton, and cinnamon of the region are the chief items of export to the fatiguingly distant plateau towns.[12] The zone of potential development is limited by the steepness of the higher mountain valleys on the one side and by distance and a tropical climate on the other, with scarcity of labor and bad transport conditions straining the ingenuity and sapping

[12] Joseph H. Sinclair: In the Land of Cinnamon: A Journey in Eastern Ecuador, *Geogr. Rev.*, Vol. 19, 1929, pp. 201-217.

the strength of those outpost dwellers who have been attracted by cheap land.

Sinclair made surveys in the "Oriente" of Ecuador in 1921 and 1927, and his notes on settlement in the eastern valleys are most valuable. The whites are Spanish-speaking people from the highlands. For ninety miles along the eastern borders of the Andes there were but 600 whites, and most of these lived in the town of Macas, "distant eight days from the upland civilization by the most difficult travel on foot, in mud, and up mountainous cliffs."[13] Only a healthful climate and the great productivity of the soil tempt people to remain. There are no mosquitoes, the water supply is pure, and the mean yearly temperature probably does not exceed 72° F.

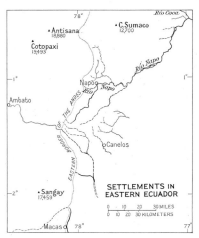

FIG. 221—The Oriente of Ecuador, showing localities mentioned in the accompanying text. Based on Sinclair and Wasson, *Geogr. Rev.*, Vol. 13, 1923.

The labor supply is gathered about white "patrons" who exercise spheres of influence among the Quechua-speaking Indians north of the Napo River. Only wild forest Indians live south of the river. Protection and supplies are the main inducements held out in exchange for work—the carrying of goods between the valleys and the highland towns.

The settlers of the Napo are described as "pioneers of a high type." They are remarkable for purity of race in a land where the white stream is much diluted. No Indians reside in the settlements of eastern Ecuador "except as servants and laborers for the white families." Otherwise the Quechua-speaking Indians live in small clearings along the streams where they raise yuca and plantain, catch fish, and pan gold. "We found the families at Napo to be remarkably intelligent, strong and healthy," says Sinclair, "but, as in the case of all pioneers, forced to depend on themselves in all emergencies. The children are educated at home, and there are no doctors or priests in the region."[14]

[13] Joseph H. Sinclair and Theron Wasson: Explorations in Eastern Ecuador, *Geogr. Rev.*, Vol. 13, 1923, pp. 190–210; reference on p. 210.
[14] *Ibid.*, p. 192.

Cattle ranches are established where grass and access to streams provide favorable sites. There are seven in the ninety-mile stretch by river between Napo and the mouth of the Coca. The cattle ranch of Umberto Garcias is seventeen miles below Napo and "consists of 290 acres of pasture land on the left bank and 125 acres on the right bank, the large ranch house having a beautiful location. . . . We were told the owner had 500 head of cattle, the market for which is far east on the Rio Aguarico, a tributary of the lower Napo."[15]

The Tropics as a Pioneer Zone

We have been viewing the border valleys of the eastern Andes. What of the pioneer zone presented by the tropical lowlands of South America? Is not the Amazon Basin itself one of the greatest seats of potential agricultural settlement? If tropical agriculture in South America is carried on under exceptionally difficult conditions of enervating climate and deficient labor supply—and the eastern valley regions of the cordillera, which has just been described, are the most favored—I think one need not regard the tropics as a pioneer land that will some day have a development akin to that of the temperate lands with which this book deals in the main. The figures of production of tropical lands are of course imposing. They show a steady commercial growth of increasing importance to us all. But the growth is in the main *commercial*, not social or political, and the manual labor is not done by whites. So long as this condition obtains, the white man will be the manager, not the settler; and that means in turn that the individual will stay for a relatively short time and then make way for another.

Tropical development of this sort means an isolated life for the manager and political problems for the government. Native labor has benefited in a rough way—greater security of life through public health measures, a greater number of things to enjoy as the white man's wares are more and more widely distributed, better housing.

The strongest argument against the tropics as homes for white men is the trend in pioneering today. Even if science should prove all sorts of good things about its ability to cure tropical diseases, or avoid them, it is still true of whites in general that they prefer a cool climate to a hot one. The agricultural folk of the

[15] *Ibid.*, p. 193.

world have grown up in modern times in the temperate zones; and this means, for the present at least, that inertia will carry them into all corners of those zones before they venture to make a grand assault upon the tropics. A certain way of living and a familiar culture system can be continued here and will fail there. *What people desire, and not merely what they can or could do, determines the trend of population.* They may even do the quite unreasonable thing and prefer it, as when the plateau Indian of Bolivia throws aside the wheelbarrow supplied him by the railroad engineer and returns to the carrying of earth in a blanket. The modern plow has often met the same fate in rivalry with the crooked stick.

Comfort is also a condition of the good life. If the heat of the sun *seems* oppressive, that is all there is about it to many men. President Lowell once asked "Who can set bounds to science?" He was referring to the future that the Amazon country might have. So thought Humboldt more than a hundred years before, when he pictured teeming cities in the abundant tropics and bridges across the Amazon. The abundance is there, and the fertility of the soil is there, and tropical medicine does advance; but comfort and human society and the accustomed way conspire to keep the tropics a world apart. *A specialized way of living cannot be a popular one.* Active pioneering by white men is still restricted almost wholly to the temperate lands or to those sub-tropical lands more favorably endowed, like the southern part of the United States or the eastern valleys of the Andes at suitable altitudes, or the cooler altitude zones of the "white man's lands" of Africa.

The Piedmont Border South of Santa Cruz

The haciendas of Santa Cruz de la Sierra (founded in 1560) at the eastern border of the mountain country of south-central Bolivia are situated 400 miles from the Upper Paraguay; and there is today only the roughest oxcart track, passable for a few months of the year, between city and river. Two months may be required for the trip from Puerto Suarez on the Paraguay to Santa Cruz, though the journey has been made in two weeks in the dry season. Westward a mule trail leads from Santa Cruz to the mountain valleys and basins, to Cochabamba, and to the lesser towns about Cliza. Until 1916 there was no railway nearer than the Oruro line, 700 miles from Santa Cruz. Rails have now crept to within 360 miles. The first section of the Cochabamba-Santa Cruz railway (to Arani) was completed in 1929. The airplane has jumped over the centuries here as in so many other isolated places in the world. The Bolivian Lloyd Airline has a service from Cochabamba to Santa Cruz and one from Santa Cruz to Puerto Suarez. But the airplane is still in the stage of preliminary exploitation. It cannot yet displace the oxcart and the pack train in the common services that are the foundation of community living.

Upon so distant a frontier it is to be expected that pioneer conditions would be continued down to our times, because the scale of production has permitted no revolutionary change in transportation which might have sent its wave of economic effect through the community. The planter has been drawn to a remote situation by the union of favorable climate and alluvial soil. As for the economics of the place, it is directly comparable to that of the Kentucky moonshiner. From cane juice the planter makes *aguardiente* (brandy), a much more valuable product than

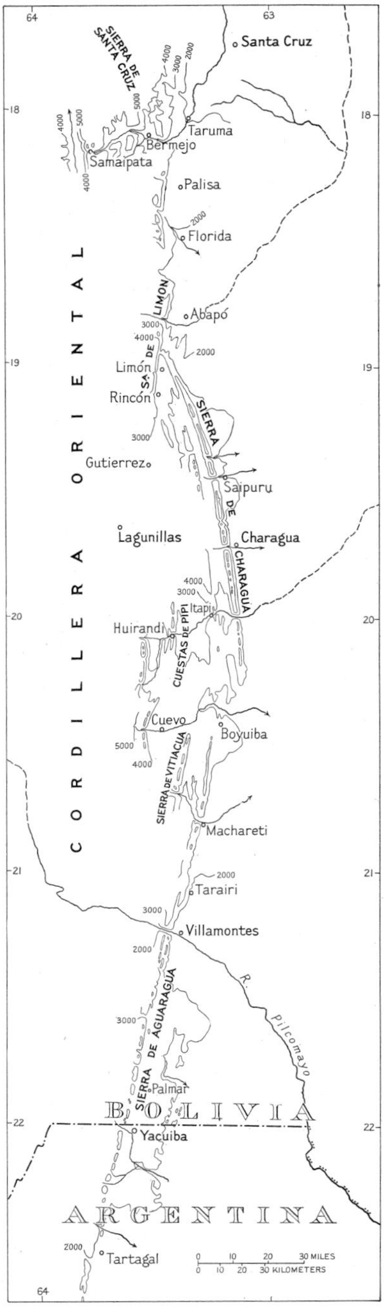

FIG. 222—The pioneer fringe along the eastern border of the Bolivian Andes from Santa Cruz de la Sierra southward to the Argentine Chaco.

sugar and one that will bear a higher rate of transportation and yield a greater net profit. If sugar can be exported, well and good; if not, it can be used to produce brandy which will support heavier transport charges. Coca leaves and cacao also reach distant markets. Both require more labor than sugar, but they are lighter in bulk and incur a smaller transportation cost in proportion to their value.

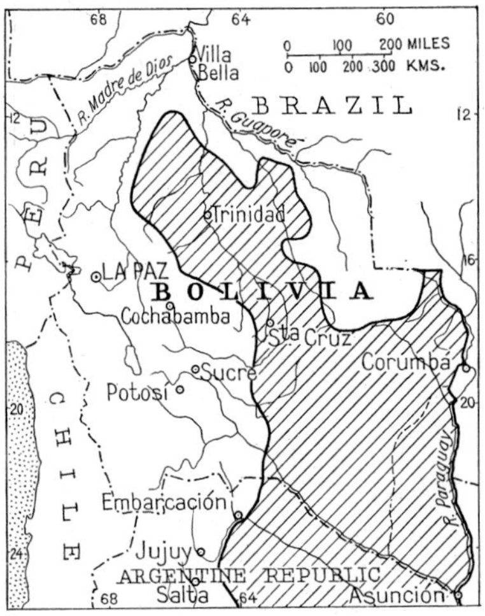

The most marked frontier conditions in south-central Bolivia are found in a belt of country that runs from the Argentine boundary northward to Santa Cruz (Fig. 222), with cattle ranches and farms developed in the most incredibly isolated and distant situations and life to a high degree self-contained except for the export of a few products such as tobacco, sugar, and rice that will stand the long haul to market through the medium of cheap labor.

FIG. 223—The shaded area of the map includes all of the potential grazing areas between the Andes of Bolivia and the Paraguay River. The northern part has much forest, and the grassy tracts are small and scattered. The southern part is grassland interrupted by "gallery forests" along the streams and about the lagoons and by a wide though broken woodland fringe along the piedmont on the west and bordering the Paraguay on the east.

"Cattle paths lead everywhere," wrote Mather[16] less than ten years ago, "and all the Indian and Bolivian settlements are connected by a network of fairly good trails. In very few localities is it necessary to spend much energy cutting paths through the jungle, as there is ordinarily plenty of open country through which the trails may easily go." He found, near the larger towns, that trails were used by two-wheeled oxcarts almost as freely as by saddle animals, unbridged arroyos and small stream courses providing obstacles that kept carts to a zone seldom more than twenty miles from a town. He noticed but a few four-wheeled wagons with metal tires and hubs but thought that better methods of transportation were gradually advancing northward from the Argentine.

[16] Kirtley F. Mather: Along the Andean Front in Southeastern Bolivia, Geogr. Rev., Vol. 12, 1922, pp. 358–374; reference on p. 371.

"For the traveler on horseback or with mule train the only difficult parts of the journey from Santa Cruz to Embarcación are the river crossings. . . . The Rio Grande and the Rio Pilcomayo, however, are seldom low enough to be forded with safety. At the more important trail crossings there are little settlements of Indians who make it their business to assist in the passage of the river. Luggage, saddles, and all equipage are ferried across in crude flat-bottomed boats which are carried a half mile or so downstream before the frantic efforts of the Indian oarsmen bring them to the farther bank. Mules, horses, and cattle are forced to swim the river . . ."[17]

Genial and well-favored, Mather terms the climate of the Andean foothills of south-central Bolivia, still in an early stage of pioneering. Southern Colorado is the nearest counterpart in the United States. The wet season lasts from November to April, and the dry season from May to October. The smaller streams disappear in the dry season, and the weather may be quite cold, ice being reported from one point only 2000 feet above sea level. The warm and the wet periods coincide.

"This is preëminently a cattle country," continues Mather. "The sparse vegetation of the lowlands resulting from the somewhat meager rainfall is nevertheless sufficient for the sustenance of vast herds of cattle . . . upon the nutritious grasslands." Cattle ranches are found all about the larger Bolivian settlements. Corn and sugar cane are cultivated at almost every center of population: "many *estancieros* have crude stills where alcohol is made from the cane syrup." Hides and alcohol are exported and cattle are driven southward to the markets of northern Argentina. "In the vicinity of Yacuiba . . . cheese is manufactured as the only nonperishable milk product suitable for export from an iceless region, into which the condensery and its tin cans have not yet come." Most of the large estates are managed by *administradors*, with little capacity for thrift or industry. The owners live in Buenos Aires or Paris. "It is quite evident that the absentee landowner system is utterly failing to make the most of the opportunities offered by this land."[18]

Mather's eye was open to the possibilities of the land, though his field studies were concentrated on oil. "The excellent kitchen gardens and vineyards maintained by the Franciscan padres

[17] *Ibid.*, p. 372.
[18] *Ibid.*, p. 374.

Fig. 224

Fig. 225

Fig. 226

Fig. 224—The Santa Cruz plains stretch monotonously southward along the eastern margin of the Andean Cordillera. (Photographs 224 and 225 by Kirtley F. Mather.)

Fig. 225—The northern end of the Limón Valley, with the Sierra de Limón in the distance.

Fig. 226—The gaucho of the Gran Chaco. The huge leather flaps (*guardamontes*) hung over the saddle are for protection against the thorny scrub that is common in the Gran Chaco.

Fig. 227

Fig. 228

Fig. 229

FIG. 227—Tree-dotted grassland of the Gran Chaco, "sufficient for the sustenance of vast herds of cattle."

FIG. 228—Farmhouse on the bank of the Paraguay River, Gran Chaco.

FIG. 229—Typical grassland, lagoon, and tree cluster composition, Gran Chaco.   (The photographs for Figures 227–229 were supplied by W. L. Schurz.)

at many of the missions" he takes as proof of the capacity to grow "a great variety of farm and garden products." "The rain-drenched mountains" have a border that supplies ideal sites for dams and reservoirs to feed the widespreading lowlands.

The backwardness of the region appears to be due not to climatic conditions but mainly to remoteness from the centers of civilization. The settlement of the land by "energetic and ambitious pioneers" is presaged by the railroad survey for the line to run from Embarcación to Santa Cruz by way of Yacuiba. The Bolivian government has opposed construction until after the completion of the projected Cochabamba-Santa Cruz Railroad "because of the fear of increasing the already close co-ordination of eastern Bolivia with Argentina before the contacts of eastern Bolivia with western Bolivia are perfected." The frontier of civilization is seen creeping northward along the mountain front; and "in the next few years one may confidently expect great changes in this pioneer land."

The government of Bolivia has been slow to attempt actual colonization of the eastern frontier regions and recently has put renewed effort into the increase of its main agricultural production in areas now under cultivation. It has granted land for colonization in the eastern piedmont and plains region and has considered schemes frequently proposed. Settlers have not been lacking, but their attempts at colonization have largely failed. Capital is required to clear the land and buy seed and implements. Tropical diseases, with which the colonists have no experience and against which no effective means of resistance are provided, and an almost complete lack of transportation facilities, have been the principal causes of failure. It is the present purpose of the government to study the eastern pioneer areas thoroughly, "so that, when the time for colonization comes, it can be accomplished without waste of life and capital; and to plan for the development of each section according to the agricultural activities best suited to it."[19]

Romecin, a Bolivian agricultural expert, believes "that colonization of the frontier when it is undertaken must be on a large scale with provision for broad communal organization if the great physical obstacles that have defeated all prior attempts are to be overcome. Meanwhile companies with large capital will be allowed to study particular areas and create settlements under scientific principles."

[19] Eduardo Romecin: Agricultural Adaptation in Bolivia, *Geogr. Rev.*, 1929, Vol. 19, pp. 248–255; reference on p. 248.

The Savanas of the Gran Chaco and Paraguay

Between the Matto Grosso of Brazil and the zone of upland farms and pastures of northwestern Argentina is a broad belt of country that includes Paraguay, the Gran Chaco of Bolivia, and

Fig. 230—Park landscape in northern Paraguay. ("Handbuch der geographischen Wissenschaft," Potsdam, 1930, Süd-Amerika, pp. 65–142. Photograph by Carnier.)

central-northern Argentina. Pioneering here goes forward in spotty fashion on a rather wide front. From the standpoint of both rainfall and temperature the region is tolerable for settlement, but it is no paradise. Insects are one of the main sources of discomfort. Paraguay has been called the garden of South America, as we should expect from nine months of high temperature and a rainfall well distributed through the year. Upon the highest of the uplands of northern Paraguay there are open savanas, extensions of the Brazilian grass and *caatinga* country, that is, grassy country with local stands of palms, cacti, and leguminous plants. The savanas are surrounded by denser masses of rain forest which grow on the adjacent heights, hence the term *campo cerrado* or "enclosed" plains, as we might describe them.

In contrast to the wide distribution of haciendas and *chacras* (farms) of earlier times, the principal zones of settlement are now

FIG. 231—Quebracho forest. ("Handbuch der geographischen Wissenschaft," Potsdam, 1930, Süd-Amerika, pp. 65–142.)

limited rather closely to the railways, the principal highways, and the streams. This gravitative pull of highways of every sort is much more marked in the modern world where transportation costs so often affect competition in distant markets. The grassy areas of Paraguay are suitable for cattle raising rather than for conquest by the plow. The forest region has its special production also, and between the two extremes of grassland and forest are produced the characteristic products of the region, the beans, rice, coffee, sugar, and bananas, while the extensive plantations of the same zone produce for export tobacco, cotton, groundnuts, and oranges.[20]

The cattle of Paraguay are a tough creole breed adapted to local conditions of high temperature and insect pests. They are not of high grade, and while their hides are exported their flesh is principally used for dried beef or *charqui* for local or at least for

[20] Franz Kühn: Die La Plata-Länder, in "Handbuch der geographischen Wissenschaft," Potsdam, 1930, Süd-Amerika, pp. 65–142.

South American distribution. Cattle ranchers are the pioneers of the grassy country on the north, their holdings running, according to the disposition of the grass, right up to the Brazilian border.

In recent years the Chaco grasslands have been developed by Paraguay. The extension of ranching interests on the west side of the Paraguay River has been one of the factors in the critical situation between Paraguay and Bolivia with respect to their common boundary. Immediately west of the Paraguay River is a zone of low-lying swampy country, and it is only beyond this and where lagoons supply permanent drinking water, that the Chaco grasslands are capable of development in the immediate future. Cattle raising and quebracho gathering go hand in hand on some of the large estates. Until a better breed of cattle is produced—and this possibility has still to be proved under prevailing climatic conditions—nothing like an intensive development of the ranching industry can take place. Nor can agriculture hope to grow in the absence of roads and railways, even if the soil were more favorable for the products suitable to the climate.

The most substantial settlements of the Chaco are in that section that constitutes central-northern Argentina. The quebracho industry, the cattle industry, and agriculture are the leading types of development. About three-fourths of the surface is covered with forest or woodland. Quebracho was the first product to draw settlement and it still leads in the list of Chaco products. Cattle raising has engaged the native and the settler on the Chaco border since the seventeenth century. When sugar and cotton drew the planter it was natural that large estates should be the rule and recent agrarian laws have sought to effect a better balance between the earlier system of *latifundia* and concessions to the favored and powerful few and the ideal of the small farmer as conceived by political leaders in recent years. The holdings of agricultural colonies now embrace about a third of the territory of the Argentine Chaco.

The social and economic life of the region is still in the experimental stage—life on the isolated *chacras* is monotonous and narrow; a series of bad crop years caused by drought, as in 1925, 1926, and 1927, spells the ruin of the man without capital reserves; and the labor difficulties of both plantation and quebracho exploitation keeps the capitalist owner in an anxious state over production costs in relation to prices in the ever uncertain world market. The work is hard and the temperatures during the cotton-growing period

excessively high. Mixed farming, rather than monoculture, would
at least provide subsistence for the small landowner and free him
from dependence upon his money crop for food supplies. Planter
and farmer have still much to learn about agricultural technique
and of adaptation to the special circumstances of a dry spring and
little winter rain. In a period of six years, one fifth of the months

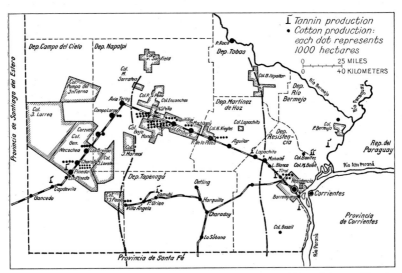

FIG. 232—A part of the Argentine Chaco bordering the Paraguay and Paraná rivers. (Theodor
Brinkmann: Ackerbau und Kolonisation im argentinischen Chaco, *Berichte über Landwirtschaft*,
Vol. 12 (N.S.), 1930.)

were dry at Resistencia, one third at Campo Largo, and one half
at Charata.[21]

The soil has received little attention from the Chaco planter.
Its adaptability to different crops, the tillage methods that will
best conserve the moisture of the wet season for the benefit of growth
in the dry season, and the balance between possible crops best
calculated to give security to living—these are still remote matters
to the farmer and planter accustomed to primitive types of cultivation and a land-culture system that has few technical studies to
guide it. The colonization pattern of one of the eastern sections
of the Argentine Chaco is shown in Figure 232, drawn from Brinkmann. This is the cotton- and quebracho-region in contrast to the
sugar and cattle belt on the western side as described on page 320.

[21] Theodor Brinkmann: Ackerbau und Kolonisation im argentinischen Chaco, *Berichte über
Landwirtschaft*, Vol. 12 (N.S.), 1930, pp. 499–540; reference on p. 503.

Matto Grosso

The Brazilian Matto Grosso, like the Gran Chaco of Bolivia and Paraguay, is destined one day to be a great cattle country. Its cheap land and extensive grassy plains will draw capital and

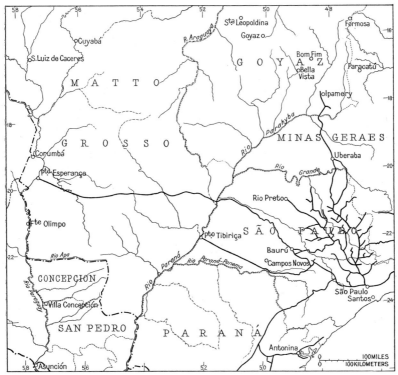

Fig. 233—Location map of the Matto Grosso region in relation to the Paraguay River and the railway net of São Paulo.

ranchmen when the rising price of hides on the shrinking grasslands of the world inspire a keener interest in the pastures that remain undeveloped. Roosevelt, in "Through the Brazilian Wilderness," describes the climate of the Plan Alto as healthful: "The country is excellently suited for settlement, and offers a remarkable field for cattle-growing." Here and there on the route leading north to San Luis de Cáceres were "little clearings with palm-thatched houses." The town of Cáceres is "on the outermost fringe of the settled region of the state of Matto Grosso." Mosquitoes were absent, the air was clear and fresh, the sky brilliant, and the nights

(January) cool and pleasant after the hot midday sun. Cattle raising on the grassy uplands and agriculture in the valleys—such was the future, as Roosevelt saw it, when it eventually should become the homeland of "a healthy, highly civilized population."

The same grassy plains extend far to the eastward—in fact, with modifications, right to the coast of Ceará (Fig. 38). But it is in western Matto Grosso that the climate is best suited to a balanced population. Farther east it becomes drier. Dyott found a great contrast between wet and dry seasons in the Plan Alto region east of Cuyabá (Fig. 233). July to September or November is the period of dryness—every stream bed a gravelly or stony band—"the entire country as dry as parchment."[22] In February, water is abundant— "every gully has an angry torrent." It could be made a great cattle country—for there is plenty of grass even in the dry season—if drinking water were provided by wells or reservoirs for the stock. Only in the low ground and along the streams are there trees, "gallery forests" as the botanists call them. Dyott describes the country between the Araguaya and the Rio Roosevelt as suitable for cattle raising, the land being at an elevation of 1500 feet, grassy, open, and healthful.

In the present state of prices and of distances to market, only the smallest use can be made of the natural pastures. Farther south and within launch navigation of Corumbá a few cattle ranches of large size have been established. Roosevelt mentions 70,000 head of stock on the ranch of the Brazil Land and Cattle Company between Corumbá and Cáceres. The small rancher has a primitive existence; profits are to be made only by large-scale operations requiring a substantial capital outlay. The company form of development is the only feasible one here when it comes to populating the region as a whole. The reason for this is the absence of a continuous belt of population connecting with southern Brazil and the coast or with the riverine ports on the lower Paraguay. The organization of transport and market supply bears a critical relation to profits. The experience of cattlemen in Australia for many years past shows how important is organization in securing the special facilities of water, transport, loading, and market deliveries at seasonable periods. Company management is like government in serving the whole interest of a region in process of development.

The grasslands of Matto Grosso are far from ideal. Parts are

22 G. M. Dyott: Man Hunting in the Jungle, Indianapolis, 1929.

afflicted with a saw-edged grass that lacerates the mouths of the cattle. The sandy soils of other parts do not hold sufficient water at economically recoverable depths. The outposts of settlement in other places are occasionally paralyzed by banditry. Until

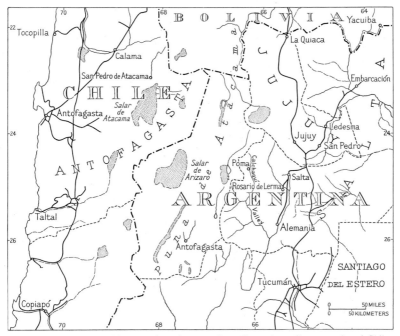

FIG. 234—Location map of a part of northwestern Argentina and an adjacent section of Chile.

railroads, local constabulary, and an effective population density are assured, the grasslands will be the resort of political refugees and outlaws who organize an occasional local "revolution" as they have done on the grasslands of the Orinoco hinterland in Venezuela. A ragamuffin army accustomed to a meat diet finds a cattle country excellently adapted to a simple commissariat, with cattle to be got here and there or driven along slowly from one temporary camp to another.

In the vicinity of Bom Fim, northwest of Bahia, notably where the Itapicuru flows down to the coast from the São Francisco divide, there is an upland belt that continues to attract settlers. Neighbors are still far apart, mostly squatters; and there are "no doctors here, no medicine," wrote one experimenter at Villa Nova da Rainha, a few miles northwest of Bom Fim, whose ranch was an

FIG. 235

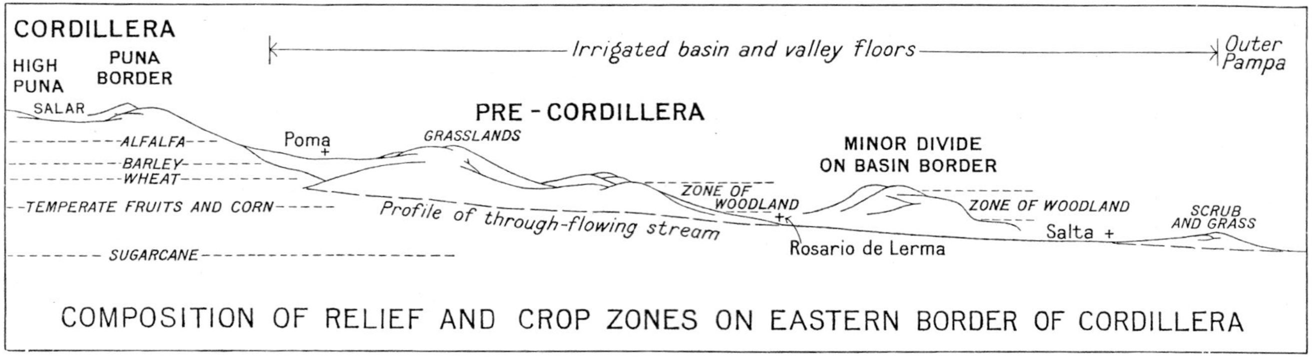

FIG. 236

FIG. 235—The Salta basin: cornfields in the foreground, pastures in the middle distance, swamp along the river course, northwestern Argentina.
FIG. 236—The narrow woodland belt is characteristic. Above and below the woodland are grassland and irrigated agricultural tracts.

utter failure owing to the losses incurred in a "perpetual war against ants" and to lack of capital for implements and stock.[23]   The clearing of the ground proved to be unexpectedly hard and coffee trees take four years to come into bearing.   The lower country, the *caatinga*, is "desert" to the upland dweller, but it is grazing country and here are the "rich cattle owners."   This is a part of the zone of experiment in the hinterland of the great eastern projection of South America.   The world map of pioneer belts (Fig. 38) shows its relation to the Matto Grosso region.   Cultivation nearer the eastern coast, and notably in Ceará, has here sought help to an increasing degree from the climatologist and the irrigation engineer.[24]

PIEDMONT BORDER IN NORTHWESTERN ARGENTINA

On the Andean flank of northwestern Argentina there has persisted for centuries a strongly marked frontier life.   Through the passes in the Andean wall the Inca rulers sent their military forces to gain the southernmost outposts of empire.   The first white conquerors of the sixteenth century came over routes made familiar by the Inca advance.   Salta, Jujuy, and many smaller towns were settled by men who arrived from the north and had their trade affiliations with the high *puna*.   For two centuries commerce with the Pacific was mainly by way of Chile and Peru (including Upper Peru or Bolivia), and a boom in the Chilean mining industry invariably produced an expansion in pastoral colonization in the Argentine.   Meat for the mining population of these two countries and mules for the ore carts established the livestock industry of northern Argentina as far back as the close of the sixteenth century. Only after Argentina became a republic and its boundaries extended to the cordillera was control exercised from Buenos Aires.   At that the orientation of the northern valleys was determined less by natural boundaries than by the railway that came long after independence.   To the pampa landowner of the La Plata region the northwestern grasslands of the Andean border valleys and basins were only a degree less remote than their wild mountain hinterland.

Today as in the past the livestock trade into Bolivia from the

[23] Evelyn Scott: Escapade, New York, 1923, pp. 194, 205, and 222.

[24] A bibliography of material on the droughts of northeastern Brazil is given in *Ibero-Amerikanisches Archiv.*, Vol. 3, 1929, pp. 99–105.   The causes of the droughts are discussed by J. de Sampaio Ferraz: Causas provaveis das seccas do nordeste brasileiro, Ministerio da Agricultura, Industria e Commercio, Rio de Janeiro, 1925.

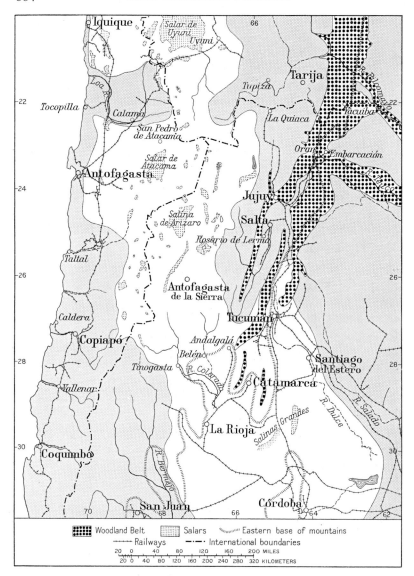

FIG. 237—Woodland and drainage relations in the southern part of the Central Andes.

Notable is the close association of dry interior-basin belt and woodland about Tucumán. The woodland means a heavier rainfall on the mountain flank than on the plains and basins below, a steadier stream flow, irrigation, towns, a more complex life. To the east of the woodland belt, particularly in the Chaco, are patches and bands of tree growth, but their distribution is uncertain; and on the map above only the denser belts are shown. The area with through-flowing drainage is stippled; the area with interior-basin drainage is unshaded.

south focuses in mountain border towns in Argentina. Cattle is the main business of Salta, which is served by a railway. Alfalfa meadows, irrigation ditches, and crude cultivation all serve the cattle business. Corn is raised for fattening cattle. The elevation of the basin (4000 feet) is great enough to bring frost, and sugar cane will not mature. The land is in a first stage of development.

Fig. 238—The Nevado de Cachi on the western side of the Calchaquí Valley, northwestern Argentina. Below the snow cover of the higher mountains is grassy vegetation down to the main valley border, but the valley floor is dry except where irrigated. (See Isaiah Bowman: Desert Trails of Atacama, New York, 1924, Fig. 65.)

Salta has not yet been in touch with outside markets long enough to have more than begun the development of its agricultural and pastoral resources. Its tributary streams of commerce are still of the casual, primitive sort and lack organization and development. The haciendas of the Lerma Valley on the southwest where the railroad ends, the possibilities of the Calchaquí Valley, and of the plains country naturally tributary to Salta, are in a state of mere beginning; and they are regions well adapted to a wide range of temperate and subtropical products. In addition, there are many smaller tributary areas capable of supporting stock and now developed only to a slight extent.

As in many places elsewhere in Hispanic America, the "fair" is still a thriving institution in the Salta region as a medium for

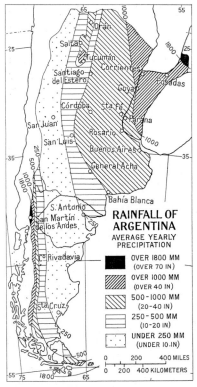

FIG. 239—The rainfall of Argentina. (Franz
Kühn: Die La Plata-Länder, reference cited
in footnote 20.) For a corresponding map of
Chile see Figure 218.

exchange as well as purchase
and sale, though the regular
July meeting of the traders has
now been transferred to Suma-
lao, twenty miles south of
Salta. It might be supposed
that the railway would alter
this old trading device, but
the railway freight rates are
so high, and the standard of
living of the peon class so low,
that the railway service is chiefly
for what might be called the
overhead business of the region.
With low wages and abundant
and cheap forage a pack train
is cheaper than the railway—
in fact, its main purpose is to
feed the railway. The mule
can forage by night and endure
very hard work. The llama
is equally well adapted to extreme conditions. With these
two adjuncts the railway draws
to it the trade of a vast region
that supports only a scattered
and low-grade population. Cargo
mules, llama trains, and two-
wheeled carts come and go from the end of the railway at Rosario
de Lerma, 9 miles southwest of Salta.

Chief among the settlements west of Salta is Poma (Fig. 234)
in the Calchaquí Valley which runs parallel with the main front
of the cordillera. Cattle bound north to the silver and tin mines of
Bolivia or west to the nitrate fields and copper mines of Chile
rest and feed in the Calchaquí Valley before being driven across
the high and dry puna and the cold windy passes of the Andes.
No corn is grown in the valley—the elevation (9800 feet) is too
great: but barley, potatoes, and alfalfa are grown and, locally, wheat.

The number of white inhabitants in the Calchaquí Valley is
still very small, and they remain, as a rule, only during the summer
season. For the rest the management is left to superintendents

of mixed blood who employ Indian labor. The main cultivated part of a ranch has the buildings and corrals. The outlying parts of the estate are composed of pasture lands and locally irrigable tracts that are rented to *arrenderos* (renters), Indian folk who have no land of their own and who require a *pied à terre*. This they find on the small alluvial fans at the mouths of the tributary valleys where they, like the owner, grow barley, potatoes, and alfalfa. Although they pay a rent for their land they have free grazing rights and therefore spend a large part of their time drifting with their flocks along the moister borders of the ravines and the deepsunk gully floors. Generally they are bound, by the terms of a contract, to give a month's labor on the main ranch at a stipulated wage. The conditions of the contract are often unsatisfactory, and in time an *arrendero* will rent another place that he thinks more favorable. As a class they move about a great deal, spending a part of their time as traveling traders while their families stay at home to guard the flocks, till the soil, and protect the hut and its belongings.

The whites are in the lower

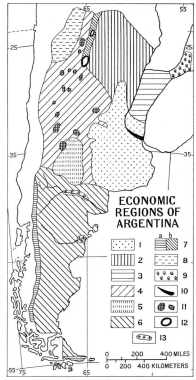

ECONOMIC REGIONS OF ARGENTINA

FIG. 240—The economic regions of Argentina, in diagrammatic and generalized form. (Franz Kühn: Die La Plata-Länder, reference cited in footnote 20.)

The numbers in the legend have reference: 1, pampa region of agriculture and cattle raising; 2, Chaco region of quebracho, cattle, and local subtropical agriculture; 3, mesopotamian region of forest, cattle, and subtropical agriculture; 4, woodland and scrub zone of light and extensive grazing; 5, central Argentine semiarid region with little population; 6, Patagonian plains and uplands, sheep grazing; 7(a), forest zone of the Patagonian Andes; 7(b), subtropical mountain forest; 8, Puna de Atacama, high basin country with thin pasture and widely scattered and small habitations; 9, tropical forest of Misiones with tropical agriculture in favorable localities; 10, delta of the Paraná; 11, cultivated oases of the northwest; 12, sugar plantations; 13, valley oases of northern Patagonia.

country, the Indians mostly in the grassy tracts of the mountain zone. The Indians have a low and primitive mode of life, a shy-

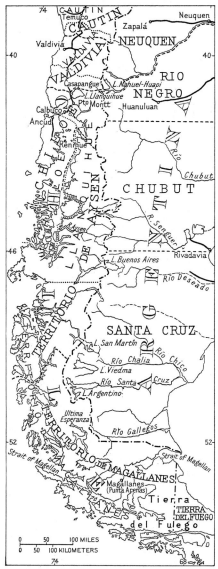

FIG. 241—Location map of a part of the Patagonian region. The new territorial divisions in Chile (1927) are shown by heavy lines and lettering, the old divisions by light lines and lettering. (See William E. Rudolph: The New Territorial Divisions of Chile with special reference to Chiloé, *Geogr. Rev.*, Vol. 19, 1929, pp. 61-77.)

ness with respect to the whites, and a marked preference for the high country that has been their ancestral home. Neither their products nor their requirements are sufficient to attract a railway, and rails are absent except for lines connecting the larger towns. Without a railway the trade and manner of life will remain pastoral and primitive in many districts capable of much higher cultivation. Down to 1905 there were many farms in the Calchaquí Valley that were in a low state of production and could still be bought cheaply. Farm values increased from three to five times in a few years in response to the temporary rise in prices of farm products that culminated in the abnormally high figures attained during the World War. Everyone was then trying to get land. Never before had Argentina shared so fully in general world prosperity. The period 1904, 1914 was marked by great commercial activity, the steady extension of railways, agriculture, and cattle raising, and by a net migrational increase in population of 1,484,000.[25]

[25] International Migrations, Vol. 2, Interpretations, New York, 1931, p. 150.

PATAGONIA

Patagonia is no longer world's end, a no-man's-land, a symbol of remoteness. The best of the country south of the Rio Negro (Fig. 241) is overrun by sheep that find on the semiarid grassy plateaus, 3000 to 5000 feet above sea level, much better feeding grounds than one would suppose existed, judging by the more arid plains along the Atlantic coast. If the scanty waters are wisely used, says Bailey Willis,[26] the region could support millions of beasts, the pasture of the upland pampas being of wide extent. Wasteful and destructive grazing practices are still the rule throughout Patagonia except in the case of a small number of the better-managed *estancias*. The control of public ranges is as needful as in our western country to prevent overgrazing and to give edible plants an opportunity to seed.

Fortunately the snowfall of winter is light and infrequent on the Patagonian upland pastures. Livestock can be wintered on the ranges without other shelter than the canyon walls that mark the transverse drainage of the region. While the Andes on the west receive a heavy winter and summer precipitation, the flatter eastern country is in the "rain shadow" of the mountains. The pampas are both drier and warmer than the high country on the west. Windiness is a great drawback, not merely from the standpoint of the comfort of man and beast but also because it increases evaporation and reduces the value of the little precipitation that falls. Winter ranges require a sunny northern exposure protected from the westerly winds.

Land values in Patagonia are determined by the degree of abundance of the pasture. It is the principal "elemental resource." In northern Patagonia bunch grass is common, growing in separated tufts and reaching a height of two feet. Though coarse and spiny when old, young shoots sprouting among the older ones supply good forage. The algarrobo (acacia) has a delicate edible foliage, and the beans are eaten by both cattle and sheep. The *jarilla* and chañar are also useful, the former for its foliage, the latter for its fruit. The bush *zampa* and the shrub *tomillo* are both eaten by sheep. The *neneo* grows on open porous sands and gravels and depends on the deeper soil water. Some of the flowering plants form rich if temporary elements of the upland pastures.

The chief interest of agriculture in the Patagonian pioneer fringe

[26] Bailey Willis: Northern Patagonia, New York, 1914.

FIG. 242

FIG. 243

FIG. 244

FIG. 242—Lake Nahuel Huapi at the outlet, Limay River. On the right of the picture, above the houses, rises the terminal moraine that encloses the lake. (Bailey Willis, Northern Patagonia, 1914: Figures 242 and 243 supplied by the Ministerio de Obras Públicas, Buenos Aires.)

FIG. 243—Looking south over the high grass-covered plateau of the western Rio Negro region.

FIG. 244—Sheep range and water hole in Sañico Hills, northern Patagonia. Vegetation is of the type common to most of central and southern Patagonia, but limited in northern Patagonia to a narrow dry zone just east of the open woodlands of the Andean border.

Fig. 245

Fig. 246

Fig. 247

Fig. 245—Valcheta station, in the dry sheep-ranching country of northern Patagonia. (Figures 244–249 from photographs by Wellington D. Jones.)

Fig. 246—Ranch center near Piedra de Aguila on the Limay River, in the extreme western part of the sheep-ranching region of northern Patagonia.

Fig. 247—Oxcarts near Rio Collon Cura, in the extreme western part of the dry region of northern Patagonia, on the return trip to San Martín de los Andes from Neuquen which is on the Ferrocarril Sud (Fig. 241).

is to grow feed to support cattle in winter when the restricted
grazing makes it difficult to carry cattle to the number sustained
by the more abundant summer pastures. The production of oats,
wheat, and other grains for local consumption is a natural development that follows the fuller use of the ranges. Local irrigation has

FIG. 248—Cattle ranch on the eastern border of the Andes, near Junin de los Andes.

been practiced for many years, but it is not successful in an economic
sense as an independent enterprise. Joined with ranching, irrigation
results tell a different story; and the same is true of dry farming.

The quick spread of the grazing industry in Patagonia to the
point where all the best ranges were occupied took place between
1900 and 1915. By the latter date the best and the most accessible
districts were overstocked. First there were the private properties,
huge ranges acquired from the government, and then the nomadic
cattleman whose principle is that possession is nine points of the
law. He is not concerned about the general welfare, establishes
himself on the best summer pastures in the valleys, which ought
to be left for winter feeding when the uplands are bare, and even
fences government land and puts up buildings without any legal
right whatever. Up to 1913 the squatter flocks had grazed on public
lands without paying a tax, though since then there has been
collected a modest tax of a few cents a head on cattle and horses,
and even less on sheep. With the rapid growth of grazing it is

more apparent that flocks should migrate from season to season
from the thinner upland pastures of summer to the better valley-
floor pastures of winter.

With the increase in flocks and herds to the full capacity of
the ranges it is necessary to recognize a law that has had ample

FIG. 249—Ranch center, with fields of alfalfa and orchards irrigated from hillside spring, near
Junin de los Andes, in the extreme western part of the dry region of northern Patagonia.

illustration in the western United States, namely, that if useful
grasses and shrubs are kept nibbled down the flora will change,
and useless thorny and bitter plants will be given direct encouragement. The laws of conservation have been well worked out elsewhere; and it is to the interest of government and rancher alike
that the grasses, the permanent asset of the region, should not be
destroyed. There is also the question of water. The division
of the lands into units that control the water supply without making
a maximum use of the ranges farther afield is harmful. Each lessee
should have a just share of the water of the country and reasonable
access to it. This is the principal reason why the small proprietor
should not be encouraged. The land should be divided into large
blocks each of which contains a proper share of winter and summer
range and of water supply. The equalization of winter and
summer ranges is effective only when the herds are required to
migrate through moderate distances. All of this requires a sense of
responsibility on the part of the proprietors and of intelligent survey-

ing, land classification, and administration on the part of the government.

About the borders of the lakes that lie in a chain along the foothills of the Andes and represent the dammed river courses where the ice of an earlier period built transverse moraines there is land suitable for settlement, and permanent occupation is assured. San Martín de los Andes at the end of Lago Locar is adequately sheltered from the west winds and has become an attractive resort (Fig. 214). It lies on one of the principal routes across the cordillera and is a center of communication of growing importance. Elsewhere in the lake region of Argentina—a thousand-mile stretch between latitudes 38° and 52° S.—the elements of good soil, accessible forests, and a sheltered location are combined in a way that invites settlement.

Fifty years ago Patagonia was Indian country. Although a mission was established on Lake Nahuel Huapi in early times, it was destroyed in 1655. Reëstablished, it was again destroyed in 1716. In 1879 Moreno, the Argentine geographer, barely escaped death from his Indian hosts. The year 1884 saw the dispersal of the Indians by a military force under General Roca, and directly after that came the frontiersman who occupied the sites of the old Indian villages along the shores of the lake. Bailey Willis, who visited the region nearly twenty years ago, found clearings and cabins scattered all about the lake, the hardy frontiersmen having made their houses in the upper valleys, their cattle ranging in the forests and on the alpine pastures or dense canebrakes. Bariloche is a famous settlement, a village of wooden houses built on the lower and upper terraces of the southern lake shore at the foot of a wooded hill. The site is near the border between the wooded heights of the cordillera and the grassy hills of the pampas. At the outlet of Lake Nahuel Huapi we have the center of a region of great geographical diversity. There is an abundant and excellent water supply, conditions favorable for water-power development, a genial climate, and a wide diversity of resources. In the region roundabout there may be practiced agriculture with irrigation, cultivation without it, and grazing over an immense realm. West of this point the rainfall exceeds forty inches a year; wheat, oats, alfalfa, potatoes, onions, etc., have been cultivated successfully, and hardy fruit trees also thrive and bear well. For fifty years cattle and sheep have been grazed on the lands roundabout.

Like every other pioneer region, Patagonia has felt the impulse of the larger interests of government and business in the distance. "The land is all fenced right up to the Cordillera, and grazed by domesticated animals," says Barrett, who traversed the southern sections north of the Strait of Magellan in 1928.[27] "Streets" provide a passage for herds or flocks driven to port on the eastern coast or south to the strait. To be sure, the fences are "leagues and leagues apart," and there are still many wild guanaco and ostrich. Posts to support the smooth wire are widely spaced and this permits the wires to be pressed down and crossed at will.

The best pastures are on the west near the mountains, and here too are the best breeds of cattle. Wild cattle are still to be found— in the Lago San Martín region (Fig. 241) and between lakes Viedma and Argentino "back of the fences, right up against the Cordillera." Huge wool carts take the "crop" of the sheep ranches over what pass for roads. Both Chile and Argentina own parts of southern- most Patagonia and both have moved against the large ranch owner and capitalist by reducing the size of the holdings. One company had its holdings reduced from a hundred leagues to thirteen. The larger companies had bought out settlers upon the best lowland patches in "the canal country" of Ultima Esperanza in Chile, east of the Andes, where there are some of the finest natural pastures in the region. Flocks of sheep numbering several millions and horses for handling them up to the number of 10,000, besides many oxen for hauling the wool, are reported by a single company. Life is here of the old frontier type, on the grand scale, despite reduc- tions in the size of holdings. The ample ranges have few counter- parts in the world and no other region has more picturesque features than the drives and the seasonal visits of the shearers from Buenos Aires or from Chiloé, the latter coming via the Aysen Valley across the Andes to Lake Buenos Aires and thence south 150 miles afoot or on horseback to return before snow closes the Andean passes.

There is little prospect for the farmer in southern Patagonia— the seasons are not favorable except in sheltered situations. At best, land tillage will be a purely local thing. There can be no thrust of agriculture in a wide foothill zone. The upland plains to the east are permanent pasture which to be used economically must be held in large units and managed by central ranch organ- izations. Up to the present they have been based on the ports of the east coast and the northern coast of the Strait of Magellan.

[27] Robert and Katherine Barrett: A Yankee in Patagonia, Edward Chace, Boston, 1931, p. 49.

INDEX

Abadie, Maurice, 240

Abandonment, 29; farm, Oregon (ill.), 94; New Hampshire town, 30

Acknowledgments, vii

Aconcagua (province), 309

Adaptations, 51

Adin, California, 104

Adventure, 17, 34, 35

Afghanistan, 75

Africa, 61–62; native agriculture, 229; white colonization, 201. *See also* Southern Africa

Agricultural revolution, 220

Agriculture, 83, 153, 251; economic law and, 87; government and, 140; machinery in, 113, 220; range, 37; science and, 84; scientific management, 139

Airplanes, 166; eastern valleys of the Andes, 319; northern Canada, 167 (map), 168; Russia and Siberia, 265

Airways, 80

Aktyubinsk, 261

Alaska, 4, 248, 253; railways and mines, 226; wagon road (ill.), 71

Alberta, 148, 152, 153, 157, 159; grain-belt town (ill.), 157; seeding (ill.), 86

Alcock, F. J., 72

Algarrobo, 339

Alice Springs, 73, 191, 192, 193

Amazon Basin, 317, 318

American Geographical Society, vii

Amur River, 265, 282, 284

Andean valleys, eastern, 312, 313 (diagr.)

Andes, 314, 345; eastern valleys, 312; woodland and drainage relations in southern-central part (map), 344

Angola, 206, 211, 219, 235 (with map), 236, 237

Angoniland, 232

Anta, 297

Antofagasta and Bolivia railway, 308

Araguaya River, 330

Aral Sea, 261

Araluen Farm, Northern Rhodesia (ill.), 223

Arani, 319

Arctic Sea, 264

Argentina, 10, 45, 52, 327; agriculture and grazing, 303; Chaco country, 65; economic regions (map), 337; land use, 53; livestock industry, 333; northwestern (map), 331; northwestern, pasture and woodland (map), 334; northwestern piedmont border, 333; rail transport, 73–74; rainfall (map), 336

Arid lands, 169, 172; Russian Central Asia, 260, 261 (map)

Aristocracy, 300

Arrenderos, 337

Artesian wells, Australia, 182

Australia, 36, 51; central part, 185; deserts, 172; drought, 170; economic Australia (map), 173; forecasting rainfall, 184; gold excitement, 179; lack of mountains, 175, 176; land on lease (diagr.), 179; location map, 174; northwestern coast, 180; population, 173; prospect, 169; railway scheme (map), 175; rainfall, 61, 177–178; rainfall belts (map), 171; rainfall variability (map), 172; settler's home in irrigation area (ill.), 183; stimulating settlement, 61; water and cattle, 178, 182, 190; wheat and rainfall correlation, 184; white Australia, 74, 174

Australians, 2–3

Austria, 33

Automobiles. *See* Motor cars

Avilion Farm, Rhodesia (ill.), 217

Aysen Valley, 345

346

Bacon, Sir Francis, 35
Bacon's Two Bit Flop (ill.), 24
Baddeley, J. F., 241
Bailey, L. H., 34, 36, 37, 46
Baker, O. E., 32
Ball, John, 4
Banditry, Matto Grosso, 331
Barbed wire, 157
Bariloche, 344
Barkley, Henry, 184, 185
Barkly Tableland, 178, 189
Barns, T. A., 235, 236, 237
Barren Grounds, 152, 168
Barrett, Robert and Katherine, 345
Barrows, H. H., 7
Bateman, Alan, 226
Bauxite, 232
Beerburrum (ill.), 181
Beira, 211, 230
Belgian Congo, 64, 208, 211, 219, 221, 226
Bend, Oregon, 93, 96, 97, 98, 99, 102, 139; freighting by wagon southeast of in 1913 (ill.), frontispiece; pioneer country, 101; section of country near (diagr.), 96; view over the town (ill.), 99
Benét, S. V., 11
Benguella Railway, 219, 236, 237
Bering, Vitus, 248
Berkey, C. P., 267, 269
Beveridge, A. J., 30
Bieber, California, 104, 107, 139
Biel, Erwin, 60, 204
"Big Dry" creek, Montana (ills.), 134
Billings, Montana, 129
Black earth, 242, 249. See also Chernozems; Russia
Black labor, 213–214
Blantyre, 229, 230, 232
Boer War, 208
Boers, 3, 237
Bolivia, 299, 314; Argentina and, 324; boundary with Paraguay, 327; climate of eastern Andes, 321; colonization, 324; Gran Chaco, 58; grazing, 320 (with map), 321; Indians, 297
Bom Fim, 331
Boman, Éric, 251

Boomlaager, 228
Boone, Daniel, 13
Border, 1; appeal of, 5; extent, 48; land and people, 112
Border living, 3
Boundaries, 48
Bourne, E. G., 6
Bourne, R., 221
Bowman, Isaiah, 62, 335
Brandy, 313, 319
Brazil, 17, 51, 52; early transportation, 21; frontier, 299; settlement, 306; southern, 302
Brazil Land and Cattle Company, 330
"Breaks," 116, 119, 126, 131
Brinkmann, Theodor, 328
British, in Southern Africa, 213
British Columbia, 155; transport, 73
British South Africa Company, 208, 214
Britstown (ills.), 207
Broken Hill, Rhodesia, 211, 224 (with ill.), 226, 227
Brooklands Estate, W. A. (ill.), 41
Brooks, A. H., 71
Bryce, Lord, 80, 169
Buchanan, Sir George, 186, 189, 190
Buck, J. L., 270
Buell, R. L., 230
Buenos Aires, 333, 345
Buenos Aires, Lake, 345
Buffalo grass, 127, 156
Bunch grass, 95
Burns, Oregon, 93, 107 (ill.), 108; sign post west of (ill.), 66
Bushnell, Horace, 1, 18
Buxton, L. H. Dudley, 278

Caatinga country, 325, 333
Cacao, 320
Cáceres, 329, 330
Caink, T. G., 233
Calchaquí Valley, 335 (with ill.), 336, 338
California, northeastern, wheat farming, 104; range country (ill.), 107
Calvinia, 239, 240
Camels, 172; grain transport, Southern Rhodesia (ill.), 219

Campo cerrado, 326

Campo Largo, 328

Canada, 47, 58, 143; Clay Belt, 149, 151; colonization companies, 157; conveyance old and new (ill.), 16; eastern, types of farming (map), 147; Fertile Belt, 152; forest belts and railway net (map), 145; fringe of settlement, 143; immigration, 156, 160, 161; industry, 159; lumber industry, 148; migration from, 85; mining, 151; northern pastures, 165; power, 152; prairie provinces, rainfall (with map), 153; prairies, 147; railways, 160; railways, transcontinental, 148, 158–159; rainfall (maps), 150, 151; settlement, committee on, 154; sub-Arctic fringe, 164; temperatures (map), 144; timber and settlers, 150; western, 144; western, types of farming (map), 146; western prairies, 152; wheat, 143, 147, 157, 162; wheat pools, 88, 167

Canada Wheat Board, 162

Canadian National Railways, 148, 159

Canadian Northwest, 20, 22, 36, 84; immigration, 161; settlement, 85

Canadian Pacific Railway, 22, 148, 155, 156

Canadian Pioneer Problems Committee, vii

Canadians, 143

Cape of Good Hope, 206, 219

Capital, 23; immigrants and, 161; Southern Rhodesia, 213

Caribou, 165

Carnarvon, W. A., wool teams (ills.), 196

Carts (ill.), 72; Manchuria, 286, 293. *See also* Ox teams

Casapangue, 311

Cascade Mountains, 95, 99 (with ill.); pasture (ill.), 100

Caspian Sea, 260

Cattle, 88, 95, 122; Australia, 190; Bolivia, 320 (with map), 321; Canada, western, 155; Hereford (ill.), 130; industry in Canada, 156;

Jordan country, Montana, 127, 130, 131; Manchuria (ill.), 279; Matto Grosso, 330; Oregon, 102; Paraguay, 326; Patagonia, 339, 342; small owners, 132; Southwest Africa, 235, 236, 237, 238

Ceará, 53, 330, 333

Census, U. S., vanished frontier and, 111

Central Africa, 240

Central Andes, woodland and drainage relations in the southern part (map), 334

Central Australia, 187; disadvantages, 192; new government, 191

Chaco, 65; grasslands 327, 328 (map)

Chadron, Nebraska, range country (ill.), 117

Chañar, 308, 339

Chances, 3

Changchun, 293

Changlopu, 270

Character, 25

Charata, 328

Cheap land, 21, 94

Chernozems, Russia (map), 244

Chestnut soils, Russia (map), 244

Children, 23; asset or burden? 251

Chile, 310; agriculture, 309, 311 (map); Huasco Valley, 169; rainfall (with map), 311; southern frontier, 308; territorial divisions, new (map), 338

Chiloé, Island of, 310

Chiloé, Province of, farms reclaimed (ill.), 44

China, 38; agriculture, 44; government and Chinese pioneers in Mongolia, 278

Chinese, 2, 6, 36, 37, 267; economic order, 273; migrating into Manchuria 281, 284 (ill.), 293; pioneers, 59

Chinese Eastern Railway, 285, 292; importance, 290

Chisamba, plowing (ill.), 223

Chongoni Mountains, 232

Chosen, 285, 290

Christmas Lake Valley, 106

Churches, 18, 20, 81

Churchill, Manitoba, 167; wireless station (ill.), 67
Chüyungkwan, 272
Cities, 14, 25, 32, 39, 40, 41, 82, 83; Canada, 160; Siberia, 245; South American frontier, 307
Civilization, 17, 19, 42, 49, 154
Clairmont, Alberta, road near (ill.), 7
Clapp, F. G., 180, 270, 274
Clay beds, Canada, 149
Cleinow, Georg, 248, 249, 250, 251, 256
Clifford, B. E. H., 238
Climatic trends, 62
Cliza, 318
Coal, Canada, 151
Cobalt region, Canada, 151
Coca River, 317
Cochabamba, 315, 318, 319
Cochabamba-Santa Cruz railway, 319, 324
Cochrane, Canada, 151
Coffee, 302, 333; Brazil, 53
Colchagua (province), 309
Colebatch, H. P., 197, 198
Collon Cura, Rio, ox carts near (ill.), 341
Colombia, 39, 42, 312, 314
Colonization, Canada, 157; Oregon, 100, 101
Columbus, Christopher, 34, 296
Comfort, 40, 318
Communities, 142; religious, 81; Russian colonizing in Siberia, 249
Condover Estates, 228
Connecticut, roads, good and bad, 68
Connecticut Valley, 17
Continental interior, 144
Coolgardie, 179
Coöperation in Hispanic America, 301
Coöperative marketing, 162
Copiapó, 169, 307
Copper, 64, 307; Northern Rhodesia 226
Corn, Garfield County, Montana, field (ill.), 137
Cornelius, C. G., 302
Correlation, wool clip and rainfall in Australia, 184
Corumbá, 330

Cotton, 87; Russian Central Asia, 258
Coward Springs, Australia (ill.), 73
Cox, A. B., 121
Cranberry Portage (ill.), 24; nursing home (ill.), 12
Cream separator, 82
Cressey, G. B., 268, 271
Crops, decrease and increase in 1919–1924 in the U. S. (maps), 82, 83; effective economic distance for hauling, 64, 70, 255
Crown Hill oasis, South Australia (ill.), 59
Culliton, J. T., 148
Cultivators (ill.), 207
Cunene Valley, 236
Cuyabá, 58, 330
Cuzco, 8, 297
Czechoslovakia, 33
Czechowicz, Paul, 243

Dafoe, J. W., 155
Dairen, 285; soy beans, storage (ill.), 285
Dakotas, 182
Darby, H. C., 86, 222, 227
Darwin, Australia, 186, 187, 190
Dawson Valley, Queensland, settler's home (ill.), 182
Day, T. E., 187
Deerfield, Mass., 17
De Grey River, 178
Denison, Sir Hugh, 188
Denmark, 33
Denmark, near Albany, W. A. (ill.), 41
Deschutes River, 96, 100
Deserts, 77, 170; Australia, 172, 177; California, 104; Oregon, 97; rain in, 153; Westralian, 180
Dewey, John, 142
Dixey, Frank, 230, 231, 232
Dodoma-Fife route, 240
Drakensberg, 234; farms on eastern scarp (ills.), 210
Drayton, Muriel, 220
Dreamers, 200
Drought, 169, 170
Dry cycle, 106, 108

Dry farming, 8, 94, 95, 106, 112; Glasgow, Montana (ill.), 137
Dry-land country, 171; settlers in, 169
Dukhobors, 2, 5
Dutch, 19, 238; early settlers, 206
Du Toit, A. L., 238
Dwight, Timothy, 1; on pioneers, 18
Dyott, G. M., 330

Earth, bounty, 46
Economic density, 9, 10
Economic distance for hauling crops, 64, 70, 255
Economic realm, 88
Ecuador, Oriente, 315, 316 (with map)
Edmonton, Alberta, 158
Edwards Plateau, 114 (map), 119
Egypt, 43
Eliot, Sir John, 170
Ely, R. T., 33
Embarcación, 65, 321, 324
Emerson, R. W., 4
England, 33
Englishmen, 2, 3
Enterprise, 39
Eskimo Lakes, 166
Eskimos' children, 251
Esperanza. See La Esperanza
Esquel Valley, wheat (ill.), 57
Experimentation, v, 9, 29, 36, 46, 82, 84, 154; American frontier, 111; Oregon, 110; science and, 85; western United States, 93
Eyre, E. J., 175
Eyre, Lake, district, 175
Eyre's Peninsula, 194, 195 (map)

Failures, 25
Fairbanks, Alaska (ill.), 17
Fairs, 335
Fairview (Waterhole), town of, 163
Far East, 248, 282; pioneer, railway, and government, 293
Farmer-ranchers, 102, 112, 116
Fear, 34
Fences, 132, 133, 156
Fenner, Charles, 196
Ferraz, J. de S., 333

Fifth dimension, 14
Folk movements, 280
Forecasts, 62, 80, 84, 140, 183; Australia rainfall, 184
Forests, 106; devastated, in eastern Canada, 151; Siberia, 264; Yenisei Valley (ill.), 262
Fort Albany (ill.), 54
Fort Churchill, 148; bank building (ill.), 24. See also Churchill
Fort Jameson, 225
Fort Nelson, 167
Fort Rock, Oregon, 102, 106, 108
Fort Rock Valley, 106; looking east to Fremont (ill.), 28
Fort Simpson, 152, 166
France, 38
Frankel, S. H., 228
Free range, 132
Freedom, 39
Freighting by wagon in Oregon in 1913 (ill.), frontispiece
Fremont, Oregon, 28, 108
Fringe of settlement, 7
Frontera, 310, 311
Frontier, v, 14, 42; American, 111; dangers, 13; metes and bounds, 48; present interest in, 32; United States, 306

Gabet, Joseph, 269, 272
Galway, Sir Henry, 187, 188
Gama, Domicio da, 34
Garcias, Umberto, 317
Garfield County, Montana, 113, 123; cornfield (ill.), 137; general setting (map), 129
Garland, Hamlin, 11
Gauchos, 65, 322 (ill.)
Germans in South America, 302
Ghanzi, 238
"Giant Farm," Russia, seeding (ill.), 87
Gilbert, A. W., 88
Gilbert Creek, Montana, 13
Gillman, C., 240
Glasgow, Montana, 123, 129; farm near (ill.), 137
Gobabis, 238

Gobi Desert, 270, 272, 275

Godsal, F. W., 143

Gold, Australia, 179; Canada, 151

Goldthwait, J. W., 30, 31

Gonzalez, A. R., 308

Goose Lake basin, Oregon (ills.), 101

Gordon, South Australia, 194

Gordonia, 238, 239

Government, 21, 33; land classification and, 140; pioneers and, 85, 86; settlement and, 10, 38

Grama grass, 127

Gran Chaco, 5, 56; Bolivia, 58; farmhouse (ill.), 323; gauchos (ill.), 322; grass, lagoon, and trees (ill.), 323; savanas, 325; tree-dotted grassland (ill.), 323

Grand Prairie (ill.), 157

Grande, Rio, Bolivia, 321

Grant, H. C., 161

Grass, the Land of, 267, 272

Grasses, Australia, 177; Jordan country, Montana, 127

Grazing country, 88; Canada, northern, 165; Montana, 127

Great Basin, 94, 96, 103, 104

Great Bear Lake district, 166

Great Plains, 83; central, 112; central and northern, 121; drier western part (map), 114; life, 142

Great Slave Lake, 164; region, 154

Great Wall of China, 269, 270, 271

Gregory, J. W., 171

Group settlement, 20; Western Australia, 198, 199

Guardamontes (ill.), 322

Guessing, 22

Gwelo, 217

Haciendas, 66, 301, 302; eastern Peru, 313, 314 (ill.)

Hall, Francis, 17, 39, 42

Hall, R. B., 57

Hammond, F. D., 72, 216, 217

Hansa Colony, 2; church festival (ill.), 15; farm (ill.), 15; German immigrants (ill.), 40; public square of Humboldt (ills.), 40; team and mountain road near (ill.), 2

Harbin, 281, 282, 291, 293

Hartebeestpoort farm, 239

Haude, Waldemar, 270

Haxby, Montana (ill.), 136; land profile near (diagr.), 128

Hay River, 164–165

Heilungkiang, 281

Hemon, Louis, 21

High Desert, Oregon, 93, 101; abandoned farm (ill.), 94; region, 109; road from Bend to Burns (ill.), 98

High Plains (with map), 114; farm buildings, panhandle of Oklahoma (ill.), 120; slopes of western Kansas (ill.), 120; western part, 114

Hill, J. J., 46

Hoe culture, 273

Hofmeyr, Jan, 204

Hokkaido, settlement on Tokachi Plain (ill.), 57

Homesteaders, 132–133; Canada, 156; Montana, 109, 128; Oregon, 98; Saskatchewan, 160

Hoover, Herbert, 11, 12

Hope, 1, 25, 27, 169

Horses in Siberia, 256

Hosie, Alexander, 285, 287

Hospitality, 132

Houses, Montana, 135; sod house in Kansas (ill.), 13

Howe, C. D., 149

Huasco Valley, 169

Huc, Abbe, 267, 269, 272

Hudson Bay, 166

Hudson Bay Railway, 148, 159, 167; buildings along (ills.), 24; country at mile 42 (ill.), 37; crossing the Nelson River (ill.), 69; steel laying (ill.), 161; telephone line (ill.), 6

Hudson's Bay Company, 155

Humboldt, Brazil (ills.), 40

Humboldt, Alexander von, 39, 318

Humpata, 237

Hurley, P. J., 11, 12

Hutterians, 2

Icelanders, 2

Ideas, 34; opposition to new, 47

Illinois, 7

Immigration, Canada, 156, 160, 161;
science and, 85–86

Impey, Lawrence, 273

Imrie, J. M., 163

Incas, 307, 333

Indians, Argentina, northwestern, 337;
Bolivia, 297; Brazil, 306; eastern
valleys of the Andes, 315; Ecuador,
315, 316; Patagonia, 344

Inducement, 33

Ingomar, Montana, 128; main street
(ill.), 136

Inner Mongolia, 59, 267; Chinese
immigrants, 273

Innis, H. A., 24, 68, 69, 162, 163, 167

Insects, 56, 325

Institutions, 38

Instruments of power, 48

Inventions, 87

Invitation of the land, 34, 38

Inyanga Estate (ill.), 215

Ireland, 5

Irrigation, 76; Australia, 182, 183 (ill.);
South America, 301; United States
projects, 77

Isotherms, 143

Italians, 20

Itapicuru River, 331

Jaeger, Fritz, 235, 236

Jamaica, 42

James, William, 76

James Bay, 150

Japan, Manchuria and, 280, 285, 291,
295; Russia and, 290, 292

Jarilla, 339

Jefferson, Mark, 143, 306, 308, 310,
311; on Argentina, 303; on San
Carlos, 26; South American books,
302

Jennings, A. C., 212

Jigalong, country near (ill.), 193

Joerg, W. L. G., 230

Johnson, W. D., 115, 116

Jones, Wellington D., 341

Jordan, Montana, 123; combining
wheat near (ill.), 79; life in and
near, 138; panorama (ill.), 134

Jordan country, Montana, 122; cattle,
130, 131; farming, 123, 126, 128,
130; general setting (map), 129;
land classification map, 124; location
map, 125; railless condition (map),
123; schools; mothers; houses, 135;
sheep (with ill.), 131; transportation,
138

Jujuy, 333

Junin de los Andes, cattle ranch near
(ills.), 342, 343

Juniper, 93, 97; sagebrush and (ill.),
100

Kafue River, bridge (ill.), 225

Kahlotus-Connell region, farm (ill.),
27

K'ai-yüan Hsien, 286

Kakamas, 239

Kalahari Desert, 206, 208, 209; border,
grazing, 237

Kalgan, 267, 272; traffic on the pass
into Mongolia (ill.), 275

Kalgoorlie, 177 (ill.), 179

Kalomo, 219, 223

Kansas, 115, 122, 132, 162; farm land
(ill.), 120; sod house (ill.), 13

Kansas City Southern Railway, 70, 305

Kansu, 270; abandoned farm (ill.),
271

Kaoliang, 274, 288 (map)

Kapuskasing farm (ill.), 155

Kara Sea route, 264, 265

Katanga, 238

Katun River, 249

Keeble, Sir Frederick, 205

Keetmanshoop, 236

Kenai Peninsula, railroad (ill.), 71

Kentucky, 26

Kenya, 208, 240

Keyserling, Count, 273

Killenges, 236

Kindle, E. M., 54

Kipling, Rudyard, 46, 200

Kirghiz, 260

Kirin, 281, 284

Kirin-Tunhua Railway, 284

Kitats, 269

Kitto, F. H., 163, 165

Knoche, W., 311
Korea, 285, 290
Kruger National Park, 234
Kühn, Franz, 326, 336, 337
Kusnetsk-Altai, 252

Labor, 24; Africa and, 213–214
La Esperanza, 21, 305
Laessoe, H. de, 235
Lakeview, Oregon, 96; Goose Lake basin near (ills.), 101
Land, 5; allotment, 297; cheap, 5, 21, 94; government and, 140; honoring, 46; Indians and, 297; invitation of, 34, 38; love of, 38; new, enticement of, 84; occupation, 46, 47; problem, 32
La Plata, 333
Latifundia, 308, 327
Lattimore, Owen, 272, 273
Laurentian Highlands, 145, 148, 149 (map), 151, 154
Laurier, Sir Wilfrid, 143
Lena River, 265; Valley, 253
Leppan, H. D., 206
Lerma Valley, 335
Lewistown, Montana, 129
Leydsdorp, 234
Liaotung Peninsula, 281
Liard River, 165
Lien-en Tsao, 293, 294
Life, quality, 14
Limay River (ill.), 340; ranch center on (ill.), 341
Limon Valley, northern end (ill.), 322
Limpopo Valley, 211
Lismas, Montana, ferry (ill.), 137
Living, 41, 141; standard of, 37, 45, 142
Livingstone, Rhodesia, 211, 227
Livingstone Mountains, 232
Llanquihue, Lake, lands bordering (ill.), 309
Lobito, 219
Locar, Lago, 344
Loram, C. T., 230
Low Desert, Oregon, 106, 109
Low Veld, 233 (map), 234
Lowdermilk, W. C., 270
Lowell, A. L., 318

Lower, A. R. M., 149
Lubango, 237
Lucerne, wagons loaded with (ill.), 207
Luck, 81
Lumber industry, 46; Canada, 148, 150; frontier in Manitoba (ill.), 163
Lusaka, Northern Rhodesia, irrigation channel (ill.), 86
Lyme, New Hampshire, 30; deserted schoolhouse (ill.), 31

Macas, 316
McBride, G. M., 297, 308, 309
Macdonnell region of Central Australia, 187
Machinery, 10; agricultural, 113
MacInnes, C. M., 156
Mackenzie River, 166; district, 166; Valley, 164
Mackintosh, W. A., 145
Madigan, C. T., 177
Magellan, Strait of, 345
Maier, Hans, 294
Mail, 49, 82, 135
Maize, Southern Rhodesia, 217
Makeri Farm, Lusaka (ill.), 86
Manchuria, 36, 59; average annual rainfall (map), 286; cattle on grassland (ill.), 279; Chinese bound for (ill.), 284; Chinese farming methods in, 293; Chinese migration into, 281; divisions, towns, railways (map), 291; frost and the growing season (map), 287; immigrants walking to (ill.), 9; Japan and, 295; kaoliang and Italian millet (maps), 288; northern, 281, 282, 286, 287, 290; pioneers of, 280; population, 281; soy beans (map), 289; wheat, 287, 289 (map), 290
Manda, 240
Manitoba, 11, 30, 159, 161
Manitou Rapids (ill.), 69
Marbut, C. F., 87, 244
Marginal living, v, 11, 18, 112, 122
Maritime Provinces, 145
Marketing, 10; coöperative, Canada, 162; distance from markets, 66, 70, 255

Mashonaland, 208

Massachusetts, 17

Matabeleland, 208

Mataco Indians, 65

Matadi, 237

Mather, Cotton, 17

Mather, K. F., 320, 321, 322

Matto Grosso, 56, 58, 329; grasslands, 330, 331; location map, 329; western, 330

Mazabuka, farm (ill.), 217; Research Station (ill.), 223

Meat, 45, 88, 131

Medical care, 13

Melsetter, 211, 234

Mennonites, 2, 5

Metes and bounds, 48

Mexico, 32, 67

Michigan, timber cutting, 29, 45–46

Middle West, 11, 16, 18, 22, 23, 81, 82; hopes, 25

Mier country, 238, 239

Migrations, government power over, 280

Mildura, settler's home (ill.), 181

Miles City, Montana, 123, 129, 138

Mill, H. R., 23

Millet, Italian, in Manchuria (map), 288

Minerals, 179; Canada, 151; railways and, 226

Missouri River, 126

Mlanje Mountains, 230 (with map), 232

Molopo River, 238

Mongolia, 258; carts (ill.), 274; China and Russia and, 280; Chinese farm-house group (ill.), 275; climate, 276; farming of Chinese colonists, 276, 278 (ill.); habitations, 274 (ill.), 278; pioneering in, 267, 268 (map); Russia and, 279; villages, 278. See also Inner Mongolia

Mongols, 267, 269; civilization, 272; nomads, 279; withdrawal under Chinese pressure, 275

Montana, 122, 143; central settlement, 111; homesteading, 109; log school-house (ill.), 13; Red Cross relief in

1930–1932, 113; ridges and slopes near Rock Springs (ills.), 126, 127

Monte, 312

Moose Factory, 150

Moreno, F. P., 344

Morris, F. K., 269

Moscow, 243, 259

Moss, 166

Mossamedes, 237

Motor boats, northern Canada, 168

Motor cars, 16, 82, 135, 142; com-munity ruined by, 29–30; Oregon, 96

Motor roads, 70

Mountains, rain and, 175

Murakoshi, Nobuo, 286, 287, 290

Murchie, R. W., 11, 161

Murray, Walter, 161

Murray-Hughes, Robert, 221

Murrumbidgee, settler's home (ill.), 183

Musselshell River, 126

Nahual Huapi, Lake, 49; mission on, 344; outlet, 340 (ill.), 344

Namaqualand, 236, 239; wheat, 239, 240

Nankow Pass, 272

Nansen, Fridtjof, 34, 241

Napo River, 316, 317

Nash, Roy, 21

Natal, 228

National Research Council, vii

Native carriers, 64

Natives, 201; eastern valleys of the Andes, 313, 314; rights, treatment, etc., 228

Nature, conquering, 77, 80

Navigation, 76

Nebraska, 122; topography (ills.), 117

Negro, Rio, Argentina, 239; plateau of the region (ill.), 340

Neighbors, 9, 132, 142

Nelson, Helge, 144, 151

Nelson River (ill.), 69

Neneo, 339

Nevado de Cachi (ill.), 335

New England, 17–18, 20, 22, 81; com-munity ruined by the motor car, 29–30; food, 88

New Mexico, High Plains, 118
New South Wales, 170, 178; wool-carrying teams (ill.), 176
Ngami, Lake, 208, 238
Nickel, 151
Nile, 43, 44
Niobrara Valley, Nebraska (ill.), 117
Nitrate, 307, 310
Nkana Railway Bridge (ill.), 225
North Africa, 240
North Australia, 185
North West Territories, 164, 165 (map)
Northern Rhodesia, 201, 211; bush; copper, 226; country and population, 221; farms in railway belt (map), 227; irrigation channel (ill.), 86; native question, 222, 228; products, 221, 222; railways, 222, 225, 226, 228; settlement, 224
Northern Territory, Australia, 56, 178, 185, 187; boom periods, 188; isolation, 190
Novo-Sibirsk, 245, 248 (ill.)
Nuanetsi, 217
Nyasa, Lake, 221, 230, 232
Nyasaland, 208, 220, 225; distribution of natives (map), 231; land and people (with map), 230; products and natives, 232; rainfall, 231; tea growing, 229 (ill.), 231; water supply, 232

Ob River, 245, 253, 263, 264, 265; farm in this valley (ill.), 251
Oklahoma, 121; farm buildings in western (ill.), 120
Omsk, 245
Ontario, 150; farm (ill.), 155; rural slum, 149
Oodnadatta, 191, 192 (with ill.), 193
Opportunity, 37
Orange Free State, 204, 206
Orange River, 236, 238, 239
Ordos Desert, 270
Oregon, 65; central, occupation, 102; central and southeastern, 93, 105 (map); colonization, 100, 101; early settlers, 99; experimentation, 110; remoteness from railways (map), 97;

southern termination of wheat belt (ill.), 95; southeastern, 108
Oriente, 315, 316 (with map)
Orinoco River, plains, 45
Orleans, Father d', 267
Orleans, Island of, oxen (ill.), 79
Orroroo, 194
Ossipee mountaineers, 26
Outer Mongolia, 279
Overcoming, 34
Overseas Settlement Board, 213
Ox teams, 16, 17, 206, 224–225, 227, 228, 319; New South Wales (ill.), 175; Patagonia (ill.), 341; plowing in Northern Rhodesia (ill.), 219; plowing in Quebec (ill.), 79; wagon and team in Northern Rhodesia (with ill.), 218

Pack trains, 64, 66, 307
Pampas of Patagonia, 339
Panama Canal, 22
Paper industry, 151, 152
Paraguay, 325; boundary with Bolivia, 327; cattle, 326; landscape in northern (ill.), 325
Paraguay River, 58, 318; Chaco bordering (map), 327; farmhouse (ill.), 323
Paraná, German farm (ill.), 57
Paraná River, 21
Parkman, Francis, 65
Pas, The, Manitoba, 68 (ill.), 167; air base (map), 167; lumbering frontier (ill.), 163; pioneer town (ill.), 162
Pasco, Washington, 104; sheep ranch near (ill.), 100
Pasture lands, 88
Patagonia, 49, 52, 310; agriculture, 339; grazing industry, 342; location map of part of, 338; ranches (ills.), 342, 343; sheep, 339, 340 (ill.), 345; sheep-ranching country (ills.), 341; southern, 345; view in northern (ill.), 298
Patton, H. S., 150
Peace River (ill.), 26

Peace River country, 51, 69–70, 160; farmhouse (ill.), 159; pastoral land, 164; root drag (ill.), 79; settlement, 163, 164; social life, 164; wheat and farming, 163; wheatfield (ill.), 27

Pecos Valley Railroad, 118

Peel Estate, Western Australia, 197

Peking, 270

Peking road through the Nankow Pass, 272

Pembina Mountain, 155

Peonage, 297

Peons, 67, 303, 314

Peru, 299, 301; Coast Range, 171; eastern valleys and basins, 312

Peter the Great, 245, 255

Phillips, P. D., 198

Physicians, 13, 96, 133, 192

Piedra de Aguila, ranch center near (ill.), 341

Pilcomayo, Rio, 321

Pioneer belts, 50 (map), 58

Pioneer lands, vi, 49; government and, 51; value, 47

Pioneer living, 141; definition, 48

"Pioneer Settlement," vii

Pioneer Woman, 11, 12

Pioneering, v, vi, 35, 80; America, 1; Australia, 174; Canada, western, 158; definite business, 16; end announced, 35; government and, 85, 86; modern, 11, 46; railroads and, 74; science and, 84; tropical, 317; uncertainties, 110

Pioneers, 1; character, 4, 26; freedom, 39; modern, 25; nations of today, 2; sturdy qualities, 18

Plan Alto, 329, 330

Plantation system of agriculture, 214, 299; South America, 303

Plata, 333

Plummer, F. E., 204, 205

Point Barrow, 253

Poletika, W. P. von, 253, 262

Political action, 141

Poma, 336

Ponca City, Oklahoma, 11, 12

Population, flow of, 280, 318

Population density, 9, 10

Porcupine region, Canada, 151

Porsild, A. E., 166

Port Arthur, 291

Portuguese, 3, 236, 237, 296

Portuguese West Africa, 206

Potosí, 64

Powell, J. W., 182

Powers, Justice, 186

Prairies, 7; Canada, 155

Preface, v

Price, A. G., 188

Prices, vi

Priestley, H., 189

Principe, 237

Prineville, Oregon, 96

Propiedad Austral, 311

Proudfit, S. V., 109

Puerto Montt, 310

Puerto Suarez, 318, 319

Pulpwood, 149, 150

Puna, 333

Quality, 14

Quebec (province), 149, 150

Quebracho, 66, 327; forest (ill.), 326

Quechua Indians, 251

Quechua-speaking Indians, 316

Queensland, 56, 189; settler's home (ill.), 182; soldier settlement (ill.), 181

Quiros, P. F. de, 4

Radio, 80, 82, 123, 142, 154

Railways, 64; Canada, 148, 158–159, 160; economics and politics and, 75; effective economic distance, 64, 70; ends of new lines, 64; Hudson Bay route, 168; mining and, 226; Northern Rhodesia, 222, 225, 226, 228; Oregon, southeastern, 96; part in pioneering, 69; politics of, Far East, 290; Rhodesia, 219; Siberia, 256, 257 (with map), 264; South America, 304 (map), 305; southern Africa, 228; Southern Rhodesia, 216, 217; "Turk-Sib" line, 75; West and, 139

Rainfall, 51; Australia, forecasting, 184; Canada, prairie provinces, 153; central Great Plains, 112; Chile, 311; dependability, 62; mountains and, 175; Nyasaland, 231; Southern Africa, 202 (maps), 203 (map), 204, 205 (with map); taking chances with, 169; variability, 153; world variability (map), 60

Ranching, 121; Canada, 156; Edwards Plateau, 121; Oregon, 101

Range country, 88; California, northeastern (ill.), 107

Reading, Vermont, abandoned farm (ill.), 31

Reclamation Service, 77

Red Cross, 113

Red River (of the North) Valley, 146; Canadian section, 155; carts (ill.), 72

Red River (of the South), 119

Reenen, F. J. van, 239

Reindeer, 165, 168

Reindeer moss, 166

Religious sects, 81

Reñihue, 311

Rents, 23

Resistencia, 328

Revolutions, 35

Rhodes, Cecil, 46, 200, 208, 238

Rhodes Inyanga Estate (ill.), 215

Rhodesia, 10, 11, 22, 36, 51, 204; ox teams (with ills.), 218, 219; settlement, 208; social life and schools, 220

Rio de Janeiro, 21

Rio Grande do Sul, 306; grassy plateaus (ill.), 306

Rio Negro, Paraná, farm (ill.), 57

Risks, 17, 18, 33, 113

Riverina, Bishop of, 170

Roads, 22; Connecticut, good and bad, 68; economics, 22; Jordan country, Montana, 133; Oregon, 103

Roan Antelope Mine, 226

Roberts, S. H., 195

Roca, General J. A., 344

Rock Springs, Montana, slopes (ill.), 127

Rockyford, Alberta, seeding (ill.), 86

Romecin, Eduardo, 320, 324

Roosevelt, Rio, 330

Roosevelt, Theodore, 18, 329, 330

Rosario de Lerma, 336

Rostov, Russia, 87

Roxby, P. M., 283

Rudolph, W. E., 309, 338

Rural free delivery, 82

Russia, 32; agricultural regions, natural (map), 244; Chinese Eastern Railway and, 290; famine belt, 260; Japan and, 290, 292; Mongolia and, 279; outlets, 255; population density and chief towns (map), 246; population regions (map), 243; seeding (ill.), 87; Siberia and, 241; transportation, means of (map), 247; wheat, 258, 260, 262

Russian Central Asia, 75, 241, 266; cotton, 258; political divisions (map), 242; railway net (map), 259; southeastern dry region, 260, 261 (map)

Russian Hydrographical Expedition, 264

Russian Turkestan, 258

Russians, 3, 20; settlers emigrating to Siberia (ill.), 3

Ruthenian home, Alberta (ill.), 158

Sabi River, 234

Sagebrush, 93, 97, 106, 127; juniper and (ill.), 100

Sahara, 170, 240

Sahuayaco, 8

St. Louis, Mo., 65

Salisbury, Southern Rhodesia, 209, 216

Salta, 333; cattle, 335

Salta basin, 335; cornfields, grasslands, etc. (ill. and diagr.), 332

Saltation, 200

Samara, 260, 261

Sampaio Ferraz, J. de, 333

San Carlos, 26

San Luis de Cáceres, 329

San Martín, Lago, 345

San Martín de los Andes, 298 (ill.), 341, 344, 345

San Pedro de Atacama, 308

Sand, Ordos Desert, 270, 272

Sandburg, Carl, 1, 17
Sañico Hills (ill.), 340
Santa Catharina, 306
Santa Cruz de la Sierra, 65, 318; piedmont border south of, 318, 319 (map); plains (ill.), 322
Santayana, George, 22
Santiago (province), 308, 309
São Bento, 2
São Paulo, 53, 302, 305
São Thomé, 237
Saratov, 260
Saskatchewan, 148, 153, 159; elevator at Wawanesa (ill.), 160; immigrants, 160–161
Savanas, Gran Chaco, 325
Savings, 23, 26
Saw grass, 56
Sayce, R. U., 228
Scandinavians, 2, 20
Schoolhouses, frontier (ills.), 13
Schools, 18, 20; Montana, 135
Schultz, Arved, 243, 250, 253
Schurz, W. L., 323
Science, pioneering and, 6, 8, 76
Science of settlement, vi; new phase, 8
Scotch, 2
Scott, Evelyn, 333
Seattle, 98
Semenov-Tian-Shansky, Benjamin, 245, 246, 247
Serrania de Guadalupe, 64
Settlement, 7; advertising, 22, 23; border type, 111; Canada, study of, 154; government and, 38; group, 20, 198, 199; railways and, 74; science of, vi, 8
Settlers, 1
Shaler, N. S., 26
Shangtu, 273
Shaniko, 106
Shankaikwan, 270
Shansi, 270, 272
Shantung, 281, 282; refugees from, bound for Manchuria (ill.), 284
Sheep, 95; Australia, correlation with rainfall, 184, 190; Jordan country, Montana (with ill.), 131; New South Wales, 170; Oregon, 102; Patagonia,

339, 345; ranch in Washington (ill.), 100; range and water hole in Patagonia (ill.), 340; transport by rail, 97–98
Sheep herder's wagon (ill.), 136
Shensi, 270
Shiftless, 25, 26
Shire Highlands, 230
Shire River, 230; valley, 232
Siberia, 3; Arctic coast, 265; background of the pioneer in, 241; central, 253; colonization, 242; communism, 256; community organization, 249; crop land (map), 254; eastern, 292; lands and cultivation, 252, 253; life, 250; life at a standstill, 256; northern limits of agriculture, 253, 255, 263; political divisions (map), 242; railways and transportation, 256, 257 (with map), 264; rivers and their commerce, 265; roads, 241; special products, 255; transport, 73. See also Russia
Sickness, 96, 133
Silver Lake, Oregon, 96, 106, 107 (ill.)
Sinclair, J. H., 315, 316
Skinners of the earth, 46, 149
Skvortzov, B. W., 290
Slave River, 164
Smith, Guy-Harold, 31
Smuts, J. C., 229
Social Science Research Council, vii
Soil, love of the, 38
Soils, 10; Russia, 245
South Africa, 19, 47, 201; white man and natives, 213. See also Southern Africa
South Africa, Union of, 201, 205, 206; political map, 204; railways, 228
South America, 32; aristocratic system, 300; early settlement, 296; frontier conditions, 305, 306; hinterlands, 296; railways, 304 (map), 305; southern part, 51, 52 (map)
South Americans, 299–300
South Australia (map), 195; Crown Hill oasis (ill.), 59; drought and

relief, 178, 193, 194; settlement, 195, 196; starving stock, 194

South Manchuria Railway, 291, 292

Southern Africa, access to railways (map), 203; climate, 208, 210; highlands, rainfall, and rain reliability (maps), 202; location map, 203; rainfall expectation (map), 205; subtropical fringe, 233; summer rainfall (map), 203; temperatures, line of tolerable (with diagr.), 208–209; west coast highlands, 235; white man's lands, 200

Southern Manchuria, 282; plain of (ill.), 283

Southern Rhodesia, 201, 209, 212 (map); farm land and ranch land, 216; immigration, 212; land use, 211; maize, 217, 218; mining and agriculture, 214; plantation system, 214; population and production, 212, 218; public assistance, 220; railways, 216, 217; road improvement (ill.), 218; settler's home (ill.), 216; transport, 72

Southwest Africa, 235 (with map), 236

Soviets, 241, 250

Soy beans, 286, 294; Manchuria (map), 289; open storage (ill.), 285

Spain, 300

Spaniards, 296, 300

Spencer's Gulf, 194, 195

Spirit, 29, 81

Spring Creek, Nebraska, farm buildings (ill.), 120

Springfield, Tasmania, bush home (ill.), 181

Spruce, white, 164

Squatters, 8, 21, 252, 299, 310

Srosk (ill.), 249

Standard of living, 37, 45, 142

State, 10, 140, 141

Statistics, 36

Stefansson, Vilhjalmur, 143

Stevenson-Hamilton, J., 233, 234

Strathcona, Lord, 64

Sublette, Kansas (ill.), 117

Sudan, 44, 61, 240

Sudbury region, Canada, 151

Sugar, 302, 320, 321, 327

Sungari River, 282, 284, 290; winter scene in the valley (ill.), 283

Swamps, Siberia, northwestern (ill.), 263; Yenisei Valley (ill.), 262

Sydney, G. H., 169

Taiga, 264

Talca (province), 309

Tanganyika, 208, 225, 240

Tashkent, 258, 259

Tasmania, bush home (ill.), 181

Tatars, 249, 250

Taxes, 21, 22, 30, 122, 142; pioneer lands, 32; rents and, 23

Taylor, Gordon, 198

Taylor, Griffith, 59, 73, 171, 172, 173, 176, 197

Tea, 248, 264; growing in Nyasaland, 229 (ill.), 231

Technology, 140

Telegraph, 48, 123

Telephone, 49, 123

Temperate zone, 143

Temperature, 51; Southern Africa, line of tolerable (with diagr.), 208–209

Tennessee, 7, 13, 26

Terry, Michael, 187, 188

Texas, 13, 119; panhandle, 114, 115

Textiles, 87

Thomas, Sir W. B., 35

Thoreau, H. D., 19

Timber, 149; stripping in Michigan, 29

Tobacco in Northern Rhodesia, 222, 228 (ill.)

Tokachi Plain, Hokkaido, settlement (ill.), 57

Tomillo, 339

Tomsk, 250

Tractors, 83, 168, 223 (ill.)

Trans-Caspian country, 75

Transehe, N. A., 264

Transhumance, 96

Transportation, 38, 49; Canada, old and new (ill.), 16; effective economic limit, 64, 70; need, 67; wagons in Oregon in 1913 (ill.), frontispiece

Trans-Siberian railway, 75, 242, 264

Transvaal, 182, 204, 206; citrus farm (ill.), 210; eastern border, 234; settlement, 209

Trekking, 19

Trewartha, G. T., 286, 287, 290

Tropics, 56; Australia, 188, 189; pioneering in, 317

Tsetse fly, 221, 226, 235, 238

Tsin pien, main street (ill.), 271

Tucumán, region (map), 334

Tulaikov, N. M., 260

Tule Lake, floor of, California (ill.), 87

"Turk-Sib" railway, 75, 258

Turkestan, 258, 260

Turkestan-Siberian railway, 75, 258

Turner, F. J., 18

Turtle Mountain, 155

Tzaneen, 234; district (ill.), 210

Uganda, 240

Uintah Basin, 70

Ukrainians, 2; church and school in settlement north of Winnipeg (ills.), 12; houses in settlement north of Winnipeg (ills.), 158; truck farm north of Winnipeg (ill.), 36

Ultima Esperanza, 345

United States, crops, changes in 1919–1924 (maps), 82, 83; frontier conditions, 306; western zones of experiment, 93

U. S. Reclamation Service, 77

Umtali, 211; farm near (ill.), 215

Umvukwes, tobacco field (ill.), 215

Union of South Africa. See South Africa

Urubamba Valley, 7; hacienda (ill.), 314

Utah, 70

Valcheta station (ill.), 341

Valdivia, 310, 311

Vallenar, 169

Valparaiso (province), 308

Vegetables, 88, 154

Vegreville, Alberta, 158

Veld, farm land (ill.), 207

Venezuela, 41, 42

Vernal, Utah, 70

Victoria, settler's home (ill.), 181; sheep and rainfall, 184

Villa Nova da Rainha, 331

Volcanic ash, 93, 103

Volga River, region, 262, 263

Walvis Bay, 208

Wants, v, 14, 142

Washington, dry-land farm (ill.), 28

Wasson, Theron, 316

Water, 43; Australia, 178, 182; High Plains, 115; regulation, 301; rights, 170

Water holes, 208

Water power, Canada, 152

Waterhole (Fairview), town in Peace River country, 163

Wawanesa, elevator (ill.), 160

Wealth, 45

Weather forecasting, 62, 80, 140, 183

Webb, W. P., 113

Webster, Daniel, 48

Wellington, Duke of, 34

Wells, 109, 121

Welsh, 2

West, United States, 141; railways, 139

Western Australia, 10, 180; character of the land, 196; country near Jigalong (ill.), 193; crop of Dutch clover (ill.), 45; group settlement, 198; group settlement, houses, and State Farm (ills.), 41; group settlement, land and trees in (ill.), 7; Peel Estate (ills.), 78; school (ill.), 13; settlement, 61, 197; settlers at post office (ill.), 197; stock routes and water, 178; transport, 73; wheat, 197

Westphalia Estate, Drakensberg (ill.), 210

Westralian Land Law, 180

Wheat, 94, 112–113; Australia, 184; California, northeastern, 104; Canada, 143, 147, 157, 162; Canadian pools, 88, 162; combining (ill.), 79; export from Canada, 167; field in Alberta (ill.), 27; Jordan country, Montana, 128, 129; line in Oregon,

95 (ill.), 103; Manchuria, 287, 289 (map), 290; Namaqualand, 239, 240; new strains, 8; Oregon, 98; Patagonia (ill.), 57; Peace River country, 163; prairie provinces, 162; prices, 113, 122; Russia, 258, 260, 262
White, David, vii
White, J. H., 149
White, John, 1
White, Langdon, 96
White man, in Africa, parts of, 201; in Australia, 74, 174, 190; in southern Africa, 200; in Southern Rhodesia, 214; in the tropics, 317
White River, Transvaal, citrus farm (ill.), 210
White Sea, 253
Wildcatters, 8
Wilkins, Sir Hubert, on Australians, 179; on the Northern Territory, 190
Williams, Robert, 187
Willis, Bailey, 57, 298, 339, 340, 344
Williston, Montana, 129
Wilm, Paul, 275, 276, 277
Wilson, H. F., 31
Wind, 116; chinook, 153; Oregon and Washington, 104
Windhoek, 236; native location (ill.), 210
Windhoek Plateau, 236
Windmills, 115, 116, 121

Winnipeg, 12, 36, 158; Grain Exchange, 162
Wireless, 67; Churchill station (ill.), 67; Siberia, 264–265
Wisconsin, abandoned land reclaimed (ill.), 31
Wolff, S. M., 274
Women, 11, 20, 99, 135, 220–221
Wood, G. L., 189, 198
Wool, 87, 225; Australia, 184; Australian team (ill.), 196; teams carrying, in New South Wales (ill.), 176
Wooton, E. O., 93, 118
World, 14; pioneer belts, 50 (map), 58
Wynne, W. H., 197
Wyoming, 122

Yacuiba, 321, 324
Yakutsk, 253
Yenisei River, 265; isolated settlement on (ill.), 55; valley, forest and swamp (ill.), 262
Young, C. W., 281, 282
Youngblood, B., 121
Yugoslavia, 33
Yülinfu, 270

Zambezi River, valley, 211, 221
Zampa, 339
Zoa Tea Estate (ill.), 229